CREATING GERMANS ABROAD

Creating Germans Abroad

Cultural Policies and National Identity in Namibia

DANIEL JOSEPH WALTHER

Ohio University Press
Athens

Ohio University Press, Athens, Ohio 45701
© 2002 by Daniel Joseph Walther

Ohio University Press books are printed on acid-free paper ⊖

10 09 08 07 06 05 04 03 02   5 4 3 2 1

An earlier version of chapter 4 appeared as "Creating Germans
Abroad: White Education in German Southwest Africa, 1894–1914"
in the *German Studies Review* 22, no. 2 (2001).
Reprinted here with permission.

Library of Congress Cataloging-in-Publication Data

Walther, Daniel Joseph, 1965–
Creating Germans abroad : cultural policies and national identity in
Namibia / Daniel Joseph Walther.
p.   cm.
Includes bibliographical references (p.) and index.
ISBN 0-8214-1458-5 (alk. paper)—ISBN 0-8214-1459-3 (pbk. : alk. paper)
1. Germans—Namibia—Ethnic identity. 2. Germans—Namibia—Politics
and government. 3. Namibia—Ethnic relations—History. I. Title.

DT1558.G46 W35 2002
320.54'089'3106881—dc21

2002027071

To my wife, Linda

Contents

Contents

Tables

Tables

Acknowledgments

This project began nearly eight years ago, and there are numerous people who have assisted me in various ways on it. To begin, I would like to thank my dissertation adviser, Thomas Childers, and the other members of my committee, Lee Cassanelli and the late Jack Reece, for their initial encouragement, comments, and insights into the study of German history and colonialism. Without their support, I would not be where I am today. During the revision and expansion process, Robert Gordon and Woodruff Smith gave me invaluable and expert assistance. Indeed, their suggestions and interpretations have truly turned this into a study that has much more breadth and appeal. I feel the debt that I owe these two men can never truly be repaid. I would also be remiss if I forgot to mention my good friend Kenneth Holston. I thoroughly enjoyed our conversations in graduate school, and continue to enjoy them today.

Many others helped with various aspects of the project. For example, comments made by the members of the Transatlantic Doctoral Seminar in German History—especially Armin Nolzen, Hans Mommsen, and Roger Chickering—enabled me to clarify aspects of the argument. I am also indebted to Lora Wildenthal and Krista O'Donnell for encouragement, assistance, and their own work on German colonialism. I benefitted immensely from the advice and experience of Richard Dale: never in my life have I met a more pleasant individual.

The bulk of the research would have been impossible without the generous financial and logistical support of the Mellon Foundation and the German Academic Exchange Service. In addition, my colleagues and friends at Wartburg College have been truly supportive. Most notably I would like to thank my colleagues in the History Department Cheryl Jacobsen and Terry Lindell. In various ways, often intangible, they enabled me to finish the manuscript.

I would also like to express my gratitude to the people at Ohio University Press for facilitating the review and production process. I especially thank Gillian Berchowitz, who was an invaluable advocate for the manuscript from the beginning, and Dennis Marshall, whose copyediting skills enabled me to sharpen my arguments and make the book more anglicized. Their assistance helped make the project a reality.

Last, and foremost, I thank my wife, Linda. Without her love, support, encouragement, and patience, I would not be the scholar and husband that I am today.

Abbreviations

AA	Auswärtiges Amt (German Foreign Office)
ADV	Alldeutscher Verband (Pan-German League)
AO	Auslandsorganisation der NSDAP (NSDAP's foreign office, Hamburg)
BAK	Bundesarchiv Koblenz (Federal Archive, Koblenz)
BAP	Bundesarchiv Potsdam (Federal Archive, Potsdam)
BdM	Bund deutscher Mädchen (League of German Girls)
DA	*Der Auslandsdeutsche*
DB	Deutscher Bund (German League)
DKG	Deutsche Kolonialgesellschaft (German Colonial Society)
DKGfSWA	Deutsche Kolonialgesellschaft für Südwest Afrika (German Colonial Society for Southwest Africa)
DKZ	*Deutsche Kolonialzeitung*
DSWAZ	*Deutsche Südwestafrikanische Zeitung*
DSWB	Deutscher Südwester Bund (German Southwest League)
DtSchA	*Die Deutsche Schule im Auslande*
FB	Frauenbund (the women's league of the DKG)
FBuE	*Frauenberuf- und Erwerb*
FWG	Farmwirtschaftsgesellschaft (farm economic corporation)
HLA	Helene-Lange-Archiv (Helene Lange Archive, Berlin)
KORAG	Koloniale Reichsarbeitsgemeinschaft (Colonial Reich Syndicate)
KPA	Kolonialpolitisches Amt der NSDAP (NSDAP's colonial political office, Munich)

KZV	Koloniale Zentralverwaltung (the colonial central administration, part of the Reich Ministry for Reconstruction)
HJ	Hitlerjugend (Hitler Youth)
KuH	*Kolonie und Heimat*
LAB	Landesarchiv Berlin (State Archive, Berlin)
LdDS	Landeschulverband der Deutschen Schulvereine/Landesschulverband (Union of the German School Associations/ Territorial School Union)
NP	National Party (South Africa)
NSDAP	Nationalsozialistische Deutsche Arbeiterpartei (National Socialist German Workers' Party)
RKA	Reichskolonialamt (the imperial colonial office)
RWA/RfA	Reichswanderungsamt (the Reich migration office; after 1924, Reichsstelle für das Auswanderungswesen, the Reich office for emigration)
SfDSWA	Siedlungsgesellschaft für Deutsch-Südwestafrika (Settlement Company for German Southwest Africa)
SfsS	Syndikat für südwestafrikanische Siedlung (Syndicate for Southwest African Settlement)
SWA	Southwest Africa
SWB	*Südwestbote*
WN	*Windhuker Nachrichten*
UNSWP	United National Southwest Party
VDA	Verein für das Deutschtum im Ausland (Overseas Association for Deutschtum)
VdB	Verband deutscher Berufsgruppen (Union of German Vocational Groups)
VdR	Verein der Reichsdeutschen (Association of German Citizens)
ZAfA	Zentrale Auskunftsstelle für Auswanderer (Central Information Office for Emigrants)
ZfKKK	*Zeitschrift für Kolonialpolitik, Kolonialwirtschaft, und Kolonialrecht*

CREATING GERMANS ABROAD

Namibia

Introduction

In most newly established nation-states, issues of national identity, of nation building, arise. This applies to Namibia (the former German colony of Southwest Africa), which gained its independence in 1990, as the united Federal Republic of Germany (FRG). Both are relatively new polities facing a number of dilemmas such as the creation of a national consciousness, the presence of minorities, and integration into a larger comity. Obviously there are also differences between them, but in another way each is still linked to the other: each is inhabited by a German-speaking population in search of a definition for itself in a new atmosphere. For the FRG this is rather obvious, but not for Namibia. Namibia and Germany have a long history together, a history that begins with the Scramble for Africa in the 1880s and continues to this day.

In the 1880s, Germany, under Otto von Bismarck, embarked upon a program of colonial expansion.[1] In the ensuing rush for colonies, Germany gained control of Southwest Africa along with several other territories. Of all the German colonies, experts and opinion makers determined that SWA, due to its climate, was the most suitable for colonization; nevertheless, it was not until the establishment of direct government rule and administration over the territory in 1894 that serious attempts began to establish German hegemony in the region. These efforts occupied a salient position in German popular culture even though German settlers in the region numbered only in the thousands. And, despite the loss of the colony in 1914 at the end of World War I and its transference to South African control under the mandate system, Germans remained in SWA to fight for the preservation of their status and privilege with continuing assistance from the homeland. Consequently, the histories of these two regions collectively provide insights into the development of German national identity, both in the motherland and abroad.

While the connection between imperialism and nationalism in Germany and in other European countries has been investigated,[2] the role of settler colonialism as a distinctive field of study remains underexplored.[3] This field of inquiry provides a venue to examine how different groups tried to construct their ideals of citizenship and the nation in a region populated by a large indigenous population.[4] For Germany, this was particularly important since many nationalists felt that the political unification of 1870 remained "unfulfilled." Indeed, despite that unification, Germany still suffered from social, regional, and confessional cleavages,[5] and colonialism became a vehicle to unite the nation:[6] Southwest Africa, because of its favorable climate, was seen as a place to create a truly united German nation.[7] Such a place would provide not only a place for Germany's many emigrants to settle and preserve their *Deutschtum* but also a model for the old *Heimat*.[8]

Like other European colonies,[9] SWA became a laboratory for sociocultural, as well as economic, experimentation.[10] For German authorities and colonial enthusiasts, it became a place to create a specific image of Deutschtum; namely, a hard-working, parsimonious, Protestant agrarian class filled with staunch nationalist values and devotion to the emperor, with the "traditional" German family at the core of society. It was a decidedly preindustrial vision of Germany pursued by the educated and propertied members of the middle *Stand*.[11] And by 1914, it appeared that they were on the road to success for there were many visible signs of the German presence, both physically and culturally.

However, from the beginning the project was skewed. First, despite claims to being a nonpartisan, universal project, it was predicated upon the ideals of only one segment of the German population.[12] Moreover, local conditions slowly and subtly undermined the entire project. This process began during the German colonial period. Many Germans quickly fell in love with the wide-open spaces and freedom that the land offered. In fact, the region offered, to both men and women, opportunities unavailable in the homeland, and the presence of Africans and other Europeans confronted the Germans with issues and problems, as well as solutions, that were almost exclusively applicable to SWA. On a more subtle level, the environment influenced and affected the German community: it was forced to adapt to different weather conditions, seasons, and local foodstuffs. By the outbreak of World War I, many came to see SWA as their new homeland and referred to themselves as Südwester.[13]

In the 1920s and 1930s, despite South African rule and hence an increased desire to express their Deutschtum, Südwester identified increasingly more with Southwest Africa than with Germany. Admittedly, they did this without renouncing their German linguistic and cultural traditions, which became increasing static; nonetheless, they eventually believed and felt their future lay in the territory. This applied especially to the older generation—to people who had lived there for decades—and not as much to newcomers whose ties with the homeland were still fresh, but the process of transforming Southwestern Germans into German Südwester continued. In fact, the experiences of the interwar period accelerated and accentuated this tendency. By 1948, the Südwester were firmly attached to the land and its future.[14]

While similar in a number of ways to the factors governing the experiences of other colonial Europeans (most notably in Kenya and Southern Rhodesia),[15] several things distinguished the German experience. Unlike in Kenya and Rhodesia, the Germans in Namibia had to contend with a competing white population, namely, the Afrikaners.[16] Migrating from the neighboring colonies of Angola and South Africa, the Afrikaners were initially seen during the period of German colonial rule (1894–1914) either as a manageable nuisance to be assimilated or as distant cousins because of their Low German heritage. However, after World War I the situation changed drastically for the German population.[17] As a condition of the Treaty of Versailles, Germany had to relinquish sovereignty over its colonies. Control of Southwest Africa passed to the South African Union in the form of a mandate. The Germans perceived the South African government's actions to integrate them and to promote its own citizens as an attempt to relegate Südwesters to being second-class citizens. Thus, unlike settlers from other colonial powers, the Germans went from being the rulers in the land to being the ruled.

This book fully explores this unique feature of the German colonial experience in Namibia, and to facilitate such a study it is divided into two parts: the period of colonial rule, 1894 to 1919, and the mandate years, 1919 to 1939 (the former including the relatively brief interlude of World War I). Part 1 examines the German attempts to establish themselves and to become the dominant culture in the region. For the middle Stand, this was the period of experimentation, of the attempt to create their vision of Deutschtum, while for the government it was a time of establishing German hegemony in the region. A definite confluence of goals existed here. Important issues addressed in part 1 include the nature of German rule, the use of culture not only to establish hegemony but also to create a particular image of German culture there, and the role that race and the local environment played in defining Deutschtum. These chapters focus on the apparent threats to Deutschtum during this period and the responses to these threats both by Germans in the colony and in the homeland. These supposed dangers included an increase in Afrikaner settlers entering the colony, the presence of undesirable elements, the rise in miscegenation, and the growing mulatto population—the latter challenging the definitions of race and blurring the distinctions between rulers and ruled. I examine German reactions to these ostensible threats and why Germans pursued the actions they did. These included promoting increased German settlement, deporting unwanted individuals, denying mulattos their legal rights as natural-born German citizens, introducing social and legal measures against those who went against the norm and cohabited or married African women, the sending of German women to the colony, and increasing demands for support of local German schools and of the German language. Part 1 concludes with an examination of the incipient Southwestern German identity.

World War I suspended most activities in Southwest Africa, the years 1914–1918/19 constituting an interlude in the territory's development. For the Southwestern German community, the outbreak of war ushered in a period of both hope and dissatisfaction. The dissatisfaction came in 1915—the result of German capitulation to the Allies, who thereafter occupied the colony for the duration of the war. Many of the activities undertaken prior to the conflict were stopped. For example, settlement ceased and schools closed. Despite this situation, a great deal of optimism reigned in the territory. Germans there, as well as in the homeland, believed and assumed that once Germany won the war the situation would return to normal. Colonial officials in Southwest Africa even made plans for the years after the war, in particular in the realm of education, where plans for reform were discussed. At the close of part 1, chapter 5 examines both the feelings of dissatisfaction and the German hopes and plans for the future.

Part 2 explores the ways in which the German community, reduced to minority status, fought to survive and preserve its position in Southwest Africa against the background of colonial revisionism.[18] Their struggle for survival focused primarily on maintaining pillars of German culture and identity, above all schools and the presence of women, as well as obtaining certain political rights. This was deemed necessary in light of the South African administration's perceived attempts to reduce the significance of the German presence while promoting its own citizens' efforts to gain a stronger foothold in Southwest Africa. For the German community, holding onto its Deutschtum became a means to combat the supposedly seditious efforts of the South Africans. Furthermore, by invoking German culture and identity, the effort to preserve Deutschtum acquired the status of rallying point and tool to enforce conformities within the German population. The fact that some Germans in the mandate felt that this was necessary reveals that the community suffered divisions, including over the path it should pursue. The Germans normally split along generational lines and years of residency in the territory. This became particularly acute after the National Socialists seized power in Germany. Obviously, German measures to preserve their status and position in the region were intricately tied to colonial revisionism and the hoped for return to the Reich.

In addition to fighting South Africans culturally, which included the founding of German private schools and the resumption of German settlement in the colony, the Germans also extended their struggle into the political realm. Here they fought for political rights—above all the recognition of German as an administrative language—and voting rights, as well as against naturalization and the incorporation of Southwest Africa into the Union of South Africa. The Germans viewed their actions as essential to their survival as a German community. They saw that Southwest Africa was quickly becoming dominated by South Africans, especially Afrikaners, through increased immigration and enfranchisement, which the Afrikaners acquired more easily than German immigrants. Ultimately, the Germans lost this struggle with the outbreak of World War II. More significantly, the self-reflection resulting from their internal struggles caused many Germans to recognize where their hearts and future lay. They had made the final transition from being Southwestern Germans to German Südwester.

Part I
German Colonial Rule, 1894–1919

1

The Settler Colony

German Southwest Africa is the only one among
our colonies that appears suitable to satisfy one of
the main demands of the creators of Germany's
colonial movement, namely to possess our own
overseas territories that are partially capable of
absorbing the current of German emigration.

—*Deutsche Kolonialzeitung*, 19 August 1893

T heodor Leutwein's arrival in South-
west Africa on New Year's Day, 1894, presented colonial officials and enthusiasts with a unique opportunity to influence directly the development
and character of the protectorate. Before that year, various concession
companies had essentially run the region from 1884 to 1890, with little
official German interference.[1] However, these private companies possessed neither the capital nor the means to secure and make the territory
productive. This was especially true after the Herero and Nama uprisings
in the early 1890s, which required greater state expenditures to suppress
them. After several years of imperial German administration, rising costs,
continued conflict with the African societies, and a public debate over the
worth of the colonies, the imperial chancellor, Leo von Caprivi, announced
before the Reichstag his intention to keep Southwest Africa as a German
colony; but he also stated that the government would continue to provide

only minimal financial assistance to it. Shortly thereafter, he dispatched Leutwein (territorial captain, 1894–98; governor, 1898–1905) in late 1893 to take control of the situation and turn the colony into an economically viable possession.[2]

German officials were primarily concerned with finding ways to turn SWA into a productive colony that not only would pay for itself but also would greatly enhance Germany's prestige as a world power. Of paramount concern was securing the territory as a German possession. Officially, the protectorate belonged to Germany, yet several concession companies active there stood strongly under British control.[3] Furthermore, the protectorate contained not only large African populations, but also a number of Afrikaners and colonial Britons. Officials feared that more Afrikaners and Cape colonists might emigrate from Cape Colony to SWA. Chancellor Otto von Bismarck had already, in 1890, contended that the best means to counter these influences was to colonize SWA with Germans:

> The question of the settlement of the protectorate through immigrants . . . is of the greatest importance for [its] future. A speedy settlement of the areas suitable for farming would contribute to a faster development of the country. . . . On the other hand, one cannot overlook that also here exists the danger of the prevalence of *non-German* interests in the protectorate. This danger is all the more so present, as the regions suitable for agriculture . . . are relatively limited and consequently the immigration of Boers and Cape colonists in large numbers would present serious impediments to a future German settlement.[4]

The presence of these non-Germans motivated authorities in Berlin and Windhoek (the capital of SWA) to pursue a policy of settlement in Southwest Africa to secure it as an economically viable German colony.

Meanwhile, colonial enthusiasts, most notably members of the Deutsche Kolonialgesellschaft, were also interested in the acquisition of colonies. They believed colonies would not only enhance Germany's status as a world power, but they would also provide a means to help preserve the German character of the country's emigrants. Moreover, colonies became a place to save the worthy aspects of the "old system" in the face of industrialization and urbanization. These modern developments were already under way and could not be stopped in Germany, but colonies offered a locale, away from the homeland's cultural and social changes, to preserve a preindustrial,

Table I.I. Professions of DKG Members, 1 April 1893

Professions	Number	Percentage
Noblemen	149	.9
Scholars, writers, and artists	209	1.2
Government officials	2,298	13.1
Military and naval officers	1,462	8.3
Judges, lawyers, and notaries	1,115	6.6
Physicians	826	4.7
Clergymen and teachers	1,063	6.1
Merchants, manufacturers, and businessmen	7,099	40.5
Farmers (Landwirte)	421	2.4
Pensioners	370	2.1
Miscellaneous	2,477	14.1

Source: DKG, Jahresbericht, 1892, 5; quoted in Richard V. Pierard, "The German Colonial Society, 1882–1914" (Ph.D. diss., Iowa State University, 1964), 109.

agrarian vision of Germany society.[5] The majority of DKG members belonged primarily to the educated and propertied elites (government officials, military/naval officers, merchants, shopkeepers, small factory owners) and thus were "notables" in German society, "men who represented the dominant political and social institutions in Germany and who embodied, defended, and disseminated the values and conventions that supported these institutions."[6] Like the members of other patriotic societies, they viewed themselves as custodians of German culture. As such, they represented and guarded the values, virtues, and attitudes of the nation, transmitting them by "what they did in the classroom or pulpit and by the authority of their example."[7] DKG members felt that too many Germans emigrated to non-German places and too easily and quickly assimilated into foreign cultures; hence, to prevent German emigrants from losing their Deutschtum and their ties with the Heimat, the society pursued a national campaign for the acquisition and settlement of German colonies.[8]

Experts and officials designated Southwest Africa as the most suitable of all the German colonies for large-scale settlement. Numerous scientists, notably Dr. Richard Hindorf and Dr. Karl Dove, had published reports in the 1890s under the auspices of the Colonial Department in Berlin, debating the suitability of the protectorate for European settlement. They explored not only issues such as land arability, rainfall, and water sources,[9] but also the effects of the climate upon Europeans. Although the former information was relevant to the economic latency of the region as well as to the country's capacity to accommodate potential settlers, the latter issue seemed to occupy an equal, if not greater, significance in terms of public debate. The concern about the effects of a tropical and subtropical environment on the European constitution was to be found among both scientists and lay people, the worry being primarily about the potentially detrimental side effects of extended exposure to such a climate. In the case of Southwest Africa, the experts concluded that its climate was conducive to European settlement.[10]

German officials and the DKG used reports such as Hindorf's and Dove's both to justify keeping SWA and to demonstrate the best means of developing it. They actively cooperated in advancing the settlement of Germans in the territory, although the government retained the upper hand in formulating policy.[11] Both groups, officials and the DKG, maintained that colonization would not only contribute to turning the region into an economically viable German colony but would also provide emigrants with a place to preserve their cultural identity. In essence, the cultural guardians desired to create a second Germany, a place where their vision of Deutschtum could be realized. They wanted to build a new German nation in SWA, away from the anxieties and dislocations resulting from industrialization and the dissatisfaction over the "incompleteness" of German unification— that is to say, a Germany without social, regional, and confessional divisions. While in Germany colonialism became a rallying point around which the entire nation could gather, Southwest Africa itself became not only a model for the Heimat but a laboratory for the actualization of Deutschtum ideals (much as Kenya became a place for some Englishmen to preserve their "self-perceived status as gentlemen.")[12]

Although colonial enthusiasts, both private and governmental, were united in their desire to populate SWA with German settlers, they debated the best way to accomplish this task. These discussions centered around two key issues: public vs. private involvement and small vs. large holdings. Even though no consensus was reached on these issues, elements of all views ultimately found their way into policies.

Before Leutwein's arrival, development and settlement of SWA was left entirely to private concession companies. Even after 1894, the companies continued to play a significant role. This was largely because the majority of land was under their control. For example, in 1900, concession companies controlled approximately 295,000 sq. km of land (out of a total area of 824,269 sq. km).[13] Many of these companies were speculating on land prices and hence holding onto properties until the expected big "colonial boom"; they were obliged, however, to sell land to white settlers.[14] By 1904, when the major companies had sold approximately 3.2 million hectares (12,530 square miles) to white settlers, these companies still controlled more land than the imperial government.[15] And the settlers still occupied very little.

Because of these limited achievements, settlement policy came increasingly under state control. "Patriotic" colonial officials and opponents of concession companies, recognizing that the companies were incapable of colonizing SWA rapidly and on a large scale, were the primary forces behind this shift. These people maintained that only the state with its extensive resources could quickly and extensively colonize a region as vast and as geographically hindered as SWA. A contributor to the *Deutsche Zeitung* wrote, "Today things have completely changed; the colonization must be carried out in greater style according to a uniform plan. Only the government can carry out this task with large sums."[16]

This trend toward greater state involvement started with the arrival of Leutwein in 1894. Shortly after landing in SWA, he undertook a comprehensive and directed effort to develop the colony as a productive German possession. In his eyes, this required establishing peace with the Herero and Nama and turning Southwest Africa into a settler colony. To Leutwein, both were essential: without peace, Germans would not settle there; and without German settlers, the colony could not be developed as an economically independent territory. Peace was Leutwein's top priority. His predecessor, Major Kurt von François, had shown the futility of using force in trying to pacify the Africans, so Leutwein employed another tactic: the use of concessions. "Concessions, in form if not in substance, had to be made to the chiefs' desire for political independence."[17] Leutwein took care to present himself as the representative of a legitimate government and simultaneously built a comprehensive and efficient bureaucracy, the result being "to move into the sphere of administrative procedure many of the decisions that his predecessors had tried to force on the Africans by military action."[18]

After pacifying the Africans, Leutwein moved onto the greater task of settling SWA with Germans. He envisioned the state playing a key role in making the colony suitable and attractive for settlement. In formulating his policy, Leutwein was strongly influenced by Hindorf's report on the agricultural value of the colony. Of primary importance to Leutwein was Hindorf's emphasis on the role of the state in developing the colony. Leutwein took this one step further by seeing "state finance as an investment, the profits of which should return to the Exchequer and not, as Hindorf had argued, to the private companies." Thus, Leutwein believed that the eventual taxation yield resulting from the state's initial involvement in the colony's economic development would be the government's return on its investment.[19]

Leutwein knew that the Herero successfully raised cattle, and based on their experience he decided that the future of the colony lay in raising livestock for the world market.[20] But this required considerable start-up capital for the acquisition of large tracts of land and herds, and early on Leutwein recognized that it would be difficult to lure individuals with the requisite means to the colony; he therefore allowed colonial soldiers to start farms with less capital. Justifying his position, he pointed out that the colonial troops'

> already acquired knowledge of the country alone was worth several thousand Marks. They also did not have to carry the costs of emigration and could make the selection of their plots during their service time, also cost-free. Furthermore, for a certain time before leaving the colonial army they were permitted to watch their own cattle posts, so that in reference to purchasing breeding stock they could ascertain the best prices as well as the most practical opportunities.[21]

Thus from the beginning of Leutwein's administration, former servicemen comprised the majority of settlers. In reflecting upon his decision to promote the settlement of former colonial soldiers, he admitted that "in fact, these have prospered, in any case better than in the homeland, where they would have almost without exception belonged to the propertyless classes."[22] Leutwein believed that the colony offered such individuals a better future than they could expect in Germany. However, colonization by former soldiers was for him a temporary measure until more suitable immigrants— settlers who could establish a profitable cattle industry—would arrive.[23]

The availability of land itself was not an issue. Through the pacification of the Africans in 1894 and an agreement with the German Colonial Company for Southwest Africa (a concession company), the government had acquired extensive tracts of land.[24] Moreover, the imperial government declared in 1894 that, with the permission of the territorial captain, settlers could buy land directly from the Ovaherero people. The following year, several transactions were approved. For example, in the Windhoek region, Ernst Rutsch purchased a farm known as Lichtenstein, Josef Sichel received Haris, and

August Schmerenbeck obtained Claratal. That same year, the Herero leader Zacharias Zeraua, in Otjimbingwe, sold a farm named Karibib (20,000 ha) to the Haelbich family. In 1896, Gustav Voigts acquired 22,000 hectares.[25] While such transactions did contribute to the colonization of the territory, their overall impact was minimal.

Leutwein saw the price of land as the greatest hindrance to large-scale settlement, especially since most farms, if they were going to be successful, needed to be large. Originally the government pursued the concessionary policy of offering land at 2.0 marks per hectare. However, Leutwein abandoned this practice when he realized that only wealthy individuals could afford such a price, and he could count on the immigration of the wealthy only in the rarest of cases. Consequently, the colonial government set the lowest price for a hectare at 1.0 to 1.50 marks. In 1898, Leutwein lowered the price even more, to between 0.50 and 1.0, and for imperial citizens liable for military service to 0.30. Former colonial soldiers were not required to pay anything. Leutwein also set up the conditions of sale so as to prevent speculation in inexpensively acquired land (unlike the terms for a concession company). For example, the conditions prevented the buyer from selling the land, without government approval, for a period of ten years. Moreover, the purchaser was required to begin working the land within six months from the date of purchase; if this did not happen, the farm would be returned to the government. In such instances, the buyer had no right to reclaim the initial investment.[26] Leutwein wanted to ensure a long-term commitment to the development of the colony.

The German government pursued other avenues to accelerate the colonization of SWA. For instance, the Reichstag authorized 100,000 marks in the colonial administration's 1901 budget for settlement aid. According to Leutwein, twenty-eight soldiers were settled with this money, each receiving an advance of 3,000 to 4,000 marks in the form of livestock, building materials, and agricultural implements. Each applicant had to prove that he possessed at least 2,500 marks. The governor remarked that this was "a sum that a frugally managing soldier could save during his period of service." He reasoned that "only if [the soldier] put his own money in his enterprise will he have the necessary interest to stick to it."[27] If Leutwein could not have wealthy farmers, he wanted at least ones who had a commitment to the land. Still, somehow Leutwein had to find ways to encourage and promote the settlement of Germans with greater means.

With more experience, the colonial administration concluded that, if it wanted to accelerate colonization of the territory, a settler would require, in addition to low land prices, considerable cash support. In 1902, Leutwein commissioned an expert to determine just how high the initial costs would be for a farm of 5,000 hectares purchased at the old rate of 2.0 marks/ha. The expert concluded that under such conditions few farmers could be expected to survive: the purchase price of the farm, initial start-up costs, and the first year's livelihood required the new colonist to bring with him 30,000 to 40,000 marks. Leutwein was aware that, even though they were the most desirable, such individuals would rarely immigrate to SWA.[28] Therefore, Leutwein requested more financial aid for settlement to accelerate colonization.

Colonial enthusiasts in Berlin recognized the necessity of Leutwein's request, and in 1903 the Reichstag, at the formal request of Colonial Director Dr. Oskar Stuebel, allocated 300,000 marks for this purpose. The Reichstag designated 100,000 marks of this money for the creation of a settlement commission to make practical suggestions for the general colonization of the territory: there was to be a thorough investigation, which would include studies of neighboring colonies; and the remaining 200,000 marks were to be used as state advances of 10,000 to 20,000 marks per applicant. The latter sum was to be based on the purchase price of the land and personal capital of no less than 10,000 marks, giving each farmer between 20,000 and 30,000 marks start-up capital. Leutwein concluded that "while [the farmer] was only a moderately wealthy man at home, in the protectorate he entered the ranks of the well-to-do, especially since he did not have pressure from the government regarding the repayment of interest and principal."[29] Under the conditions of settlement (i.e., through state support), not only did the government contribute to the development of the colony, it also hoped to raise the social status of its colonizers. These funds enabled twenty-six Germans to settle in Southwest Africa.[30] Leutwein, however, desired more Germans to come.

The settlement commission made several practical recommendations to the government for improving and increasing the colonization of the protectorate, suggesting that colonial officials take greater care in selecting farm sites, provide building materials for farmers, accommodations for newly arrived colonists, and find good sources for breeding stock, provisions, and other necessities.[31] In essence, the commission argued that the colonial authorities needed to create an environment more enticing to potential settlers. Leutwein believed that despite the difficulties of farming in

SWA, settler-farmers could still succeed. After reading the report, he wrote the Foreign Office's Colonial Department

> that despite all obstacles a local farmer can with the passage of time make something of himself, if he is the right man. This fact would be especially informative for new settlers and give them clarity over the character traits to bring with them. They must combine self-reliance and frugality with a work zeal that does not shy away from anything. As far as possible, I request that value be placed upon this in the selection [of settlers].[32]

Not just any man could make it in SWA; only a certain type of man. And this was the man Leutwein wanted to settle in the colony. In order to ensure that this would happen, he asked the colonial officials in Germany to select only independent, parsimonious, and hard-working individuals to settle in SWA. However, in 1904, before any of these measures could be carried out, hostilities broke out between the Germans and the Herero and Nama.

Although the uprisings interrupted Leutwein's settlement program and ended his career as governor of SWA, his policies resulted in dramatic change. The German government under his administration had taken not only an increased interest in the colonization and development of the territory, but also a more active role in the settlement of it. It went from a position of keeping state financial involvement to a minimum and allowing private enterprise to develop the colony to the realization that any rapid development required greater government involvement. The state believed that its financial commitment to settle SWA quickly would ultimately reduce its responsibility for the protectorate by turning it into a self-sufficient, productive colony. It was thus in the state's own interest to make investments in the region. From the beginning, Leutwein held and pursued this position, believing that the state's investment would pay off in the form of greater tax revenues from a productive economy. Because of his efforts (and those of his allies in Berlin), between 1898 and 1902 the government sold 1,093,694 hectares of land to settlers[33]—a figure that, nevertheless, lagged behind the sales made by the concession companies.

The Nama and Herero revolts were primarily a result of Leutwein's policies. Increasingly, Africans experienced political and social discrimination, including (and most importantly), the expropriation of land. Though the actual fighting in the uprising was brief (it took place roughly between 1904 and 1905), it was nonetheless devastating for the African populations.

Accurate population figures for the Herero and Nama prior to the conflict do not exist, but it has been estimated that 75 to 80 percent of the Herero and 35 to 50 percent of the Nama perished.[34]

After the wars the Germans were the undisputed masters of the colony, and serious attention could again be given to settlement. For colonial officials and enthusiasts, there were now new opportunities, and demands, for settlement. Most notably, the situation included the availability of large tracts of Herero and Nama land, the implementation of a new type of settlement, and the question of indemnities to farmers who had suffered during the conflict. With Germans finally the true masters, there could be the beginnings of full-scale colonization. The Germans had reduced the Africans to a subservient position and relegated them to reservations. Dr. Paul Rohrbach, the new settlement commissioner, wrote that "with the return of regulated conditions and with the beginning of a new epoch for the protectorate through the change in government, the colonization question has now moved most decisively into the foreground."[35]

Because of the damage done by the conflict, SWA needed a new beginning to improve its economic situation. Consequently, Bernhard Dernburg, the new director of the Colonial Department in Berlin and later state secretary in the Colonial Office (the RKA), decreed that, to set SWA on its own feet, a long-term program (to last approximately ten years) of economic and agricultural development had to be implemented. The program had to confront numerous issues, among them the development of the transportation system (railways, harbors, roads, and so forth); the promotion of agriculture (cotton, rubber, corn) and the appropriation of livestock (cattle, sheep); forestry; the water supply; the discovery and exploitation of minerals; the "native" question (the "workers" question); and colonization. Dernburg expected the governor to provide a report on these subjects.[36]

The importance Dernburg placed on the resolution of these issues revealed the government's intense desire to continue Leutwein's policy—that is to say, to promote large-scale settlement in order to receive an eventual return on its initial investment in SWA. In response to Dernburg's edict, the new governor, Friedrich von Lindequist (1905–7), ordered officials in SWA to conduct studies and report to him. The results of these studies, which drew heavily from similar experiences in South Africa, found their way into a memorandum that Lindequist sent to the Colonial Office. Like his predecessor, he recognized the importance of livestock breeding for Southwest Africa's future, a program that required extensive colonization. Therefore, settlement of the colony assumed top priority. In his memorandum, Lindequist wrote that "it is at the moment one of the most important tasks of the colonial and protectorate administration to make German Southwest Africa an object of attraction for German emigration." Though he stated that the natural conditions of the country would themselves be an incentive, he recognized that certain prerequisites were missing; therefore, it became the colonial administration's task "to create these requirements and arrange them as favorably and as beneficially for the colonization as possible."[37] Drawing from the findings of Leutwein's commission and the work of Rohrbach, these preconditions included the need for water reservoirs, a good transportation system, land surveying, and, above all, the easy acquisition, under favorable conditions, of farms by settlers.[38]

However, Lindequist had reservations concerning state involvement in the life and activity of settlers. He believed it was imperative for the government "to awaken and promote the independence and spontaneity of the settlers as much as possible instead of not allowing them to develop or of hindering them in their development through direct interference." According to Lindequist, this was especially a problem for the German, because "due to his nature and to the conditions at home [he] is as inclined to be cared for, to call for the state's help and to expect from the state everything, as he is prepared to criticize the measures of the government and be sensitive to patronizing treatment."[39] Thus, the government believed it had to assist settlers, but not to the point of destroying their self-reliance.

Despite these reservations, the colonial government, aided by funds allocated by the Reichstag, embarked upon a comprehensive program to prepare SWA for extensive colonization. Drawing on his knowledge, through reports, of the South African experience, Lindequist had the rail system extended, increased the number of surveyors, and aided settlers in searching and drilling for water. The latter was particularly important since SWA was a water-poor country. Lindequist also advocated the granting of state settlement aid. Lindequist justified this based upon conditions in SWA and because the Reichstag had already allocated money that had not been completely used up.[40]

Under the provisions for granting state financial assistance, a German citizen could receive up to 6,000 marks, interest free, with the first of ten annual payments due after the sixth year. Former colonial soldiers were to receive preference; then aid would be available to other German citizens. In addition, and rather importantly, the applicant had to possess certain character traits. Not only did the individual have to be a German citizen, living on his own farm or homestead and not cohabiting with a "native," but he also had to possess the "necessary knowledge and characteristics for an orderly agricultural enterprise" and "be held in good repute."[41] If an applicant did not have these qualifications, he could be denied aid.[42]

To offset state assistance and preserve the settler's independence, the colonial government increased the settler's role in building his business. First, it advocated reducing the cost of land, a factor made possible by the expropriation of huge tracts of African land after the suppression of the Herero and Nama. Lower land prices would reduce the amount of settlement aid a farmer would require, and consequently the settler's reliance on the state would be reduced.[43] Second, the colonial government provided settlers with healthy, inexpensive livestock. This came from two sources: Lindequist ordered both the sale of confiscated Herero livestock and the import and sale of South African livestock at minimal profit to the state.[44] Both of these actions, while ostensibly raising the farmers' self-esteem and independence, in fact only increased their reliance on the state. They were superficial, not truly substantive actions since the colonial government still took care of the farmer's needs and reduced his risks and costs.

In an attempt to increase the German population density, Lindequist also supported small-scale settlement (*Kleinsiedlung*) by granting homesteaders (*Kleinsiedler*) financial assistance.[45] Essentially, Kleinsiedlung corresponded to the homestead program begun in the early 1890s by the Syndicate for Southwest African Settlement (SfsS) with small-scale, intensive farming.[46] Against the recommendations of Rohrbach, the settlement commissioner,[47] in early 1906 Lindequist had thirty ten-hectare lots prepared around Osona near Okahandja. Additional plots were surveyed near Windhoek, Omaruru, Otjiwarongo, and elsewhere. By April, five "qualified, reliable people" had already begun operating the plots in Osona, three of which came from the German Kleinsiedlungen in South Africa. Lindequist maintained that more would follow them. Intents to buy had been submitted for the remaining plots. By 1908, there were seventy-five white settlers in Osona.[48]

Lindequist deflected criticism by admitting to the difficulties involved in this type of settlement. But he noted that in South Africa, Germans had already successfully overcome such difficulties. He pointed out how quickly settlers had snatched up the available plots and said he saw a potential increased demand once the number of the colonial soldiers had been reduced. Lindequist justified his position by claiming to have finally done something about the colonization of SWA—not merely to have talked about it. Furthermore, he argued that this method would "give those with few means the opportunity to settle and thereby . . . make a start producing domestically the requirements of the country for grain and garden products to a larger extent than before."[49] He argued that not only would more people thereby be able to settle in the colony, but another need would also be fulfilled.

Despite Lindequist's patronage of the program, small-scale settlement became the object of an intense debate. After three years, the enterprise disappointed supporters. It either did not experience the success expected or it did not contribute as substantially to the colonization of the territory as people had hoped. Without a doubt, successes were registered, and many people continued to support the program. Nevertheless, debates surfaced over why it had failed to provide a livelihood for homesteaders, dividing supporters into various camps. Some argued that the conditions for settlement were wrong or too restrictive. Others contended that the fault lay with the type of settlers; Kleinsiedlung needed patient, devoted, hard-working men, not individuals interested in a quick return.[50] Despite the controversies, the program continued, with state subsidies, until World War I.

Lindequist, an able administrator, was also an enthusiast for agrarianism. He believed the true German was an independent small farmer—one with pitchfork in hand and his feet in manure.[51] Thus his support of Kleinsiedlungen came as no surprise. But he took an essentially European idea, the peasant farmer, and transplanted it to SWA, where it was obviously economically unsuitable. It failed, as Rohrbach pointed out it would, and survived only through state subventions. Admittedly, from the beginning Lindequist saw it only as an adjunct to the primary goal of developing the colony through large-scale farming.[52]

Another method utilized to aid the settlement of Germans in the colony and to provide them with knowledge of local conditions was the concept of farm volunteers. Introduced by the Colonial Society's settlement company, Lindequist incorporated the practice into his overall colonization program. In early 1907, farmers reintroduced the program because they needed help on their farms. Under the program, farmers took in interested individuals for an accommodation fee. These volunteers would essentially work on the farm as apprentices for a specified time, after which they would have hopefully acquired the knowledge necessary to run their own farms successfully. Although the colonial government ran the program, the DKG readily supplied information about positions.[53]

In one instance, the colonial government went to great lengths to find a position for a student of the German Colonial School in Witzenhausen, Oskar Kisker. In his memorandum concerning the settlement of the region, Lindequist praised the work of the school in preparing Germans from the middle stratum of the educated ranks for a life in the colonies. He regretted, though, that there was little opportunity for them in German SWA. The two most obvious means for them to gain experience in the colony as preparation for a long-lasting settlement there were either through military service with the *Schutztruppe* or as a farm volunteer, and they were either unavailable to older students or too expensive. He supported the suggestion of the school's director, Fabarius, to grant students positions in state enterprises.[54] Fabarius believed his students, members of the educated ranks, "know better what awaits them out there than the simple land folk and craftsmen or even the urban factory population, and . . . are also capable of subsequently assuming economic and intellectual leadership among the following settlement population."[55] The fact that Lindequist backed Fabarius's request indicated that the governor, in addition to his bent for agrarianism, was also interested in seeing the better-educated elements of German society settle in the colony.

Lindequist's successors continued his settlement programs. There were slight variations, but the intent remained the same. For instance, Bruno von Schuckmann (governor, 1907–10) found it necessary to demand that settlers prove they possessed a certain amount of capital before they purchased land and started a business; he was concerned that unqualified individuals without means who purchased a farm—which occurred occasionally—could become an agricultural proletariat and would not contribute to the development of the country or, worse, would become more radical. He also realized that regulations could hinder the colonization of SWA; consequently, he commanded local officials to sell land to wealthy individuals and allow them to seek their own fate. Furthermore, he ordered them not to demand proof of a person's material value if that person already knew the land, could guarantee that he knew how to handle the "natives," and was prepared to lead a frugal life. In all other circumstances, they were to require verification of an individual's wealth. He ordered a similar procedure regarding the granting of settlement aid.[56]

In 1909, Schuckmann ordered that farms could not be occupied if they did not already have a water source on them. Apparently, a few overanxious young men, in their desire to become independent, had taken possession of their farms and had only then begun to establish a water source. In the process, they had expended a great deal of money, time, and energy. So much, in fact, that little or nothing was left for purchasing livestock or building a house. Such individuals then became an economic burden for the state. Consequently, Schuckmann decided that the colonial government would assume responsibility for establishing the first water source on farms; such endeavors cost a great deal of money.[57]

Schuckmann acted more discriminatingly toward Kleinsiedlung. In a circular to local authorities, he wrote, "It appears to me questionable to continue with the Kleinsiedlungen at this time," and he ordered them to give financial aid only to homesteaders who had invested in their business and accomplished something. He said that whether an individual wanted to become a Kleinsiedler or not was his own business, but assistance would not be given until the individual proved that he could make it.[58]

Schuckmann did reverse one policy begun by Lindequist—the importation at public expense of livestock from South Africa. He ordered local authorities to turn such importation over to farm associations. The government, he said, was prepared to aid these groups, as well as to grant aid to farmers who purchased good livestock for their own breeding; however, aid would go only to those farmers who could not afford to import livestock themselves. The governor did not think they were poor farmers—merely farmers without substantial amounts of capital.[59]

For the colony's next, and last, governor, Theodor Seitz (1910 to 1915/18), the most important issue was, as for his predecessors, finding a solution to the water question. The success or failure of the region depended upon this issue. He devoted considerable energy to this problem. He also shared with his predecessors a concern over the character of the colonists, believing that the colonization of SWA required hearty, unassuming men; he advised those who were accustomed to urban life to remain at home.[60] Surprisingly, in 1910 Seitz allowed certain landowners who were in financial trouble to sell farms obtained from the government; thus, farmers with little capital who were unable to develop their land adequately could sell. This enabled wealthy individuals to establish large farms more easily; the government also encouraged failing farmers to set up new businesses from their sale receipts.[61] Moreover, it suggested that the colonial government was less concerned with speculation and sought ways to facilitate the growth of large, productive farms.

By 1913, it was obvious that economic policy favored large ranches.

Table 1.2. White Farms, 1 April 1913

District	No. of Farms	Owners	Tenants	Size of Farms (ha)	Cattle	Small Stock
Grootfontein	173	165	16	777,077	16,931	21,399
Outjo	63	74	3	431,125	8,686	13,984
Omaruru	175	146	17	1,020,497	23,737	54,489
Karibib	78	57	9	931,551	12,351	35,918
Okahandja	103	89	5	788,899	23,831	33,564
Gobabis	108	87	6	773,473	11,428	30,037
Windhoek	138	129	11	1,569,703	33,516	78,712
Rehoboth	105	75	8	902,915	8,736	57,022
Gibeon	82	70	4	1,187,312	7,588	88,896
Maltahöhe	60	58	2	952,855	5,115	68,309
Keetmanshoop	73	37	23	1,209,353	5,507	58,018
Hasuur (Aroab)	63	54	7	849,462	4,609	42,452
Warmbad	47	39	11	1,081,781	2,941	46,223
Bethanien	41	23	11	507,253	3,636	37,572
Lüderitz Bay	16	11	1	358,579	339	3,769
Swakopmund	6	5	1	51,771	26	150
TOTALS	1,331	1,119	135	13,393,606	168,977	670,514
		1,254				

Source: *Die deutschen Schutzgebiete in Afrika und der Südsee, 1912–13: Amtliche Jahresberichte,* 94–95.

Although the policy of Kleinsiedlung was not abandoned, by April of that year 1,331 white farms covering approximately 13.39 million hectares were owned by 1,119 people (see table 1.2). Moreover, other large farms comprised an additional 10.9 million hectares (420 farms that had already been surveyed and were available for sale, plus 145 farms that had not yet been surveyed but were nonetheless sold or leased).[62] In contrast, 337 homesteads owned by 294 people occupied only 3,737 hectares (see table 1.3).

The increase in occupied farmland was a direct result of increased immigration to the colony. In 1898 there were only 1,242 German males in the protectorate; by 1902 the number had more than doubled, to 2,595. Following the suppression of the uprisings, the German population increased significantly. In 1908 there were 6,215 Germans (males and females), while the following year saw 9,288 Germans in the colony. By 1913 more than 12,000 Germans inhabited SWA. In comparison, the total white population

Table 1.3. Small Settlements, 1 April 1913

District	Settlements	Farmers	Tenants	Size of Farms (ha)
Omaruru	33	25	5	781
Karibib	8	8	–	22
Okahandja	59	52	5	672
Gobabis	12	11	–	138
Windhoek	165	143	10	1,448
Malthöhe	1	1	–	5
Keetmanshoop	10	9	1	65
Bethanien	21	18	–	42
Swakopmund	28	27	1	564
TOTALS	337	294	22	3,737
		316		

Source: *Die deutschen Schutzgebiete in Afrika und der Südsee 1912–13: Amtliche Jahresberichte*, 96–97.

was 2,499 (1,532 males) in 1898, 4,635 in 1902, 8,213 in 1908, 11,791 in 1909, and 14,830 in 1913. Thus the Germans not only increased their actual numbers, but also their percentage of the total white population. In 1898 they comprised 81 percent of the colony's white male population. In 1902, in figures showing percentage of the entire white population, the German share dropped to 56 percent, but subsequently this percentage rose steadily, reaching 83 percent in 1913 (see table 1.4).

In most regions and towns, Germans formed a majority by 1913. This was true even for the southern part of the colony, where most of the Afrikaners settled. For example, in Gibeon and Keetmanshoop, respectively, between 1900 and 1913 Germans went from 32 percent and 38 percent of the population to 67 percent and 85 percent. Thus, Keetmanshoop, Bethanien, Warmbad, and Gibeon all boasted German majorities; only in Aroab (Hasuur) did German citizens make up less than half of the population (see table 1.5).

Of course, not all SWA immigrants stayed. For example, in 1908, when 3,627 immigrated to SWA, 2,641 left the territory. In 1910 an even higher percentage left: 5,766 entered and 4,835 left.[63] The net increases in the white population were 986 in 1908 and only 931 in 1910. Despite such statistics, the region nonetheless became a predominantly German possession with the passage of each year.

Table 1.4. European Population Statistics, 1894-1913

Year	Total*	Germans	% of	Foreigners
1894	969			
. . .				
1896	1,992			
1897	2,628			
1898	2,499			
1899	2,827			
1900	3,339	2,104	62	1,284
1901	3,607	2,223	61	1,420
1902	4,635	2,595	56	2,079
1903	4,640	2,998	64	1,684
. . .				
. . .				
1906	6,366			
1907	7,110	4,929	69	2,181
1908	8,213	6,215	76	1,998
1909	11,791	9,288	79	2,503
1910	12,935	10,226	79	2,709
1911	13,962	11,140	80	2,822
1912	14,816	12,135	82	2,681
1913	14,830	12,292	83	2,538

* To achieve uniformity in statistical measurement, for the years 1891–96 the number of African women married to European men has been subtracted. In official statistics from 1891–96, the African women married to European men were counted in the "white" population; after 1907, official statistics counted these women as "natives."

Source: Herbert C. Nöckler, *Sprachmischung in Südwestafrika* (Munich: Max Hueber, 1963), 134; Hans Berthold, "Die Besiedlung Deutsch-Südwestafrika," *Jahrbuch über die deutschen Kolonien* 4 (1911): 160; *Bevölkerungsstatistik D-SWA, Anlage D.1. zur Denkschrift über die Entwicklung der deutschen Schutzgebiete in Afrika und der Südsee, April 1903–March 1904 an den Reichstag*, 11. Legislatur-Periode 1, Session 1903-5, BAP R101/1096; *Bevölkerungsstatistik, Anlage zur Denkschrift über die Entwicklung der Schutzgebiete in Afrika und der Südsee, 1908-9, an den Deutschen Reichstag*, 12. Legislatur-Periode 2, Session 1909-10, BAP R101/1101; Karl Dove, *Die deutschen Kolonien IV: Südwestafrika* (Berlin; Leipzig: Göschen'sche Verlagshandlung GmbH, 1913), 66; *Die deutschen Schutzgebiete in Afrika und der Südsee: Amtliche Jahresberichte 1912–13*, 24–25.

What these figures did not reveal, however, was the type of individual encouraged and aided in settling in the colony. Nor did they expose the anxieties about the stability of German hegemony in the region. Colonial officials and the DKG as well as the Southwestern German community consciously promoted the settlement of a specific type of German, while simul-

Table 1.5. **Percentage Relationship between Germans, Afrikaner, and British, 1900 and 1913**

District	1 Jan. 1900			1 Jan. 1913		
	German	Afrikaner	British	German	Afrikaner	British
Aroab (Hasuur)	—	—	—	28	72	—
Bethanien	—	—	—	86	11	3
Gibeon	32	63	5	67	33	—
Gobabis	88	11	1	94	5	1
Grootfontein (mit Ovamboland)	—	—	—	94	5	1
Karibib	—	—	—	98	1	1
Keetmanshoop	38	50	12	85	13	2
Lüderitz Bay	—	—	—	88	9	3
Maltahöhe	—	—	—	78	22	—
Okahandja	—	—	—	97	3	—
Omaruru	70	20	10	98	2	—
Outjo	—	—	—	96	4	—
Rehoboth	—	—	—	86	14	—
Swakopmund	75	4	21	95	2	3
Warmbad	—	—	—	60	39	—
Windhoek	82	14	4	94	5	1

Source: Herbert C. Nöckler, *Sprachmischung in Südwestafrika* (Munich: Max Hueber, 1963), 131–33.

taneously implementing measures to exclude undesirable elements and to combat potential threats to Deutschtum in SWA.

2

The Model Settler and Challenges to Deutschtum

> Whoever has seen the country knows that a German new land can be created here, with an active population . . . and knows that the way is open to give a form to German life that would make it a joy to live in this country. In the not too distant future, may German South Africa blossom into such a land that it is a blessing to itself and the Motherland.
>
> —Wilhelm Külz, architect of self-government in Southwest Africa, writing in 1909

In the eyes of many colonial officials and enthusiasts, the ideal settler would belong to a particular segment of society; namely, the upper-middle Stand. This was evident in the amount of start-up capital deemed necessary for success in SWA. Indeed, Dr. Paul Rohrbach, the former settlement commissioner, adamantly advised individuals who did not have at least 50,000 marks to stay at home.[1] Colonial enthusiasts believed that if an individual possessed that type of money, and hence belonged to that socioeconomic strata, and bred livestock, he would almost automatically be endowed with the preferred characteristics—that is, he would be self-reliant, parsimonious, prosperous, adaptable, patient, loyal to the empire, aware of racial differences, and in possession of a good reputation. In other words, he would be a solid representative of Deutschtum. Thus, the colonial endeavor in Southwest Africa had a socioeconomic, predominantly nonindustrial character, especially because it intended to exclude elements of the working class. The inclusion of personality criteria for the allocation of state funds gave officials an additional means to prevent exceptions from slipping through the screening process.

Both public and private means were employed to attract appropriate colonists. As early as the 1890s, the Syndicate for Southwest African Settlement issued a brochure outlining what colonists required to settle and to begin a business in SWA.[2] Their advice ranged from what to bring in terms of clothing and farm implements to acquiring livestock and building a house and how much everything cost. It also included information regarding conditions for raising livestock, planting fields, and the availability of water. Obviously, the pamphlet was intended to prepare the individual by describing what awaited him. Yet it served a double purpose: it also discouraged undesirable colonists.

Once the Reich became involved, in the later 1890s, it too wanted to inform and attract settlers. Initially the Foreign Office assumed responsibility for providing information for interested emigrants as well as for screening them. The DKG took over this role in 1902 when, with state funding, it created the Central Information Office for Emigrants (Zafa), providing brochures for those who were interested in settling in the German colonies and who possessed the right traits. Most of the requests for information came, however, from people who were deemed unsuitable because they did not even possess the necessary travel money; that is, they were from the lower strata of society, and thus were discouraged from immigrating.[3]

As interest in the colony increased after the suppression of the Nama and Herero revolts, in 1908 the German government published its *Amtlicher Ratgeber für Auswanderer* (official guide for emigrants), updating it annually. The guide contained descriptions of the various areas of the colony, what was needed to settle there and start a farm, how to breed cattle, handle the "natives," and so forth.[4] Through the details, it discouraged those without means.

The press—colonial periodicals as well as daily newspapers—also disseminated colonial propaganda. Like the SfsS and official publications, its articles encouraged interested and, more importantly, appropriate individuals to emigrate.[5] For example, a personal account, by Hubert Janson (a Südwester), published in *Kolonie und Heimat* (organ of the DKG's Women's League), acted as both a warning and an invitation:

In this country one must be everything, gardener, livestock breeder, farmer (I have corn fields on the farm), hunter, trapper, smith, cartwright, mason, plumber, glassblower, yes even photographer. Only tailoring and cobbling have I not yet tried. One thing, however, is not allowed to be extinguished, and that is the entrepreneurial spirit and the humor—even on days when there is only thick rice and a piece of dry bread with coffee, our national bread. . . .

The man who easily loses the desire, who is fearful and accustomed to good living and social life, who always must have spiritual refreshment and cannot endure loneliness and exertion, in often great heat—it is preferable that he remain with mother at home. However, the man who does not shun work and who has a little bit of the devil in his body, he is the right man for our Southwest![6]

As the statistics given in chapter 1 indicate, officials and enthusiasts turned SWA into a German colony with an ever increasing German population. More importantly (see tables 1.4 and 1.5), the territory developed apparently according to plan: the number of farmers continued to increase. In 1898, farmers numbered only 278. By 1904 their numbers had risen to 813, and by 1911 to 1,388. On the other hand, the number of government employees continued to remain higher, as did the number of craftsmen, workers, and miners. In 1898 there were 801 government employees (civil servants and military personnel) and 183 craftsmen, workers, and miners. By 1909 the number of government employees had fallen to 768; the craftsman/worker/miner group had risen to 1,979[7]—a significant increase attributable primarily to the discovery of diamonds in the protectorate.

Many of the farmers appeared to possess the necessary character traits. One notable example was the Voigts family. In 1896, Gustav Voigts purchased a farm of 22,000 hectares and went on to be a prominent individual in SWA politics. Family members were also involved in the extremely successful trading company Wecke & Voigts, which had offices in Okahandja (1892), Windhoek (1894), Swakopmund (1908), and Grootfontein (1908). Albert Voigts, involved in the company until 1906, purchased Voigtsgrund (which lay between Mariental and Maltahöhe), which was one of the largest farms in SWA.[8]

However, not all groups in the colony embodied the good-German ideals exhibited by the Voigts; in other words, they did not possess the appropriate socioeconomic character traits that would allow them to develop the colony economically as a German possession. Colonial officials promoted the settlement of individuals with lesser means, most notably former colonial soldiers and Kleinsiedler. Although these were not the most desirable settlers, colonial authorities could not deny them the opportunity to settle in SWA, especially the ex-servicemen. Officials believed their presence would contribute to strengthening the German character of the colony. Either because of acquired knowledge through years of service in the colony or because of the nature of the enterprise, the colonial government reduced the minimum wealth stipulation for these two groups.

Officials like Leutwein and Lindequist argued that SWA would offer these people opportunities they would never have had in Germany. Thus, the possession of land would allow them to rise into the ranks of the middle Stand. The character requirements for state assistance existed to make certain that they possessed the qualities necessary for inclusion in this group. However, Leutwein saw the settlement of such individuals as merely temporary until more appropriate colonists had arrived.[9] While Lindequist also believed that livestock breeding would be the backbone of the economy, he nonetheless was more adamant about supporting the settlement of Kleinsiedler than both his predecessor and successors.

The settlement of Afrikaners from South Africa proved to be more problematic. Almost from the beginning of German control, Afrikaners practically occupied center stage in discussions about colonizing the protectorate. Many colonial enthusiasts welcomed the immigration of Afrikaners into the colony. Unlike newly arrived farmers from Germany, the Afrikaners already possessed the knowledge necessary for a successful farm enterprise and could thus contribute immediately to the economic development of the colony. Furthermore, their knowledge could be passed onto the fresh, young German farmers. The *Alldeutscher Verband* (ADV), a middle-strata nationalist Pan-German league, favored the settlement of Afrikaners in the region; in fact, it aided the settlement of twenty-four Afrikaner families in the colony. For the ADV, the Afrikaners belonged to the German race because of their Low German heritage; their settlement in SWA would supplement the German stock.[10]

Although colonial officials recognized the utility of settling Afrikaners in the protectorate, many had reservations about it. In fact, as early as 1890 Bismarck perceived the Afrikaners as a potential rival for mastery of the colony. Several years later, Caprivi, while simultaneously acknowledging their usefulness in a report before the Reichstag justifying the colonial government's policies toward Afrikaners, also expressed concern about their moving into the region:

> Also among the South Africans and especially among the Boers a strong inclination exists to migrate to our territory and come into the possession of farms there. It is undeniable that the Boer is a good pioneer in South Africa; Boers know the country and people, and from them the German colonist can learn something. In principle the administration also has in no way the intention to keep the Boers out of the protectorate. It will only prevent Boers from moving into the country in closed groups and more or less establishing independent, political communities. It will further not allow a Boer proletariat in, but rather only those Boers who possess sufficient wealth in cash or herd animals.[11]

Later, Leutwein shared views similar to Caprivi's. However, Leutwein believed that once new arrivals from Germany had become acquainted with local conditions they would ultimately achieve more than the Afrikaner. He foresaw that there would eventually be enough experienced Germans later to advise and help those Germans who followed them, thus negating the need for the Afrikaners.[12]

Concerns about the Afrikaners went beyond colonial officials: colonial enthusiasts and settlers also voiced opposition. However, their worries manifested themselves in conspiracy theories and perceived threats to Deutschtum and German authority. They viewed any dubious action by an Afrikaner as an attempt to overthrow German rule. This perception increased as more Afrikaners trekked into SWA, settling primarily in the south. There the Afrikaners constituted the majority, and concerned individuals demanded action from the government to defuse this threat and control the type of Afrikaner who could settle in the territory.[13]

In order to reduce their own concerns, and possibly to placate colonial enthusiasts and settlers, officials implemented measures to control the entry of Afrikaners into the territory and to incorporate those already there into the German population. Beginning in 1902, government authorities demanded from Afrikaners proof of enough wealth to start a small farm (although not as much as was required from newly arrived Germans), granted them German citizenship (which some availed themselves of), and inducted their sons into the colonial army. In general, the government discouraged

Boers from immigrating to SWA. The authorities had to grant the Afrikaners the right to maintain their Reformed Dutch religion and their African Dutch language (Afrikaans), but they hoped that Afrikaner children would attend German schools. Unlike German settlers, Afrikaner colonists received no financial assistance from the government. Most importantly, officials realized that the best means to offset the Afrikaners' presence was to promote the settlement of Germans.[14]

Despite the ever increasing German and European population, another group continually threatened German rule and notions of Deutschtum. Before the arrival of Europeans, various African societies had already settled there. Once Germans and other Europeans began settling in the region, these Africans posed a direct challenge to German hegemony. The Germans met this challenge by claiming that their skin color—"white" *(weiß)*—entitled them to rule the land, especially after the brutal suppression of the Nama and Herero between 1904 and 1907. They invoked "the European-Principle"—"the national race and legal conditions of the colonizing powers in Europe and the world"[15]—to justify the subjugation of the Africans and the expropriation of their land. In other words, they believed that their white skin, a symbol of their supposedly "superior" culture, gave them the authority to rule over those inferior to them—in other words, those with dark skin.[16] Hence, because of their skin color Europeans claimed the right to manage the world's resources as well as to assume a moral obligation to care for those "less civilized." However, the Germans were not fully able to establish their claims and take control of the land until 1906, when they had subjugated the indigenous populations. Thereafter, the Germans controlled and regulated the lives of the Africans essentially to the benefit of European farmers. They issued discriminatory regulations regarding where the Africans could live and work as well as limiting their mobility.[17]

To the Germans, the Africans were not only a potential danger but also an important resource and an essential part of the colonial economy. This was evident in the various official reports detailing the colony's development that placed statistics about the African population after the white-population statistics and before those enumerating livestock. The authorities and settlers saw Africans as a cheap source of labor that would carry out the most menial tasks for the white population. Yet this "special resource" was in short supply after General von Trotha nearly annihilated the Nama and Herero in his campaign to suppress the uprisings in the early 1900s—a slaughter deplored by the farmers. Thereafter, colonial authorities gave special attention to ensuring a constant labor supply. Simultaneously, fearing incitement to further revolt, they took care to ensure that Südwester did not blatantly mistreat Africans. As in British South Africa,[18] this dual function of the colonial government—developing the colony while protecting the indigenous population—was obviously contradictory and revealed the regime's hypocrisy. Especially evident in officials' attempts to promote the local economy, it was complicated by farmer demands for more laborers and missionaries' advocacy of fair treatment for Africans.[19]

Though the German government had defeated the Herero and Nama and had implemented regulations to control and exploit them, threats to its rule continued. As in other European colonies with small white populations and significantly larger numbers of Africans,[20] the threat came from the behavior of whites who crossed the boundaries that separated Europeans from "natives."[21] In European colonies, for whites to maintain mastery it was imperative that Africans respect them;[22] however, not all Europeans honored this unwritten code, especially poor whites of questionable character. Since such individuals were not good examples of "whiteness," they endangered German domination. At the turn of the century, colonial officials considered limiting the entry of these so-called "questionable" elements into SWA (i.e., those not representative of their image of Deutschtum),[23] but policies were not implemented. By 1905 the situation had changed. In a report to Berlin, Lindequist pointed out the need for a decree to limit immigration to "suitable" settlers.[24]

The biggest threat for colonial authorities and enthusiasts came from those whites who cohabited with or married African women. Such relationships were deemed pernicious to the maintenance of German rule in the colony, especially in light of the general belief of the time that the "more primitive" partner would bring down the "more civilized" one:

> It is a known matter, that mixed marriages between whites and coloreds pass the bad characteristics of the parents onto the children to a higher degree than the good. . . .
>
> The woman and the offspring do not rise to the educational level of the man and father, but rather the man sinks back to that of the woman. His house does not become a place of German ways and German family life, but rather he comes down in the world and degenerates more or less in his hut that maintains its mark through the essence of the woman and finally pulls the man down, after perhaps initial resistance in his thinking

and actions, to the level and sphere in which the woman was born and feels whole.[25]

Settlers, the authorities in Southwest Africa, and government officials and colonial enthusiasts in Germany all shared racist interpretations of such contact.[26]

The progeny of such relationships further exacerbated fears. Because German law entitled the wives of German nationals as well as their children to German citizenship, "male half-castes would be eligible for conscription and be able to occupy public office" such as that of a police or military officer or even governor. Because of their split loyalties, if the crunch came these offspring probably would side with the "natives." Authorities and enthusiasts alike interpreted this as a threat to not only "the purity of the German race . . . but [to] the power of the white man."[27] To racial purists, the mulattos *(Mischlinge)* embodied the moral and cultural degradation experienced by white men who lived with "native" women. An assault upon the values embodied and promoted by the upper-middle Stand in its conceptualization of Deutschtum, they represented all that was bad in German society. They posed a threat to bourgeois visions of the German race and German rule in SWA; consequently, the alarm was sounded.[28]

In the 1890s, Leutwein and Lindequist had expressed concern over increases in cohabitation and intermarriage as well as over the rise in the mulatto population.[29] After 1907, these worries were vocalized more, especially with the sudden growth of the single, white, male population due to the presence of colonial troops and the heightened racial tensions following the suppression of the African uprisings. Lindequist had recognized this potentially dangerous situation in 1905 after most of the fighting had subsided:

> As a result of the reinforcements caused by the bellicose unrest and through the expected numerous departures [to civilian life] of soldiers of the imperial colonial army, a considerable increase of the white population, especially of the German element will result.
>
> As experience has taught, many of the young men are inclined to enter into a conjugal relationship with native, namely Bastard [sic] girls, in the absence of white girls. They are moved simply through the circumstance that the Bastard girls quite often bring a herd of livestock, an oxen wagon, and not seldom also a farm into the marriage.[30]

Officials and settlers felt compelled to counteract this "unacceptable" situation.

The anxieties over the quality of settlers, miscegenation *(Mischehen)*, and the mulatto population exposed the larger European bourgeois concern with class status and degeneracy. This was especially true in light of the dislocations due to industrialization and the increasing proportion of non-European populations compared with the European. Both factors threatened the status of the European middle class. A growing proletariat accompanied industrialization, and a decline in the European population and rise in the non-European signaled a possible non-European ascendancy at the cost of European prestige and power—a further blow to the custodians of culture. In SWA, as in other European colonies with a large middle class, these factors threatened to undermine white rule.[31] Therefore, to combat this threat and to encourage racial solidarity, it became imperative for officials and enthusiasts to emphasize the "inherent" differences between the races. Quite often, references were made to the "natural" or "God-given" order of things in order to justify the differences. Writing in *Zeitschrift für Kolonialpolitik, Kolonialrecht und Kolonialwirtschaft* (an organ of the DKG), High Privy Councillor Schreiber stated that "in the interest of colonies and of our people the preservation of the *natural* [emphasis added] racial differences between the whites and natives—the 'coloureds'—must be and remain the highest principle when taking positions regarding the racial question."[32] To Schreiber and others like him, not only did "differences" between the races exist, but the differences enabled one race to rule over another. In order to preserve this "natural" ordering of the world—an order based on middle-class insecurities and supported by pseudoscientific notions of race—Schreiber advocated that "keeping the German race pure must be our aim, so that the Germans in the colonies can protect their . . . ruling position."[33]

To prevent catastrophe and to eliminate such affronts to Deutschtum, colonial officials and enthusiasts pursued a variety of measures—legal, political, social, cultural, and legislative.[34] For example, there were the stronger measures to control the type of individual who entered the colony—Lindequist's comprehensive decree in 1906 to regulate immigration, a move supported by enthusiasts in Germany.[35] Based on a survey of similar ordinances in British and Dutch colonies, the order empowered officials to deny entry to individuals who did not meet a set of requirements. Those who were "nonwhites," who "could not provide enough information about themselves," who were "unable to prove a sufficient livelihood for himself and his family," who were "apparently not in the position to support themselves because of their physical condition," who "pursue[d] or abet[ted] prostitution," or "pose[d] a danger to the peace of the protectorate or the public security" were prevented from entering SWA. Those who traveled from countries that had immigration limitations had to obtain permission from consular authorities. The order allowed persons of questionable character to enter the colony, but only if they made a security deposit and claimed they could prove their worthiness. In an apparent effort to reduce Afrikaner immigration from South Africa, immigrants from there had to pay more.

Registered SWA residents were permitted to enter without difficulty.[36] After the discovery of diamonds in the territory, one zealous official attempted to demand proof of possession of £90 to prevent the entry of "undesirable" elements. He was ordered to stop this practice since he might have "scared away very desirable German immigrants" and, besides, "other undesirable elements, for example really dubious Semites, were absolutely not hindered" by the official's actions.[37]

Despite the concentrated efforts to control the type of individuals entering, "unwanted" elements did find their way to the colony—or their circumstances once there reduced them to that status. These included the destitute, the ill (primarily mentally), criminals, and those considered dangerous to "public security." In SWA as in other European and German colonies, colonial officials wanted to remove such "undesirables."[38] Toward this end, German colonial governors were empowered to deport such people from the colony, including German citizens.[39] Cautioned by the Colonial Office not to make extensive use of this power, they did so when they believed the public security and welfare of the protectorate were threatened, especially when the situation involved a threat to the appearance of white "supremacy."[40] Authorities and colonial enthusiasts believed that anyone who undermined white authority was obviously not a "good German" and did not belong in a Germany colony, anyway. In one case, technician Karl Ernst Bartenwerfer was expelled after conviction for selling spirits to Africans; it was feared that his destitution, laziness, and alcoholism might have led to renewed attempts to violate the ordinances passed for the "protection" of the "native" population, which "endangered the order and security" of the colony.[41] A trader named Rosinger was deported in 1912 because "his idleness and his inclination to drink created a danger for the order and security of the protectorate and his entire behavior is suited to lower the appearance of the white race in the eyes of the natives. Especially the last circumstance makes the expulsion of Rosinger urgently desirable."[42]

Perhaps the most noteworthy deportation case involved a thirteen-year-old boy, August Martin. A Dr. Fock, headmaster of the Okahandja school, wrote in a report that Martin "through lying, thefts, burglaries, conversations and expressions of the meanest kind about sexual things and through similar conduct . . . is a great danger to the moral development of his fellow students." Fock said he had tried all means to correct the boy's behavior, including hard corporal punishment, but it had had no influence; Martin's behavior would only become worse as he grew older. Fock described Martin's behavior as a "disturbance of the inner life" and attributed it to the time the boy, at the age of seven, spent with troops during the uprisings of 1904; such an abnormal experience, "especially the alcohol [and tobacco] to which the boy had been exposed," had a strong effect on the boy's development. Martin was expelled from the school and sent to a reform school in Germany.[43]

Pivotal to the decision were details about the boy's family life. The local district officer reported that the boy's mother had prostituted herself. He claimed that the boy had himself brought soldiers to his mother for this purpose. Martin's father he described as a weak man who admitted to having no control over his son. The mother ran the family; she provided a bad example and obviously did not properly raise him as an obedient German boy. The official concluded that "an improvement of the young man . . . in another family is very improbable."[44] In light of the reports, the authorities considered that "an improvement . . . in this land, where the young man always comes into contact with natives and where he will always have the opportunity to run away" would be "impossible."[45] Officials were particularly concerned that an individual like Martin would undermine white rule; he spent time with Africans—behavior that for a white boy was socially unacceptable.[46]

Because of these reports and a conviction Martin had for theft,[47] the government expelled the boy from SWA and sent him, with the father's approval, to Rauhe House, near Hamburg, where he received training in farm labor. At the institution, Martin was to be turned into a productive member of society. But Martin remained unchanged. Initially deported for only five years (normally expulsions from the colony were forever, but it was hoped that Martin would improve), he stayed at the school, at RKA expense, until 1917, when he joined the military.[48]

Young Martin and his parents embodied everything Germany's cultural elites feared. The Martins, in the eyes of prevailing bourgeois thinking, symbolized an "unGerman" family: the father did not provide order in the family but was weak and dominated by his wife; he did not act like a respectable "man"; and the wife was not a good spouse and mother, was not subservient to her husband, and did not possess a virtuous nature.[49] In the minds of colonial officials, the boy's comportment—which undoubtedly was contributed to by the household conditions—was particularly worrisome since his generation was supposed to provide the future leadership of the colony and Germany. His behavior, they believed, undermined that cause; August, and his parents for that matter, were a danger to the colony, and hence the nation.[50]

The authorities' "solution" to the dilemma can give us a good deal of insight: officials felt they needed to "correct" this "deviant" behavior by sending the boy back to the homeland. However, they did not send him just anywhere: they sent him to the Rauhe Haus, where they hoped he could learn skills that would enable him to become a contributing member of society. For them, that meant training in a preindustrial vocation.[51]

In addition to placing controls on the type of character who entered the colony, officials found legal means to forbid or inhibit transgressions against the color divide. In 1905, in response to an increase in applications for marriage between white men and African women, colonial officials used language in article 7 of the 1900 Protectorate Law to argue that since different laws governed "nonnatives" and "natives," marriages between them could not exist. Armed with this legal interpretation, the government prohibited Mischehen.[52] In 1907, they extended such efforts by nullifying all such marriages performed before 1905, including those where the family had maintained a European household. In a landmark decision, the high court in Windhoek in 1907 ruled that marriages contracted before the ban were null and void. It based its decision on the same article that allowed government officials to forbid such marriages. According to the court, if the law legally separated Europeans and Africans, then legal unions between them could never have occurred. The court's ruling included women of mixed parentage, the court defining them as African, no matter how much "white" blood they had. Therefore, courts refused to hear any cases involving "natives," even divorce cases dealing with Mischehen, since in their eyes the marriages did not exist.[53]

Some Germans circumvented this ban by going to South Africa. The colonial administration declared marriages between whites and "natives" performed there legal because English law recognized such conjugal bonds and thus the ban had no effect upon them; nor could courts throw out cases involving Mischehen or the progeny of such unions, a fact realized by the RKA and contested by officials in SWA. This legal position backfired on a Mrs. Denk, an African woman who went to court in Windhoek to have her marriage declared invalid. She wanted to get away from her abusive German husband and hoped the court would rule that her mixed marriage was invalid. However, since the two had married in South Africa, the courts declared the marriage valid.[54]

Because of the limitations of the marriage ban, colonial authorities felt compelled to employ additional methods to control such unacceptable behavior. For instance, the decree establishing self-government in SWA denied voting rights to those German citizens who were married to Africans. In effect, this excluded them from the colonial political scene and from deciding the future of the colony. Furthermore, the colonial government did not grant settlement aid to Germans living with "natives" since they constituted an unwelcome element in SWA.[55]

In 1909, Governor Schuckmann attempted to introduce an exception to the colony's self-government decree. He wanted to allow certain Germans— those who had married in a church before 1890 with a Rehobother Bastard woman and maintained a European household—to retain their political rights. Though the RKA turned down his request, it did bestow upon him the power to make exceptions. Like his counterparts in French and Dutch Southeast Asia, Schuckmann was empowered to grant electoral eligibility to those nationals who conducted their marriage and household in "an especially recognizable" and "moral" manner. However, the colonial secretary told Schuckmann to make limited use of this power, and only when no doubts existed as to the moral fiber of the family.[56] The governor was glad he had this power, otherwise he feared the colony might have lost hard-working, loyal Germans. For example, Becker, a farmer who was married to a Rehobother woman, wrote to Schuckmann that his "joy" and "interest" in the country would be extinguished if his civil rights remained denied to him and his marriage went unrecognized. He stated that he ran an orderly farm and maintained that his wife could measure up to any white woman in the colony in terms of morality and intelligence.[57] German nationals like Becker—people who met property qualifications and could demonstrate that their households were respectable in terms of language and culture— regained their civic and family rights; their children, however, did not always receive social equalization.[58]

The white community itself imposed measures on its members to enforce conformity, something not uncommon in other white settler societies in Africa (e.g., Kenya and Northern Rhodesia).[59] Those who cohabited or even married "natives," were excluded from the colony's social life. This was most evident in the protectorate's club life. Typical of any Germany community, these clubs constituted a significant component of the colony's social fabric and hence were essential in maintaining one's position in society.[60] Therefore, when these associations excluded from membership those who either lived with a "native" or behaved in a manner detrimental to Deutschtum,[61] they struck a mighty blow. In doing so, they embodied the ideals of "proper" German culture and behavior.

The missionaries were divided on the subject of miscegenation. Though all of them—missionary organizations in Germany as well as those in the field—opposed miscegenation and cohabitation, some took a pragmatic approach to the subject. The hard-liners, primarily the missionaries in SWA, stood staunchly behind the ban of Mischehen. In their eyes, "the mixed marriages are not only undesirable, but rather nothing less than amoral and a slap in the face to Deutschtum." The hard-liners viewed miscegenation as "a sin against racial awareness," and welcomed the government's ban on mixed marriages.[62] Pragmatists on the other hand—Missionary Director T. Öhler, chairman of the Committee of the German Evangelical Missions in Basel, and Pastor G. Haussleiter, the inspector of the Rhenish Mission—while concerned about the moral behavior of the colony's inhabitants, believed that cohabitation was unavoidable. They thought men should not be punished for behaving responsibly.

Haussleiter wrote that a white man "who would publicly legitimate his relationship with a native" was "more honorable than all the white men who debase themselves and colored women through unregulated relationships and cast aside the care for their offspring without hesitation." To missionaries like Haussleiter and Öhler, declaring marriages to African women invalid and banning future marriages freed white men to cohabit with African women (and in some cases to have children) without their having to take responsibility for such action. They saw in such measures the means to allow men to live a life of debauchery without facing the consequences. They wanted the colonial government to hold such men accountable and not to punish those who acted honorably—those who lived conjugally with African women. Despite such opposition, the government did not retreat from its position.[63]

In conjunction with measures to curb miscegenation and cohabitation between Germans and African women, the colonial authorities took steps to reduce the perceived danger to Deutschtum posed by the mulatto population. Mulattos were relegated to the status of "natives" and segregated from the white community. The colonial courts declared all Africans and anyone of mixed blood—regardless of the proportion of white to African—a "native."[64] From the settler perspective, this had the added advantage of increasing the African population and, hence, the labor force available to whites—a labor pool that, as discussed earlier, was nearly annihilated in the German response to the 1904 uprisings.[65] Moreover, State Secretary Dernburg, in Berlin, prohibited the registration of mulatto children into German birth registries, a step he thought necessary to retaliate against those who circumvented the ban on mixed marriages by marrying in neighboring colonies. In a decree to Schuckmann, Dernburg ordered this prohibition "in the interest of the preservation of the white race . . . even if it leads to hardships."[66] Dernburg saw this decree as a means of preventing such children from ever attaining status or a position of authority in the colony.

Despite this policy, the mulatto issue remained a problem, much to the consternation of colonial authorities and settlers, albeit for different reasons. Settlers desired greater control over the African population; the colonial administration saw them as a threat to German culture and, hence, to German hegemony in the region. It also did not want to incite the indigenous population to revolt again.[67] Although the colonial government was unwilling to go to the extremes demanded by settlers, it shared their desire to control the mulatto population. Thus, in 1912, after long consultation with the Southwest African Territorial Council and strong farmer input, Governor Seitz issued the Regulation for the Mulatto Population, requiring the registration of all children born of "non-native" men and "native" women. The children were to be kept in the care of the mother; that is, away from the white community. The regulation also authorized the police to separate couples that provoked "public scandal through the illegitimate cohabitation of a non-native with a native."[68] The deputy governor, Oskar Hintrager, in his implementation guidelines, ordered local officials to represent, decisively and emphatically, the official point of view: "The white man who has sexual intercourse with a native woman degrades himself."[69]

The move to exclude children of mixed German-African parentage from the white community was wholeheartedly welcomed by the settlers. The colonial authorities nonetheless realized that such segregation was not always in the best interest of the colonial society. Dernburg had already empowered the governor to make exceptions regarding the political rights of German men married with "native" women; in a similar move, Governor Seitz permitted local officials to do the same regarding "natives" who had been seen and treated as whites. In his decree to the district officer in Bethanien, he stated that

> If value must also be laid on the strict separation of whites and natives in the interest of racial purity, so it is from the perspective of the administration not advisable to conduct for official purposes investigations into the lineage of such persons who have so far been seen as whites and in view of their education and social position stand on the same level as whites.

Seitz feared that if this happened, not only would it bring considerable disadvantages to the investigated individual, but also to his creditors and associates (i.e. to the white community). He warned local government officers, however, that when treating such individuals as whites they should not come into conflict with the judicial system (i.e., do not contradict its decisions concerning racial heritage).[70] Seitz and some Südwester requested the RKA to establish a formal avenue for treating mulattos who stood culturally equal to whites as Europeans, which it refused to do. Nevertheless, a way had been introduced to include those mulattos who were perceived as white without bringing embarrassment and discredit to business associates, but this happened rarely. It wasn't much, but Seitz had created space for them to operate in the realm of the whites, even though he was probably more concerned with the interests of business associates; and even with this loophole, the prevailing conditions for including mulattos in SWA society remained more ambiguous and stricter than in other European colonies.[71]

The primary motivation behind official and settler measures was obviously racist. Helmut Bley argued that settlers did not care about checking the growth of the mulatto population or reducing the number of illicit liaisons with African women. "Their real intention was to include this group of the population in the inferior status of 'natives' and permanently take away their power."[72] The various regulations set up by colonial authorities did indeed relegate the Mischlinge to "native" status and prevent them from posing a threat to the social and political status of the white population. Yet Bley's assertion ignored the additional steps taken by settlers and colonial officials; it hence overlooked the other component of social engineering taking place in SWA: not only were servants being created, but also masters. Thus, administrators and colonial enthusiasts actively worked to prevent illicit relations between white men and "native" women (and consequently to reduce the number of their progeny) through legal, political, social, and cultural measures.

Admittedly, the ban on miscegenation did allow men to escape their paternal obligations arising from such encounters, but mechanisms were in place to discourage such behavior. For instance, access to the political and social life of the colony was denied those who disgraced the white community by living with an African. For those who tried to bypass the ban by marrying in a neighboring colony, government officials did not enter their children into the birth registries. The Regulation of the Mulatto Population provided local authorities with a sociocultural tool to discourage such relationships and bring shame onto both parties. All these measures—as well as the encouragement and assistance to suitable colonists and the exclusion or expulsion of undesirables—pointed to a conscious attempt by officials and colonial enthusiasts in both SWA and Germany to establish a certain "German" element that would contribute to the development of the colony as a German possession and reduce potential dangers to their power. They recognized that their authority in the colony depended on their skin color and nationality. Not only did this mean the establishment and promotion of Deutschtum, but also of a specific notion of Germandom. To be German meant to behave a certain way: work hard, be prosperous, maintain German traditions (linguistic and cultural), and preserve racial distinctions. Accordingly, they worked to preserve the racial and national barriers and threatened punishment to those who considered crossing them.

Nevertheless, cracks in the racial barrier existed. These exceptions revealed that the lines were not as rigid as some would have preferred. Governors were given the latitude to include in the settler society those Germans who were making contributions to the colony, even if such colonists had "betrayed" the white community by living with an African. Moreover, their authority allowed them to ensure that the racial barriers remained fluid enough for those rare cases when it was actually in the best interest of the white community to include mulattos. These cases were rare, but a doorway into the white world existed.

On the whole, the issues surrounding Afrikaners, poor whites, miscegenation, and mulattos demonstrated how insecure German males were in their position of power in the colony and how concerned they were with creating a certain image of Deutschtum. This image included some while excluding others—the "suitable" and the "undesirables." Only certain types were encouraged and aided in settling in SWA. Those who did not conform to certain standards of behavior or threatened to undermine German culture, and hence German authority, by virtue of their behavior (e.g., the Martins) or their nationality or race (e.g., the Afrikaners and the mulattos) were either excluded or attempts were made to control them. However, the cultural guardians in Germany and in SWA, like their peers in other European countries and colonies, believed that the presence of women, as carriers of European culture, would combat these perceived threats. More German women would guarantee an enduring German presence in SWA. Thus, for colonial officials and enthusiasts it became necessary to settle more German women in the colony.

3

Female Settlement and Ideals of German Womanhood

The German soldier conquers the land with the sword, the German farmer and businessman searches for its economic utilization, but the German woman is alone called to and capable of keeping it German.

—Adda von Liliencron, "Die Frauenfrage in den Kolonien," in *Kolonie und Heimat,* 1908–9

Early in the colonial endeavor, colonial officials and enthusiasts recognized that the presence of German women was necessary for Southwest Africa. Their role was to serve as bastions of national culture, to resist the potential dangers to Deutschtum, and to ensure an enduring German presence in the region. They were to do this by marrying German men and establishing German homes. This notion of women as carriers of culture was not limited to the colonial endeavor, and did not originate in it. In fact, this image of the woman was the product of late eighteenth-century and early nineteenth-century European nationalism and bourgeois fears of degeneration. The need for such a representation arose out of the desire for symbols that would provide unity in a world searching for norms in the face of the dislocations and anxieties wrought by industrialization.[1] Industrialization eroded the financial security of segments of the middle class and created a proletariat (especially as it became increasingly associated with Marxist rhetoric) that threatened the way of life of the middle strata—the middle *Stand.*

In Southwest Africa, fears of degeneracy and feelings of insecurity resonated even more loudly than in the homeland. Colonial officials and supporters of colonialism—most notably the Colonial Society and its auxiliary the Women's League *(Frauenbund)*—worried not only about the creation of a proletariat; the presence of poor whites, Afrikaners, Africans, and mulattos amplified their fears. Consequently, they used legal, social, cultural, and political measures to prevent the creation of a proletariat and to diffuse these threats. These steps nevertheless proved insufficient to offset these challenges to German rule and to guarantee continued German hegemony in the region. Women were needed to prevent the cultural and economic degeneration of German males. Clara Brockmann, a German woman who lived in Africa for many years, writing in 1910, observed, "Out of the disheveled bachelor economy an orderly family life emerges as soon as the woman passes over the threshold of the house."[2] Brockmann claimed that "a farmer with a wife comes ten times farther than one without one."[3] Other writers noted that "the German man is only able to reach the highest that he wants to hand in hand with the German woman,"[4] and a male settler would "through his marriage with a racial comrade raise himself not only ethically, but also economically."[5]

In addition to raising men to their cultural level and contributing to the economic vitality of the protectorate, German women would also make certain that future generations would be raised as good German citizens and maintain ties with the Heimat. While it was the father who passed his citizenship onto his children, the educated and propertied class maintained that "the mother gives them, in most cases, their language and therefore the feeling of affiliation to their race."[6] In other words, "the attachment to the homeland and racial consciousness are raised through the stabilization of family life,"[7] a creation unfathomable without German women. According to Roger Chickering, "the domestic sphere was but a metaphor for German culture; it stood for order, discipline and cleanliness—for civilization in the highest sense."[8]

Thus to colonial authorities and enthusiasts, German women were essential for the colonial endeavor. According to Dr. Külz, the architect of self-government in SWA, "only one thing is missing: German women. One first notices that the German woman inextricably belongs to true Deutschtum when she is missing."[9] The custodians of culture believed that women would diffuse these threats as well as sustain and perpetuate the existence of a loyal German population by supplying it with specific German culture and customs—that is to say, the middle Stand ideal of Deutschtum. As carriers of German culture, they would help transform SWA into a New Germany away from the divisive homeland. Oskar Hintrager succinctly made this point when he said, "She is in fact the most important—that is not only supposed to be a complement—because without her, without the family there is no lasting German culture in the new country."[10]

Because of the dearth of women in the colonies—the so-called woman question *(Frauenfrage)*—and the significance of their role, colonial officials and the German Colonial Society viewed it as imperative to dispatch women to the protectorate.[11] Initially, the DKG embarked upon the program of sending German women to Southwest Africa in response to Leutwein's and the SWA officials' calls for assistance in 1897. Prior to this, in 1892 the imperial government had granted colonial ex-servicemen who stayed in the colony a subsidy of 350 to 600 marks to bring over their brides. Beginning in 1897, the German Colonial Society provided financial support for German women who had relatives in the colony (for example, husbands, brothers, fathers) and wanted to travel there. This was on a case by case basis, and it was not until 1898 that the DKG, in conjunction with the colonial government, began sending women to the protectorate more frequently and regularly.[12]

This expanded role included sending not only female family members but also domestic servants for German farmers. Thus, the DKG provided a means for young, interested women to go to the colony, and indeed the sending of servants constituted the greater part of the society's efforts to increase the number of eligible German women in the protectorate. Since settler families were willing to accept maids, cooks, and so forth, there was justification for sending out these single women. But, out of concern for the women's welfare, the DKG sent them only if they had an employer or relative there who could care for them.[13]

The colonial government had the final say on every request. In one case, Deputy Imperial Provincial Officer Heilingbrunner spoke out vehemently against the sending of a woman of questionable moral fiber. He argued that she was not worth the cost of the free passage to SWA. In another case, Governor Leutwein deemed it imperative that a particular request be granted; therefore, he endorsed sending the wife of an inspector-general in the colonial army, Mrs. von Hagen, because she possessed "a sound personality that . . . will also raise sound children." Leutwein noted in addition that "the support of such a woman would be advantageous to the comparatively character-weak . . . husband in every sense, especially with regards to fulfilling his duties."[14] The DKG agreed to subsidize the wife's transportation to SWA.[15] In other cases, the relatives of some farmers had no desire to emigrate to SWA.[16]

Since the primary goal was for these women to marry, the DKG had to provide suitably desirable brides for the settlers. But there also was concern about finding women with the right level of expectation. In the years before the uprisings of 1904, the majority of settlers were former servicemen. One DKG official wrote:

> The settlers in question are merely small farmers, cattle breeders, traders, etc. who in education correspond somewhat to our small farmer (*klein-bäuerlichen*) Stande and are recruited overwhelmingly from former members of the colonial troops. A young lady, who came from a better family circle and enjoyed a better education, would have difficulty finding a husband who only approximately corresponds to her demands.[17]

Because of the cultural and educational level of the white male population and the rigors and demands of life in SWA, the DKG sent only "simple," healthy young German women (*einfache Mädchen*) who were not afraid of hard work. Furthermore, they had to possess knowledge of agrarian labor (e.g., cattle breeding, gardening, planting) as well as of basic household chores like cooking, ironing, washing, and sewing. The society believed that this was the type of woman settler that SWA needed and wanted.[18]

To ensure that only suitable candidates went to the colony, the DKG screened applicants. A candidate needed to submit a health certificate, a character deposition from either the police or a minister, a recommendation from her last employer, and proof of her nationality and religion. In addition, the candidate had to have the permission of her parents or guardian. Those selected had to sign a two-year contract; only then would the DKG pay for passage to SWA. If the woman received a marriage proposal, she could get out of her contract before it expired if she gave six months' notice.[19] When the conditions of female employment came under harsh criticism, some changes were introduced.[20] However, the DKG was unwilling to budge on the issue of servants' wages. Vice President Sachse argued that it was "not an employment office for maids; its intention was . . . to facilitate the emigration of German women and girls to SWA with the intention to provide the settlers there with the possibility of marriage with white women." To Sachse, the conditions did not appear "so very unfavorable" since it was about a "transitional relationship"—a job that preceded finding a husband.[21]

In 1907, the selection of women passed to the DKG's Women's League—the FB. Founded that same year by Baroness Adda von Liliencron "to rally feminine support for German colonialism,"[22] the FB saw its primary task to be, in close cooperation with the DKG, the preparation and maintenance of a secure place for the German family spirit and German ways and customs in the colonies, above all in Southwest Africa: "Strengthening the feeling of home, strengthening of racial consciousness, protection of the physical and moral entirety, preservation of a healthy German progeny, those are the great national and cultural tasks of the German woman in Southwest Africa."[23]

Though the FB assumed responsibility for the careful selection of "worthy and healthy" young women for employment in SWA, the DKG retained financial control over transportation subsidies for the women the FB selected (it also retained responsibility for selecting and sending family relatives to the colony). The DKG hoped that eventually the FB would reach a degree of financial independence that would allow it to pay the costs of sending not only these women to SWA but also family members. The Women's League worked toward this goal by continually attempting to increase its membership (therefore its coffers), an act that brought it into conflict with the DKG. The FB never achieved the financial self-reliance that it and DKG president Mecklenburg desired, but neither was there a split between the two organizations. Both realized they needed each other.[24]

When selecting candidates, the Women's League continued using the DKG's screening process. Like the DKG, the FB considered only "healthy and well-reputed girls, who have the best credentials" for positions in SWA.[25] And the league selected women only after receiving validation of an employer's credentials. Pursuing the DKG's policy of choosing primarily "simple girls" from the country, the FB assumed that such women did not have too many expectations and were accustomed to hard work.[26] Initially, the FB sought women between the ages of twenty and thirty-five, but beginning in 1913 changed to between twenty-one and thirty because it believed that cohort would make better candidates for marriage.[27]

Although the greatest demand was for young women from the country, the Women's League also desired to dispatch "educated" (*gebildete*) young women; in fact, it preferred to send such women. Gertrud von Hatten, general secretary of the league, believed that what the protectorate really needed were "physically, mentally, and morally *high standing* [emphasis added] women who take the true German spirit with them over there."[28] The DKG shared the FB's opinion on this. Franz Strauch, DKG deputy president, wrote that "it can . . . only be requisite for the development of German Southwest Africa when also a greater number of people who belong to the educated ranks settle down there and found families."[29] The cultural guardians saw these women as the "proper carriers of national culture." They believed that the "simple girls" required the presence of educated women as role models—women they could look to in order to carry out their national and cultural obligations in SWA. The "higher standing" women would show those of the lower classes how to behave and act.[30]

But employment opportunities for such women were limited. Imperial Provincial Officer Brill, in Windhoek, reported that "above all a demand for educated young women is not existent; servant girls from the lower Stand are always valued." He also noted that the chances for superior marriages were also limited because "the educated farmer, for whom these women search, are very few."[31] Von Hatten attributed the situation partially to the hesitancy of SWA's educated families to request a social equal because they did not feel comfortable making place in their families for an unknown person. Von Hatten believed the situation would improve once the cultural level of the protectorate rose.[32]

An undeniable factor was that these women were deemed useless in the colonial setting: they did not possess the appropriate skills and background. In order to make these women more suitable for colonial life, several schools for women were founded in Germany, the goal being to prepare them for colonial life. These institutions primarily educated the wives of colonial officials and officers but also took on "young women of *good education* and *irreproachable reputation* [emphasis added] in the age from twenty to thirty years." Such young women had to "be physically healthy, strong-minded, and energetic."[33] The curriculum would encompass both theoretical and practical instruction. Women would be taught such things as infant care, women's hygiene, tropical health care, cultural and colonial science, zoology and botany, accounting, and law. At a practical level, they learned, among other things, gardening, farming, animal breeding, cooking, baking, and sausage making. The range of abilities was deemed necessary because, in the words of Countess Zech, director of the Colonial Women's School in Witzenhausen, it must be emphasized that the demands that are asked of a woman out there . . . are by far greater than . . . here. We want the women in the colonies to assume, from the beginning, the roles that she should have in the old homeland, but unfortunately quite often does not have or does not occupy. The woman in the colonies must be the true comrade, the understanding helpmate of the man, who works and creates shoulder to shoulder with him and who, when the conditions require it, represents him in the management or overseeing of a great farm enterprise.[34]

Thus Zech argued that, with proper preparation, women could achieve more in the colony than at home.

There were several venues for assisting "educated" women in finding employment in SWA. The Colonial Women's School in Weilbach, for example, under the leadership of Privy Councillor Hoffmann, chair of the school's supervisory board, established a job service for its students, in consultation and cooperation with colonial governors.[35] Helene von Falkenhausen, the first director of the Colonial Women's School in Witzenhausen and earlier an inhabitant of SWA, in 1909 founded the teaching farm (*Lehrfarm*) for young women in Brakwater, near Windhoek, her goal being to provide temporary accommodations and practical experience to women seeking employment in SWA.[36] Falkenhausen assisted women in finding employment as teachers, housekeepers, lady's companions, farm assistants, and so forth, or in establishing independent enterprises such as a laundry, a candy store, or a seamstress shop.[37]

Assistance was not limited to facilitating settlement. The Women's League and colonial enthusiasts, especially other women, provided advice, tips, and institutional assistance. For example, the articles in the FB's *Kolonie und Heimat* covered a range of subjects from preparation for the journey (such as what clothes and cooking equipment to bring and hygienic conditions)[38] to chores on a farm (gardening, caring for chickens, cooking, baking)[39] and how to handle African servants and raise children properly in the colony.

In a sense, colonial women, and men, were "forced onto a stage."[40] They constantly had to demonstrate their "superiority" and present themselves as rulers in front of the "native" population. In this regard, they had little control over their lives. Like their counterparts in other European colonies, the conditions of the regime forced them to be constantly aware of their behavior and not to do anything that might jeopardize white rule.[41]

Nowhere was this more apparent than in handling "natives." According to experienced Südwester women, the most important aspect of running an orderly household was the proper handling of the African servants.[42] Clara Brockmann wrote in *Kolonie und Heimat* that "the young housewife who is used to having . . . her perfect girl at home . . . will have to reckon that she has to deal with servants who often in the true sense of the word are 'wild,' who neither know her language nor have any clue of her service obligations."[43] In order to have any chance of success with African servants, experienced Südwester women admonished farmers' wives to observe the racial differences. "The natives are like children. They must be sternly but fairly treated."[44] Above all, these wives must "inspire respect for the white woman" "through . . . worthy behavior."[45]

Colonial women found that female African servants required special attention if they were particularly attractive. For example, one day Brockmann found Johanna, one of her servants, walking in a provocative manner. Around the same time she claimed that Johanna increasingly disliked working. Brockmann said she let Johanna go because she was no longer a useful servant. To Brockmann, the cause of this transformation was "not difficult to find, it is an accusation which falls back onto the men."[46] She believed that without men's desire these servants would behave in a manner she deemed appropriate—in other words, obsequiously.

The abundance of white men relative to the small number of white women provided African women with the opportunity to ameliorate their position by making themselves attractive to white men; a relationship with a white man had obvious advantages. While this often turned them into "useless" servants (as Brockmann thought Johanna's behavior demonstrated), it also made them direct competitors with white women. However, white women believed they had a distinct advantage: only they could bear white children for German men, a factor imperative for the future of German rule in the colony. This competition among women for male attention also extended to African men. However, if a white woman risked such a liaison, "she paid with a loss of respect, honor, and status; such a woman would be expelled from the white colonial community and therefore from participation in authority."[47] No incidents were reported, but the threat of exclusion remained very real.[48]

Precisely because of the importance of offspring to the future of the colony as a German possession, authorities and colonial enthusiasts expected women to bear and raise "German children to be brave German citizens [i.e., men] and women."[49] As part of this endeavor, the Women's League and other metropolitan organizations established maternity homes in the colony. The FB became involved in order to enable pregnant German women, far from home and medical care, to feel comfortable in their hour of need, and then to help them care for the newborn.[50] The FB and experienced Süd-wester women also provided wives with advice and guidelines to follow in order to rear German children properly under colonial conditions. "More than at home, the upbringing of children here rests on the shoulders of the mother, because the husband has his sphere of influence—which amply makes demands of him—outside the house."[51] Consequently, women were expected to become involved in and were responsible for all aspects of their children's development. In the years before a child went to public school, its German mother was to develop its character and instill in the child a sense of discipline and racial consciousness. For example, Maria Karow advised mothers to develop a child's fantasy by giving them simple toys. She also suggested that mothers should give children pocket money so that they learn thriftiness and generosity. When it was time for the child to go to school, it was the mother's duty to make sure she or he attended daily for the required number of years.[52]

One of the most important tasks for a mother was to cultivate and supervise the child's use of German, language being "a metaphor for culture." Those who knew the language had access to the culture and customs of a nation, which in turn gave one entry into the national identity. In other words, language equaled national identity, an identity based on cultural prerequisites.[53] Therefore, colonial officials and nationalists believed it was imperative to preserve the purity of the German language in the colony, a task made particularly difficult by the presence of non-Germans—namely, Afrikaners and Africans.[54] In the eyes of many Germans, the presence of Africans exacerbated the mother's work, especially if she employed them as servants. Articles therefore advised her to limit the contact a child had with an African nanny and to keep nannies under constant surveillance. This was intended to reduce or even prevent the nanny from gaining any spoiling influences or bringing the child unobserved into contact with "native" children. Karow did point out, though, that some contact was desirable: "Because the German children easily feel superior to the colored ones, a pronounced rulerdom is formed, which one must check a little in good time." That said, too much contact was still undesirable.[55]

Because the colonial setting demanded so much of a mother's time, it was not always possible for her to care for children all the time.[56] But since leaving them in the care of "natives" was considered to be potentially dangerous, the FB in 1911 built a children's home *(Jugendheim)* in Lüderitz Bay to relieve "busy mothers of the care of their children for a part of the day."[57] Windhoek, too, acquired a children's home, in 1902, through its own efforts and the German Women's Association for the Colonies. The Lüderitz Bay Jugendheim claimed that children there would be secure from "native" influences; equally important, colonial supporters saw to it that children in the home would "learn the ways of the homeland and German customs" and "acquire a certain discipline that formed the basis of their character development."[58]

The duties of a German housewife went beyond just running an orderly household and being a mother. Antonie Brandeis, writing in *Kolonie und Heimat,* maintained that "the woman must entirely live her domestic sphere of duty." For Brandeis, this meant that the woman's influence "must stretch over the sphere of her domesticity and beyond and offer friends of the house a place where they can physically and also spiritually recuperate after the burden of work."[59] Middle Stand women expected colonial housewives to be prepared and genuinely willing to receive guests—known and unknown—at any time and to give them the best she had to offer: such was SWA hospitality. One woman wrote that the hospitality extended to guests was "unquestionably something beautiful that our colonies have ahead of the old homeland."[60] In other words, she felt (as did others) that Germany could learn something from the behavior of the German element in its colonies.

Despite the efforts of the Women's League, the Colonial Society, and other colonial supporters, not all women fulfilled their national obligation. This applied perhaps especially to women selected by the DKG and the FB.[61] For instance, one woman broke her contract because she found the conditions in the colony unbearable. She complained that she had too much work to do, received too little pay, it was not clean enough, there were "no amusements, no theater," and she was too lonely.[62] Another left her employer to live, out of wedlock, with a man in Windhoek. The local government official repeatedly tried to get her to establish an "orderly household" by marrying the man.[63]

Colonial authorities also took an unsympathetic view of women who decided to return to Germany after their contract had expired. They usually attributed such decisions to the women's lack of ability. For example, in 1914 local officials explained that the reason for an inordinate number of women leaving was not because of a lack of work opportunities but rather because of "illness, nervousness, a personal unsuitability for use in the local businesses, disappointment over life in Africa . . . or nonfulfillment of marriage wishes."[64] One provincial officer wrote that if women left the colony it was probably because "they either did not tolerate the climate or did not measure up to the demands made upon them."[65] In other words, these women did not possess the proper character traits: they were either not healthy, did not have an amenable personality, had too high expectations, or did not know how to "get a man." Thus, women were at fault, not the conditions in SWA.

Not all women went to SWA with the immediate goal of marrying and raising German children, of course. Indeed, some went there to earn enough money in order to achieve independence in a predominantly male world. Female teachers in an SWA public school received a decent salary, vacation in Germany, and pension rights. Opportunities also existed for office workers, seamstresses, cooks in the larger hotels, telephone operators, nurses, and barmaids. Some women stayed after their two-year contract expired and set up their own businesses as seamstresses or owners of laundries, hotels, or cafés, or even as speculators in the diamond market. But despite these new chances, the "climate" in SWA was by no means emancipating.[66] Women were expected to marry and devote themselves to their families. Women sent out by the DKG were expected to give up their positions once they married. Furthermore, Brockmann argued that a single woman ran the risk of being the object of rumormongers, which would have serious consequences for her standing in the community.[67]

One option for women who did not marry was prostitution. Because of the large European male population and the dearth of white women as well as the relative abundance of African women, white prostitutes provided an important service. Colonial officials regularly imported them in their fight against the growth in the mulatto population and against the spread of sexually transmitted diseases.[68] European prostitutes, preferably German, provided safe entertainment, and their skin color did nothing to damage the status of the white race. In other words, the authorities preferred that white men go to white prostitutes, who stood under police and medical supervision, rather than to "native women." In his application for establishing a bordello in Seeheim, near Keetmanshoop, Karl Bambers justified his request before the Provincial Council by claiming that "the establishment of a bordello . . . is definitely necessary in the interest of public health and to the preservation of the appearance of the whites."[69]

Although white prostitutes served an important function, colonial authorities nevertheless strictly regulated their lives. This was particularly necessary to maintain the image of white superiority: not wanting to upset the rest of the population, officials issued regulations governing where white prostitutes could live and work as well as how they could dress and behave in public. These prostitutes also had to follow doctor's orders, and the doctor had to report examination results to the police.[70] Moreover, ordinances existed that prescribed the location and layout of bordellos.[71]

Women who did not follow these regulations suffered prosecution and imprisonment of up to six months. In one case, three women wrote the provincial office that they had given up prostitution and had begun living and working in a bar; however, the local official warned them that they still stood under police supervision and would remain so until he had decided otherwise. They essentially ignored this and were indicted for not following the ordinances governing women under moral control *(Sittenkontrolle)*, regulations that required them to have weekly medical exams and forbade them from living in a bar. In convicting the women, the judge explained "that a prostitute under moral control simply declaring she wants to give up prostitution is insufficient to release her from her . . . obligations. A declaration of the police that the control is canceled must supervene, otherwise every possibility of the supervision of prostitution would be fully illusionary."[72]

On the whole, though, colonial officials were little concerned with their ability to control prostitutes. Like their counterparts in Germany and neighboring South Africa,[73] they passed various ordinances to regulate the lives and livelihood of prostitutes, thus making the presence of these women more bearable to the more "respectable" members of society. In addition, these regulations provided colonial officials with another way to pursue racial and social control; instead of forbidding prostitution, authorities controlled it. And, most prostitutes followed the ordinances. Lindequist's decree in controlling entry into the colony provided local officials with a means to deny prostitutes entry; however, if a demand existed, they could grant them entry—provided the women left a security deposit.[74] Of greater concern for officials was their ability to control pimps.[75]

One way or another, either through the offices of the DKG or FB, by traveling with spouses, or on their own initiative, women did immigrate to Southwest Africa. Indeed, from 1894 the number of women in the protectorate increased almost annually. In 1894 there were only 78 adult women in the colony; by 1900 there were 403. The years 1900 to 1909 witnessed a more than

Table 3.1. The White Population, 1891-1913

	Men		Women		Children		
Year	Number	% of Total Population	Number	% of Total Population	Number	% of Total Population	Totals
1891	246	49.4	59	11.8	193	38.8	498
1892	199	22	48	8	375	60	622
1893	225	40	55	10	278	50	558
1894	573	59	78	8	318	33	969
1895	917	53	190	11	625	36	1,732
1896	1,080	54	209	11	703	35	1,992
1897	1,564	59.5	310	11.8	754	28.7	2,628
1898	1,532	61	291	12	676	27	2,499
1899	1,840	65	306	11	681	24	2,827
1900	2,146	64	403	12	790	24	3,339
1901	2,181	61	481	13	945	26	3,607
1902	2,569	55	633	14	1,433	31	4,635
1903	2,804	60.4	670	14.4	1,166	25.1	4,640
1904							
1905*							
1906	4,842	76	717	11	807	13	6,366
1907	4,899	69	1,079	15	1,132	16	7,110
1908	5,295	64.5	1,491	18.1	1,427	17.4	8,213
1909	8,010	67.9	1,826	15.5	1,955	16.6	11,791
1910	8,451	65	2,173	17	2,311	18	12,935
1911	8,915	64	2,468	18	2,579	18	13,962
1912	9,046	61.1	2,808	20	2,962	20	14,816
1913	8,530	57.5	3,058	20.6	3,242	21.9	14,830

* No statistics available for 1904–5 due to Herero and Nama wars. Figures for 1906–8 exclude colonial troop dependents.

Source: Karen Boge Smidt, "'Germania führt die deutsche Frau nach Südwest': Auswanderung, Leben, und soziale Konflikte deutscher Frauen in der ehemalige Kolonie Deutsch-Südwestafrika, 1884-1920. Eine sozial- und frauengeschichtliche Studie" (Ph.D. diss., Otto-von-Euericke-Universität Magdeburg, 1995), 430; and author's calculations.

fourfold jump, to 1,826, and by 1913 there were more than 3,500 adult females in SWA. Women also increased as a percentage of the population. In 1894, they constituted only 8 percent of the population and thereafter, until the uprisings, the figure rose every year (there was a dip during 1904–7 because during the war colonial troops' dependents were excluded, whereas before the conflict they were included). Although their total numbers rose, as well as their percentage of the population, they never achieved the status of a majority; indeed, the most they ever constituted was nearly 21 percent, in 1913.

Table 3.2. **Women and Dependents Sent to SWA by the DKG, 1898–1911**

Year	Wives	Sons under 16	Daughters	Other Relatives	Brides	Domestic Servants	Total
1898	2	1	1	1	2	12	19
1899	0	0	0	10	3	10	23
1900	4	4	1	4	8	0	21
1901	5	0	1	2	11	0	19
1902	6	0	1	16	7	1	31
1903	6	1	1	8	12	6	34
1904	11	1	2	5	4	2	25
1905	12	3	18	11	4	8	56
1906	26	17	18	8	16	24	109
1907	43	27	23	9	15	48	165
1908	30	19	33	15	27	56	180
1909	35	26	29	26	21	72	209
1910	43	37	29	26	19	75	229
1911	56	42	55	21	15	99	288
TOTAL	279	178	212	162	164	413	1,408

Source: Winkler, "Zur kolonialen Frauenfrage," *DKZ,* 20 April 1912, 258.

As we have seen, not all women traveled to SWA via the Women's League and the Colonial Society, but these two organizations, going to extensive lengths to recruit, select, and dispatch women for "duty" in SWA, had the opportunity to try to influence the nature of the colony—that is, the character of its white inhabitants. As the numbers indicate, an increasingly large number went each year, especially after the FB became involved and the Germans had established themselves as the apparent rulers of Southwest Africa. This was especially true of the number of domestic servants sent, and eventually this became the largest group dispatched (see table 3.2). By 1 January 1913, the DKG had enabled 1,696 people to travel to the colony: 701 wives, brides, and sisters of settlers, and so forth; 468 children; and 527 servant women.[76] By way of comparison, private organizations in Britain and its colonies, in particular in South Africa, achieved significantly greater success. For example, the British Women's Emigration Association (BWEA) assisted more than 8,000 women to emigrate to Canada, Australia, and South Africa. In 1907 alone, the founding year of the German Women's League, the BWEA helped more than 900 women to travel abroad. The South Africa Colonization Society aided more than 3,700 women and children (predominantly women) to emigrate to South Africa between 1902 and 1908.

Table 3.3. **Percentage of DKG-Sponsored Emigrant Workers Married in SWA**

	1898	1899	1903	1905	1906	1907	1908	1909	1910	1911	1912	1913	1914
# wed	10	5	3	5	9	24	27	35	31	14	22	2	1
total	12	10	6	9	23	49	55	72	75	99	109	116	77
% wed	83	50	50	55	39	49	49	48	41	14	20	2	2

Source: BAP 61Ko1/156–60, 170–79, 607–9 passim; BAP, R151F/FC14858–59; cited in Krista O'Donnell, "The Colonial Woman Question: Gender, National Identity, and Empire in the German Colonial Society Female Emigration Program, 1896–1914 (Ph.D. diss., SUNY Binghamton, 1996), 244.

These activities did not go unnoticed in Germany. In fact, Dr. Kuhn and Lieutenant W. Harbers published them in a DKG periodical, with the obvious intention of motivating colonial enthusiasts to greater action in the settling of German women in SWA.[77]

Official statistics indicate that a fair number of the women who went to SWA did carry out their duty; namely, they married white men. Between 1898 and 1914, 188 female servants dispatched by the Colonial Society and the Women's League had married in the colony. This constituted only 26 percent of the total sent, but during the first decade of the program, the number hovered around 50 percent.[78] These organizations also assisted 393 wives and 224 brides to travel to Southwest Africa.[79] It should also be noted that some wives and brides traveled to the region without the assistance of the DKG and the FB. Thus, while it was by no means completely satisfactory, the number of married men in the colony did increase over the years. In 1902 there were only 588 married males, and in 1903 only 622. But by 1908, officials reported, there were 1,354 wedded men, and 1,574 in 1909.[80] By 1913, the number had risen to 2,514 married men.[81]

Although they were not absolutely successful, colonial officials and enthusiasts tried to control the type of woman who emigrated to SWA. They appealed to them in both nationalistic and practical terms. They explained to them their national and cultural duty and pointed out the benefits of living in the colony. The cultural custodians claimed that German women were essential for the cultural salvation and preservation of the German community and the economic development of the protectorate. They also argued that women would enjoy greater status and prestige in the colony than at home; some of them might even be able to afford domestic servants for the first time.

In making their nationalistic appeals in various articles and speeches, colonial enthusiasts intentionally left the term Deutschtum vague. By doing so, they gave the appearance that the colonization of SWA was a national task and that everyone possessed the ability to fulfill it. They attempted to turn the colonization of SWA into an inclusive, nonpartisan endeavor.[82] Yet, when it came to the actual colonization of SWA, the term became imbued with a specific sociocultural definition—that of the middle Stand. Thus, in SWA the term was not inclusive, but exclusive—as, in fact, the colonial movement in Germany actually was.[83]

Indeed, differences existed among the German women in the colony. Since women depended upon their husbands for social status, they entered and represented their spouse's social position in the colonial community. Thus, social differences existed between the wives of missionaries, settlers, craftsmen, and colonial officials, for example. "Simple" women did not move in the same social circles as "educated" women.[84] In fact, these women often made these differences strongly explicit. This was particularly evident in the overabundant amount of gossip and mudslinging in the colony, much of which was directed at the transported working women.[85] However, they were united in one aspect: "They were all German, the colonies were German, and they should also remain German."[86] Colonial enthusiasts assumed that their female social equals would act as role models for those of lesser status, via their own comportment. More significantly, they arrogantly expected "simple" women to follow that example.

Despite the salience of their task, colonial officials and enthusiasts envisioned women occupying an implicitly passive role. "The national symbolism implied the passivity of women and the virtues of their confinement to the domestic realm."[87] As in Germany, women in SWA enjoyed no political rights, and publicly they were relegated to the domestic sphere. Men feared political activity would have distracted women from their primary "vocation"— namely, to be "priestess[es] of the house." Not surprisingly, the introduction of voting rights in 1909 excluded women.[88] Many middle Stand women accepted this, though not all. Only unofficially did women give advice to their husbands: she was to be there to support him, to help him recuperate from a hard day's work, and to raise his children.[89] "The private sphere was transported abroad, so that feminine virtues might flourish there within their accustomed confines."[90]

This subservient role was exemplified in the notion that women "were sent" or "dispatched." Essentially, women were commodified. Such language implied that the "dispatched" women did not rule their lives; rather, that was the role of the DKG and colonial officials. Men were the ones taking action to address the need for women in SWA. Yet, by using such terms, they treated women not as human beings but rather as goods to be selected and sent to customers—the settlers in SWA. Men in SWA even referred to the first shipments of women as "Christmas packages."[91]

Even women in the FB and in the colony, such as Eckenbrecher and Karow, openly advocated this passive, domestic role. Yet, by publicly using these national symbols and rhetoric, they were able "to extend and defend the autonomy of their public roles and claim a measure of public equality with men."[92] Their patriotism enabled them to break out of the domestic realm and achieve greater equality with men in the public sphere. More important, however, like European women in other colonies, the economic role assumed by women allowed them to break out of their passive, domestic role.[93] They played an important part in turning SWA into an economically viable German colony. Colonial enthusiasts even publicly admitted that the protectorate's economic development was inconceivable without German women. Thus, women did more than transplant their "feminine virtues" to SWA. Similar to European women in other colonies,[94] they toiled in the fields and the household; they helped with bookkeeping and running the business, especially if their husbands became incapacitated or died. Some women even opened up their own businesses. Men's recognition of the significant role of women in the colony's economic development and in securing and maintaining German rule did greatly enhance their status and prestige in SWA. Not only was their social status improved—many housewives were able to afford servants for the first time—but as economic partners and protectors of German culture their privileged status was guaranteed. Only they could bear white children, and German men and women believed that only white progeny secured German hegemony in the colony for the future.[95]

Because their newly achieved status depended almost exclusively upon race, German women became some of the most vocal supporters of racial purity. Racial tensions between ruler and ruled existed before their arrival as well as accounting for their presence in SWA. Although German women may not have held racist attitudes prior to their arrival in the colony, once there they opted to adopt and support racism as a means to maintain white rule and their status.[96] According to Chickering, race "placed them in a superordinated position in a public hierarchy and required that they take on attitudes and characteristics appropriate to domination."[97] Thus, race helped these women achieve a form of status and importance in an otherwise male-dominated world at the cost of moral dignity.

However, not all women represented the ideal German housewife, and some did not even care to try. Some women decided not to marry but instead opened up their own businesses, although the number of women who owned their own farms remained limited; in fact, most were widows of men who died during the Nama and Herero Wars.[98] Others did not possess the requisite mentality and values and either left the colony disgruntled or raised their children improperly. In the eyes of colonial officials, the mother of August Martin clearly exemplified a mother incapable of properly rearing her child. The result of her inabilities was the deportation of her son from the colony. Conversely, individuals like Mrs. von Hagen represented the type of woman that colonial authorities and enthusiasts wanted in the colony—supportive of their spouses and interested in the upbringing and well-being of their children.

Colonial enthusiasts viewed those who did not conform to the expected behavior as social deviants and unacceptable examples of German womenhood. Nevertheless, according to colonial enthusiasts and officials, the majority of German women in the colony did conduct themselves properly, and they came to enjoy the benefits of their improved status. These women contributed to establishing and maintaining Southwest Africa as a German colony in a manner reflecting the middle Stand ideal: a new Germany populated predominantly with loyal, hard-working, racially conscious Germans. As carriers of German culture and language, they worked to achieve this. In doing so, they greatly enhanced their position in an otherwise male-dominated society. They were not, however, alone in their national and cultural task: they were aided by the educational system, a system that built upon the achievements of the mother in turning the white youth of the colony into loyal citizens of the empire.

4

White Education

Foundations and Curriculum

With the increase of the white population, the
number of school-age children according to German standards has also multiplied. These children grow up without partaking of the necessary
instruction to some extent. Even in places in
which government schools exist, parents send
their children to school only irregularly.

—Friedrich von Lindequist, the SWA governor,
  in 1906

$\mathbf{G}$erman officials and private institu-
tions in both Germany and Southwest Africa assisted German mothers in
inculcating the youth of the colony with German values and traditions. Together they strove to win them over to Deutschtum and thus secure them
as a loyal German population; in turn, this would guarantee that Southwest
Africa remain a German possession. The most active among these groups
was the colonial government. It implemented preventive measures to ensure the moral safety of SWA youth by keeping potentially corrupting
young individuals out of the colony or expelling the morally dangerous ones
(like August Martin; see chapter 2). But more importantly, the colonial government took a proactive approach by establishing an educational system.

Mothers could teach their children at home for only so long, and schools played a salient role in the education of colonial children. Eventually mothers would want to send their offspring to school for further education—a move that was desired and encouraged by colonial authorities and the enthusiasts for colonial development. In schools, the children would not only receive a basic, practical education but would also be taught to be good German citizens. In fact, both aspects were primary goals of European educational systems. In Germany, the curriculum aimed at securing the loyalty of the masses by combating social democracy and creating a sense of fidelity to the fatherland and the emperor, of what it meant to be German, as well as providing Germany with a better-qualified workforce. Students would learn "order, obedience, discipline."[1]

In Southwest Africa, the educational system played a similar if not more important role. Not only was it to turn the colony's youth into good, useful Germans, it had the added task of preserving the colony's German character. While the first settlers still had close ties with and memories of the homeland, their children grew up in a decidedly different atmosphere in the first decades of the territory's existence as a German colony. Many of these children were either very young when they arrived in SWA or were born there. For them, the old homeland was nothing but an abstraction, made only somewhat familiar by the accounts of their parents and the little education that their mothers provided. In the pre-1914 period, only a few had ever been to Germany, and in general even those who had been "home," had visited only briefly. Moreover, though it was not readily admitted, questionable, lower-class elements had settled or grown up in the territory. They challenged definitions of "proper" German comportment. In addition, the region was populated by Africans and Afrikaner. Their presence—especially that of the Africans—raised fears that impressionable young Germans might "go native," and this might ultimately lose SWA for Germany. Like their peers in British Kenya and Southern Rhodesia,[2] these circumstances became an acute concern for colonial officials and enthusiasts.

In order to assuage these worries, the German colonial administration in SWA, with assistance from pedagogues and institutions in Germany, embarked upon a program to turn the colony's white youth into productive and loyal members of the German Empire. According to the pedagogue Hans Amrhein,

> the German school abroad, as a true custodian, is called to give, through
> a national education in the foreign country, maternal protection to the

holiest achievements that our people created in the homeland. The school leads the struggle out there against the dangerous, foreign spirits that court the German heart of our youth. The care of German manners and integrity helps the advancement of German work by leveling the way and retaining new markets. In those foreign places where our brothers have erected for themselves a German hearth, the school aspires to maintain and strengthen the humanity in the German character. How soon would the inheritance of our fathers be made apparent and our people be made poor if the school, as conscientious trustee, did not always anew convey our ever-increasing cultural assets to our progeny![3]

Thus colonial schools in SWA were seen by Germany's cultural elite as essential for "saving" youth, and therefore the colony, for Germany from "dangerous, foreign spirits." Moreover, the type and quality of education became a means to distinguish Germans from the indigenous population.

The school system in SWA also served another important function—namely, the Germanization of the Afrikaners. A culturally strong, cohesive Afrikaner element posed a considerable and unwanted threat to German hegemony in the region. Officials believed that their schools, as carriers of German culture, were one of the better avenues to achieve Germanization. Although efforts were made to acculturate the adults, greater emphasis was laid on winning over the Afrikaner young. Colonial officials realized that this process would not happen overnight, but nonetheless predicted it would occur. "Pursued with the right means and necessary consideration, it will be a question of only decades to make out of the Boers in German Southwest Africa true German Africans (*Deutsch-Afrikaner*)."[4]

In their efforts to realize their dream of creating a cohesively strong and loyal German population and thus ensuring the continued loyalty of SWA to the empire, Germany's cultural guardians and the organizations for which they worked took a fairly comprehensive and aggressive approach early in the colony's history. This was especially true in comparison with other white settler colonies. For example, in both Kenya and Southern Rhodesia officials did not institute comprehensive educational programs until the late 1920s, and even then they tended not to match the scale or degree of German efforts in SWA.[5]

In the German protectorate, the state was actively involved in education as early as 1894, though a comprehensive program was not instituted until 1906. Indeed, a German official, Ministerial Councillor Gerstenhauer, argued strongly that the educational system in the colony should remain under the control of the government. "The German government wants to and must keep in hand the schools of the colony as the most important means for the promotion of Deutschtum."[6] In assuming primary responsibility for educating the white population, Germans and non-Germans alike, the colonial administration introduced and expanded compulsory education, built schools, instituted a uniform curriculum and monitored its implementation, controlled the hiring and quality of teachers, and relegated African education to the missionaries. The education of the "native" population was left to the various mission societies, who attempted to convert Africans and mold them "into semiskilled and obedient" workers "capable of attending to the needs of the colonial government system and the expanding settler population." In contrast, the German administration in East Africa assumed responsibility for educating both Africans and whites. There, the governor recognized the need for a "loyal and literate local staff in the vast colony devoid of many white settlers." Thus it was more dependent on the indigenous population to fill the lower ranks of the bureaucracy.[7]

In 1894, the same year that Leutwein arrived in the colony, the colonial administration opened the first state school (*Regierungsschule*) "for white children" in Groß-Windhoek at the request of its inhabitants. The school was maintained by a state subsidy, supplemented by school fees. However, the school lasted only until 1898, when it was closed due to a lack of students. The closing was attributed to the strenuous relationship between the teacher and local parents, especially over the content of the lessons.[8] But despite this failure, the colonial administration continued along the path of state education. In fact, the first Windhoek school was said to have laid the "kernel of a prosperous development" in the SWA educational system.

Several years later a new school opened in Windhoek. As the settler population continued to grow, especially around Windhoek, the necessity for renewed instruction had made itself apparent. The colonial government summoned a teacher from Germany in 1899, and the Windhoek school reopened in January 1900. Although the school did not require parents to pay fees, tensions again rose between parents and the teacher, which threatened the continued existence of the school. The arrival of a second teacher in 1902—an appointment that coincided with the transfer of the first teacher to the south, with its prolific Afrikaner families—helped alleviate these difficulties. In April 1902, a boarding facility was added to the school in order to allow out-of-town (*auswärtige*) children the opportunity to attend school.

The annual cost of boarding was 600 marks, but the government partially defrayed the costs by giving parents 300 marks a year for each child.[9]

Soon after the opening of the school in Windhoek, the colonial government founded other schools in the colony: one in Gibeon in 1900 and one each in Keetmanshoop, Swakopmund, and Grootfontein in 1902. In building these institutions, the administration recognized the pressing need for German schools in the south, where there were Afrikaners with large families. In Keetmanshoop, for example, in 1899 there were 186 boys and 162 girls, half of whom were Boers; one-quarter were English, the other quarter, German. By January 1901—the year before the school was built—there were 231 boys and 185 girls.[10] At the insistence of the DKG, the German Colonial Office allocated 25,000 marks to build the school.[11]

The Nama and Herero uprisings in 1904 essentially brought the educational development of the colony to a halt. Many teachers were called up for military service, the schools were used as either military quarters or hospitals, and the general uncertainty in the country forced parents either to flee or to keep their children at home. But, as colonial troops slowly restored order to the region, schools again opened. The restoration of peace also brought increased settlement to the protectorate, which meant more children in the colony.[12]

Indeed, after the uprisings the government took a more active role in the development of the region. It had reduced the Africans to a subservient position and relegated them to reservations, thus freeing up large tracts of land for white settlement. In essence, the defeat of the Nama and Herero marked the beginning of the full-scale colonization of SWA. The situation presented new opportunities and demands, for state-sponsored education as well as in other areas. But despite the return of peaceful conditions and the increase in population, attendance at schools was minimal. This was especially true in areas where most of the children lived outside of town.

The low attendance was a result of both Afrikaner resistance to German acculturation efforts and, as in Kenya and Southern Rhodesia,[13] the presence of lower-class whites. In several regions, especially in the south, Afrikaners constituted a sizable percentage of the population, and with the cessation of hostilities, numerous former soldiers (i.e., members of the lower classes) settled in the region. Already, in the years prior to the war, Leutwein had expressed concern about allowing the lower classes to settle in the region; nevertheless, he ultimately justified it in the belief that SWA offered heretofore unprecedented opportunities for them. The settlement of such individuals was supposed only to be temporary, until more "appropriate" elements arrived.

Because of the poor attendance—and another reason for it was that the rebellion had imposed economic hardships on families, undoubtedly making it difficult for many of them to send children to school—it became necessary to mobilize the widely dispersed children. These efforts included increasing parental involvement, increasing the number of schools, and building more boarding facilities for children who lived far away. Above all, Lindequist believed that the most suitable means to accomplish increased attendance was to introduce compulsory education, a measure supported by local officials and some members of the community.[14]

Lindequist issued a decree in 1906 regulating school attendance—the so-called School Act *(Schulgesetz)*. The law required white children between the ages of six and fourteen within a four-kilometer radius of a town with a public school to attend the school. The governor selected this distance based on medical reports about the effects of walking to school. If schools existed outside of populated areas, the government determined the radius of the corresponding school district. Lindequist believed that holding parents or guardians responsible for their children's attendance was the best means to administer compulsory education. Those who neglected their obligations faced either a 150-mark fine or up to six weeks' imprisonment.[15]

Shortly after the introduction of mandatory school attendance, prominent individuals in the colony worked toward expanding the spatial criterion for attendance. The most vocal proponent of such a move was Dr. Alfred Zedlitz, director of the Windhoek *Realschule*:

> The School Act . . . has so far worked beneficially and must be seen as the beginning of a systematic Germanization of our colony. In order to turn the country into a true German one, in order especially to accustom a not insubstantial part of the population . . . the Boers and their offspring . . . to German language, manners, and customs, one is not allowed to stand still on the well-traveled road, but rather must take a step forward and this step forward is a further spatial expansion of the compulsory education.

Zedlitz accordingly called for extending the radius from four kilometers to fifty. Moreover, he believed that four years of instruction was enough to accustom an Afrikaner child to the German language, customs, and traditions. "Less than four years might appear as inappropriate, and to take away a child from an Afrikaner family [for longer than this] would not go well with the ideas and customs of the Boers."[16] In response to Zedlitz's comments, Governor Seitz issued a decree in 1911 that extended compulsory education to the entire colony.[17]

When drawing up plans for the 1906 School Act, Lindequist concluded that the primary reason for low school attendance lay with the lack of participation in school affairs by the civilian population. In order to increase public participation, he had the local official in Windhoek call an assembly for January 5, 1906, ten months prior to the proclamation of compulsory education. At Lindequist's suggestion, the participants established an organization whose members would elect the school board. Every interested white person could join on payment of a 10-mark fee, to be renewed annually. The organization's stated purpose was, 1. the promotion of the general interest for the German school system; 2. the enhancement and expansion of the German school in Windhoek; and 3. the acquisition of funds for school necessities.[18] In subsequent years, other communities founding school associations looked to Windhoek as an example, and by 1911, the major areas of settlement had established associations. These associations, by assuming responsibility for construction and maintenance of schools, expedited the expansion of the educational system.

Then in 1909, with the introduction of self-government, financial responsibility for schools and dormitories passed into the hands of municipal and district governments. The state provided a one-time grant (up to 10,000 marks) to financially weak communities or associations, and it aided communities by paying teachers' salaries.[19] Schuckmann saw this as essential for the promotion of German culture in SWA: "For us the school is so important as the means of conveyance of Deutschtum that we cannot leave to others the hiring of faculty without running into the danger that instruction at schools is often completely stopped due to a teacher shortage or is inaptly taught by insufficiently trained faculty."[20] Thus colonial government retained control of the important teacher element—the means to ensure that the schools maintained standards commensurate with German schools and to carry out its Germanization program.

In 1910 officials still felt that the colony's inhabitants exhibited too little interest in the educational system. In order to correct this situation, Privy Councillor Brückner, assistant to the deputy governor, ordered teachers to hold a public examination at the end of the school year. He believed this would "rouse and keep awake" interest for the schools in the population. Brückner required teachers to invite their superiors, the local government official, the community council, and citizens to these exams.[21]

With the creation of school associations (later, the local governments) and the introduction of compulsory education, the groundwork had been laid for the actual construction of schools and boarding facilities in the colony. The establishment of new schools was especially important since SWA's young population was growing rapidly and also contained non-German, white elements. Lindequist, on a trip through the colony in 1907 on behalf of the Colonial Office, wrote that "the young progeny in the colony multiplies so that next to the already existing schools it is an urgent necessity to build new ones." He also noted that "good German schools are the best means to join the non-German elements to us."[22]

Meanwhile, the dormitories attached to schools served several functions. First, they were a means to accommodate children who lived outside the town where the school was located. By boarding their children in these hostels, parents did not have to worry about getting their children to classes each morning.[23] From the perspective of colonial authorities, boarding was a means to include more children in the educational system. Indeed, these facilities often contributed to the success of a school, as was the case in Windhoek.[24] And since many of the Afrikaner families lived outside population centers, officials viewed boarding as an integral part of the Germanization process. As late as 1913, Seitz recognized the salient role dormitories played toward this end when he remarked, "Boer children must be accommodated in German boardinghouses in which a good German is spoken."[25]

However, boarding children in dormitories was often too expensive for many parents. Many farmers, despite government efforts to colonize the territory with a particular type of settler, were not wealthy. So the government continued to provide subsidies, even after it transferred responsibility for schools to local communities in 1912, for destitute families who had to send their children away to school. Officials in Windhoek granted assistance amounting to an average of 500 marks per child annually. The government also subsidized construction of boarding facilities, and the Reichstag allocated 50,000 marks for building and expansion.[26] In addition, several private, nationalist organizations assisted poor families. Indeed, both the Colonial Society and the Pan-German League saw in the supporting of families with school-age children a means to strengthen the German presence in the region.[27]

By 1908, in addition to there being the secondary school in Windhoek (the *Kaiserliche Realschule*), local communities, with government assistance, had built schools in Lüderitz Bay, Karibib, Warmbad, and Okahandja. In that same year, the Higher Catholic Mission School for Girls began operation in Windhoek. These openings were followed by Omaruru (1909), Maltahöhe (1910), Kub (1910), Klipdam (1910), Klein-Windhoek (1910), Gobabis (1911), Aus (1912), and Usakos (1912). In addition, Swakopmund, in 1910, and Lüderitz Bay, in 1911, also had established secondary schools. By 1910 dormitories existed in Windhoek, Omaruru, Grootfontein, Keetmanshoop, Warmbard, Gibeon, Kub, Maltahöhe, and Klipdam, and by 1913 there were boarding facilities also in Aus, Gobabis, and Okahandja.[28]

Colonial officials viewed the founding of schools in border regions with their relatively large numbers of Afrikaners as imperative. For example, in Klipdam, an Afrikaner stronghold, officials feared that local children would grow up without an education. Even more threatening was the possibility that a new school would come under the influence of the Afrikaner community and thus contribute to strengthening "Boer culture." Accordingly, officials authorized the construction of a school there and made funds available in an attempt to raise the Afrikaner children as loyal German subjects.[29]

The establishment of secondary schools in the protectorate was significant. Many parents desired to send their children to Germany after primary school for further education, but for most it was financially unfeasible. However, such education was necessary if they wanted their sons to receive the so-called One-year Certificate, which would qualify them for a year's voluntary military service[30]—"an essential requirement for the advancement . . . into the reserve officers' corps or the officers' corps"[31] (i.e., for entry into a significant milieu of German sociopolitical life). As the population of the colony grew, so did the demands from parents for a secondary school, and the government opened the Imperial Realschule in Windhoek on January 18, 1909, with Dr. Alfred Zedlitz as its first director. They decided upon the Realschule style of education because of its emphasis on English and French.[32] Latin, used in more classical forms of education, had little practical application in the colony. Furthermore, officials selected a Realschule since it accepted young women; they thus hoped to eliminate the need for a separate secondary school for girls.[33] Additional Realschulen were opened in Swakopmund and Lüderitz Bay.[34]

In addition to the high school, Swakopmund hosted another private secondary school. As an expression of the colony's business needs, a continuing education school (Fortbildungsschule) opened in 1913 in the town. Operating under its own supervision, the school offered evening courses to apprentices in the commerce and trade industries, according to demand. It was able to support itself and received only minimal assistance from the city for building and lighting.[35]

In October 1907, the Catholic Mission opened two secondary schools in Windhoek, one for boys and one for girls, both with boarding facilities. According to the School Law of 1906, the government decided if such institutions provided education equivalent to the government schools and whether the faculty was qualified; in other words, the law gave them the power to control and interfere in the affairs of private schools. For the school for young women, this presented no problem: two sisters gave instruction, and one of them was qualified to instruct girls at middle and higher levels, the other to give handicraft courses at primary, middle, and secondary levels; consequently the government approved the girls' school.[36] Government approval of the boys' school, however, proved to be more complicated.

The boys' school instructor, Father Kalb, did not possess the qualifications necessary to teach. Nevertheless, in recognition of the mission's service to the colony, Schuckmann granted permission for the institution to operate under the condition that it have a state-examined teacher sent from Germany by August 1907. At the mission's request, the governor extended the deadline to December. The mission also asked for permission to hire privately examined teachers if they stood under the supervision of a qualified one. Schuckmann did not authorize this request because he was concerned it might set an unwelcome precedent. He feared it would lead to the government losing its ability to ensure "that disagreeable and unsuitable elements are kept away from providing instruction . . . especially hazardous in areas heavily populated with Boers and other foreigners." Schuckmann finally forced the school to close when it was unable to find an appropriate teacher after the allotted time had expired. The governor saw no real need for it in the first place since the "Catholic Mission School is a competing enterprise against the emerging secondary government school and because the possibility now exists for boys who attend the government school to receive adequate instruction."[37]

The governor obviously placed greater importance on the education of boys than girls. He apparently did not have any problem with girls receiving an education in a "competing" Catholic school; girls, like boys, were able to receive "adequate instruction" in the Realschule, but he apparently preferred to have boys educated in schools under the watchful eye of state—predominantly Protestant[38]—employees.

Despite the government's efforts, the SWA education system did not include all school-age children. Parents living far away from government schools often did not want to send their children away to dormitories, especially if they needed them to work on the farm. Consequently, many farmers continued to hire private teachers to instruct their children, as settlers had done since the 1890s. Although the government opposed these so-called farm schools, forty existed in the protectorate by March 31, 1914.[39]

Once the schools and dormitories were built and compulsory education had been introduced, it became necessary to turn the white pupils into good German citizens, regardless of their parents' nationality or wishes. In general, this entailed providing an appropriate environment and curriculum as well as hiring suitable teachers. However, not until 1911 did colonial authorities issue guidelines for teachers in their preparation of lessons plans and curriculum. They delineated how many hours per week teachers should devote to the various subjects. Prior to this, teachers had taught in the ways to which they were accustomed. Since the teachers came from different parts of Germany and had varying systems, this meant that instruction varied widely. This created difficulties for students transferring from one school to another, both within the colony and between the colony and Germany. The government-issued guidelines alleviated this problem, essentially instituting a Prussian-based curriculum.[40]

As in Prussian schools, the SWA educational system placed great emphasis on teaching German language and history, as well as instilling a sense of "order, obedience, and discipline" in the pupils.[41] However, because of the requirements and demands of the colony, the SWA curriculum also stressed physical education and vocational training. Such a curriculum would introduce children to German culture and values as well as train them practically, most often through sensory experiences. The guidelines also provided information about how teachers should instruct these subjects as well as the goals they should attain with the children.

Because of the belief that language provided access to cultural identity, German language instruction occupied a salient position in the curriculum. This was especially true in areas with a large Afrikaner population, like Keetmanshoop. There, German authorities saw their worst fears materialize: even in German households, Dutch and Nama was the colloquial language. The fact "that often six-year-olds of pure German parents spoke Nama and Dutch at enrollment" made the teacher's task more difficult. Consequently, "the command of the German language was aspired to as the main goal of instruction," and hence seen as the best means to maintain the German identity of the German pupils and to create that identity in Afrikaner children. In Keetmanshoop and elsewhere, therefore, German remained the language of instruction, even in those schools where Dutch was permitted in religion class and for beginning Afrikaner students.[42]

In 1913 colonial officials introduced the teaching of local histories *(Heimatkunde)* in government schools. Emphasis on local histories did not necessarily reflect a blatant form of provincialism but rather a new approach to teaching nationalism. Begun in Germany around the turn of the century, local studies, as well as local geography, were seen by pedagogues as more interesting to children, and therefore more meaningful. More important, "one of the major justifications for teaching about the homeland was that love of homeland was the 'root' or 'seed' of love of fatherland."[43] Over time, children were supposed to transfer their love of Heimat to a love of their native region and, eventually, to love of the entire German nation. According to Katharine Kennedy, "educators argued that by reinforcing children's emotional bonds to their homes, schools could help to ensure their unflinching loyalty to Germany and willingness to sacrifice for it."[44] Thus, Heimat would evolve to embrace "both the beloved local places and the beloved nation; it was a comfortably flexible and inclusive homeland, embracing all localities alike."[45] In Southwest Africa, officials believed local studies would engender a feeling of belonging to the "new" Germany while simultaneously strengthening the bond to the old homeland.

Intended as an introduction to the history and geography taught in the Realschulen, local studies did not initially receive adequate attention in primary schools. Government officials worried especially about the lack of documentation describing the schools and their localities. They attributed this to the frequent changes in the faculty. In order to rectify the situation, in 1913 the deputy governor, Oskar Hintrager, ordered government teachers to begin a comprehensive chronicle of their institution and its location. He gave specific instructions about what it should include: the school chronicle should contain information about its founding, why it was needed, government and private contributions, a layout diagram of the school, its dedication, the first pupils, the faculty, festivals, the dormitory (if there was one), lesson plans, and so on. The chronicle about the town was supposed to describe, among other things, the first settlement, good and bad rain years, public buildings, the names of colonists, the town's fate during the uprising, and inhabitants' occupations.[46] Such studies were intended to provide students and future generations with a sense of their past and thus create an affinity to the region.

The Windhoek government requested Bernhard Voigt (teacher, and later school inspector) to write a local history of SWA for the 1913 academic year. His *Land und Leute: Eine Heimatkunde für Deutschlands Jugend und Volk* was adopted as the required textbook for Southwestern local studies. "The book owed its origin to the need of Southwest African schools for a local study." Voigt intended the book "to bring the country that had become a new homeland for many Germans closer to the understanding and heart of the old homeland." In other words, he wished to fortify the bond between the colony and Germany. Thus, his essays were intended to establish an affinity between the territory and its new inhabitants as well as between the colony and Germans in the homeland, who would also supposedly have access to the book. Consequently, the book contained essays about, among other things, the colony's early history and descriptions of its landscape, the Afrikaners, examples of Germans taking holidays in SWA, indigenous flora and fauna, a hunting expedition, Africans, and the uprisings.[47]

As an integral part of history education, various institutions in Germany also assisted instructors in the teaching of natural history and geography, especially when these subjects touched upon animals indigenous to Germany. In 1912, Dr. Oskar Wallberg, director of the Swakopmund Realschule, in an effort to improve the curriculum, appealed to the colonial government for assistance in acquiring stuffed animals from Germany. Dr. Wallberg argued that such material was particularly important for visual instruction *(Anschauungsunterricht)* in geography and natural history instruction. He pointed out that "our children hear in stories, fairy tales and poems continually about the fox, the rabbit, the weasel, the hedgehog and the types of birds, but for most of them it remains an empty word, they have no picture of it before their eyes because they have never seen the animals." Numerous museums throughout Germany agreed to help the colony by sending extra specimens to the colony. Some, like the Bavarian Conservatory, offered only to exchange Bavarian fauna for Southwest African examples. The colonial administration collected the various shipments and distributed them to the secondary schools in Windhoek and Swakopmund.[48]

Physical training played an important role in the education of children, both in SWA and in Germany. Educators believed physical exercise was essential to the development of national character because it symbolized "the vigor and manliness of the nation."[49] Furthermore, according to Eduard

Moritz, a Berlin educator, "in a young settlement country, where the physical prowess still plays a larger role in professional life, physical training is rightly granted a wider acceptance in the school than in the culturally higher standing motherland."[50] In 1913, the Territorial Council felt that not enough attention was given to physical training *(Turnunterricht)* for either boys or girls and requested the governor to correct this situation. Seitz thus instructed schools to provide instruction, either in a hall—if one was available—or outside. Moreover, true to the biases of his time, he decreed that "if a female faculty member is available the boys' training is supposed to be separated from the girls. If that is not the case, both sexes can be united in physical training. Of course the individual exercises then had to be selected carefully and tactfully."[51]

The colonial government also believed that boys and girls in SWA required lessons in handiwork and finishing work *(Handarbeitsunterricht* or *Handfertigkeitsunterricht).* As in Germany, such instruction would prepare them practically for the necessities of life.[52] One individual disagreed when he wrote in the *Windhuker Nachrichten* that handiwork classes were not intended "to prepare them for a trade, but rather to train spirit, eyes, and hands harmoniously." He did concede that practical instruction in such areas as metalworking and carpentry would be beneficial to the future farmer.[53] At any rate, the colonial administration devoted its attention early to such studies. Initially, it provided only boys with handwork instruction, though as early as 1908 young women also participated; not until 1912, however, did the authorities officially regulate girls' courses and provide sufficient teachers. Of course, because their future roles differed from those of the boys, the content of the course emphasized handicrafts, like sewing.[54] Colonial officials assumed that such skills would make young women better candidates for marriage.

By 1914, the curriculum at the secondary schools resembled that of a Prussian Realschule. Initially, officials tailored the course of study to correspond to local conditions. This meant that students first learned English, rather than French, since more English than French was spoken in the colony. However, in 1913 the Territorial Council requested that the syllabus resemble the Prussian curriculum in all respects, meaning that students would start with French. Members of the council saw this as particularly important since students transferring to an equivalent school in Germany did not possess the necessary knowledge of French. Similarly, students coming from Germany lacked adequate preparation in English. Essentially, authorities accommodated the children of colonial officials and business-men who had only a brief tenure in the territory. The Colonial Office in Ber-lin approved the council's request and thus brought the Southwest African curriculum at the secondary level into line with Prussia's.[55]

In addition to the curriculum guidelines, colonial authorities instituted other measures to monitor instruction and enforce conformity. Governor Seitz required all schools to submit their syllabi and overviews of course dis-tribution to the colonial government. The government even requested every faculty member to submit a lesson plan, annually, in order to gain a better overview of the activities of teachers at government schools.[56] Furthermore, in 1913 it created the office of school inspector to make sure that all schools followed the colony's educational laws and statutes.[57]

Since colonial officials believed that the quality of education depended on the character of the instructor, they took great care in selecting them. In general, most of the teachers employed in government schools were male civil servants on an extended leave of absence. Often colonial authori-ties preferred married teachers so that their wives could run the dormitories. Because these teachers were state-educated and state-examined instruc-tors, officials could assume that they possessed the necessary pedagogical qualifications.[58] Moreover, because they were civil servants, these teachers swore before God to be loyal and obedient to the emperor as well as "to fulfill loyally and scrupulously" their duties according to the laws and in-structions and to promote "the best of the empire and its protectorates."[59] The colonial government did occasionally hire private individuals for teaching positions in its schools, but only after a thorough examination of their credentials.[60]

This scrutiny also extended to the hiring of teachers in nonpublic schools. In fact, because of the importance attached to teachers and educa-tion, officials consistently exercised this hiring authority since it was the ad-ministration's only means to supervise instruction in these schools. As in the case of the secondary Catholic Mission School for Boys, colonial officials withheld approval for the school due to the absence of a qualified instructor. In another instance, the local official in Grootfontein, Berengar von Zas-trow, forbade a private teacher named Claussen from exercising his profes-sion because of his moral character. Claussen had earlier worked for a Mr. Poolmann, but eventually ran off with the man's wife; on a previous occasion he had seduced a servant girl, a Ms. Bosse, in Kubas. The official had regrets about his decision since Claussen was very talented and "the children had learned very well by him"; however, he said in his report to Seitz, "one cannot leave children to such an objectionable man in moral affairs."[61]

The responsibility of government employees for the upbringing of children extended beyond the classroom. For example, in the boarding facilities, strict rules existed to instill a sense of order, discipline, and personal hygiene.[62] The colonial government also believed it was necessary to supervise children's extracurricular activities, especially those influencing their moral character. This became particularly important after it came to the attention of the Territorial Council's school commission that young individuals had been frequenting inappropriate places without their parents or late at night. Not surprisingly, Seitz requested local officers "to forbid pupils the visitation of bars without the accompaniment of their parents—further, the late visitation of bars, movie theaters, roller-skating rinks, and dance halls, and when necessary to inform owners that they keep children away from such establishments."[63]

One other step was taken to help establish and preserve the emerging German character of the colony; namely, the education of the African population. Unlike German East Africa, where the government provided education for both Europeans and Africans, the administration in Windhoek relegated instruction for the Africans to the missionaries. Here was a conscious attempt to segregate whites and Africans. Such a situation was intended to protect white children from the supposedly "bad" influence of the Africans[64] and at the same time to create a diligent and obedient workforce to be exploited by the white population. In their role as educators, missionaries provided religious and German-language instruction as part of their Christianizing and civilizing efforts. They supplemented their curriculum by emphasizing diligence, obedience, honesty, hard manual labor, and personal hygiene. In essence, they prepared them to become conscientious workers capable of understanding and communicating with their masters.[65] Such education, authorities believed, would turn them into "good German subjects"—that is to say, obedient to their white masters, and productive workers.[66]

Despite the fastidious attention given to pedagogy in SWA, there were still calls by individuals both in the colony and in the Heimat for sending young Germans to Germany to supplement and continue their education; they were worried about the limited learning possibilities. Moreover, some saw it as means to acquaint the Southwestern youth with Germany and Deutschtum. To remedy this situation, Dr. Eduard Moritz, a secondary-school teacher in Berlin and author of a study on the SWA school system, suggested that educators in Germany should promote exchanges between German and Southwestern schools instead of the usual ones with French or English schools. Although the costs of such an endeavor were potentially high, Moritz contended that they would not compare "to the moral gain, the national fortification that our nationhood experiences through the education of our kinsmen [abroad] into Germans." Because of the importance of such a program, he expected the government to provide financial assistance.[67] The government did not institute a program toward this end, but some parents undoubtedly sent their children to the homeland for pedagogical purposes.

In retrospect, colonial officials took an active role in shaping and influencing the educational system. They worked to inculcate the protectorate's youth, both Germans and other Europeans, with "German" values and traditions in an effort to win their loyalty for Germany and thus ensure that the colony remained a German possession. They introduced regulations and offices to monitor and control the type of instructors and curricula. This supervisory role extended even to private schools. Moreover, they provided the African population with inferior education, separate from that of the whites, that was intended to create good, obedient, subservient workers.

Statistically, the government could point to significant successes. By 1914, there were seventeen government primary schools in SWA, twelve of which were built after the institution of compulsory education in 1906. In addition, the educational system included three secondary schools—the imperial one in Windhoek; the municipal one in Swakopmund (with, briefly, another in Lüderitz Bay); and the Higher Catholic School of Girls in Windhoek. There were also fourteen boarding facilities attached to schools in the protectorate, including one run by the Catholic Mission.

Without the building program, especially the building of dormitories, the SWA educational system would not have been able to absorb the increased student population after the introduction of compulsory education. In 1908 there were 287 pupils in school; by 1911, 548 children attended classes. After the introduction of territory-wide compulsory education in 1912, 671 students went to school—an increase of 123 children and the largest jump in attendance between 1908 and 1913. By 1913 there were 775 pupils attending school in SWA (see table 4.1). In 1914, nearly 1,000 children went to school out of a total youth population of 3,000. School Inspector Voigt contended that approximately two-thirds of the children had not yet attained school-age,[68] thus, the education system enjoyed a relatively high percentage of attendance.

Table 4.1. Development of Public and Private Education in
Southwest Africa, 1908–1913

Schools (public & private)	Students	Boys	Girls	Protestant	Catholic	Jewish	Local	Out-of-town	In Dormitory	Germans	Foreigners	Teachers Secondary	Teachers Male	Teachers Female
31 March 1908	287	139	148	246	29	12	211	76	62	252	35	—	9	4
31 March 1909	377	181	196	325	31	21	272	105	84	311	66	—	12	9
31 March 1910	470	221	249	401	48	21	359	111	82	377	93	—	12	12
31 March 1911	548	269	279	467	53	28	415	133	99	436	112	—	17	11
31 March 1912	671	361	310	577	65	29	484	187	164	536	135	4	15	15
31 March 1913	775	370	405	657	85	33	530	254	210	622	153	5	18	16

Source: Eduard Moritz, *Das Schulwesen in Deutsch-Südwestafrika* (Berlin: Dietrich Reimer, 1914), 43–46.

Similarly, the number of children who boarded at school increased annually. There were 62 students in dormitories in 1908; by 1911, the boarding establishments had 99; by 1912, 164, and in 1913, 210. Of the entire school population, 22 percent lived in dormitories in 1908–9, 17 percent in 1910, 18 percent in 1911, 24 percent in 1912, and 27 percent in 1913.[69] The boarding system contributed considerably to the growing attendance of school-age children in the colony.

Compared with Germany, the Südwester educational system offered smaller classes and more teachers per student (see table 4.2). In 1912, Berlin had an average of 42.53 students per class; in 1911, Brandenburg had 43.9, the Kingdom of Prussia, 51.1, Schleswig-Holstein, 42.2, and Braunschweig, 44. In Southwest Africa, in 1911 there were 18 students per class, and in 1912, 19.2. On average, the number of students per teacher was 42.5 in Berlin, 51.2 in Brandenburg, 57.4 in Prussia, 55 in the empire, 50 in Schleswig-Holstein, and 61 in Braunschweig. In SWA, the figure was 23.[70]

After a comprehensive inspection tour of the German schools,[71] Inspector Voigt reported that these circumstances contributed to satisfactory, if

Table 4.2. **Development of Public Education in German Southwest Africa, 1908–1913**

	# of Pupils in Public Schools	Classes	Pupils to Classes	Teachers	Pupils to Teachers	Schools	Population	Population to Pupils	Population to Schools
1908	253	11	23.0:1	11	23.0:1	8	8,213	28.6:1	1026.6:1
1909	322	18	18.0:1	17	15.0:1	12	11,791	31.3:1	982.6:1
1910	437	22	19.9:1	22	19.9:1	14	12,935	27.5:1	924.0:1
1911	518	29	18.0:1	25	20.7:1	19	13,962	25.5:1	735.0:1
1912	634	33	19.2:1	31	20.4:1	20	14,816	22.1:1	740.8:1
1913	732	37	19.8:1	31	23.6:1	20	14,830	19.0:1	741.5:1

Source: Eduard Moritz, *Das Schulwesen in Deutsch-Sudwestafrika* (Berlin: Dietrich Reimer, 1914), 46.

not above-average, results in the SWA school system. He even argued that the children in SWA had a distinct advantage over their counterparts in Germany. Not only did they have smaller classes and competent teachers, but the children almost never came "from such miserable conditions as those in German industrial centers." According to the school inspector, "that makes a big difference." He admitted that "many young children grew up in monotonous areas . . . poor on impressions"; however, when they started attending school they gained exposure to many new things "in the correct way." They comprehended things with "surprising eagerness." After one year they made advances "hardly possible in the Heimat." This even applied to the Afrikaner children, especially those of well-situated parents. For example, Voigt noted that after only two years of school, the Afrikaner pupils in Klipdam (aged twelve to fourteen) could already read and write almost perfect German. He conceded that the results at the Realschule were not particularly noteworthy. He attributed this to the fact that many children attended the higher school who would not have been able to do so in Germany (he added that this observation applied only to a small number of children, not to the majority at the Realschule).[72]

Some students did indeed come to see SWA as their new homeland. One notable example was Anna Rohlig. Born in the colony, Anna went to Germany in order to continue her studies. Longing for her "true" home, she wrote a poem in 1908 that was published in the *Windhuker Nachrichten,* an SWA newspaper. She writes in the first stanza of her "Meine Heimat" ("My homeland"),

> How much the yearning for the land
> That is across the sea seizes my heart!
> How my heart always beats on high full of jubilee,
> When the home sounds touch my ear
> Where many an affectionate bond ties me to the soil,
> There is my home, the Hereroland![73]

Whether it was the authorities that had succeeded in inculcating a bond, a loyalty to SWA, Deutschtum, the poem does not say. But an idea of Heimat was indeed a trait cultural elites sought to instill in the region's youth: they believed that loyalty to a particular region could ultimately be transferred to the larger Heimat—namely, the German Empire.

Despite these academic achievements within a relatively short period of time, Voigt regretted that some German and Afrikaner children lagged behind in one notable area: in the development of their emotional characteristics. In other words, their inner "good German" qualities remained underdeveloped. He stated that many children were disorderly. "The picking up of toys and school books, the orderliness of the clothes and hair, the unpunctuality, the forgetting of books, folders, and writing instruments also gives reason to complain." He added that they were guilty of not being chaste, honest, and truthful. Many lied, stole, and cheated. When such children entered the dormitories, he said, they constituted a danger for the "still unspoiled children." Yet, he contended that this behavior did not originate in some notion of youthful rebellion because "the [German-]African children are noticeably obedient and easy to manage." No, he argued, it was due to "negligence," "general indifference," "bad habits," and "bad examples."[74]

Voigt laid the blame squarely on the parents' shoulders. He noted that "already before school age, much is neglected." He claimed that some unscrupulous parents allowed "natives" to take care of their children entirely, thus "irritating incidents do not fail to materialize." He pointed out that when the children grew older, they spent time with the "natives" and learned their language "to the joy of the parents." Voigt believed that in a young colony like SWA, the presence of such individuals could not be avoided: "It is the lot of all young settlement countries that unsuitable and low-quality people in overabundant numbers stay in them, give wicked examples from mean, unGerman nature, dishonesty, indulgences, treason, and lies, and therefore spoil good customs."[75]

In order to correct this situation, Voigt emphasized the importance of upbringing. Therefore, all those who played a role in raising children—parents, teachers, dormitory directors—had an important task to fulfill. Not only did they need to counter the deficiencies Voigt noted, but they also had to instill notions of "courtesy," "modesty," "piety," "devotion to duty," and "love for the fatherland" in the colony's children. Voigt stressed that this was imperative "if in the future a mentally and spiritually healthy generation should grow up here." He argued that families and schools should view this as their "highest task" and contribute to a solution.[76]

In blaming the parents, Voigt shifted culpability away from the system and the measures that had been instituted. In other words, the problem lay with those responsible for the pupils *outside* the classroom. Thus, the colonial administration failed to prevent "unsuitable" elements (i.e., lower-class Germans) from settling in the territory. If they were "good" Germans (i.e., members of the educated and propertied classes), they would contribute to instilling the values and behaviors every "proper" German possessed.

Voigt, though not admitting it outright, recognized the salient role parents played in developing children's character. He realized the limitations of the education system, if not state education in general, in creating citizens. Nonetheless, he seemed to be hopeful that the children could still be raised as "proper Germans." That was why he emphasized that not only school officials but also that parents needed to become more involved in the education process. This may have meant that the state would have to take additional measures, beyond those already in existence, such as the penalties for truancy, to ensure the compliance of parents.

Nonetheless, Germany's cultural elites had achieved a degree of academic success, even though they were not completely satisfied with the results. Through various means, the colonial government and other organizations had tried to introduce the colony's children, both German and Afrikaner, to German culture, traditions, and values through a predominantly Prussian model. In classrooms and dormitories, colonial authorities and educators intended to convey to SWA's youth, primarily through the senses (sight, sound, movement, touch), what it meant to be a German. In other words, they believed the territory's youth would experience Deutschtum. Learning and speaking the language gave them access to German culture. History and geography lessons as well as stuffed animals would help them attain an affinity for both their local environment and the fatherland. In addition, they would learn about discipline, hard work, and physical training. This—combined with practical skills obtained through vocational training—was supposed to enable them to become contributing members of the empire, adding their strength to that of the nation.

The fact that the colony's cultural elites and their allies in Germany undertook such measures early in the colony's history, in contradistinction to what occurred in other settler colonies, illustrated a perceived need. They were concerned about the potentially detrimental influences of living in a region so far from the homeland and populated by "questionable" Germans, Afrikaners, and Africans; they ostensibly feared for the future of the colony as a German possession—fears that, in the light of Voigt's report, still seemed real. Therefore, they believed it was necessary to extend the school system, involve the colonial population in the education of the territory's youth, and provide an "appropriate" education for their children, in particular for those living in rural areas. And, as the population increased, so did the comprehensiveness of the measures.

According to the stated aims of the educational system, the authorities did achieve a degree of success. German and Afrikaner children, even if they did not all possess the character traits of a "good" or "idealized" German, could read and write the German language. Voigt attributed the unsatisfactory results to the "quality" or character of some parents and, to a lesser degree, the local conditions. He implied that public education could achieve only limited successes if parents did not support the middle-class, nationalist agenda. But Voigt did not give up hope. He saw nothing wrong with the programs or the means: he encouraged German educators and, equally important, parents to work harder if they wanted to save the colony as a German possession for future generations. Hence, he appealed to German patriotism in an effort to win over reluctant, resistant, or indifferent parents.

It should be noted that the more comprehensive aspects of the system had been introduced only since 1906. The outbreak of war in Europe and the establishment of a mandate over the territory under South African administration created new problems and concerns for the Southwestern German population. But the immense energy and sacrifices made to preserve the German educational system during that period (1914–39, and especially 1919–39) indicated that perhaps the program did succeed, at least in establishing a firm sense of affinity for the "new" homeland among the region's German population.

5

Southwestern Germans

German is . . . who feels German culture as his
own culture, to whom the great presentiments of
the German spirit are his own presentiment; German is . . . who feels the experience of his people
as his own experience; German is . . . who has in-
ternally witnessed the great personalities and the
great deeds of the German history. . . . German
is . . . an enormous cultural concept, is a value of
humanity and an idea of humanity, without
which humanity would not be what it is today.

—Reichstag member Dr. Wilhem Külz, speaking
    after World War I

By the outbreak of World War I,
Southwest Africa had become a predominantly agrarian colony populated
largely by German men and women. Some had lived there more than two
decades, others even longer. Many had come to feel an affinity for the
land—to identify with it. For them the colony had become their new homeland, and their destiny became intertwined with that of the protectorate.
They called themselves Südwester, in much the same way that Bavarians
and Saxons referred to themselves. Yet, again like Bavarians and Saxons,
they were distinctly German and part of the larger German Empire. These

two components, their Deutschtum and their strong affinity to SWA, were inextricably linked in the Southwestern German identity.

In many ways, Southwest Africa revealed itself as a German possession. One readily noticeable expression of this was in the place-names. Over time and particularly during the period of colonial rule, beginning with the early missionaries, Germans had given names to various geographical and human-made locations. Within three decades, there were approximately one thousand German place-names and names of farms. This led undeniably to a Germanization of the region. Some of the names were simply brought over from the old Heimat; others were influenced by local conditions.

Three motives can be detected behind the nomenclatures. First, names from the homeland were used directly for nostalgic, cultural, patriotic, or historical reasons; thus, missionaries named Bethanien and Rehoboth after biblical names. Secondly, family names were often used to honor or remember family members; for example, Lüderitz Bay, Maltahöhe, and Keetmanshoop: the former was named after Alfred Lüderitz, the founder of the colony, Maltahöhe after Martha Beathe Luise von Dallwitz (Malta von Burgsdorff), the wife of a district officer, and Keetmanshoop after the missionary Keetmans; and many farms also carried family names (e.g., Voigtsgrund, Voigtland, Marienhof, Amalienhof). Thirdly, Germans named locations for topographical reasons, geographic and geological factors or characteristics playing a salient role in the designations; thus, we find names like Kalkfeld (literally, lime field), Salztal (salt valley), and Tiefland (deep land). Germans also utilized animal or plant designations to name places, such as Giraffenberge (giraffe mountains) or Pavianskopf (baboon head).[1]

The Germanization of the colony was also apparent in the efforts of colonial officials to create an infrastructure comparable to states in the German Empire. Not only did these include establishing an administrative and judicial apparatii, but also facilitating a healthy economic development. Officials believed that the provision of efficient services would also attract immigrants to the region.[2] By 1914, noticeable advances had been made in administrative, judicial, economic, and community development. For instance, there were sixteen administrative districts, eight independent town administrations, one high court, and five district courts.[3] The administration also introduced and expanded postal and communication systems.[4] SWA had seventy post offices and 4,000 kilometers of telegraph lines at the end of the German colonial period.[5] The state also assumed an active role in constructing a railway system. Begun in 1897 (in that year, rinderpest wiped out large numbers of livestock, including transport oxen), the public railway between Swakopmund and Windhoek was completed in 1902. This initial stretch was complemented by a southern line that connected Lüderitz Bay with Keetmanshoop (completed 1908) and a north-south line (completed 1912) that connected Keetmanshoop and Windhoek. In 1910, the government nationalized the Otavi railroad (from Swakopmund to Tsumeb, with a branch line to Karibib) and added another stretch between Karibib and Windhoek.[6] By 1913, the region possessed 2,104 kilometers of active rail lines.[7]

With the expansion of the railroad and increased immigration, Southwest Africa's urban centers grew as well. And as the populations of Windhoek, Swakopmund, Lüderitz Bay, and Keetmanshoop expanded, so did the services and social, cultural, and economic opportunities that they offered. Places like Windhoek by the end of the German colonial era assumed the character of a small German town—although not everyone would have agreed with such an assessment: in 1907, M. J. Bonn, traveling to SWA at the insistence of the University of Munich, offered an unsympathetic view of the city, describing it as a "big village with sandy streets."[8] Even by 1911/12, the city still lacked pavement and lighting, a condition that often resulted in the unprepared evening traveler sinking into deep sand.[9] Nevertheless, these towns exhibited a strong German character, as was immediately visible in the architectural style employed in governmental and private building projects. In a book about architecture in SWA, Walter Peters wrote that the period after 1907 gave architects and master builders "the opportunity to furnish the country with a long-lasting imprint."[10]

The German style was most evident in the increasing number of administrative buildings. Over time, the government built various state buildings, including a new administrative building *(Tintenpalast)* in Windhoek, housing for civil servants, post offices, court houses, district offices, jails, schools, hospitals, train stations, and a new pier in Swakopmund. Officials emulated the architectural styles of Germany by building massive structures similar to those from *Gründerzeit* or *Jugendstil* periods.[11] Many individuals and private construction companies also contributed to development. In 1906–7, forty-seven private homes were built in Windhoek, and the following year, an additional seventy-seven. Between 1910 and 1914, the government issued between thirty-six and seventy-four building permits annually in the capital city.[12]

The new structures symbolized the colonization of Southwest Africa as a German possession; the message was: the territory belongs to Germany and is populated by Germans. In a sense, the German architecture was a testimony to the German will to tame this new homeland and to demonstrate long-term commitment to this new German region. Many of the structures erected during the colonial period still stand today: for instance, the train station in Swakopmund (built 1901), the Princess Ruprecht Home in Swakopmund (1914), the *Tintenpalast* in Windhoek (1913), the post offices in Swakpmund (1907) and Keetmanshoop (1910), the gymnastics hall in Windhoek (1909), the gymnastics hall and Lüderitz memorial and reading house in Lüderitz Bay (1913), government housing and other buildings, and many private homes and businesses.[13]

Especially after the suppression of the Nama and Herero and the discovery of diamonds, the urban centers continued to grow. In 1894, the white population of Windhoek (excluding nearby Klein-Windhoek) was only about 34; in 1900, it was 227 civilians and an increasing number of civil servants. By the beginning of 1903 the number of civilians had more than doubled, to 457, and the garrison in Windhoek during these years numbered between 100 and 200 men. In 1907, the town counted 1,521 white inhabitants, and by 1913, 2,186.[14] With the rise in population came increases in the number of businesses. Windhoek in 1903 had only fifteen businesses (among them, seven stores, a butcher, a hotel, a wagon smith, and the headquarters of a concession company, the Settlement Company for Southwest Africa). By 1909, two years after the return of peace to the colony, there were sixty businesses (two hardware stores, two barbers, a butcher, a bakery and confectionery store, a shoemaker, a watchmaker, a drugstore, fifteen other shops of various kinds, a shingles factory, two locksmiths, two banks, a bookstore, and, among other establishments, several concession companies and farm corporations). By 1913, there were ninety-eight businesses— the mix by this time including two stores for ladies, a tailor, two bakeries, two plumbers, two saddle makers, two lawyers, a notary, a bookstore, and eight hotels.[15]

Swakopmund, too, experienced growth. In 1894, this coastal town had only 19 whites (10 soldiers and 9 civilians); two years later, the number had jumped to 113, and by 1910 there were 1,212. Over the next few years, Swakopmund's population increased steadily, though not dramatically. In the last year of German control, the white population reached 1,463.[16] As in Windhoek, the number of businesses multiplied. In 1900, there were only 19 businesses (several stores and bars, as well as a hotel, a butcher, and a bakery). Three years later, the number had jumped to 35 (two hotels, two bakeries, a café, several restaurants). In 1909, 112 businesses operated in

Swakopmund—among them, three bakeries, two barbershops/beauty salons, two butchers, a drug store, three tailors, a plumber, five laundries, two watchmakers, and three cabinetmakers. But by 1913, the number of businesses had dropped to 100.[17]

Throughout the colony, social life duplicated Germany's in many ways. For instance, alcohol consumption, especially beer consumption, was prominent, as was evident in the introduction of beer evenings at a casino in Windhoek around 1908–9. Such events were tolerated if they "did not lead to class prejudice and arrogance"; they represented "good customs of the homeland transplant[ed] to the colony."[18] The predilection for alcohol was apparent in the increasing number of taverns and breweries and the decreasing number of people per establishment. In 1900, there were only nine bars; thus, for every 238 adult males there was a bar. By 1905, the number of taverns had leapt to twenty-nine and there were now three breweries. By 1907, thirty-nine bars and five breweries operated. Even though the population had increased, the number of people per tavern had decreased, to only 125 males per bar. In 1911, there were eighty-two bars and seven breweries, with only 109 males per bar. In 1914 there was a small decline in the number of bars but an increase in the number of breweries, to nine (three of them in Windhoek, two in Swakopmund).[19]

Bars and breweries could be found throughout the colony, but they were concentrated in the larger towns. In 1903, Windhoek had only two bars (*Gastwirtschaften*) and one brewery, but by 1909 the number of taverns had expanded to ten. The one brewery by then was a new one: the Felsenkeller, founded in 1907. In 1914, there were only eight bars, but in addition to the Felsenkeller Brewery, there were now two wheat-beer breweries.[20] Swakopmund had a larger tally of drinking establishments than Windhoek. In 1903 there were six bars and a brewery, and 1911 appeared to be a heyday in the town for taverns: eighteen operated there, as well as three breweries and a distillery. By 1914, there were only ten bars and two breweries, but the distillery continued to operate.[21]

Probably nothing was more indicative of the establishment of German culture in the colony than the number of clubs. The colony had a healthy associational life. Throughout the territory, there were gymnastic, shooting, singing, veteran, bowling, and occupational clubs. One of the first was the shooting club in Windhoek, founded in 1895. By 1914, Windhoek had twenty-four associations, including a gymnastics league and a veteran's organization.[22] Similar clubs existed in Swakopmund, Lüderitz Bay, Usakos, Keetmanshoop, and Tsumeb. In some clubs, social order played a significant role. For instance, in the Swakopmund bowling clubs, groups bowled on a specific day, determined by "rank and worth."[23] These associations not only provided social activities and distractions from everyday life,[24] but in their assumed cultural role they acted as guarantors of Deutschtum. Along with schools and women, these associations claimed to preserve "German thoughts, German ways, and German customs."[25] Notwithstanding the social divisions that could be found in some Southwestern clubs, they were said to be above the din of partisan politics—a direct reference to the special-interest politics in Germany.

The numerous taverns and associations, as well as other social institutions like movie theaters, dance halls, and racecourses, allowed many Südwester to replicate their former social lives in Germany—and some to attain a previously denied social existence. Moreover, the increasing number and variety of businesses also offered greater consumer choice and more comforts. Clara Brockmann could say of the colony that

> in the large stores of Windhoek one can obtain everything that moves the heart, and luxury extravagance is cultivated enough in the elegant, small towns. One lives like in Germany. The social activity stands in bloom, athletics and formal questions play a role.[26]

But there was another side to this: "A more discriminating social life grew up . . . based on the social hierarchy of a German provincial town."[27] This was in sharp contrast to the supposedly generous hospitality farmers that readily extended to any European. The hierarchical behavior was particularly evident in Windhoek, but it existed also in Swakopmund and Lüderitz Bay. Different quarters, based on profession, emerged in the towns.[28]

Meanwhile, those in the countryside—where most Germans lived—did their best to duplicate German life, but their isolated situation hindered them significantly. They were confronted daily with the territory's wide open spaces and African population. Unlike the inhabitants of Windhoek or Swakopmund, who saw the Africans as "strange and dejected laborers . . . uprooted from their homes and drifting aimlessly through the town,"[29] farmers and tradesmen in the country were more intimately involved with Africans. Before 1904, they needed African headmen, for they did not have a European market for their goods; nor did they possess the means to provision their laborers. African headmen assisted them in both areas. This left the colonists uncomfortably dependent on those they deemed "inferior." However, the suppression of the 1904–7 uprisings was accompanied by the issuance of regulations controlling the Herero and Nama, and this gave farmers greater power over the Africans. Nonetheless, Europeans in the country continued to lead lives very different from those in towns, even as they occasionally gathered to celebrate some German festival or holiday.[30]

Although Southwest Africa exhibited strong characteristics of Deutschtum, local circumstances also played a significant role in shaping the nature of the Southwestern Germans. Many had lived in the region for decades, the so-called "old Africans." Over time, they, and even newcomers, developed a strong affinity for the land. In addition, the Southwest African environment affected the attitudes and behavior of Germans. They called themselves Südwester and were referred to as such by people in Germany. Though they felt themselves tied to the old homeland through their Deutschtum, many nevertheless kept a distance to the fatherland: "In personal and material respects they oriented themselves on Southwest Africa."[31] Thus, Südwesters often found themselves more at home in the colony than in Germany, despite the strong nationalistic devotion to the European homeland.[32] This situation often manifested itself in strained relationships between the protectorate and the metropole. Some even threatened revolt when they felt that Berlin was not meeting their demands.[33]

The colony attracted many people back to it who had at some point returned to Germany. For individuals like Falkenhausen and Eckenbrecher, Southwest Africa was their only true home. Falkenhausen went back to Germany after losing her husband, only to return to SWA in 1909 to open the learning farm in Brakwater. Eckenbrecher traveled to Germany at the outbreak of hostilities in 1904, but wanted to return to SWA with her husband and two sons. "I had fought, worked and suffered for the Southwest," she wrote. "We and both our sons belonged there." However, her husband had no desire to go back to the colony, so she divorced him and returned with her sons. Back in the colony, she began a career as a schoolteacher.[34]

Many notable Südwester tried to immortalize their attachment for the land in words, offering readers personal and sometimes idyllic visions of the territory. Falkenhausen, Eckenbrecher, Brockmann, Höpker, Voigt, and Paul Leutwein (son of Governor Leutwein), depicted life in SWA either through their own eyes or through fictional characters.[35] Many, if not all, of their books were works of propaganda (especially those written after Germany relinquished control of SWA in accordance with the Treaty of Versailles in 1919), but they were nevertheless expressions of the authors' affinity for the colony. A dominant theme throughout the literature was the land. Southwestern German colonial writers devoted long, poignant passages to the Southwestern landscape. They praised its wide-open and free spaces and longed for its unspoiled, idyllic beauty. Lydia Höpker emotionally wrote,

> Everything was so dewy fresh and untouched, round about loneliness and quiet; only from afar did the call of a bird resound now and again. We hiked silently through this beautiful morning. A dreamlike feeling enveloped me, and I felt enchanted, as if in another world.[36]

The purity and freedom of Southwest Africa were in conscious contrast to the overpopulated and industrialized Germany. Eckenbrecher, shortly after her arrival in the colony, euphorically wrote,

> The Namib offered a most glorious view, veiled in blue haze, above which rested, rosy in the gleam of the sun, the enormous mass of the Brandberg. It is among the most beautiful things I have ever glimpsed in my life, so splendidly exalted and yet so desolate and lonely . . . I felt it with my senses. . . . Heavy tears streamed down my face. I could have clasped my hands and said: "Dear God, I thank Thee for vouchsafing to me that I might see Thy beauty in the wilderness. I will gladly endure hunger and thirst and privation, but let me enjoy the wonder of their creation far from the hustle and bustle of mankind.[37]

Eckenbrecher, like her contemporaries in SWA, desired "to escape the industrialized European world . . . and Germany's crowdedness,"[38] and the protectorate offered them a welcoming and enticing alternative.

Underlying this romantic, idyllic motif were elements of hardship and even death. Although they praised the country's beauty, writers also recognized that Southwest Africa was a hard and demanding land. Only the hardiest and most determined of men and women could make it there, and even those qualities did not guarantee success. Those who lived in the wide-open spaces had to struggle for their existence and survival. They had to combat drought, disease, loneliness, and sometimes death. Their struggle was not limited to the natural environment. Between 1904 and 1907, many Germans lost their lives during the Herero and Nama wars—albeit a good many fewer than the losses to these African societies. In addition, farmers had to deal with government officials, missionaries, large companies, and reluctant African laborers as they tried to eke out an existence. Yet, after surmounting or coming to terms with these hardships, an individual—according to these writers—could find satisfaction and joy.

Indeed, the struggle with the land brought the colonists to it. Their labor, sweat, and blood had mixed with the soil. This mixing created a bond and a sense of ownership; they felt they had paid for the territory and thus it belonged to them. As Clara Brockmann wrote, "This land must remain German, German to the very core; it has truly been purchased dearly enough through all the noble blood that its soil has absorbed."[39] Such statements obviously served as both an invitation and a warning. Writers like Brockmann repeated the theme that only those who could overcome or endure the rigors of the new land could claim ownership to it, and only such people were "true" Germans. This physical and almost spiritual relationship with the land undeniably played a role in the character development of the Southwestern Germans.

Equally significant, the presence of non-European populations also influenced the nature of the Southwestern Deutschtum. In the colonial literature, authors (especially women) portrayed the "natives" as "uncivilized" and inferior, in stark contrast to the more "civilized" and "cultured" ways of the Europeans.[40] After the suppression of the Herero and Nama uprisings, settlers demanded greater control over the indigenous population. The Africans were indeed regulated and exploited. Their land was expropriated and they were essentially reduced to the status of second-class citizens in order to serve as a readily available and inexpensive labor force for the white community.

Through their control over the land and the indigenous populations, settlers believed that they would become masters of the land (Herrenmenschen). In SWA, they struggled daily to tame this wide-open, pristine country. And unlike their peers in Germany, where the industrial working classes increased in numbers and their political representative, the Social Democratic Party, increased its power, these new "aristocrats" exercised considerable control over the "masses" (i.e., the indigenous population).[41] Thus, all whites in the colony, if they played the skin game, could achieve and enjoy a special status, a position they may not have acquired in the homeland.

The difference in status opportunity applied equally well to the position of women in the colony. SWA was, admittedly, a decidedly male-dominated society, but more was expected of women there than in Germany. Not only did they have to perform their reproductive function, bearing and raising children, and provide a regenerative haven for their spouses, but they acted as helpmates in the daily running of the family businesses; and if she lived on a farm, a woman's tasks were further multiplied. However, because only they, as whites, could bear white children, whereby they were deemed essential to upholding the racial boundaries, many white women achieved an enhanced and in many respects irreplaceable position in colonial society. Many women were able to employ domestic servants (African or German) for the first time, a situation inconceivable for all but the wealthy in Germany. The colony also opened up unprecedented employment opportunities for a number of women. Many independent-minded women were able to establish and run their own businesses in SWA (although they had to face the gossipmongers, a situation that might damage reputation). Thus, although they did face many hardships, life in the region provided German women (as well as men) with opportunities and recognition not available to them in Germany. Much of this was due to the blatant racism practiced in the colony.

Despite their wish to become masters[42]—and after the suppression, they did have control over the indigenous population—the settlers, especially the farmers, were actually "dependent masters" *(abhängige Herren)*.[43] Farmers had come to expect the government to help them whenever they needed it (and at other times to leave them alone). Moreover, they expected their position and needs to take precedence over others. If this did not happen, they quickly blamed the government. Officials began to fear that instead of the settlers becoming self-reliant individuals, many had become too dependent on state assistance, and they resented the farmers' selfish, ungrateful attitude. It was in order to silence farmers, while at the same time to increase their share of the burden, that the colonial authorities decided to introduce limited self-government in 1909.[44]

Settlers perceived self-government as the means to achieve complete control over the colony's—and hence their own—destiny. Farmers' initial enthusiasm turned to opposition as two demands remained unfulfilled. First, the plan called only for the indirect election of representatives to the new Territorial Council—not direct, as settlers had hoped. Second, the council itself, like its predecessor, the Governor's Council, remained essentially an advisory body, albeit with limited legislative powers.[45] One individual warned the colonial authorities not to drive a wedge between

Southwest Africa and Germany through their actions.[46] Meanwhile, Dr. Wilhelm Külz, the architect of self-government, cautioned both sides, noting that they needed each other and belonged to each other:

> In the Motherland lie the roots of our energy, politically and economically: this conviction must become common to all German-South Africans. Conversely, in the motherland the conviction must become even more pronounced, that the economic and political life of German-South Africa must be developed unrestricted, freely and generously.[47]

Schuckmann and the deputy governor, Hintrager, convinced farmers that it lay in their own best interest to accept the plan. They reminded farmers that, alone, they could not achieve their goals, especially since the colony was financially dependent on the Reich. In addition, officials promised to broaden self-government and authorize discussions to extend the settler's political power.[48] Thus, in accepting the authority of imperial colonial officials over SWA, farmers were able to increase their power and status disproportionately. By the outbreak of World War I, the Territorial Council had complete control over African employment and labor questions as well as power over other aspects of the colony—much to the satisfaction of the farmers.[49] But although farmers gained a good deal of control over the indigenous population and enjoyed a status well beyond their numbers, they did not exercise as much authority as they wanted. Berlin and the administration in Windhoek had the final say in many matters. Moreover, when a crisis emerged, such as during and after the 1904–7 uprisings, the settlers turned to the imperial government, and thus revealed their subordinate position.[50]

In other ways, too—ways perhaps not readily apparent—the colony affected and molded settlers' lives. For example, although women made conscious efforts to cook as in the homeland, local conditions and foods prevented them. They used indigenous foods and prepared them in ways appropriate to local circumstances; and *Kolonie und Heimat* printed an article about the preparation of menus based on agricultural products in the tropics.[51] Since the colony's climate and seasons were different from Germany's, Südwester moved to a different rhythm; for instance, the Southern Hemisphere school year began in January, the middle of summer, whereas in Germany it started in the fall. The presence of Africans also affected the settlers' mentality. Because they based their rule upon their skin color and nationality, Germans became extraordinarily conscious of their cultural heritage. Like white rulers in other colonies, they lived in a situation that constantly tested them and forced them to assume the air of superiority and ruler. Not surprisingly, given the pressures and the ratio of taverns to population, many imbibed large quantities of alcohol (supposedly, average beer consumption was 50 percent higher than in Germany).[52]

Despite the differences, the impact of Southwest Africa on the German community's sense of identity could not be separated from its connection to the old homeland. Although their efforts to make SWA a German territory and the time they spent there resulted in tying their future to the future of the colony, for the most part Südwester remained loyal to the fatherland, or at least to the greater notion of Deutschtum. To ensure that this would always remain so—to cultivate further a sense of community and belonging among the settlers—the cultural elites, in Germany and SWA, utilized the media, activities, and structures to demonstrate this ambiguous, at times tenuous, connection. German periodicals, for example, created links between Südwester, both to each other and to Germany.[53] Organizations in Germany, notably the DKG and the FB, provided the protectorate's inhabitants with periodicals from "home," and thus those who could read German gained access to the larger world of Deutschtum. Through language—and consequently culture—they were not only inextricably tied to their fellow Southwestern Germans, but also to the rest of the German-speaking community, in particular to the locus of Deutschtum, Germany. The colony itself had three regional newspapers: the *Windhuker Nachrichten,* which was succeeded by the *Südwestbote,* represented farmers' interests; the *Deutsche Südwestafrikanische Zeitung,* printed in Swakopmund, was supportive of the colonial government and businesses; and the *Lüderitzbuchter Zeitung,* an organ of local mining interests.

The protectorate had its own territorial anthem, which people sang at festivals and on other occasions.[54] Because German music possessed a "socially inclusive" character, it was a "key, and possibly the most important key, to the identity of Germans."[55] The anthem extolled the virtues of the new Heimat, but it also reminded people of their duties to the colony and of their obligations to the homeland. It was sung to the same tune as the German national anthem, "Deutschland, Deutschland über alles." It was both an expression of the unique Südwester identity and an identity intricately linked to the former homeland. Schools contributed to the creation of a feeling of affinity for SWA while maintaining the one with Germany. One

Südwester said, "We view as one of the most beautiful tasks of educating our youth, next to the love for the old German fatherland with its cultural value for German Southwest, the cultivation of the Southwest African sense of homeland."[56] Pedagogues believed that through local studies, students would attain a feeling of Heimat for SWA, a feeling that, as they grew older, they would transfer to the empire.

This duality in the Southwestern character found expression in poetry. Anna Rohlig, longing for her "true" home in 1908 while studying in Germany, described Southwest Africa in detail and with great emotion. Even though she "linger[ed] far away on the shore of the Rhine," her heart was really "where many an affectionate bond ties me to the soil."[57] Another writer of verse, a Southwestern farmer, A. Hermkes, praised the opportunities his "new" home gave him. He used his poem to encourage others, pointing out that they, too, could achieve success through hard work. Hermkes simultaneously recognized the colony's bond to the Reich. He noted that only he who worked hard would enjoy his own "kingdom" in Southwest Africa under the "black-white-red" flag of Germany.[58]

The celebration of German holidays and festivals provided a means to establish a feeling of community in the colony and strengthen the ties between it and the metropole. In Germany, such events "provoked feelings of community and definition,"[59] and this applied equally well to German SWA. Thus, such occasions acted to bridge metaphorical gaps between the different groups in the colony as well as the distance between protectorate and metropole. The colony celebrated the larger national holidays to demonstrate the inhabitants' loyalty to the Reich—the Emperor's Birthday (January 27), Sedan Day (September 2),[60] and the Christian holidays of Easter and Christmas. Such occasions, especially Christmas—"the most German of German holidays"—evoked notions of national solidarity. "Christmas images pictured the German nation as a harmonious community ostensibly stretching from the Kaiser's palace to the poorest peasant farmhouse; the impossibility of this image did not damage its appeal."[61] These feelings were emulated in Southwest Africa.[62] As a sign of the colony's loyalty and a reminder to the inhabitants of Germany of SWA's importance, the protectorate's veterans' association attended the 1913 unveiling in Leipzig of the monument commemorating the 100th anniversary of the Battle of Nations against Napoleon.[63]

The construction of churches and the creation of confessional communities also constituted an important component of the colony's cultural and spiritual identity. These, too, symbolized the ties between colony and old homeland. In 1914, there were six Protestant parishes, seven Catholic, and one Dutch-Reformed. Pastor Siebe, dispatched by the Rhenish Mission, in 1896 founded the first Protestant community in Windhoek at the behest of Governor Leutwein. This church fell under the supervision of the Supreme Church Council of the Evangelical Church of Prussia in Berlin. Others Protestant parishes followed, in Swakopmund, Karibib, Lüderitz Bay, Omaruru, and Otjiwarongo.[64] Leutwein's initial involvement, followed by other administrative actions, clearly indicated that the colonial government, in conjunction with Protestant church officials in Germany, was extremely interested in "preserving their conception of German Evangelical Christian culture." The Protestant church became an important component of German nationalism and hence identity.[65]

Churches and religious communities not only served spiritual needs but also acted as community builders. Indeed, the building of churches was accompanied by festivals in which the entire citizenry was expected to participate. Following the erection of a new Christ's Church (the Christuskirche) in Windhoek, for example, consecration festivities began on the morning of October 10, 1910. After the first tolling of the new church bells, the colony's acting governor, Privy Councillor Brückner, as representative of the emperor, awarded the Crown Order, fourth class, to the pastor, Pastor Hammer; to the architect and the director of finances, he presented the Red Eagle Order, fourth class. The following day, six hundred people gathered to celebrate the official dedication of the church. That Sunday morning, a procession moved from the old church hall to the new Christuskirche, children dressed in white carrying the key on a velvet cushion, to the accompaniment of music by an army band. Pastor Hammer consecrated the church and the men's choir sang the One Hundredth Psalm.[66] In the afternoon, soloists from Windhoek, a men's choir, the voluntary church choir, and an orchestra gave a concert, which concluded with Beethoven's "The Honor of God." That evening, two hundred and fifty guests attended a banquet.[67]

This celebration—in addition to bringing together large numbers of Südwester and symbolizing a significant milestone in colony history— demonstrated the strong ties between the protectorate and the homeland. Joint efforts by individuals in the homeland and the colony had built the new church; indeed, financing of the project was made possible through church offices and organizations in Germany, collections in Southwest Africa, and private contributions. Hammer's predecessor, a Pastor Anz, held a church bazaar that collected nearly 10,000 marks, and "the old Süd-wester Schmerenbeck, Gustav Voigts, and August Stauch as well as the Evangelical Mission in the country made large contributions."[68] In 1912, the community gave the church a clock tower.[69] The colonial administration and the homeland also contributed in other ways: Governor von Linde-quist placed the government architect, Gottlieb Redecker, in charge of designing and constructing the church, and the colony's official surveyor, Dr. Lotz, tested the ground structure. Later, in 1914, Governor Seitz's wife donated the altar piece (a copy of Peter Paul Rubens's painting of the resurrection of Lazarus). Emperor Wilhelm II donated the stained-glass windows for the altar apse, and Empress Augusta presented the altar Bible.[70]

Territorial fairs were another way the German community expressed their identity. These fairs, which strengthened the bonds of community, both local and transoceanic, were "the major social event" for the entire colony. Begun in 1899, they exhibited the "increased quality and range of European farm production"[71]—but they were also a great source of personal pride for the colonists, who could point to their accomplishments through hard work and commitment. In 1914, Governor Seitz commented that the fair offered "a whole picture of a young state developing upon a sound basis and can rightly so be described as the high point in the short history of the protectorate."[72] Gustav Voigts, the organizer of the event, claimed that "the exhibition became a success," and said "it was as if the immense and excellent work which Germany accomplished in a few years in an apparently bleak and despised country should be displayed before our eyes once again"[73]—a reminder that helped them to realize what they could accomplish and that the outcome belonged to them. These fairs became a means to show critics in the homeland the value of the endeavors in this overseas territory.[74]

Southwestern Germans were particularly sensitive to negative publicity in Germany. They constantly felt that they had to prove their loyalty to the homeland and that they were true representatives of Deutschtum. Undoubtedly this was a result of an unfavorable press in Germany that questioned the value of the protectorate and the character of its inhabitants, including various rifts in the German community. In direct response to such criticism, the organizers of the 1909 Territorial Fair—commemorating the colony's twenty-five years of existence—claimed that the guests at the inaugural festival represented all classes, and their "hearty tone" demonstrated "undeniably the good understanding between the population and their governor."[75]

In response to renewed criticism,[76] a participant at the 1914 Territorial Fair felt compelled to note that German Südwester were a "model of Deutschtum, who only differentiate . . . [themselves] from . . . Germans born in Germany by the fact that . . . they are born on African soil."[77] Another individual, reacting to accusations of the unreliability of Südwester nationalism, claimed that one could not find a more perfect example of a loyal German than a Südwester, writing: "We call out to those who doubt the reliability of the German colonists: Imitate it, but imitate it exactly!"[78]

Significant for the emerging Südwester identity were the struggles of conquest over the territory. While the spilling of German blood was often used in colonial propaganda as justifying German claims to the protectorates,[79] such acts also created a sense of devotion to the land and to the memory of those who died to make it German. It gave the survivors a sense of meaning:[80] in the case of SWA, to make and maintain it as German territory. This implied a commitment, and consequently a connection, to the colony as well as the fatherland.

Nowhere was this more evident than in the erection of monuments. Their construction in SWA, as in Germany, contributed to creating a "national" consciousness.[81] While several monuments had been built to commemorate the dead in service to the colonial agenda,[82] none had as powerful and long-lasting an influence as the "Rider of Southwest." Built between the Christuskirche and the Old Fortress, the monument became a symbol not only for Windhoek but for German Southwest Africa. Like the Christuskirche, the monument was built with financial and material resources from both the colony and the homeland. The dedication took place on 27 January 1912, the Emperor's Birthday, followed by a celebration on the 28th. It was built to remind people of the sacrifices made to secure the protectorate as a German possession—the shedding of German blood on Southwestern soil, which inextricably linked SWA to Germany. Simultaneously, it commemorated the blood shed for this new Heimat;[83] it thus became a symbol of Südwester identity. The establishment of a local museum served a similar function. While the museum "embodied the uniqueness of the locality," it also gave "meaning to the national whole" because Southwest Africa was a part of the greater German Empire. Thus, not only the Southwestern Heimat museum but also the 197 other such museums founded in Germany between 1871 and 1914 contributed to the construction of a "national narrative," whereby the locality became "the location of the origins of the nation."[84]

These institutions—festivals, holidays, fairs, the German architecture and monuments, the sociocultural and economic opportunities—all worked to establish and maintain Deutschtum in SWA. They reminded Germans from whence they came and, simultaneously, strengthened their connection to the land. They celebrated and contributed to the construction of the local identity and at the same time strengthened the bond to the old homeland. The Germans in SWA thus created a hybrid identity that combined Deutschtum with a strong dose of Southwestern conditions and life.

Members of the educated and propertied classes—the self-designated cultural elites—contributed considerably to the establishment of a German presence in SWA. In their capacities as colonial officials, businessmen, scholars, and members of the various patriotic societies (notably, the Colonial Society and the Women's League), they directly influenced and made policy decisions about who could settle in SWA and how the colony would be developed. They provided financial assistance, encouraged and aided the settlement of women, tried to attract certain types of individuals and favored farmers' needs, built schools, establishing a directed curriculum, and expelled or prohibited the entry of undesirables. Life in the old homeland was replicated by building German towns and setting up familiar administrative, economic, and sociocultural institutions and lifestyles— German families, clubs, churches, monuments. Throughout the colony were place-names that owed their origin to the German occupation. As Wilhelm Külz remarked after his visit to SWA, "German South Africa is no protectorate, it is without a doubt, German land."[85]

But the German inhabitants had a dual loyalty. While they had not forgotten their connection to the homeland, they felt strongly about Southwest Africa. The land, the opportunities, and the status that the country provided influenced their behavior and hence their identity. Many of them even felt more comfortable in SWA than in Germany. Individuals like Rohlig and Hermkes demonstrated not only a strong affinity toward the region but also did not forget their obligations to the fatherland. In behavior and words, they revealed the success of programs and institutions intended both to create a local identity and to preserve ties with the homeland. Thus despite School Inspector Voigt's concern about the protectorate's young generation, Southwestern and German nationalists could point to individuals like Rohlig who exemplified "good" German behavior, guaranteeing the future German character of the colony.

The eruption of hostilities in Europe in August 1914 changed things dramatically for the Southwestern German population, however. One month after World War I broke out, South African units began to occupy territory in Southwest Africa. On July 9, 1915, German colonial troops, under the command of Governor Seitz, surrendered in Khorab, near Tsumeb. With this surrender, German rule ended in SWA; thereafter Germany lost effective control over the region.[86]

The terms of surrender worked out by Seitz and the South African minister president and commander-in-chief, General Louis Botha, were extraordinarily generous. All German reservists were released to their homes in the colony and the rest of the German population retained possession of their properties. Botha imposed martial law in the territory, but said he hoped to see an early return to normal conditions, provided the Germans obeyed the South African authorities. The German civil and criminal codes (except laws it was deemed necessary to repeal because of martial law) remained in effect. In some districts, the German criminal court system was replaced by military courts, but South Africa did not introduce its own civil courts.[87] According to Helmut Stoecker and Adolf Rüger, Botha treated the Germans sparingly for two reasons: 1. in order not to damage the "appearance of the white race" in the eyes of the Africans in Southwest and South Africa; and 2. in order to hold an internationally valid document that would give South Africa a right to claim possession of Southwest Africa.[88] Indeed, South Africa had had designs on Southwest Africa for years.[89]

Martial law gave way to civilian rule in October 1915, when South Africa's former minister of the interior, E. H. L. Gorges, became the region's administrator, but life for the German population did not return to what it had been antebellum. The Germans remained under foreign rule, and the war had interrupted traffic between the homeland and SWA. The DKG had to suspend the transport of German women to the colony; in fact, the last group had been on its way to SWA when the war broke out, and when the Allies interned their ship in Tenerife the women had to find alternative means to get back to Germany.[90] Many Südwester who had been visiting Germany were unable to return to SWA, and thus to their property. Even near the end of the war, when passage to SWA was possible, the British denied Südwester the right to return to the region.[91]

The South African occupation brought a relaxation of the regulations controlling the African population, much to the consternation of many Southwestern Germans. Africans could move about freely and could acquire or appropriate livestock.[92] Many Germans found the new situation deplorable. Lydia Höpker complained that it was a misery with the natives. They were insubordinate and lazy, but one could do nothing to correct it. Corporal punishments were banned; the new government announced that the blacks had the same rights as the whites. If therefore a native became rebellious, or if one surprised him in the act of stealing, one was not permitted to flog him in the act or get the police for this purpose. No, one had to go to the next police station and accuse the native.[93]

Höpker's comments, though exaggerated, were nevertheless representative of German sentiment at the time. Moreover, the South Africans were not exactly acting in good faith: the reinstatement of freedoms for the Africans was only temporary. The South Africans relaxed the regulations for propaganda purposes, to demonstrate Germany's brutal treatment of the "natives" and inability to rule.[94] Such measures proved to be merely a smokescreen since shortly after the occupation the South Africans moved to include and intimidate those African societies that either did not fall under German jurisdiction (the Ovambo) or were disappointed in the unfulfilled expectations that accompanied the change in power (the Bondelzwarts).[95]

Despite the Allied occupation, after the establishment of civilian rule most Germans were able to enjoy a degree of normalcy in their lives. The majority went back to farming their land or to running their businesses. The South Africans established a German administrative body, the Commission of the Former German Government, to regulate the German community and liaise between it and the occupiers. One of the most important acts was the resumption of German education—a result of School Inspector Voigt's efforts and the desire of the South Africans to treat the Germans fairly in order to win them over. The biggest problems facing Voigt were the behavior of teachers, finding enough of them, poor attendance, and a lack of coherent lesson plans, although he was able to overcome the latter.[96]

Despite the apparent setbacks, Voigt maintained an optimistic outlook. In fact, he titled his 1917 school inspection report "Foundations and Further Development of the National Education System in the Protectorate, German Southwest Africa."[97] He assumed that Germany would regain possession of the colony, and in general the German community shared his assumption. There was, however, a degree of uncertainty, especially since an increasingly large number of Afrikaners took up residence in the territory.[98] A German newspaper in Berlin, the *Deutsche Tageszeitung,* had already, in 1915, reminded Cape Town that the fate of SWA would be decided on the battlefields of Europe, not in South Africa. Secure in the belief that Germany would win the war, the Südwester, even in the face of South African administration, held firm to the belief that they would be reunited with Germany at the cessation of hostilities. Their fellow Südwester stranded in Germany would return and life in the colony would continue as before the war. According to Margarethe von Eckenbrecher, "one gets used to a lot in life. One has to. We also accustomed ourselves, even against our will, to the enemy in the land. In the beginning the thought consoled us: it is only a transition."[99] From the old homeland, sympathetic voices like Friedrich von Lindequist's called out for the return of Southwest Africa, claiming that it was in fact a German necessity.[100]

However, the signing of the Treaty of Versailles dashed all hopes for the reunification of Southwest Africa with the homeland. According to article 119 of the treaty, Germany had to relinquish control of its colonial possessions. It claimed that Germany was unfit and incapable of running colonies. Control of the territory passed to South Africa, via the mandate system established by the newly created League of Nations. According to article 22 of the League's covenant, the Union of South Africa was permitted, because of SWA's status as a C mandate, to administer the former German colony essentially as an integral part of its territory, although it had to "safeguard . . . the interests of the indigenous population"[101] (the categorization A, B, or C depended on "the supposed readiness of the inhabitants of the territory for self-government").[102]

In Germany, widespread opposition erupted against the treaty and its signers. Opponents included not only colonial enthusiasts, like members of the DKG, and businessmen, but also government officials and most members of the Reichstag (except the Communists).[103] They called for a revision of the terms of the treaty and a restoration of Germany's colonial possessions. They embarked upon a campaign to disprove the so-called Colonial Guilt Lie (i.e., the assertion that Germany was incapable of maintaining colonies) and restore German national honor. They also pointed out that Germany needed colonies for raw materials and to absorb its excess population. Most Weimar governments and many revisionists published books and reports demonstrating that Germany's rule was no different from other colonial powers, pointing out the country's many achievements in the colonies. The most widely circulated of these books were the works of Hans Grimm and Heinrich Schnee (the last governor of German East Africa).[104] Some revisionist literature argued that the mandate system, especially as it applied to SWA, was illegal or pretentious because it denied its German inhabitants the right to self-determination, while other works took up the theme of mistreatment against the German population in SWA after years of South African administration.[105]

Such arguments completely ignored the African population. The revisionists even tried—though without success—to persuade Africans living in Germany to attest to the fairness of German rule. Under the leadership of Martin Dibobe, the Africans demanded better treatment than they received under the imperial government and called for independence and equality. Such requests provided no useful material for revisionist propaganda. Despite this apparent setback, colonial revisionist efforts continued until the outbreak of World War II.[106]

The Southwest Germans strongly opposed the treaty and called for the return of the colony to Germany. However, after the end of the war and the establishment of the C mandate, they quickly realized that South Africa had no intention of relinquishing control of the region. They also feared that the new masters would try to assimilate them; they saw ulterior motives and subversion in almost all South African activities. The South Africans undeniably wanted to assimilate the Germans and to create a "white man's country." In fact, it was their desire to populate the territory with experienced white settlers that inclined them to deal gently with the Germans: they wanted to win them over (they also wanted to avoid political divisions at home).[107] Moreover, they recognized that the Germans constituted an important element for the country's economy; hence, the Union government permitted most of the German population to stay in SWA after the end of the war and tried to accommodate them.[108]

Despite the South Africans' conciliatory behavior, the Southwestern Germans never abandoned the hope that one day they might reverse their fortune, or at least plot their own course. Thus, during the mandate years, a new threat to Deutschtum was perceived to have unfolded and played itself out. It was no longer a struggle between Europeans and "natives" for control of the country; rather, it was one between Germans and Afrikaner. This new conflict enabled the German community to overcome many of the divisions that plagued it during the German colonial period. No longer did the various professions and social groups oppose each other: it was the Germans against Afrikaners. They experienced an increasing feeling of solidarity as they struggled to overcome their fate as the defeated and to maintain their privileged status in Southwest Africa. Thus, in the face of the new perceived threat, they reacted as they had done during the colonial period when they contended with African, mulatto, and Afrikaner populations. They responded by expressing their sense of self and community—this time building on their experiences under German rule.[109]

In order to accomplish their goal, they planned to gain control of a local legislature with extensive powers and eventually become an autonomous state dominated by Germans. In striving to achieve their objective, they and their supporters in Germany pursued a number of strategies, intimately similar to those employed in the days of German SWA, with the intention of maintaining a strong German character in the territory. The Germans in Southwest Africa and Germany pursued programs for the settlement of Germans (male and female) and for the maintenance and expansion of a German educational system and sociocultural milieu. The arrival of more Germans was aimed at guaranteeing numerical superiority in the face of increasing Boer and British immigration from South Africa; meanwhile, German schools, women, and associations would preserve and inculcate German cultural identity and thus secure loyalty to Deutschtum and the old Heimat.

In addition, Southwestern Germans and their allies realized that they had to secure certain political rights: they felt that the South Africans treated them like second-class citizens. Gains within the political realm would correct this and improve their chances of success in the areas of settlement and cultural institutions. Specifically, they strove for political equality, in particular with regard to voting entitlements, and the recognition of German as the third administrative language, next to English and Afrikaans. They also worked to maintain the legal status of the territory (i.e., keep the status of mandate) and to expand the authority and responsibilities of the Legislative Council, the local legislative body established in 1925. Such a condition would enable them to change the mandate status from a C to an A;[110] that is, from one deemed incapable of administering itself (a land of "uncivilized natives") to one that had the right to determine its own future (a land of whites).

The Southwestern Germans thus desired not only to increase their numbers but to make those numbers count. They hoped, ultimately, for a closer bond with the old homeland; however, in the pursuit of this goal, generational and personal divisions over the best means to achieve it emerged within the Southwestern German community. This was especially true in the 1930s after the arrival of National Socialists, primarily because "to be 'German' assumed a new meaning; it did not describe a foregone conclusion, but rather became an object of active and deliberate argument."[111] It was against this backdrop of revisionism, internal splits, and the struggle for cultural and political survival in the face of a white regime and people they perceived as hostile, that the fate of the Southwestern Germans unfolded in the interwar years.

Part 2
Struggle for Survival, 1919–1939

6

German Settlement and Cultural Integrity

However much every brother is welcome here
and is of the highest value in our fight for our national character, we must point out that only
very certain, indispensable requirements make a
living possible for an emigrant. Southwest
[Africa] is primarily a farm country. Population
growth, which we urgently need if the country is
to develop, will have to belong for the most part
to the farming class.

—German League press release, 1927

As in the German colonial period,
Südwester and their supporters in Germany believed settling German men
and women in Southwest Africa was essential in order to perpetuate the
German character of the region. Even before the signing of the Versailles
Treaty, Gerstmeyer, of the Imperial Colonial Ministry—successor to the
Imperial Colonial Office—remarked that "as soon as the peace is ratified, I
will do my damnedest to influence the [South African] Union government
in the desired way, because the preservation of the Deutschtum in the
former protectorate is of the highest interest." The "desired" way was to
convince the South Africans to allow Südwester and other Germans in the
homeland either to return to or to settle in SWA.[1]

Südwester and their allies also believed, as in the colonial period, that Germany must find a place for its excess population—a place where emigrants could maintain their culture and traditions in a closed settlement. August Stauch, of the *Vereinigung für Deutsche Siedlung und Wanderung* (VfDSW), speaking to a full assembly of the settlement organization, blamed the current tensions and unrest in Europe on overpopulation in conjunction with overindustrialization and too much organization of commerce; settlement and emigration offered a solution to the dilemmas facing Europe in general and Germany in particular. Invoking a notion of manifest destiny, he maintained that "it is a *principle of reason* [emphasis added], when we Germans look around in the world in order to find suitable room where our excess population can be accommodated in closed settlements if possible." He favored closed communities because they offered the best opportunities "to cultivate German language, German customs, and German culture" in order to maintain a "uniform German character." For Stauch and his colonial fellows, Southwest Africa, because of its climate and the presence of a relatively significant German population, offered one of the best places for emigration and settlement.[2]

But now, of course, Southwestern Germans were struggling to preserve their political and self-assumed cultural superiority in the face of a supposedly hostile foreign occupation and administration. Seitz, now DKG president, wrote, "We can only guard the Deutschtum there from the final decline if we make possible a continuous immigrating of strong German elements."[3] Women, as carriers of German culture, were essential to this formula. Oskar Hintrager, director of the *Reichsstelle für das Auswanderungswesen* (RfA)—the Reich office for emigration—and former deputy governor of SWA, wrote that

> the woman is the preserver of the language. Although German churches, schools, and associations may also contribute to the preservation of German culture abroad, the foundation and the preconditions of their activity still remain the silent work of the German woman. In the word *mother tongue*—we never say *father tongue*—lies the meaning of the woman as preserver also of the spiritual life. Already in the small child the word of the mother awakens the spiritual life.[4]

Only through the settlement of Germans, both men and women, did nationalists believe the Southwestern Deutschtum could survive. Ultimately they hoped that a large, culturally strong German community would eventually help overturn the colonial provisions of the Treaty of Versailles and return SWA to Germany. A. G. Sappeur-Flury, a farmer in Okahandja, wrote that "we [the Southwestern Germans] are striving to win back Southwest Africa for Germany."[5]

Even before the cessation of hostilities in Europe, the approximately two hundred Südwester stranded in Germany at the outbreak of the war wanted to return home. They asked the German imperial government to make inquiries with the British to see if they could go back; at this point, they still believed Germany would win the war, but they were nevertheless still concerned about their property and family members. After the German defeat, their requests became even more urgent; more than ever, they wanted to protect property and families, and now, either consciously or subconsciously, they also felt their presence was required to preserve the territory's German character, especially in light of expulsions and voluntary departures from SWA. The occupation powers, between the signing of the Armistice (November 11, 1918) and the signing of the Treaty of Versailles (June 28, 1919), expelled 4,941 Germans; namely, all military personnel, most civil servants, the police, and a number of "undesirables"; in addition, 1,433 men and their families departed by choice, leaving approximately 6,000 Germans in SWA. After the signing of the treaty, the South Africans seldom repatriated Germans.[6] Legally they could have done so, but they viewed the Germans as an important component in the sociopolitical development of the region.[7]

After the transfer of control of SWA to South Africa on October 1, 1920, the Southwest African administration under G. R. Hofmeyr loosened conditions for entry into the region. Although the mass deportations ceased, the new administration, as the sovereign power, retained the right to expel undesirables from SWA, and Germans desiring to enter the territory required a permit, obtainable only through British embassies and consulates and special offices in Germany. Normally only those who possessed property in the region, sufficient wealth, or proof of employment could obtain a permit. Over the next two years, more than 1,400 hundred Germans received entry permits.[8]

Following negotiations, in 1924 the German and South African governments reached an agreement about the treatment and status of the German population. The so-called London Agreement also regulated entry and settlement. Under this agreement, the laws governing immigration in South Africa now applied to the mandate. Now, no legal restraints existed to prevent the entry of Germans and other foreigners unless they fell under the "forbidden immigrants" category. Similar to the regulations of the German period of control over the territory, the administration denied entry to impoverished, mentally ill, or previously convicted individuals; prostitutes were barred, as were individuals incapable of reading or writing a European language (this included Yiddish). In 1930, the South Africans introduced stricter regulations, limiting immigration to individuals born in British territories, the United States, or in one of twelve European countries, including Germany.[9] South African officials recognized that Southwest Africa needed hard-working individuals in order to turn it into a productive country. The mass expulsion of Germans under Administrator Gorges in 1918–19 had banished many persons needed to develop the territory, including craftsmen, farmworkers, and women. This was one of the primary reasons for changing the immigration regulations, allowing Germans back into SWA. Premier Minister Hertzog argued that the Germans constituted a welcome element in the country. After 1937, the Union did require immigrants to obtain permission to enter (for both South Africa and the mandate)—a regulation aimed at reducing the number of active National Socialists entering the country. Nonetheless, the administration made no distinction between Germans and South Africans in the granting of state land and financial subsidies. Receipt of either depended on the applicant's "means and suitability," not nationality.[10]

Despite the South Africans' apparent generosity, Germans in SWA and in Germany distrusted them. Südwester and their allies in the homeland accused the administration of discrimination. They believed that the administration wanted South Africans to gain a numerical superiority over the Germans in order to achieve the majority required for the annexation of SWA by South Africa. They claimed that South Africans, especially Afrikaners, were given preferential treatment in the allocation of government land and in the acquisition of political rights. For example, they contended that in 1926 the administration distributed 29 of the 140 available farms to Germans, but then in 1936 gave only 12 of 89 farms to Germans.[11] In a speech before colonial supporters, Hintrager asserted that the mandate's settlement policy aimed "to settle as fast as possible the government land still available with Afrikaners." He contended that the aim of this land policy was "to obtain the majority of whites considered necessary . . . for entry into the Union." Although Germans did receive state land, many, he said, did not apply because they believed their chances were hopeless.[12] A policy put

Table 6.1. **German and Afrikaner Populations in SWA, 1921, 1926, 1936**

	Numbers			% of the Population	
	Germans	Afrikaner	Total	Germans	Afrikaner
1921	7,855	8,288	19,714	41	43
1926	8,875	11,359	24,051	37	47
1936	9,779	18,128	31,200	31	59

Source: Figures taken from 1921–1936 South African censuses, quoted in Guido G. Weigend, "German Settlement Patterns in Namibia," *Geographic Review* 75 (April 1985): 160; Dr. Johannes Paul, "Deutsche, Buren, und Engländer in Südwestafrika," *Koloniale Rundschau* 22 (1931): 202, 207; Oelhafen, Windhoek, to AA, 4 March 1938, BAP R1001/7431. There were many conflicting figures for these years: e.g., German sources indicated that in 1921, 7,979 Germans lived in SWA, and in 1936, 9,632, figures that are below the South African census figures. Even German figures contradicted each other: Paul's figures for 1926 vary slightly from the report of the German consul to the Foreign Office, 29 Aug. 1927.

forth by the *Deutscher Bund* (DB)—the German League—advising people not to apply for government farms further exacerbated the situation; as an organization claiming to represent all Germans in SWA,[13] the league's policy undoubtedly deterred many Germans from applying for these farms. Meanwhile, Robert Blank, of Swakopmund, complained that newly arrived South Africans obtained electoral rights before newly arrived Germans, who had to wait two years, and after 1926, five years.[14] The South African government's move to settle impoverished Afrikaners from Angola in the late 1920s—even to the consternation of Afrikaners already living in SWA—did little to alleviate the Southwestern Germans' suspicion that the administration wanted to reduce them to a political minority.

The German population had, in fact, risen over the years. The official 1926 census placed the number of Germans in the mandate at approximately 8,900. By 1931, German authorities estimated that approximately 12,000 Germans lived in SWA. Thus, since the initial deportation of Germans at the end of the war, which reduced the population to approximately 6,000, the number of Germans had nearly doubled. However, this figure appeared to be inflated, for by 1936 the official census stated that 9,779 Germans in a total white population of 31,200 lived in the mandate—a statistic contested by Oelhafen, the German consul in Windhoek.[15] Between 1931 and 1935, more Germans gave up their residency in SWA than emigrated from Germany, and with the passage of the Foreigner Law in late 1936, the

Table 6.2: **Percentage Relationship between Germans, Afrikaner, and British, 1913 and 1936**

District	1. Jan. 1913			1936		
	Germans (%)	Afrikaner (%)	British (%)	Germans (%)	Afrikaner (%)	British (%)
Hasuur (Aroab)	28	72	—	3	96.5	0.5
Bethanien	86	11	3	20	75	5
Gibeon	67	33	—	12	86	2
Gobabis	94	5	1	17	81	2
Grootfontein (w/ Ovamboland)	94	5	1	54	39	6
Karibib	98	1	1	39	42	18
Keetmanshoop	85	13	2	9.5	81	9.5
Lüderitz Bay	88	9	3	57	26.5	13.5
Maltahöhe	78	22	—	17	81	2
Okahandja	97	3	—	43	51	6
Omaruru	98	2	—	59	35	6
Otjiwarongo	—	—	—	25	68	7
Outjo	96	4	—	20	71	9
Ovamboland	—	—	—	21	5	13
Rehoboth	86	14	—	24	73	3
Swakopmund	95	2	3	70	22	8
Warmbad	60	39	—	4	94	2
Windhoek	94	5	1	46	34	18

Source: Herbert C. Nöckler, *Sprachmischung in Südwestafrika* (Munich: Max Hueber, 1963), 133.

number of Germans arriving in SWA further dwindled. In April 1939, administrator D. G. Conradie announced that since the law had been in effect, 206 of 468 German applicants had been refused the right to a lengthy stay.[16]

In the eyes of the Germans, the rise in numbers of the Afrikaner population was of equal, or more, importance to the number of Germans in the region. Since South Africa assumed control of the mandate, the Afrikaner community had more than doubled. In almost every district except Windhoek, Swakopmund, and Lüderitz Bay, Germans had become a minority population. These statistics reinforced Südwester fears that they were second-class citizens. Seitz argued that "through the strong Boer immigration the Deutschtum there finds itself in a critical situation."[17] Indeed, during the mandate years the Southwestern Germans went from a majority to a minority of the white population.

Südwester and their allies in Germany recognized in the early years of the mandate the precariousness of the Southwestern Germans' situation. They believed it was imperative to promote the settlement of Germans in SWA. In order to accomplish this task, they created various public and private organizations in both places to accomplish this task. These included, among others, the *Reichswanderungsamt* (RWA—Reich Migration Office), which after 1924 became the *Reichsstelle für das Auswanderungswesen* (Reich Office for Emigration); the German Colonial Society; the *Verein der Reichsdeutschen* (the Association of German Citizens), based throughout SWA; and the *Farmwirtschaftsgesellschaft* (FWG—Farm Business Corporation), in Windhoek. Although interest existed in facilitating the settlement of Germans in SWA immediately following the Treaty of Versailles, there was little these organizations could do. They could assist would-be immigrants in obtaining entry permits and provide them with sparse information about employment opportunities there, but it was not until after the London Agreement, which opened Southwest Africa to greater German immigration, that these organizations could pursue a more active role. Working independently and together, they aided new settlers on their arrival in the mandate.

According to Southwesterner Germans, farmers and craftsmen had the best opportunities for carving out an existence in the mandate, a condition that persisted throughout the interwar period. They warned Germans in other walks of life against traveling to SWA, saying they had little chance of finding a position.[18] Consequently, organizations in Germany advised only farmers and craftsmen to emigrate to SWA. While some Südwester recommended that immigrants possess financial means (between 35,000 and 50,000 marks if they wanted to buy a farm)[19] others believed character and experience were more important. H. Mehnert, a longtime Southwest resident, wrote that "the country needs practical agrarians, sons of agrarians in whom livestock breeding and farming flows in their blood from their youth . . . who are unpretentious, frugal, and orderly and can build their own home."[20] In a meeting with the German consul in Windhoek, Dr. Franz, others commented that they did not want

> to classify the immigrants . . . as desirable according to their capital. The main point is the ability to work and the level of energy in the immigrants.

Those who do not want to or are not able to work would be eliminated from the economic organism.[21]

They also expected craftsmen to have been properly apprenticed.[22] Sofie von Uhde, a former Südwester, wrote a discerning critique of those who went to SWA. In her *Deutsche unterm Kreuz des Südens* (Germans under the Southern Cross), published after a return visit in the early 1930s, she wrote that "the Southwest needs an influx of men with knowledge and culture. I have found here a hunger for intellectual stimulation and the cultural goods of the homeland that is truly astonishing."[23]

These concerns became especially pertinent after Südwester complained in 1927 about the quality of immigrants from Germany. They protested that "the young people . . . are not very hard-working, apparently have hopes of an easy life in Southwest Africa, and do not demonstrate the firmness of character that such a harsh life as that in Southwest Africa demands."[24] Similar to the concerns over poor whites during the German colonial era, they feared an unwanted agricultural proletariat would develop if too many unqualified individuals came to SWA. They also reminded officials and supporters in Germany that the mandate only had a limited capacity to absorb immigrants. Nonetheless, Südwester did not want to inhibit the desire to emigrate to SWA currently in vogue in Germany; they therefore advised those organizations providing information to potential settlers, such as the DKG and the RfA, only to be more selective. They maintained that "those willing to work" and "the competent" could find work in SWA.[25]

Consequently, organizations in both SWA and in Germany tried to improve the situation. Groups in the homeland—following the Südwester suggestions, in ways reminiscent of the German colonial period—provided better information about the situation in the mandate only to those possessing the requisite character traits. The RfA provided an official pamphlet that not only detailed the entry requirements for SWA but also described the conditions awaiting the immigrant.[26] Apparently its authors believed the hardships and difficulties they described would discourage all but the hardiest. The RfA issued another pamphlet describing how Germans abroad should behave. Ostensibly printed in response to complaints by foreigners regarding the poor comportment of Germans overseas, it in fact undeniably aimed at reminding Germans of their heritage so that they would not be lost to Deutschtum. The pamphlet commanded the German before emigrating to remember two things: "I am a German" and "I enjoy the hospitality of a foreign country." In elucidating the first point, it emphatically demanded that he "not forget . . . [his] old homeland in the new country." It enjoined the immigrant to find contact with other Germans and "cultivate in the new circle German customs and German ways." It also charged him to avoid "differences of opinion" and to urge reconciliation in conflicts. Regarding the second point, it advised him to observe local customs and traditions, directing the newcomer to act not only hospitably toward his new fellow citizens, but also with pride and dignity "when one tries to insult you as a German."[27] Apparently officials believed that an emigrant must not only preserve his Deutschtum, but that practicing Deutschtum was the best way to get along. Above all, they felt that all conflict should be avoided, not only within the German community (which would weaken it) but also with their new masters. However, they did not want them to behave as lackeys and expected them to defend their German heritage.

Private organizations also assisted in the distribution of material about the possibilities for settlement in SWA. The DKG remained the most active and, through its essential control of the *Koloniale Reichsarbeitsgemeinschaft* (KORAG—the Colonial Reich Syndicate), it was able to obtain a dominant position among the colonial organizations. Seitz, the DKG president and former governor, also presided over the KORAG. The syndicate, created at the insistence of the Weimar Government in 1922, was an amalgamation of many groups and organizations, including the Women's League and the Association for Deutschtum Abroad. It actively disseminated colonial and emigration propaganda and information. KORAG activities primarily concentrated on raising support for colonial revisionism, domestically and abroad, but it also encouraged German colonization in the mandate.[28]

In addition to their information activities, organizations in both countries introduced more practical mechanisms to facilitate settlement. For instance, the RfA—through reliable sources in the mandate—made available to suitable would-be settlers lists of farms for sale. The farms varied in location and size, and hence price, but generally were intended for individuals possessing capital. Most often the farms belonged to Germans who either could no longer manage them or wanted to get out of the business. When making these announcements, which were not intended for the press, the RfA often pointed out that the purchase of these farms served a higher national cause as well; namely, the strengthening of the Southwestern German community. To quote one RfA pamphlet, "The strengthening of the Deutschtum in our former colony Southwest Africa lies in German interests."[29]

After 1933 and the National Socialist seizure of power, conditions for the sale of farms to Germans assumed a decidedly anti-Semitic character. This was especially true after the persecution of the Jews began in Germany. Dr. Bielfeld, in the Foreign Office, believed it was in the Reich's best interest to prevent the acquisition of land in SWA by Jews. He argued that "the transfer of property to Jewish hands in the mandate-administered German colony Southwest Africa is equally undesirable as the immigration of Jews to Southwest for political reasons [and] must be prevented." He asserted that "without a doubt . . . the emigrating Jews—also when nothing unfavorable about them was known during their stay in Germany—will work against the return of the colony to Germany and therefore will support the recent growing anti-German agitation there." His assumption about (and antagonism toward) the Jews, emblematic of the situation in Germany, caused Bielfeld to order German foreign-currency exchanges to refuse transfer of the necessary funds abroad, thus preventing the sale of farms to Jews.[30]

The German Colonial Society also took steps to provide farmland for German immigrants with the RWA's endorsement. Through a company it controlled, the Overseas Industry and Trade Corporation, the DKG established the South West Land and Settlement Company in Windhoek in 1927. The company purchased three large tracts of land totaling approximately 160,000 hectares. After surveying the land, supplying each property with water, and enclosing them with fences, the company intended to sell both large 2,000-hectare plots and small 10-hectare plots. Those possessing insufficient funds to purchase their own farms could also find employment with the company: the company offered individuals a salary to manage a farm; the farm would still belong to the company and be under its supervision, but each year the net profits (after interest payments, amortization, taxes, etc.) would go into a special account. When the amount in the account reached the value of the farm (estimated to take about fifteen years), the individual would receive possession of the land, including inventory. If he could not last that long or lost money, any interim profits became the company's.[31]

In addition to establishing South West Land and Settlement, the DKG also tried to push two relatively large-scale settlement projects. The society appealed to the Foreign Office to make funds available for the settlement of twenty to thirty young craftsmen with little or no means in 1926 and for the resettlement of Volga Germans to SWA in 1927. Despite the DKG's efforts, neither plan found support in the government, primarily because of a lack of money. Officials in Germany and SWA also worried about the repercussions of sending too many people to the mandate, especially since a number of them were poor; the territory could not support a large population, and with rising unemployment in South Africa, the appearance of a group of impoverished Germans might aggravate the administration and lessen its opinion of the German community. Some officials even had reservations about the Volga Germans' ability to adapt to the local conditions.[32] Lacking support, the DKG dropped both plans.

Organizations active in the settlement of Germans in SWA, especially those in the mandate, also assisted immigrants by finding them good employment. Südwester and supporters viewed this as particularly important in order not to damage the German population's image in the eyes of the administration. No matter how diligent and willing to work an individual was, if he could not make a living he would become a burden and disgrace to the German community. The Südwester Hans Denk said that "every destitute, possibly incompetent German in the Southwest who threatens to be a burden to the general welfare is an immense detriment to the Deutschtum."[33] Südwester and German officials therefore viewed the finding of steady employment for newly arrived Germans, especially craftsmen who wanted long-term employment, as essential. However, frequent employer dissatisfaction and frustration with workers rendered the task more difficult. They complained that employees often broke their contracts, either for a better paying position or to set up their own businesses.[34]

The FWG (the revived successor of the old Syndicate for Southwest African Settlement), under the leadership of Paul Barth, and the South West Land and Settlement Company, under the direction of August Stauch, recognized the seriousness of this situation; it threatened to weaken the settlement and appearance of Germans in SWA and thus the strength of the German community there. Therefore, these two organizations, especially the FWG, took a more active role in finding employment for dependable new arrivals and for Germans who already lived in the territory and needed a job. The DKG assisted these organizations by keeping them financially afloat, especially the FWG.[35]

In its role as an employment office, the Farm Business Corporation enjoyed both successes and failures. Although it had difficulties finding jobs for craftsmen, clerks, and others already living in the mandate, it was able to locate positions for them here and there with the assistance of the Workers' Association and the White-Collar Workers' Association.[36] The FWG's greatest success was in finding positions for farm interns. Hintrager, an outspoken proponent of settling Germans in SWA, saw in this system one of the best means to accomplish this goal. In a report to the Foreign Office, he wrote that "the settlement of Germans could essentially be promoted if the German system of . . . intern positions would be introduced again." Originally instituted during the German colonial period, the system returned in 1924 after the London Agreement went into effect. It granted new arrivals the opportunity to acquaint themselves with local conditions before embarking on their own.[37] Such knowledge not only improved their chances of success but also fulfilled a prerequisite for the purchase of inexpensive government land. Furthermore, the system provided inexpensive labor for farmers. The FWG claimed to have no difficulties finding positions for such young men. It was even able to supply the RfA with a list of farmers willing to take in trainees and their conditions of employment. The terms varied. Some offered a monthly salary, others provided only free room and board and the opportunity to learn.[38]

As in the days of German colonial administration, farmers and German officials looked for "unassuming" and "diligent" individuals. Hintrager warned interested young men in Germany that "hard physical labor in farming businesses is demanded of them and that unassuming appearance, modesty, and diligence are of use to them. Whoever is inclined toward megalomania, avoid South Africa."[39] One Southwestern farm administrator, Gustav Frenzel, claimed that those who "have no great demands and are satisfied with pocket money" will always find a job.[40] After initially experiencing a period of greater demand for trainees than there was supply, the program encountered difficulties in late 1928 finding positions for them. Despite Hintrager's efforts as director of the Reich Migration Office to influence and persuade both public and private organizations to do everything in their power to support this program, there was simply a limit to the number of interns that farmers could accommodate. As low as the cost was, only a limited number of farmers could afford such help.[41]

Those who did decide to live in SWA could turn to a number of places for assistance upon arrival. In addition to the DB and the FWG, Franz, the German consul, had put together a system of reliable informants to dispense advice to newcomers about local conditions. Hintrager argued that direct German government assistance was necessary

> if the Deutschtum in Southwest Africa is supposed to maintain the same
> tempo [with the South Africans] in the competition for the settlement of

the country. A diversion of suitable German emigrants to Southwest African can only have success if a well-working advice bureau is available in the country.[42]

Initially, Franz failed to establish his system; however, in 1925 he discovered a new willingness among Südwester to assist new settlers—a change he attributed to the increase in immigration. He reported to the RfA that "the growing number of immigrants who want to devote themselves to farming here has fortunately raised the interest in the care and consultation of new immigrants."[43] He noted that he had received numerous pledges from trusted individuals, most of whom he knew personally, willing to give advice to newly arrived farmers. Once he had found people for all districts of SWA, he sent the RfA and the AA copies of the names,[44] which enabled those interested to contact experienced people directly.

The *Verein der Reichsdeutschen* (Vdr), or Association of German Citizens, was a group created to assist newcomers and protect the interests of Germans. Created in 1925, the organization was comprised solely of Südwester who refused South African citizenship. In addition to its task of fighting for Südwester political rights, "remaining true to German customs and traditions" and "true to our German fatherland,"[45] the VdR provided moral and material assistance to newly arrived Germans. It informed them about local conditions and assisted them in starting their new lives in SWA. For those who found themselves in need, either through unfavorable circumstances or through no fault of their own, the VdR also provided financial aid; consul Franz, however, pointed out that the VdR possessed limited funds and generally assisted only its members.[46] More important, the founding of the association resulted in an ongoing conflict with the German League, which claimed to represent the interests of all Germans in the mandate. Early negotiations between the two groups failed to resolve the tension. The DB described the Association as "incapable" and "pointless," an opinion essentially shared by de Haas in the Foreign Office. Meanwhile, the VdR maintained that the majority of the league's members did not share the opinions of its leaders—Dr. Fritz Brenner, school director Dr. K. Körner, and Hans Richter.[47] Although the VdR apparently enjoyed strong support in SWA, even from Franz, the consul, it never achieved the power and significance of the DB; nor did it enjoy the same level of support from Germany.[48]

Most of these programs and associations focused on the settlement of young men in the mandate. In fact, during the interwar period, men pre-dominated among immigrants from Germany to SWA. However, as in the days of German hegemony over the region, Südwester and the authorities in Germany again expressed concern over the lack of women in the region: they still believed that women were essential to maintaining and perpetuat-ing the German presence there. Agnes von Boemcken, FB deputy chair and later chair, commented in 1926 that "now after the war the dispatch of Ger-man girls in the interest of strengthening the German influence in South-west appears even more important than it was earlier."[49] Hintrager, too, saw a need for German women in SWA. He repeatedly informed the Reich Inte-rior Ministry and, above all, the Foreign Office that "the Deutschtum can only be preserved in the long run through the family and the German woman."[50] and that "the Deutschtum in Southwest Africa stands and falls with the German women."[51] Moreover, he argued that the "promotion of the women's emigration is also necessary so that the German schools in South-west Africa will have recruits again."[52] Thus, the German woman in the mandate would not only ensure that German men and German progeny re-mained true to Deutschtum, but she would sustain the German schools by continually providing them with children. According to Hintrager, "the preservation of the German character of Southwest Africa and of the Ger-man schools themselves depends upon the emigration of women and girls to Southwest Africa."[53]

In order to correct this deficiency and secure the mandate for future generations, the Reich Office for Immigration in 1926 successfully applied for funds to promote the emigration of women to SWA and East Africa. The Reich Finance Ministry made 20,000 marks available in 1926 and 30,000 marks in 1929. The Women's League again assumed responsibility for select-ing and dispatching the women and for finding employment for those with-out a position.[54]

Although the FB still retained the title of Frauenbund—the women's league of the German Colonial Society—it had achieved full independence from the DKG in the early 1920s. As a self-sufficient organization, it pursued its own colonial policy (often more successfully than the DKG). As before, it aimed "to prepare and to preserve a fertile and caring place for German fam-ily spirit and German customs and traditions in our former colonies." Specifically, it undertook the support of the German schools in SWA and of needy colonial Germans in Germany, the provision of grants to Southwest-ern children for study in Germany, and the sending of women to SWA and

East Africa.[55] In selecting women for financial assistance, the FB essentially followed the same guidelines as it had done in the 1900s and 1910s. It sought unpretentious, self-sufficient, hard-working women of "sound character" between the ages of twenty and thirty who could cook and perform all household chores. It also expected them to possess knowledge of gardening and poultry farming, especially since, as Hintrager noted, "the success of the [future] husband's business often depends upon her ability." The women had to have the necessary documents for entry into the mandate as well as a confirmed position. For those who did not have employment yet, the FB, through its representatives in SWA, found them jobs.[56] After 1933, it claimed to select only those women who stood "firmly on the foundations of the Third Reich."[57] The FB believed that women possessing sound character and practical skills could more easily adjust to the new circumstances, find employment, and eventually make good wives. If a successful candidate agreed to a three-year contract, the league would provide her with two-thirds of a third-class ship ticket from Hamburg to Africa.[58]

The FB complained that the majority of women seeking employment abroad differed considerably from those in the prewar period. Earlier they had been essentially "simple," hard-working women from the country. Such women could easily find employment in families and on farms. However, during the Weimar period, most came from the "the earlier propertied estates"; they were women whose position had changed radically in the postwar years. According to the FB's Margarete Schnitzket, they were "educated women and girls . . . most often not very young," who saw emigration "as the last means for an existence."[59] Thus, the pool of "suitable" candidates remained small.

As in the German colonial period, nationalists still expected these women to assume a passive, domestic role in SWA. Indeed, Hintrager claimed that the majority of women who went to the mandate became housewives and mothers.[60] In this capacity, Sofie von Uhde wrote, these women were not only supposed to act as a business partner for their husbands but also had to be "an attentive hostess for guests, an affectionate and happy wife for the often tired and concerned husband, [and] a never-tiring mother for the children, who in this great freedom are doubly difficult to supervise." She warned that

the house in which the woman is not vigilantly at pains to cultivate German ways and German customs, [and] the day care in which she does not keep alive with care German songs and fairy tales and games and prayers [and] out of which she does not sternly ban all African words, falls with truly unbelievable speed to that what one calls here Boerized, and the next generation is lost for Deutschtum.

For all her efforts, the German wife's only reward was "the most trusted, intimate, comradely harmony with the husband in the middle of a wonderful, boundless freedom and the beautiful feeling to be completely indispensable." According to von Uhde, this would be more than enough: "It is certainly delightful and perhaps altogether the most delightful thing that women can gain."[61] Once again, German cultural elites held women almost exclusively responsible for the fate of Southwest Africa, while at the same time expecting them to assume a secondary position behind men. With these women, the fate of the German community supposedly "rose and fell," yet it was assumed that merely being with and pleasing their husbands was reward enough.

Although the emigration of German women to SWA did increase, it never experienced the volume that Hintrager and Boemcken desired. In 1926, the year that the FB and the RfA made a conscious effort to promote the settlement of women in the mandate, 320 women moved to the region. The following year, 295, and in 1928, 309 (for 1924 and 1925, respectively, the two years prior to the resumption of the program, 110 and 219 women had immigrated). Despite the efforts of Hintrager and the FB to increase immigration by women, the number of men going to SWA, relative to the number of women, remained higher each year (1926, 477; 1927, 428; 1928, 355).[62]

The FB did report successes regarding the employment and marriage of women it assisted. For example, Frida Voigts, chair of the FB Windhoek chapter, reported in 1929 "that of the 74 women for whom the league found a position, 78 percent proved themselves first-rate, and in all cases very satisfactory news arrives from both employers and the girls."[63] The league also reported in 1929 that 48 of the 150 single women it sent to SWA in 1927/8 were already engaged or married.[64] Of the 64 single women it aided in 1929, 13 married by 1930. In that same year, it also sent out 14 married women and 10 fiancées of men living there.[65]

Of course, not all women fulfilled their "national cultural" task. Like some of their predecessors, some women went to SWA without the express purpose of marrying. Some wanted to pursue an independent career or establish a business; they went as private teachers, stenographers, nurses, hair stylists, seamstresses.[66] Not all of those sent by the FB expressed satisfaction. For instance, although only two of the women dispatched in 1929 wrote to say that they were unhappy, an additional forty-three did not notify the FB of their whereabouts.[67] When the league did not hear from "its" women, it usually attributed this to their not having been there very long,[68] they ignored the possibility that these women might not have cared about the FB's work or might not have fulfilled the terms of their contracts: these women may have merely wanted subsidized passage to SWA. However, the FB reported that it usually did hear from most of them, eventually.[69]

In 1930, the dispatching of women to SWA was almost suspended. Albert Voigts, an old Südwester and DB chairman at the time, wrote in 1929 that women from Germany were no longer needed. He said that SWA's own young women were now old enough to cover the mandate's needs. However, various people disagreed with Voigts's assessment. Frida Voigts, his sister-in-law, argued that the country's "daughters" were still too young. Those who were old enough, Frida Voigts continued, lacked the desire, the "necessity" to work in households. She noted that they preferred to work in offices, where they enjoyed "more freedom." She claimed that most farmers' wives preferred employing women from Germany.[70] Franz, the consul, agreed with Frida Voigts's assessment, reporting that "for the occupation of positions in the household . . . the girls from Germany are still considered first."[71] Hintrager contended that Albert Voigts's position corresponded "neither to the German interests nor the predominant opinion in Southwest Africa."[72]

Hintrager reported that the desire to stop sending young women from Germany came primarily from Southwestern "mothers with daughters." Apparently they wanted to eliminate any competition for their daughters.[73] Franz saw no reason for these mothers to fear: there were more than enough men, Germans as well as South Africans, to marry in the mandate. Using the same language employed to fight miscegenation, he noted that

> if in general the thesis is valid that the nationality of the wife imparts to the family her imprint, then I do not see why German women cannot also win over their South African husbands for the German way and raise their children in certain relationships as Germans.[74]

Consequently, Hintrager appealed to the Foreign Office to ignore Albert Voigts's report and to continue providing subsidies for the transportation of women to SWA. Invoking revisionist rhetoric, he warned that "a waning in

this care would lay the foundation for the cessation of the German language, the German school, and German ways in our former colony Southwest Africa."[75] Supported by Franz's report, the AA heeded Hintrager's
warning. For fiscal year 1931, it made 25,000 marks available for emigration
assistance: 15,000 for Southwest Africa, 10,000 for East Africa.[76]

In view of the stated goal—namely, to maintain German numerical superiority in order eventually to overturn the edict of Versailles—the settlement policies of German nationalists in SWA and Germany did not enjoy
success. Statistically, the German population did increase, although it only
briefly equaled the height of German colonization during the period of German rule (it reached approximately 12,000 in 1931); furthermore, the number of German women in the mandate rose. But their numbers remained
consistently below the number of men entering the country. And, most importantly, the increase in the Afrikaner population, more than doubling its
number since 1921, diminished the German accomplishments. Long before
the outbreak of World War II, the Afrikaners became the largest non-African
group in the mandate; their numbers continued to grow, while the German's
declined.

Many Südwester and their allies in Germany blamed the South African
administration for this. They claimed that it treated them unfairly and favored the settlement of Afrikaners and colonial British. They pointed to the
small number of government farms that Germans received, ignoring the
fact that newcomers were advised by Südwester not to apply for them anyway. They also noted the South African government's large financial commitment to resettling Afrikaners from Angola in SWA in the late 1920s.
Despite these assertions, by 1937 nearly three-fifths of the farms in private
possession (1,228 out of 1,950) belonged not to Afrikaners but to German
citizens, naturalized Germans, and a few foreigners. That amounted to 10.6
million hectares out of a total of 25.4 million hectares of farmland, including
government land, falling under the ownership of Germans.[77] Thus, more
than 40 percent of the land belonged to a group that comprised approximately one-third of the population.

Despite these achievements, Südwester held fast to the belief that they
were second-class citizens. They saw the South Africans as their enemies,
opponents who unrightfully took SWA away from Germany. Southwestern
Germans and their allies in Germany throughout the interwar period believed that if they preserved the German character of the region it would
eventually become a German possession again, either directly or as an inde-

pendent state with a German majority. Groups both in SWA and in Germany acted on these beliefs. They pursued various avenues in order to populate the territory with Germans. Nationalists in both places became particularly concerned with the settlement of German women there, especially since the majority of newcomers were single men who might marry outside of their nationality. In the eyes of people like Hintrager and Boemcken, women were essential to maintaining Deutschtum in the region: they would preserve German customs and traditions in German families as well as provide enough children to ensure the continued existence of the Southwestern German schools. Although these organizations experienced qualified successes, it was in another realm—namely, education—that Südwester and their supporters in Germany made more significant gains.

7

Education and the Preservation of Deutschtum

> The purpose of a school abroad must be to keep our children for Deutschtum and to prevent an absorption into the foreign nation. The children are supposed to feel German above all, otherwise the later generations are lost for us.
>
> —Report on the Development of Education, 1929

In the eyes of Southwestern Germans and their supporters in Germany in the interwar period, German schools were just as essential for the preservation of Deutschtum in SWA as settling German men and women there. One Südwester, Dr. Alfred Fock, pleaded: "We are presently fighting here most passionately for the preservation of our German schools and our mother tongue for our children and our children's children."[1] In the face of growing numbers of Afrikaners and colonial Britons, German schools were supposed to contribute to maintaining the cultural integrity of the growing German community:

> A faithful pillar supports and carries Deutschtum in Southwest; that is the German school system maintained with a thousand sacrifices. With it the local culture and the local ways stand and fall; it is the last undestroyed cell of the German spirit, from which the entire body always renews itself again.[2]

Since language was a metaphor for culture, German-language instruction (along with history, religion, and sport classes) was pivotal in the effort to secure the German heritage of the territory. This was made especially necessary for the Southwestern Germans and their supporters in Germany because they believed that the Südwester represented the true, unspoiled essence of Deutschtum that even the homeland needed for spiritual revival.

German mothers were supposed to play a salient role in introducing children to German customs, traditions, and language, but officials believed—as in the colonial period—that schools were in many respects more suited and pertinent to this important task. Schools gave the self-appointed cultural elites more comprehensive control over the curricular and behavioral development of pupils. Furthermore, children's performance and comportment in school provided authorities with a means to monitor the home environment. Like the imperial-era curriculum, it had a specific goal: to create productive and loyal German citizen.

The League of Nations' decision to place Southwest Africa under South African administration engendered apprehension among the Southwestern Germans: they feared that South Africa would make attempts to assimilate them. Their anxieties appeared confirmed when, in 1919, Sir Howard Gorges, the territorial administrator, moved to repatriate all German teachers; the administration declared its intention to take over all former German schools and dormitories on April 1, 1920. The so-called Gorges Plan required the administration's assumption of all financial responsibilities associated with schools. It also limited the years of German as the language of instruction to the first four years. After the fourth year, parents would decide between English and Dutch as the medium of instruction. Furthermore, the plan required that replacement teachers come only from the South African Union. Schools had the option of rejecting the plan, but they then had to operate as private schools, at their own cost. In addition, they would have to pay a fee to use the school facilities.[3] Because of the importance that Germans attributed to education for maintaining their culture and character, Südwester viewed this as a death blow to the future of Deutschtum in SWA. This was especially true in light of the financially weak position of many Germans. In a letter to Seitz, the German consul in Windhoek, Dr. Fritzsche, wrote that "this will contribute to the weakening of the German schools. The temptation to send the children free of charge to the English government schools is too great."[4]

In response to this threat, all of the German school associations in SWA banded together to found the *Landesverband der Deutschen Schulvereine* (LdDS, or Territorial School Union), on January 14, 1920. Originally, the school associations had been founded to assume control of the schools in 1919. They established the LdDS to represent collectively German educational interests in negotiations with the administration. Consequently, the LdDS carried on "a relentless struggle" for the survival of the German schools[5]—and thus, Deutschtum.

After much debate among members of the various school associations, and knowing that their decision would lead to hardships, the LdDS unanimously rejected the administration's offer and decided to continue operating all the schools as private institutions. Surprisingly, the "smaller, financially weaker but self-sacrificing school associations and Lüderitz Bay" were the most outspoken opponents of the administration's proposal. The two largest associations, Windhoek and Swakopmund, had internal problems, but appeals to their appreciation of a higher cause and the example the other associations enabled to overcome their differences and pettiness.[6]

In addition to its rejection of the administration's offer, the LdDS sent a letter of protest to the administrator, the premier minister of South Africa, and the South African Union's parliament. The letter not only pointed out the protection given to national minorities in Europe but also made a counterproposal: it demanded that the German language be the medium of instruction in all classes except those teaching Dutch and English and that German-language teachers be trained in Germany. The LdDS recognized that it was necessary for students to learn English and Dutch, but, for pedagogical reasons, they requested that it not be introduced until the third or fourth school year. It also wanted a guarantee that the schools would enable children to continue their education in Germany and provide them with the skills and education necessary to advance in South Africa.[7] In other words, they wanted the advantages of both the German and South African educational systems.

The plight of the Germans did not go unnoticed in the Union. Afrikaner newspapers and Nationalist Party representatives in parliament supported the Germans in their resistance to the Union's attempts to assimilate them. One Afrikaner paper, the *Volkstem,* warned that "this reluctance could grow to a resentment, a resentment for which we ourselves would be the cause." They recognized that they themselves had faced a similar predicament after the end of the Anglo-Boer War and claimed that the elimination of German culture and the German language would only make South Africa poorer.[8]

As a result of the strong opposition to the plan, within both SWA and South Africa, and in recognition of the need for unity in order to develop the mandate, the administration dropped its plans. The director of education in SWA, J. G. R. Lewis, permitted the German schools to continue to operate privately, and the repatriation of teachers was postponed for six months. However, in 1920 ownership of the school facilities passed from the municipalities and local authorities to the administration.[9] Southwestern German leaders and their allies in Germany viewed the current situation as provisional until a final resolution could be reached with the administration. When Hofmeyr replaced Gorges as administrator in SWA, it appeared that their fortunes had improved: Gysbert Reitz Hofmeyr attempted to make himself well-liked among the German population. However, his Ten Points regarding the taking over of the German schools did little to encourage hope for Südwesters. Five of the points in his offer were:

1. German would be the medium of instruction for the first six school years
2. After the seventh year, English or Dutch would be used—the parents choosing which one
3. Already in the first year there would be one hour daily of South African (Afrikaans) language instruction
4. There would be full employment for all currently employed teachers
5. The administration would assume all financial responsibilities.[10]

The Windhoek members of the LdDS found the suggestions acceptable; it was the smaller associations who again expressed the greatest mistrust of the government's intentions. In an effort to assuage their misgivings, Hofmeyr discussed his plan with them in greater detail. The replacement of teachers from Germany he said was completely out of the question; he noted that there were enough teachers in South Africa who understood German. He also pointed out that after the transfer, the school associations would have no voice in educational matters: Education Minister Viljoen would determine policy. Hofmeyr did admit, despite his assertion that a separate school system for German children was unacceptable, that currently he had no objections to the private schools continuing to operate as they had done since their establishment in 1920; he said he would provide immigration permits for the needed teachers out of Germany.[11]

After listening to Hofmeyr, the associations unanimously rejected the offer: it provided no guarantees that the schools would provide adequate German instruction, they said; the conditions were unacceptable. Voigt wrote:

> The government had clearly demonstrated that it absolutely would like to gain control of the German schools. No person trusts it to keep its promises. It will allow the extremely German-hostile Education Minister Viljoen, who has it within his power to shape the schools according to his wishes under the pretext of pedagogical necessity, to administer [the schools]. Schools and teachers in the Union are indeed very bad; but the children will be raised in a chauvinistic way, unheard of for us, to an overbearing pride of Britaindom *(Britentum)* and to the contempt of other people. It was unavoidable that most of our children would be lost to us.[12]

The school associations decided to continue running the private schools as exclusively German institutions. Nevertheless, negotiations with the administration continued in the hope of receiving more favorable terms, and Hofmeyr did eventually make concessions: special attention could be paid to Germany in geography and history classes, to the metric system of weights and masses, and to German songs in music class. However, he refused to allow German to be used as the language of instruction in the middle and upper grades.[13]

Although the LdDS continued to hold out for even better terms, the tough negotiations and the poor economic conditions of the Südwester began to undermine the resolve of the German schools union. Several members of the LdDS came to the conclusion that it might actually be in their best interest to allow the government to take them over and for them then to work within the system to maintain, and even perhaps improve, the situation of the schools. Discussions began to center around a transition period in order to facilitate the switch from purely German schools to government ones with German departments.[14] Dr. H. Lotz, chairman of the LdDS, wrote that this was possibly "the beginning of the end." However, he optimistically noted that this did not have to be, "if the German population is aware of the value of its German culture and remains economically and morally on such a level that it understands that it has to fight for it."[15] Before negotiations in this direction could be concluded, in August 1921 the administration surprised the German community by changing the financial arrangements: private schools using state-owned buildings would no longer be required to pay a flat fee for use of the properties but would pay rent—approximately £4,600 annually.[16] For the schools, this was a costlier arrangement.

Under these new circumstances and the continued economic hardships experienced by the Southwestern Germans, the LdDS and the administration came to the agreement that each school association should decide on its own whether it wanted to become a government school or remain a private one under the previously agreed terms. Those that chose to become state schools would be fully funded by the government, which meant that parents would no longer have to pay anything for their children's education. Those that remained private institutions would receive no state support and the financial burden would rest on the shoulders of parents. Despite their previous efforts and sacrifices, this new financial burden proved to be too much for most of the school associations. Thirteen associations accepted the government's offer—Gobabis, Grootfontein, Keetmanshoop, Klein-Windhoek, Okahandja, Windhoek (not the Realschule), Aus, Gibeon, Maltahoehe, Otjiwarongo, Outjo, Usakos, and Omaruru. In places where Germans comprised at least one-half the student population, the administration set up what were called German medium classes *(Deutsche Abteilungen)*, where German was the language of instruction.[17] That left seven private schools: the elementary schools in Swakopmund, Lüderitz Bay, Tsumeb, and Karibib, plus the German high schools (Realschulen) in Windhoek and Swakopmund as well as the Catholic High School for Girls in Windhoek. This meant that the German private schools existed in places "with a wealthy German rural community or in cities with a strong German professional community."[18] In general, the LdDS expressed satisfaction with the state of educational affairs. It went so far as to describe it as a victory for the Southwestern Germans, even though it had wanted more from the administration. The LdDS even sent Hofmeyr a letter of thanks in the name of most of the school associations for the way in which he gave attention to the interests of the German pupils now in government schools.[19]

In 1924, nearly three years after the government assumed control of most of the German schools, the SWA school inspector, Dr. C. Frey (a former instructor in the Windhoek Realschule), commented in a German periodical, *Deutsche Schule im Auslande,* on the healthy development of the medium schools. He wrote that German medium classes existed in fourteen towns (the Swakopmund elementary school joined later after unsuccessfully trying to maintain its independence), with twenty-one teachers instructing 520 students in German; eighteen of the faculty were German citizens and received pedagogical training in Germany. He pointed out that one change in the curriculum (extending English instruction from six to seven hours in the three higher classes—grades four through six) occurred at the wish of German parents, who normally selected English as the "foreign" language of preference. He did complain that a German reader for SWA did not exist; most had been written for Germany. Like pedagogues during the Wilhelmine period, he welcomed the addition of local history (Southwest and South African) to the curriculum: "This extension should not be fought," he said, "but rather welcomed. For most of the local German children, Southwest is the homeland. . . . And it is also the duty of the school here as elsewhere to impart to the children the history of their Heimat." He quickly noted that the lesson plan paid special attention to German history, and that in geography and the natural sciences, special lesson plans had been created to unite German and South African pedagogical goals.[20]

Frey also commented on the special treatment and opportunities given to German pupils in the state's higher public schools. He explained that these schools, in contrast to German private schools, constituted an extension of the elementary schools. "Elementary school and higher school form a unit—the unit that is being strived for by the German modern comprehensive school." In the English high schools, Frey continued, German students could take the matriculation exam at the end of four years. This exam entitled them to a number of professional positions—for example, teacher, lawyer, white-collar bank or postal employee—as well as entrance to a university. Frey pointed out that the Education Department introduced changes for 1925 in order to ease the transition from German to English as the medium of instruction; thus, German remained the language of instruction in German, history, geography, and religion through the first year of high school; and German students would receive more hours of instruction than in a German high school. In Frey's opinion, this provided Southwestern German pupils with sufficient opportunity to become familiar with Deutschtum: "It will be possible here to introduce the young German Südwester to the German cultural and spiritual life in the same manner as at an institution in the homeland." Frey maintained that such a program enabled the German students to attend not only universities in the British Empire and the United States but also in Germany.[21]

On the whole, Frey had nothing but praise for the German medium classes and the administration's actions. "The government," he said, "views the Deutschtum as an asset that they want to preserve":

The Germans in the homeland and in Southwest Africa are obliged to the mandate government for the truly generous manner in the way it did justice to the needs of the old German population in the question of the education and training of their children. In no other former enemy country was one able to decide on such an accommodating and amicable school policy.

In concluding his report, Frey maintained that

not as Englishmen or Dutchmen are our German children supposed to be raised; they are supposed to remain German, and as fully entitled citizens devote their energy to this country and thus to take part in the economic and spiritual improvement and advancement of their homeland, Southwest Africa, not as cultural dung but as carriers of civilization.[22]

In 1922 approximately 360 German students attended government schools. By 1928 the number stood at 600, and it continued to rise. Several of the private schools closed or allowed the government to take them over. Furthermore, several German medium classes ceased to exist when Germans comprised fewer than half the student body.

However, not all Germans shared Frey's sentiments. Newspapers in Germany accused German teachers in the German medium classes of being traitors and "renegades"; they described the medium schools as "Boerized" *(verburt)*. Eckenbrecher, a long-time German inhabitant of SWA and a government teacher in Windhoek, took personal offense at these accusations. Such comments, she said, "insult us teachers, the parents who entrust their children to us, and our pupils." Eckenbrecher claimed that in the face of many hardships, including public ridicule and ostracism, "we hold the outposts with a great deal of tact and deliberation and raise our children to the same Deutschtum [as the private schools] and preserve it for them."[23]

Despite Frey's report and Eckenbrecher's defense of these schools and their German teachers, many Südwester and their allies in Germany continued to mistrust the administration. They saw ulterior motives in the government's attempts to accommodate the Germans and make it easier for them to educate their children. Edmund Brückner, a former governor of Togo, maintained that South Africa's ultimate objective was to assimilate the Southwestern Germans:

I am convinced that the administration and the Union government still has the goal—and from their point of view, absolutely understandable—to allow the German element in SWA to be utterly absorbed in Boerdom (*Burentum*), and that accordingly they also would like the education of the German children in their schools to conform to them more and more.[24]

In the eyes of German cultural elites, the German private schools provided the most suitable countermeasure. Seitz wrote, "In the interests of Deutschtum, I hold the preservation of the German private schools to be absolutely necessary, for when the German private schools fall, that will

Table 7.1. **German Pupils in German Medium Classes**

School	1922	1928	1929	1930	1931	1932
Aus	10	19	12	—	—	—
Gibeon	11	20	20	20	20	20
Gobabis	20	36	37	33	29	31
Grootfontein	31	52	53	60	65	64
Keetmanshoop	27	38	48	55	62	60
Klein-Windhoek	21	—	—	—	—	—
Maltahöhe	16	—	—	—	—	—
Swakopmund	—	30	22	—	—	—
Swakopmd. (HS)	—	—	—	355	313	251
Tsumeb	—	—	—	—	105	85
Okahandja	30	34	22	51	49	43
Omaruru	53	89	92	84	85	82
Otjiwarongo	12	—	9	—	15	22
Outjo	16	16	16	11	—	—
Usakos	19	20	22	28	28	22
Walfish Bay	—	20	17	17	29	22
Windhoek	101	201	184	181	173	184
Windhoek (HS)	—	25	37	—	—	—
Totals	367	600	591	895	973	886

Source: Gries, *Dritter Bericht der Deutschen Realschule zu Windhuk, 1919–24,* BAP R1001/1953; Oskar Wallberg, *Die deutschen Schüler des Mandatslandes Südwestafrika, 1933,* BAP R1001/1954.

also be the end of German in the government schools."[25] Officials in the Foreign Office concurred with Seitz's assessment.[26]

Despite the early loss of Swakopmund, the German private schools expanded throughout the 1920s. In 1925, the schools formed a unified school system "for the purpose of mutual support [and the] elimination of competition." By 1928, three more schools, in Kolsmankuppe, Elisabethbucht, and Charlottental, had joined the system.[27] In order to eliminate "the many disputes between faculty and school boards," the chairmen of the school associations and the directors of the private schools held several conferences. The result of their discussions was a set of regulations, issued on September 2, 1926, "Service Instructions for the Directors, Headmasters, and Teachers in the Southwest African German Private Schools." Based on a Prussian document, these regulations provided specific guidelines for the general running and maintenance of the schools.[28] The curriculum in the private schools essentially followed the Prussian standards.[29] However, the schools did adjust to the South African circumstances:

> Abroad it depends more on keeping the *heart* of our children for Deutschtum than on forcing a pure German culture on them that sometimes cannot be beneficial to them in their practical advancement in the foreign country and must hinder them in actively and influentially participating in the country's public life.[30]

This was most readily apparent in the German secondary school in Windhoek. In the eyes of many officials and Südwester, this was the most important German school in the country. According to Haug, the consul-general in South Africa, "I still consider the maintenance of the Realschule in Windhoek as the center of Deutschtum and of higher German education. This is one of the foremost tasks that devolves to us in the realm of Southwest African school politics." He argued that "the German private (elementary) schools require an organic summit in the form of a Realschule that leads to the so-called matriculation exam." Only with the existence of such a system, he continued, "can it be expected that parents, who later want to keep their children in Southwest Africa in order to train them, etc., additionally for an occupation, will continue to allow their children to attend the German schools." He noted further that the Realschule was important also for those children who wanted to study in Germany.[31]

Consequently, under various directors the Realschule in Windhoek

Table 7.2. **German Pupils in Private Schools**

School	1922	1928	1929	1930	1931	1932
Windhoek Oberrealschule	155	227	267	277	272	235
Girls Catholic High School (in Windhoek)	n. a.	85	64	59	83	109
Swakopmund	129	—	—	—	—	—
Swakopmund High School	n. a.	289	288	—	—	—
Karibib	21	27	23	23	27	28
Lüderitz Bay	76	151	156	159	123	115
Tsumeb	55	97	98	117	—	—
Charlottental	—	11	15	15	—	—
Elisabethbucht	—	24	27	13	—	—
Kolmanskuppe	—	61	56	25	34	41
Farm Schools (1932–34)	n.a.	18	19	43	64	84
TOTALS	436	990	1013	731	603	612

Source: Gries, Dritter Bericht der Deutschen Realschule zu Windhuk, 1919–24, BAP R1001/1953; Oskar Wallberg, Die deutschen Schüler des Mandatslandes Südwestafrika, 1933, BAP R1001/1954.

expanded its curriculum and the school's structure to allow multiple post-secondary opportunities. Initially, students could take the *Abitur* (which would entitle them to study at a German university). Later, the school received the German status of Oberrealschule nebst Reformrealgymnasium, which certified it to prepare students for further training and study in Germany. Moreover, after several requests and enhancements in its program of study, it eventually received the right to give the matriculation exam. The changes to the curriculum included strengthening English instruction and conducting the upper geography classes in English. Director Gries (1919–24) introduced instruction in Afrikaans and English standards and measurements, policies continued by his successors Dr. K. Körner (1925–1928) and Dr. Edgar Wallberg (1928–39). Officials in Germany took the unique situation of the school and the students into consideration. In one instance, the Prussian minister for science, art and education allowed some pupils to take their German exam in Afrikaans, instead of French.[32]

In late 1933, after Hitler came to power in Germany, the Nazis tried to institute changes in the curriculum of the German schools and medium classes. The German consul in Windhoek demanded that Southwestern au-

thorities provide history instruction in the government schools "in the National Socialist spirit."[33] His request was unsuccessful, so the Nazi Foreign
Department saw to it that only teachers imbued with the Nazi worldview
were permitted to teach German youth abroad. The South African government countered by requiring private schools to obtain permission to hire
new teachers and by forbidding teachers in general from belonging to political parties or from being politically active.[34]

The issue of greatest concern, though, for the German private schools
was funding. Indeed, this was an almost constant source of frustration. The
financial liquidity of the school associations remained a problem throughout the interwar period. As early as 1920, Südwester knew they would have
to make personal and economic sacrifices if the private schools, and thus
Deutschtum, were to survive. Lotz, of LdDs, wrote, "We do not fail to recognize that the local German population must also make sacrifices if it wants
to preserve Deutschtum for itself and its children—and we obviously want
that. We are also prepared to that and will do our best."[35] Yet the decision
of the majority of schools associations at the end of 1921 demonstrated that
there were limits to what they could do.

The Southwest African administration did alleviate part of their financial burden in accordance with the London Agreement. It agreed to provide
subsidies for the schools in Swakopmund and Windhoek for two years, in return for placing themselves under government control. The two schools accepted the conditions and thus received the aid. In 1925 the administration
generously offered to extend the financial assistance indefinitely and offered
it to the other private schools under the condition that they, too, would submit to state supervision. After much resistance on the German side under
the leadership of Dr. Fritz Brenner (a staunch nationalist active in the LdDS,
the Windhoek School Association, and the German League), the administration dropped this condition, and the schools accepted the aid. Moreover,
the South Africans also provided subsidies for the private dormitories in
Windhoek and Swakopmund.[36] The government's decision to stop aid in
1935 (which it nonetheless continued until 1937) resulted in a backlash of
resentment and mistrust from the German community. It viewed the administration's decision as a blow against the Southwestern Deutschtum.
The administration justified its decision by emphasizing the necessity for
children of all nationalities to learn understanding for each other. It argued
that this could best be accomplished when children attended the same
schools. Besides, the South Africans continued, such assistance was only

temporary in nature; it was intended to assist the schools through difficult economic times. To the German population, this meant that their private schools were superfluous.[37]

Despite restrictions imposed by the South African government, the German government, via the Foreign Office, also provided financial assistance to the Southwestern German schools. A South African decree forbade the German government from directly assisting the Südwester; consequently, it annually supplied monies first through the DKG and later, clandestinely, through the German consulate in South Africa, the latter lasting until the outbreak of World War II. This was particularly necessary when, for political reasons, the South Africans finally suspended subsidies for the private schools in 1937. For example, in 1921 the Finance Ministry allocated 1.2 million marks for the schools in SWA; in 1930, more than 150,000 marks in normal subsidies were allocated, and more than 80,000 marks in special grants. By the outbreak of war in 1939, the government had granted nearly 70,000 marks.[38] These sums may seem high, but inflation and the mark's poor exchange rate with British sterling greatly reduced the significance of these numbers. The point is that the Weimar and Hitler governments both felt obliged to assist the Südwester in their struggle.

The Colonial Society provided additional assistance to the private schools. Seitz assured the LdDS that he would do everything within his power "to ensure the Territorial School Union a strong financial support for the next years."[39] Initially, the DKG assumed responsibility for finding and hiring teachers needed for service in the private schools, providing them with travel subsidies, and paying for teachers' vacations in Germany, as well as for school supplies (books, teaching materials, etc.).[40] However, despite its efforts, the hyperinflation in Germany during the early 1920s and poor fund-raising skills quickly depleted the society's resources. It continued to take an active interest in Southwestern affairs, but its ability to provide financial support was greatly handicapped. It also had other commitments for its resources.

The Women's League, now independent of the DKG, was more adept at raising money and pursued its own path in supporting Südwester. For instance, the FB, with assistance from the Colonial Society and the VDA, supplied schools with libraries and books throughout the interwar period. Hedwig von Bredow, the FB chair, believed that this was essential "for the preservation of the Deutschtum in South Africa and Southwest Africa."[41] The FB also provided subsidies for the student dormitories and the private schools.[42]

In addition to maintaining the German schools directly, numerous Südwester and their supporters in Germany still wanted the region's German
youth to study in the old homeland. They continued to believe that this was
one of the best ways to preserve the German character of the Southwestern
children. One advocate argued that

> an . . . important means for the preservation of the German of our young
> is [through] . . . the personal . . . [encounter] with the homeland. A
> young person of the second, third, or fourth generation who knows his
> homeland only from books and stories can indeed be raised and educated
> German; he will however not be able to think and feel German anymore.
> His new homeland will be dearer to him than the old one he does not even
> know, and therefore he is lost to us despite the German language and Ger-
> man education.[43]

Südwester also cited practical reasons for wanting their children to study in
Germany. They realized that the Southwestern schools offered only limited
vocational training opportunities. They believed that such training would
enable them to compete better with craftsmen from South Africa.[44] One proponent even contended that providing financial assistance to young men for
training in Germany was "an important means to preserve the German
character of the country in the future through a German upper class [*Über-
schicht*] in all professions."[45] Thus, according to colonial enthusiasts and
Southwestern Germans, a young Südwester's experience in Germany would
serve to preserve the German presence in SWA in a number of ways.

In recognition of this need and desire, the FB provided scholarships for
young Südwester, both men and women, to study and learn in Germany as
well as to experience the fatherland. In 1928 alone, it provided twenty-eight
full and twelve partial scholarships.[46] The FB intended the visits to the
homeland "to make the foreign German youth familiar with Germany so
that they, grown up, become over there in the new homeland the leaders and
pillar of Deutschtum and a connecting link between the people of the old and
of the new homeland." Thus, those who went to Germany were supposed to
be "the best, most capable, and hardest working of the country, the elite."[47]
While in Germany, the young individuals would either learn new skills—like
metalworking, masonry, or carpentry for the men, nursing, bookkeeping,
and home economics for the women—or attend university or technical high
school. During vacations and on weekends, the FB saw to it that they stayed

with relatives. For those who had no relatives, the FB found families who would care for them. In these homes, they were supposed to learn still more about German family life, customs, and traditions.[48]

Despite the FB's good intentions, some experienced individuals expressed concern over sending youngsters to Germany. Haug, of the German consulate in Pretoria, warned that "Southwestern children who visit [the upper grades] in Germany adapt themselves to Germany and do not want to return to Southwest Africa. That would mean a loss for the Deutschtum in Southwest Africa."[49] In order to prevent this from happening, the FB required its scholarship holders to return to SWA two years after completing their education or training.[50] How this was enforced is not made clear.

Some Südwester expressed dissatisfaction with their children's educational experience in Germany. Their concern was less about them staying in Germany than the "unwelcome" influences they might bring back with them. Lotte Ebers, wife of the German pastor in Windhoek, contended that "one is not completely in agreement with the educational methods and results of the modern Germany." In one instance, she reported, "one of the girls saturated with our modern German civilization recently explained after her return that she could no longer associate with her father [because] he is too petty bourgeois." She pointed out that "such persons are not needed in SWA, where one must work hard."[51] Ebers rejected the tendencies of the homeland, in particular, socialism, and desired to keep such trends out of the region. Margarethe von Zastrow had already mentioned in 1926 that "for those who have lived out there [a long time] the conditions in Germany are no longer recognizable in all the details."[52] While Germany was experiencing intellectual growth and diversity, the Southwestern Germany community continued to try to preserve its antiindustrial, antiurban, agrarian vision of Deutschtum.

In order to "save" SWA from these influences, Ebers, the pastor's wife, suggested building a continuing education school for women in the territory. She argued that not only would it prevent instances similar to the one she described from recurring, but it would also provide educational opportunity for young women unable to go to Germany. A number of young women, she said, went for training to South Africa, where they lived in hostels under English influence; on their return, most parents expressed dissatisfaction with the results and blamed it on the English. Moreover, Ebers said she encountered many women with tired and resigned features—women who, upon leaving school, had been full of spirit and enthusiasm. She argued that these women required "not only training in home economics, but also . . . cultivation of mental growth, music, and literature."[53] Such cultivation was necessary so that "Deutschtum will receive a tradition, and its preservation will be self-apparent."[54] A woman's continuation school in SWA would fill this void.

As a result of Ebers's efforts and with widespread support from organizations in Germany, the Hedwig-Heyl Haushaltungsschule (School of domestic science)—named after Hedwig-Heyl, honorary FB chairperson—opened on April 1, 1933. The school was built in Windhoek because of the women's boarding facility there (the Hedwig von Bredow-Haus), attached to the German Realschule.[55] The institution aimed to provide young German women "in the age of fourteen to sixteen from Southwest and South Africa, in addition to a general upbringing and education, a thorough training in all aspects of home and farm economics, in baby care, garden work, and crafts."[56] Like similar institutions in Germany, the institution provided both theoretical and practical instruction (in domestic science, nutrition, bookkeeping, ethnology, etc., and laundry, baking, sewing, etc.). Its proximity to the Windhoek Realschule enabled students also to acquire additional education there.[57]

After completing the one-year course of study, the women were supposed to "take with them a good concept of German domesticity and a valuable memory for their entire life."[58] They would achieve "an enrichment of the inner self, a strengthening of Deutschtum, a stimulus to spiritual growth."[59] In other words, the school would provide them with the proper education and training to carry out the duties expected of them by conservative cultural elites. The school continued to exist and educate young Southwestern women through 1943. During its years of operation, approximately ninety-five women received an education from the school.[60]

Similar to the FB's measures to enable young women to further their education in SWA, the Kösener S.C. Union in 1927 undertook the task of establishing a vocational school for young men in Windhoek. Inspired by the description of the Südwester's plight and sacrifices given by Körner (former director of the Windhoek Realschule), the Kösener S.C. Union established the Committee for Deutschtum Abroad. Since the only other opportunity young Südwester had for such instruction was in the Windhoek government school, the committee resolved to build a vocational school "for the preservation of Deutschtum in Southwest Africa and especially in order to offer the *German* children in Southwest Africa . . . the possibility to be trained in manual skills" (emphasis in the original). The committee reasoned that a similar German institution would provide parents with the option of keeping their children in German schools[61] and thus ultimately preserve them for Deutschtum.

Opened on March 14, 1931, with support from the Kösener union and local businesses, the school consisted of three departments: paper working, woodworking, and ironworking. The aim was not only to prepare students for future professions and contribute to the preservation of Deutschtum in the region but also to train mental and physical coordination.[62]

Despite such assistance and self-sacrifice, not all German schools could survive as private institutions. Shortly after 1922, the Swakopmund elementary school allowed itself to be taken over by the administration. It was not until the late 1920s that another German private school—the Swakopmund high school—faced a similar decision. Although the administration continued to provide subsidies for the schools as well as to allow the high school to use an abandoned barracks free of charge for three years, German school officials remained acutely aware of their economic tenuity and their dependence on the South Africans—an uncomfortable situation for the strongly German-minded inhabitants of Swakopmund. The high school director, Hans Wunderlich, pushed a plan to decentralize German education in Windhoek and expand it in Swakopmund. He pointed out the city's healthy sea climate and that in terms of the number of pupils it equaled Windhoek.[63] Initially, consul Haug reservedly welcomed Wunderlich's suggestions,[64] moreover, organizations in SWA and Germany sought solutions for Swakopmund's precarious situation.[65] However, the DKG determined that not enough money was available to support and expand two German secondary schools in SWA, and in its negotiations with the South African government the Foreign Office concentrated on Windhoek. It decided to effect an acceptable resolution to the Swakopmund negotiations, reasoning that such a position would free more money for Windhoek and further guarantee its existence.[66]

The Foreign's Office's decision did little to dissuade the Swakopmund Germans from trying to save their school. In fact, they redoubled their efforts and tried even harder to convince people both in Germany and in SWA that the Swakopmund high school was more essential to the future of Deutschtum in SWA than Windhoek. Most residents of Swakopmund believed Windhoek was behind the Foreign Office's decision. Robert Blank, a league member, wrote, "I take for granted Windhoek's game of intrigue that led to the known decision of Department VI [the Foreign Office's Education

Department]." The simmering rivalry between Windhoek and Swakopmund erupted into open conflict. Basing their rationales primarily on economic and health factors, each side claimed that it was better suited to serve the needs of the German community.[67]

The Swakopmund Germans eventually, in 1929, had to accept the administration's offer, albeit with changes achieved through the DB's negotiations. A. Schad, the mayor of Swakopmund, recognized the futility of their situation: "The Agreement is not unfavorable, and if the Reich does *not* want to, Southwest cannot fight successfully against *two* countries" (emphases in the original).[68] The agreement, signed on April 14, 1929, contained extremely generous terms. First, it merged 'the German medium class of the Windhoek Government High School, the school of the Swakopmund German School Association, and the German medium class of the Swakopmund government school" into the "Deutsche Höhere Schule" (the German high school in Swakopmund). In the new school, Students were allowed to take both the matriculation exam (after twelve years) and the Abitur (after thirteen years). Moreover, German remained "the language of instruction and examination," except in "Afrikaans, English, and a third subject, presumably Latin, or mathematics or arithmetic." The administration agreed to hire only "German-speaking and German-national faculty who have obtained the necessary teaching qualifications at a German teachers' college or university." Both sides reserved the right to cancel the agreement.[69]

In the following years, the administration preserved the German integrity of the school and actually went to extremes to appease students' parents. The South Africans did cancel the agreement in 1934 for administrative reasons, but it nonetheless continued to operate the school under the same conditions agreed upon in 1929. When Germany abolished the Abitur year (the thirteenth school year) in 1937, parents complied by no longer demanding this additional *(Oberprima)* year. However, this led to difficulties for the German students since both the English and German final exams occurred in the twelfth grade. In 1939, the South African examination board admitted German as the first language subject in the matriculation exam and raised the number of nonlanguage subjects that could be taken in German.[70]

In the early 1930s, Tsumeb, in northern Southwest Africa/Namibia, faced a similar dilemma. After the German Otavi Mine and Railway Corporation (Omeg) reduced employment and philanthropic contributions as a result of the Great Depression, the Tsumeb School Association found itself in a financial predicament. Most Omeg employees sent their children to the

Tsumeb school; when they lost their jobs, they were no longer in a position to pay tuition. Consequently, the association felt compelled to enter into negotiations with the administration for transferring control of the school to the Education Department. The terms agreed upon essentially preserved the German character of the school. All teachers employed at the school kept their jobs and, what was more important, the curriculum still corresponded to a German elementary school, with provisions to be added in accordance with local conditions and parents' wishes. So, on October 1, 1931, the school went under South African control.[71]

Although the terms of the agreement were more than fair, some supporters saw in the Tsumeb School Association's decision a threat to the future of Deutschtum in the region. The most vocal opponent of the agreement was the DKG deputy president, Friedrich von Lindequist, the former SWA governor and state secretary. He admonished the Tsumeb members for, despite warnings from the Foreign Office, acting alone and too hurriedly before a rescue action to help save the school could be started in Germany:

> With the greatest sorrow we took notice of this final resolution and could not conceal that we are most embarrassed from the haste in which the negotiations with the Mandate government were concluded without requesting or waiting for a relief action on the part of the homeland.[72]

Lindequist also accused the association of endangering the entire Deutschtum in the region; their actions, he said, cast doubts in the minds of those in Germany who had heretofore assisted the private schools as to whether such sacrifices were worth it.[73] To further denounce their lack of resolve in trying to save the school, he finally insulted their character and patriotism.[74] The severity of Lindequist's comments did not shake the Tsumeb association's resolve. Nor did his words influence decisions of the school associations in Elisabethbucht and Charlottental: they, too, decided to close with the suspension of mining in the diamond fields due to the worldwide economic downturn. Lüderitz Bay was similarly affected, but its association members were able to maintain the school with the assistance of the FB.[75]

Organizations other than school associations promoted Deutschtum in the territory, of course. As in the German colonial period, various associations and churches cultivated "German ways and customs."[76] Many of the older and more nationalistic organizations, such as the gymnastic, singing, and school associations, allowed only Germans to join them. Meanwhile, since their arrival, South Africans had formed their own groups. Even though they often opened their membership to Germans, few, if any, Süd-wester joined. Thus, most clubs maintained a national character. The most notable exceptions to groups practicing German exclusivity in the interwar period were the sports clubs.[77] While many clubs remained segregated, a few tried to bridge the gap between Germans and South Africans, either for practical reasons or out of recognition of their common future together in Southwest Africa.

The German Lutheran churches in Southwest Africa played a salient role in preserving the identity of the local German community. While the schools and other organizations cultivated German minds, churches cultivated both their souls and nationalism; they promoted and emphasized the white, Christian, and German character of the settlers. The church continued to do mission work for the Africans while providing pastoral care for the whites. The former activity was intended to secure the political and economic dominance of the whites over the "natives," while the latter was supposed to prevent the German settler from losing "his identity as a part of the German people" due to contact with the new rulers.[78] In October 1926, the three German-speaking synods in southern Africa established a federal body called the German Church League in South and Southwest Africa.[79] Among their stated goals, the synods vowed to cooperate with one another, to awaken "an evangelical consciousness and a brotherly unity," and to care for "the German cultural assets within the German-speaking community." This was especially important for new arrivals, from Germany, who were not aware of the local circumstances.[80] Even though the synods were loosely associated with churches in Germany, their contextual engagement found expression in several print venues. For instance, the league published the monthly newsletter, *Heimat,* and the annual church diary and calendar, *Afrikanischer Heimatkalender.* It also had its own hymnal and liturgy.[81]

Equally, if not more, significant were the youth organizations, especially because of their role in supplementing the education young Southwestern Germans received in school. The most important of these clubs were the Pathfinders. Two former colonial officers, Dr. Alexander Lion and Maximilian Bayer, founded the organization around 1909 in emulation of Baden-Powell's Boy Scouts. By 1926 several branches existed in Southwest Africa.[82] Under the control of the German League, they aimed at winning the hearts of all of Southwest Africa's German youth for Deutschtum and "the old tradition of the German colonial troop," including those who had already left school. One supporter believed that the Pathfinders could possibly achieve more than the best-planned curriculum:

> When the young boys march through the countryside with their old troop hats and black-white-red cockade, visit the graves of our fallen, fire honor salvos over these graves, when they drill according to the old German orders, make their parade march before German flags and monuments, give all German national holidays the firm setting in stiff discipline—then this often educates [them] more in the national German thought than the best German curriculum.[83]

Through various activities, these groups tried to keep alive the values and spirit of the German Empire. They rejected the principles of the new German republic.[84] A perfect example of this was the use of the imperial colors (black, white, and red), and not those of the new republic (black, red, and yellow).

After 1933, National Socialist youth organizations—the Hitler Youth and the League of German Girls—joined the conservative, old imperial Pathfinders and other youth groups (the FB's Youth League and the Girls' League of the German Church) in the task of "raising and preserving the German youth in the sense of the cultural-political and folkish Deutschtum work of the German League . . . for Deutschtum."[85] These organizations came under the direction of a single individual, the so-called Youth Guardian. The situation changed drastically after 1936 when the South African Union banned the Nazi Party and all its affiliated organizations. Through the efforts of the German representatives in the Territorial Council and the school associations, young Southwestern Germans could still join the Pathfinder groups; however, they had to agree to remain nonpartisan.[86]

At least statistically, the German community essentially preserved the German character of its children. During the 1920s the majority of German children attended the German private schools. Even after the upper-level school in Swakopmund came under the administration's jurisdiction in 1930, the German private schools boasted a higher enrollment than the German medium classes. However, after Tsumeb joined the ranks of the government schools in 1931 and several of the private schools in the diamond region closed, the number of students at the private schools fell below that of the government schools. Apparently a number of parents compensated for the lack of German schools by hiring private tutors for their children. As

Table 7.3. **Attendance at Private and Public Schools**

	1919	1922	1928	1929	1930	1931	1932	1933	1935	1936
Private	1013	436	990	1013	731	603	612	586	550	551
Public	529	367	600	591	895	973	886	954	883	828
TOTALS	1542	803	1590	1604	1626	1576	1498	1540	1433	1379

Source: Gries, *Dritter Bericht der Deutschen Realschule zu Windhuk, 1919–24,* BAP R1001/1953; Oskar Wallberg, *Die deutschen Schüler des Mandatslandes Südwestafrika, 1933,* BAP R1001/1954; and Hildegard Rutkowski, "Deutsches Schul- und Erziehungswesen," *DKZ* 53 (1941): 62.

German schools closed or came under the administration's control, the number of children attending farm schools increased. In addition, individuals like Frey, Eckenbrecher, and other government teachers of German nationality worked to preserve the heritage of those Germans attending public schools.[87] Finally, various youth organizations assisted schools in inculcating children and young adults with German values and traditions. However, the mandate did suffer a decline in the number of children attending schools.

Without a doubt, Südwester's fears that the South African government desired to undermine their Deutschtum and assimilate them and their children never materialized. Except for its initial attempt to take control of the German schools, the administration continually tried to accommodate the German populace. It allowed those who so desired to operate as private schools. It created German medium classes in the government schools for areas with large German populations. Moreover, it provided subsidies to all the private schools. It accepted the Swakopmund School Association's counterproposals and maintained the German character of the school, even after the administration officially terminated the agreement in 1934. It even introduced measures to make it easier for students at the "German High School" to pass their finishing exams. In fact, the South Africans treated the Germans more equitably than the Germans did the Afrikaners, when SWA stood under German control.

Even though the administration acted more than fairly, many in the German community could still not shake the feeling that the South African government had hidden motives. They believed that it still wanted to gain control of Südwester youth, and since the best way to do that was to educate them in state schools, they therefore worked very hard to maintain the

German private schools. They looked on uneasily as the schools in Tsumeb, Swakopmund, and Charottental came under the administration's control or closed their doors. Even the German high school in Swakopmund offered them no solace. According to Dr. Wallberg, the right of the administration to terminate the agreement provided no security for the future of German education in the colony.[88] Although his fears did not materialize, he and many others continued to distrust the South African government and fear for the fate of their children. For them, the greatest misfortune had occurred: the school may still have primarily followed a German curriculum, but with the loss of it and Tsumeb, the majority of German students fell directly under the administration's control.

Their intense dislike of the South Africans, their strong attachment to Deutschtum, and their innate paranoia caused them to see ulterior motives and subversion in all the administration's activities and offers. This feeling of insecurity extended even to fellow Südwester. These radical nationalists and their supporters in Germany accused the members of the Tsumeb School Association of not doing all within its power to preserve the school. They said German teachers at the government schools and School Inspector Frey did not behave as true Germans, but rather as "renegades." For these rigid believers in Deutschtum, perceptions of reality proved more important than reality itself. And to a degree, many Südwester shared this with them, for they distrusted the administration's intentions and worked to preserve themselves and their children for Deutschtum.

Nevertheless, some did rise above the paranoia and nationalist rhetoric, most notably Frey, to recognize and to welcome the administration's generosity and accommodating behavior. These pragmatists believed that the best way to achieve results for the German community was to cooperate with the South Africans and to work within the system. However, such behavior elicited insults and accusations from the ultranationalists. This division between the pragmatists and the nationalists was not confined to the realm of education, but spilled over into other areas of interest within the German population.

8

Nationalism, Culture, and Politics, 1919–1932

> I learned that your efforts in Southwest Africa coincide with that what we view as the goal; namely, the creation of an autonomous state in Southwest Africa in which the Germans have the majority.
>
> —Former Governor Seitz to Südwester activist Albert Voigts, 1928

After the establishment of the mandate, the Southwestern Germans quickly realized that if they wanted to achieve their goal of gaining control of the territory's destiny, they had to do more than increase and preserve their numbers through immigration and education. They were acutely aware of the necessity of making gains in the realm of politics. Accordingly, they demanded political equality, in particular voting rights, and the recognition of German as the third administrative language, next to English and Afrikaans. They believed easier access to the franchise would increase their chances of gaining seats in the Legislative Assembly, the local legislature. This would enable them to resist Afrikaner moves to turn Southwest Africa into a fifth province of South Africa and work toward their goal of creating an autonomous state with strong ties to Germany. Meanwhile, the establishment of German as an administrative language would not only legally secure it but also provide full justification for independent German schools; maintenance of the language would facilitate German sway in the region. These demands, especially the calls for equal treatment, became increasingly urgent as the powers of the Legislative Assembly expanded and the number of Afrikaners in the territory grew. However, generational and personal divisions emerged within the Southwestern German community over the best means to achieve these goals—splits that undermined the German cause and position and eventually resulted in South African intervention.

The South African administration operated under the assumption that Southwest Africa was "white man's country"; as such, the government believed, the territory should be populated and governed by whites, both Afrikaners and Germans. The administration also assumed that the groups would find common cause on this issue and would want to develop the mandate along these lines. Finally, it believed that Germans and Afrikaners could be politically amalgamated by extending British citizenship en masse to the Germans, while offering them concessions in other areas, such as in education and in settlement.[1] In a speech given in Windhoek, Premier Smuts stated in September 1920 that "political rights and citizenship go together"; as aliens the Germans had "no political rights as franchise, etc."[2] If they wanted to participate in the local government, they had to apply for British citizenship and give up their German citizenship. However, the Southwestern Germans, who deemed South Africans to be their cultural and economic inferiors, resented these people denying them political rights in a land they believed was their own. Thus, they were not inclined to take either step on citizenship; they implored the South African government to introduce a special mandate citizenship for all inhabitants of SWA. In this they were unsuccessful.[3]

This situation—namely, the Southwestern German belief in their own linguistic, cultural, and economic superiority vis-à-vis the Afrikaners coupled with every day having to confront being treated as second-class citizens— led them to overemphasize "the importance of culture and language."[4] Since this community believed that language and culture determined national identity, it responded to attacks on its power and status in cultural terms. These demands actually connoted larger struggles for "power, status, and group welfare."[5]

It was not surprising that the Southwestern Germans, from the beginning of the mandate, desired that South Africa classify German as an administrative language. They believed that this step, along with maintaining

German schools, was essential to preserving their status and position in the region. "If the German language remains preserved, so strengthen we the German influence."[6] In September 1920, they demanded that Smuts fulfill their wish. Although the premier responded that implementation of such a request was impossible, he acknowledged that attempts would be made to post bureaucrats in SWA who had knowledge of German. Indeed, it became unofficial practice to answer German communications (letters, telegrams, etc.) in the German language. Administrator Hofmeyr made this policy official in November 1920, ordering civil servants to continue this policy to the best of their abilities. Moreover, a German version of the official gazette appeared, although it was not legally binding. Even in oral communications, Germans could use their mother tongue. If the official had difficulty understanding, he would seek assistance. Despite these concessions, the German community continued to express dissatisfaction: the German language lacked official status.[7]

In order to overcome Southwestern German opposition to naturalization and to achieve his goal of creating a white nation in SWA, Smuts entered into direct negotiations with the German government. The result of the discussions was the London Agreement, signed on October 23, 1923. The South Africans made concessions in the areas of politics, language, education, immigration, culture, and economics. Among other things, the South African government specifically agreed to recognize "the Germans in Southwest Africa as a part of the population with the same rights and duties as the other citizens." Although it refused to declare German an official language, it assented to the free use of German in communications with public authorities and said responses to such inquiries would be in German whenever possible. Moreover, the South African government began the subsidization of the German schools in Swakopmund and Windhoek, later extending the subsidies to all German schools. In addition, the government admitted German representatives to the Land Board and the Land Agricultural Bank of Southwest Africa—one German to each body. It also stated that within the parameters of the South African immigration laws, "all Germans were welcome." For its part, the German government agreed to advise its citizens to accept the planned automatic naturalization and not to make use of their right to refuse it. Furthermore, it officially acknowledged that the future of Southwest Africa was inextricably connected to that of South Africa[8]—which was the position that had been maintained by all South African officials since the establishment of the mandate over SWA.[9]

Smuts hoped that the concessions he made in terms of culture, immigration, and farming would make it easier for the Southwestern Germans to accept British citizenship. However, some Südwester, upon hearing the terms, felt betrayed by the German government and expressed anger toward the agreement.[10] This opposition was downplayed by the German consul in Windhoek, however; such individuals, he said, merely took the "opportunity to criticize an achievement in which they were not involved."[11]

Nevertheless, the issue of naturalization did prove problematic for some Südwester. Many resented the fact that they had to assume British citizenship in order to obtain rights they felt rightfully belonged to them. In addition, not all knew that they could refuse naturalization or that, by accepting British citizenship, they did not automatically lose their German citizenship. Smuts, and later Premier Hertzog, did, however, declare that they would not tolerate double citizenship in SWA. Only if naturalized Südwester returned to Germany could they receive their German citizenship again. Even though the German government said that ultimately each individual had to make up his or her own mind, it nonetheless advised them to accept naturalization. It saw this as the best means to safeguard German interests and to influence the development of the country.[12] The German consul-general in South Africa, Haug, wrote to one concerned Südwester that the individual had to consider whether or not he wanted "to be able to represent the interests of the German community living there through active participation in the administration and through influence on the fate of the country."[13]

Despite these reservations, the majority of Germans accepted British citizenship on March 15, 1925: more than three thousand Germans became British citizens; fewer than three hundred rejected it. Thus, more than 90 percent of the German community in SWA became British citizens. The 1924 Naturalization Law bestowed citizenship only on whites, and they had to be of age and have lived in the mandate between January 1, 1924, and September 15, 1924; subsequent arrivals had to wait two years before they could apply for citizenship. Hence, the new law excluded German children and those Germans who were not in SWA at the time and returned after June 1926. As a supplement to the 1924 law, the South Africans passed the 1928 Naturalization Law, which naturalized another twenty-five hundred or so Germans, including children; in addition, children born after July 1, 1926, became British citizens if their parents possessed British citizenship. Under both laws, the collectively naturalized Germans held Union citizenship only in the South African Union.[14]

In 1926, the South Africans changed the residency requirements for foreigners who wanted to apply for citizenship. While the 1924 law required applicants to have only a two-year residency, the 1926 law stipulated that Germans could not make their first application until they had five years' residence; moreover, the law allowed Union nationals (and the majority of Union nationals were either British or Boer) to automatically receive the franchise after one year of residence. This new law applied to the entire British Empire.[15] Many Germans, both in SWA and in Germany, perceived this new law as a means to weaken the German position. This was especially true, they pointed out, in light of the recent German success in the first elections to the newly created Legislative Assembly.

Hugo Blumhagen, a former colonial official in SWA, claimed that "this condition pursues the goal to exclude the Germans from the elections to the Legislative Assembly and to give the Boers in the Legislative Assembly excess weight, preferably a two-thirds majority."[16] However, Blumhagen and others did not realize, or chose to ignore, that the new law applied to the entire British Empire, and not just to SWA. In the eyes of Southwestern Germans, the law was decisive and contributed to a renewal of their claims for equality in subsequent discussions with Afrikaners and the South African government. It also became a pivotal platform point in all future elections to the legislature.

The legislature itself came into existence in 1925 with the passage of the Southwest African Constitutional Act. In some respects, it was the culmination of Smut's dream, completed by Hertzog, to create a "unified white" colony with increasing powers of self-administration. He believed that eventually the inhabitants would ultimately decide for themselves to become an integral part of the Union. The act was a move in that direction and was made possible by the London Agreement and the mass naturalization of the majority of Germans. It established three governing bodies with a degree of popular participation. The legislature consisted of eighteen members, twelve directly elected and six named by the administrator. The executive was made up of the administrator and four elected members of the assembly. The act also created the Advisory Council, composed of the executive and three additional members named by the administrator. The Union parliament, however, retained the right "to legislate for Southwest Africa 'as an integral portion of the Union,'" under the terms of the C mandate, and the governor-general kept ultimate powers to legislate via proclamation. This provided the administrator with a large degree of independence from his assembly and council.[17]

Despite the limits to its power, the new Legislative Assembly was viewed by both the Germans and the Afrikaners as a vehicle to achieve their goals. However, instead of the new set-up achieving the hoped for cooperation between the two largest communities in the region, open competition broke out between them. What the Germans called a *Volkstumkampf* ("national struggle") began. Each ethnic group sought to organize itself politically in order to obtain a majority in the new legislative body. Now the German community had a third foe: the Afrikaners, in addition to the mandate administration and the South African government.[18]

The German community had already taken steps to organize itself during the discussions surrounding naturalization. Various German associations felt that a single organization was needed to represent German interests in the mandate, and the result was the founding of the Deutscher Bund (DB)—the German League for Southwest Africa—in September 1924. The new organization claimed to stand above all parties and to represent the will of the memberships of the German associations. It was an exclusively German association, permitting membership only to German corporations and individuals of "German descent" who "declare their loyalty to Deutschtum." Brenner, of the Windhoek School Association, became its first chairman.[19]

Under Brenner's leadership and that of his successors, mainly the long-time Südwester Albert Voigts, the league pursued a number of fixed goals deemed necessary to preserve the Deutschtum of the Southwestern German population. For example, one stated task was the "effective care of all German establishments and efforts in the land." This was to done with "an active contact and exchange of ideas with the old homeland," for there "the roots of our culture, our intellectual interests, and our energy lie." Because of the importance placed on ties to the homeland, the DB saw itself as the "link and clearing house for all intellectual and cultural efforts with the homeland." The organization also occupied itself with issues of youth education and immigration.[20] Moreover, the DB intended "to represent politically the German efforts in the area of culture and other specific German interests (e.g., the language question)." Above all, however, it sought to establish "unity among the Germans" and "to prevent a splintering into political parties."[21] The league was the self-proclaimed "center of Deutschtum and the primary carrier of German culture in the land."[22]

The task of preserving unity among the German community became a primary concern for the DB. Part of its concern was the desire to maintain a unified front vis-à-vis the administration; the other was to placate supporters in the homeland who might have suspended funding if they felt that their money was going to a losing cause. DKG President Seitz warned Voigts of this: "I can assure you that the activity of everyone here who is interested in the protectorate will be made extraordinarily difficult if the splintering of Germans, which is complained about so much here, should arise out there."[23] The DB, therefore, in order to demonstrate that it was not like the homeland and to show that it was taking steps to maintain harmony among the Germans, constantly pointed out successes. It also tried to eliminate potential competitors, and in its 1925 annual report proudly reported that "the results of the naturalization, in which more than 90 percent of the Germans living here accepted naturalization, show that the greatest uniformity and . . . unified action succeeded as far as it is possible to achieve in this country.[24]

However, shortly after the 1925 naturalization of Germans, another organization sprang up, the Verein der Reichsdeutschen (VdR, or Association of German Citizens). It claimed to represent the interests of those Germans who refused British citizenship and to assist newly arrived settlers. The DB, claiming to represent all Germans, viewed the association as superfluous and divisive since it worked only with nonnaturalized Germans. The league warned that the association's independence might weaken the German voting constituency. The DB feared that newcomers, buttressed by the existence of the VdR, might be disinclined to apply for British citizenship and thus be unable to participate in elections. Initially, negotiations failed to bring the two groups together, but by 1927 the VdR lost significance and had funding problems—primarily since most groups in Germany funneled monies through the DB. That year, the association joined the league and essentially ceased to exist.[25]

Despite initial successes, the DB experienced difficulties maintaining unity within the German population. Its encounter with the VdR was a small foreshadowing of some of the larger problems it would eventually face. In the late 1920s the Territorial School Association left the DB ranks, and in the 1930s it had to deal with larger divisions in the German community, especially after the arrival of the National Socialists in 1932. Ultimately it dissolved, but before that transpired the league strove to represent the political and cultural interests of the German population in negotiations with the Southwestern administration, the South African government, and the Afrikaners. Although it maintained its cultural nature, never claiming to be a political organization, it delved into the realm of politics. Thus, in addition to its activities in education, it played a decisive role in the preparations for the legislative elections. The DB was largely responsible for enlisting candidates and establishing a platform. Because of its claim to be a cultural institution and its desire to preserve at least a façade of harmony among the Germans, it resisted all efforts to found a German political party. For instance, when Hintrager, of the Reich Office for Emigration, actively pushed for the establishment of a political party and tried to enlist the assistance of the DKG to add weight to its argument, DKG President Theodor Seitz, the former governor, took a more cautious approach. Seitz wished to avoid the potential splintering of German votes and feared that the various economic and professional groups might try to found their own parties based on their own special interests[26]—a situation too reminiscent of the political landscape in Weimar Germany.[27]

For the 1926 elections to the newly created Legislative Assembly, the DB pursued a simple plan that netted good results. Selecting outstanding Germans whom the league felt had a good chance of winning and who would well represent the German element, it named as candidates men like Albert Voigts, from Okahandja, Robert Blank, from Swakopmund, and Dr. Hans Hirsekorn, from Lüderitz Bay. The platform corresponded to the league's own demands; namely, the political and linguistic equality of the Germans with other segments of Southwestern society. In other words, the DB wanted the recognition of German as an administrative language and the same conditions for obtaining the franchise granted to Afrikaners and colonial British. The election outcome clearly revealed the numerical superiority of the Germans—their chances being still further improved by the division of the Afrikaners into two parties, the National Party and the Southwest Party. The Germans won seven of the twelve seats available through direct election, whereas the Afrikaners received only five. The administrator, A. J. Werth, balanced out the result by appointing two Germans and four Afrikaners to the body; thus, nine Germans and nine Afrikaners sat in the new legislature.[28] Neither group held a two-thirds majority, which meant that if either group wanted to make any significant changes, such as applying for annexation by South Africa or for the creation of an autonomous state, they had to work together. Given the intense animosity between them, this was not likely to happen.

In fact, the animosity between the Germans and Afrikaners grew in intensity. The existence of a common enemy motivated the two Afrikaner parties to enter into discussions with one another. They worked to reach some form of consensus in order to improve their chances in the 1929 elections. In 1927 they joined together and founded the United National South West Party (UNSWP). The new party claimed to represent the "national efforts of the Southwest's [white] African population" and called for the "abolition of the mandate system" and "the Southwest's incorporation into the Union." UNSWP saw the Germans as their biggest opponent.[29]

Meanwhile, the German leadership, unlike the Afrikaner, experienced increasing personal differences. According to official reports, German members of the legislature cooperated well with one another. However, there were antagonisms between them and the DB as well as between the league and some of the larger associations, such as German association in Windhoek and the Territorial School Association. The main point of contention was who should lead the German community and thus determine the best means to achieve their goals. Dr. Bielfeld, a German official in Windhoek, noted a lack of contact with each other and of a suitable individual to unite and lead the Southwestern Germans; uncertainty reigned about the direction the community should go, he said: "This lack of feeling is also the reason why the Germans in Southwest do not found a political party—they are merely a nationality group that pursues certain cultural aims but that does not have a particular political program." Bielfeld was articulating the old fear that a political party could lead to the establishment of other, special-interest parties and thus split the Germans. The only thing they were certain about, he claimed, was that they did not want the incorporation of SWA into South Africa.[30]

The DB leadership took a number of steps to improve relations between the various groupings and thus its chances in the next election. It replaced its chairman, Brenner—a contentious personality—with Voigts.[31] Furthermore, it issued suggestions (which appeared more like guidelines) for the preparations for the upcoming elections. Although the league created a central election community, it left the organization of committees in the electoral districts to the local German associations; in addition, in districts with a good chance of electing a German, it devolved responsibility for selecting candidates to the local people. After much discussion and several changes, Germans stood for election in six districts. In three other areas, the central election committee made agreements with independent candidates in order to increase their chances of victory over members of UNSWP. Its criteria for selecting candidates rested exclusively upon their commitment to equality and the maintenance of the mandate. In two districts, suitable candidates were not found.[32]

Table 8.1. Party Formation and Realignment, 1924–1945

Party Name	Formed	Dissolved	Realignments	Attitude toward incorporation	Ethnic Group
The National Party of SWA	26 July 1924	31 Jan. 1927	Formed VNSWP w/ South West Party and Econo Party	For	Afrikaner/English
The Union Party	Sept. 1924	28 Jan. 1926	Renamed South West Party on 28 Jan. 1926	For	Afrikaner/English
Deutscher Bund	3 Sept. 1924	1 July 1937 (banned)		Against	German
Omaruru Political Society	27 May 1925	31 Jan. 1927	Became part of VNSWP	Against (as of 31 Jan. 1927, for)	Afrikaner/English
Verenigde Nasionale Party van SWA	31 Jan. 1927			For	Afrikaner
SWA Labour and Farmers Party (Labour Party)	23 Nov. 1931	1932		For	English
NSDAP	June 1932	Oct. 1934 (banned)	Exercised influence in DB and Deutsche Front	Against (Pro-Nazi)	German
Ekonomische (Bond/Volksparty)	23 Sept. 1932	1 July 1937		Against (Pro-Nazi)	German
Deutsche Front	April 1935	27 June 1937		Against (Pro-Nazi)	German
Deutsche Sudwest Bund	24 June 1937			Against/for (some pro-Nazi sentiments)	German
The SWA League	4 Nov. 1938			For	Afrikaner/German
Die Deutsche Afrikanische Partei	March 1939	8 Sept. 1939	Following breakaway from DSB aligned w/ VNSWP	For	German/Afrikaner
The National Party of SWA	28 July 1939			For	Afrikaner/German

Source: André du Pisani, *SWA/Namibia: The Politics of Continuity and Change* (Johannesburg: Jonathan Bell, 1986), 87.

The committee introduced a program that attempted to include a wider spectrum of the German populace. Many goals reflected the long-standing desires of the German community as a whole, such as the demand for equality among whites in terms of "language, cultural, and voting rights" and "equality for all immigrants of the white race for the obtainment of the citizenship in the mandate area." And for the first time, the Southwestern Germans formally expressed their desire to transform the colony from a C mandate to an A mandate. Such a change was predicated upon the assumption that Southwest Africa was not a land populated by black Africans but rather was a land of whites. Furthermore, an A mandate would give them the right to determine their own future. Their goal was obvious: the creation of an autonomous state. Finally, the program also included a number of items in an effort to win over specific segments of the German community. For example, the demand for social legislation appealed to the German working class and white-collar workers, and the reference to "native policy" was undeniably intended to placate farmers.[33]

Despite their preparations and reconciliation attempts within the German population, the Germans did not fare well in the July 1929 elections, winning only four seats in the assembly. The Afrikaners won eight. Unlike the previous time, when the administrator balanced representation in the legislature, this time he named an equal number of Germans and Afrikaners. Thus the Afrikaners obtained a majority of eleven to seven (they still lacked the two-thirds majority needed to make significant changes, however).[34]

Not surprisingly, the Germans expressed outrage over the election results and the administrator's appointments. They saw this as merely another example of the larger plot to reduce German power and prestige and bring down the Deutschtum in the region by supporting the Afrikaners, all of which would pave the way for the incorporation of the mandate into the Union. They claimed that settlement policies and access to Union citizenship favored Afrikaners and colonial Britons. The mass immigration of Afrikaners from Angola, against the wishes of many Germans and even some Southwestern Afrikaners, contributed significantly to the Afrikaners' numerical strength in the 1929 election.[35]

Southwestern Germans claimed that the unfair treatment of Germans was in direct violation of the London Agreement. Hirsekorn pointed out that the agreement guaranteed them the same rights and obligations as other segments of Southwestern society. Noting the reduction in the number of seats won by Germans in the 1929 election, rhetorically, he asked, "How then did this happen?" He answered that, unlike the Afrikaners, Germans suffered disadvantages in acquiring citizenship and thus the right to vote. Although he did not actually say so, Hirsekorn tacitly concluded that the South Africans did not fulfill the terms of the London Agreement and therefore consciously tried to undermine the German position while buttressing the Afrikaners'. Such a view did little to bring Germans and Afrikaners closer together. In fact, it exacerbated the tensions between them, and their animosity for one another grew.[36]

The Great Depression and the onset of drought, though, caused them to move closer together. Both groups realized that the Legislative Assembly needed more powers to help alleviate the situation; however, a two-thirds majority in the legislature was required to make the necessary changes. In recognition of the severity of the situation, representatives of both the DB and the UNSWP agreed to negotiations. The Germans wanted their language to become the third administrative language, the immediate naturalization of all Germans living in SWA since the end of 1931, and the naturalization of newly arrived Germans after two years. If the Afrikaners agreed to these terms, the Germans were willing to support the Afrikaner's demands for an extension of the legislature's powers; if not, they would reject any moves in that direction. The Afrikaner leaders agreed to the German requests for equality, although they admitted that only in some areas—namely, the recognition of German as an official language—did they have a direct say; the matters regarding immigration and naturalization had to be addressed by the South African government. They did, however, agree not to stand in the way on these issues.[37] Thus, both sides were able to overcome differences in recognition of a higher cause—the future of their shared homeland, Southwest Africa, a future in which both Germans and Afrikaners were interested.

Shortly after these discussions, in April 1932, the Legislative Assembly unanimously and without a debate passed a resolution making German an administrative language, calling for the fair placement of Germans on a par with the South Africans, and the extension of the assembly's powers. The matter still had to be referred to Hertzog and the Union parliament. Hertzog acceded immediately to the Germans' wish to recognize German as the mandate's third official language, and although he remained somewhat vague on the other issues, he agreed to work toward shortening the time required for Germans to obtain British citizenship.[38]

The reconciliation between the Germans and the Afrikaners was short-lived. Shortly after the agreement, some German workers' associations criticized the administration's economic and financial policies. The UNSWP provided the final blow to negotiations when its leader, Niehaus, recommenced the campaign for the incorporation of SWA as a fifth province of South Africa. The Germans responded by initiating a no-confidence campaign against the administrator, the Legislative Assembly, and the mandate system. The gains of 1932 remained unfulfilled, and animosity returned with even greater intensity.[39]

9

National Socialism, Politics, and German Identity, 1932–1939

> We find that there has been continual interfer-
> ence from the Auslands-Organisation [part of
> NSDAP, the Nazi party] in the affairs of the Terri-
> tory and that, as a result, freedom of speech of
> political association and even of personal conduct
> has ceased to exist in the Territory for a large
> number of Germans who are Union subjects.
> —Southwest Africa Commission report on Nazi
>   activities, London, 1936

The founding in 1932 of a chapter of the *Nationalsozialistische Deutsche Arbeiterpartei* (NSDAP—or the National Socialist German Workers' Party) in Southwest Africa not only further strained relations between the Germans and the Afrikaners, it also threatened the fragile unity within the German camp. The Southwestern Germans received the National Socialists with ambivalence. On the one hand, the founding of a chapter of the Nazi Party in SWA came at a time when there was widespread Südwester disgruntlement (with the administration and the South African government over the nonfulfillment of its political agenda and with the Afrikaner party for its actions); on the other hand, the establishment of a political party in SWA "violated an unwritten law of the Southwestern German whereby one wanted to remain spared from the political party quarrels of the homeland, the unpopular 'System' of the Weimar Republic."[1]

In general, most Southwestern Germans were united in their desire to have SWA returned to Germany, but they were divided in their methods. Most of the tension within the German community revolved around who should direct policy and what methods should be pursued. Essentially, the arrival of the Nazis resulted in a struggle between different personalities and institutions for control of the German population. The German community essentially split along generational lines. One side, composed primarily of older individuals who had lived in the region for decades, was more monarchical and pragmatic. They tried to improve their situation through negotiations with the administration while still hoping that eventually the mandate would be returned to Germany. The other, smaller side—consisting overwhelmingly of younger, newly arrived Germans—found the "older generation's" methods too slow and too pedantic. They embraced national socialism and demanded more radical action.[2]

These tensions became most apparent when Brenner, the ousted head of the German League, returned to the region in 1933. Replaced in 1927 by Voigts because of his confrontational and egotistical attitude, Brenner again tried to establish himself as the spokesman of the German element in SWA—supposedly armed with support from prominent Nazi officials in Germany. It was apparent that Brenner was heavily influenced by the Nazi experience in Germany, especially in his attempt to introduce the "Leadership Principle" *(Führerprinzip),* with himself as leader of the Windhoek School Association. Against the wishes of his longtime opponents, he also desired to bring into line all German institutions *(Gleichschaltung).*[3]

Brenner made his move at the annual meeting of the school association. He made a speech describing the "national uprising" (i.e., the National Socialist seizure of power) and the success of the "forced conformity of the German associations under the introduction of the leadership principle." At the end, he urged the assembly "to announce through applause that they follow the new spirit of the homeland and want to adapt themselves to it as well." After the hefty applause, Brenner declared the meeting adjourned and announced the creation of a committee that would henceforth run the association. He noted that the committee would report periodically to the rest of the association.[4]

According to the German consul in SWA, Dr. Fricke, the majority of association members registered surprise at and consternation with Brenner's actions. They did not anticipate Brenner's move since he himself attended the preparatory meeting and gave no indication of his intentions. After the initial shock, most members decided to continue the meeting that Brenner had abruptly ended. They believed the best way to resolve the issue was to ask Brenner voluntarily to give up his new position as leader of the association. He refused; therefore, the remaining members of the organization, without Brenner present, declared his period of office ended. The assembly elected a new directorate, with long-standing member Adolf Neuhaus as chair. The new directorate, on behalf of the assembly, made clear that its actions against Brenner were in no way a rejection of National Socialism; on the contrary, it maintained, it wanted to restructure the association along the party's lines. However, it wanted to do it gradually in order not to aggravate South African officials.[5]

Despite the overwhelming disapproval expressed for Brenner at this meeting, he did enjoy some support. His most outspoken proponent was H. Grönewald. At the assembly, Grönewald tried to deliver a speech defending Brenner and attacking his enemies; namely, Keller and John Meinert, the mayor of Windhoek and owner of the local German newspaper. He accused them of being "democrats" and opponents of the "new national spirit." Invoking nationalist sentiment, he further accused Meinert of being a friend of the Afrikaners and the British. He also claimed that Meinert "never sent his children to the German high school (Oberrealschule)" in Windhoek. Thus, Grönewald branded Meinert a traitor. He even took a jab at Voigts, declaring that Voigts desired to "publicly emasculate the Deutschtum."[6] Grönewald's attacks found little support among the assembled members; they constantly interrupted him and eventually he had to stop speaking.[7]

But Brenner was not yet out of the picture; nor were attacks on his opponents. He was able to gain a majority in the Germania, Ltd., a trust organization for the Windhoek School Association, which enabled him to control the association's directorship. According to the statutes of both organizations, the chairman of the school association was also chairman of the Germania directorate. However, at this point Neuhaus occupied the chair in the school association and would not relinquish it. This situation resulted in a new round of conflicts between the Brenner group and the one centered on Neuhaus, Keller, and Meinert.[8]

In addition to the personal discord between Brenner and the established Germans, differences of opinion existed between the German League and the local NSDAP chapter over who represented Deutschtum in SWA. Initially, von Schauroth, DB secretary, assumed a position of indifference and reticence toward the Nazis. Himself part of the older generation of Süd-wester, he saw a necessity for neither the Nazis nor their principles of lead-ership and conformity. He argued that the Southwestern Germans were already "essentially the best National Socialists" since the South African oc-cupation of SWA. However, beginning in September 1933, Schauroth began to look more favorably upon Gleichschaltung and the introduction of the "Leadership Principle" into the league after noticing how "liberal" the new government in Berlin was. For him, the new ideology simply meant ensuring that individuals sympathetic and supportive of the new regime occupied po-sitions in the directorate. In other words, he wanted to be more inclusive. But, even though Schauroth no longer opposed these ideas, the existence of the NSDAP chapter continued to complicate matters. The question of who truly represented the Southwestern Deutschtum remained unanswered.[9]

In this atmosphere of community disharmony, organizations in the old homeland moved to improve the situation. The *Kolonialpolitisches Amt der NSDAP* (KPA—the colonial political office of NSDAP) and the Foreign Office ordered Brenner to cease all political activity and dispatched officials in September 1933 to gain an overview of the situation and to take steps to correct it. The chief of the KPA, Ritter von Epp (a former colonial officer), selected SS-Standartenführer Hans Bauszus to go to SWA. Bauszus received complete authority over the local party officials from Hitler's dep-uty, Rudolf Hess. Emil Wiehl, the German consul-general and later envoy in South Africa, joined Bauszus on his mission. Their attempts to achieve unity among the Southwestern Germans and introduce conformity and the "Leadership Principle" met initially with success. Bauszus, though he had kind words for Brenner and his enthusiasm, declared the would-be leader as too radical and activistic: Brenner had to continue to refrain from engag-ing in political activities.[10] By November 1933, the German League was characterized by the leadership principle, individual membership instead of association membership, and the designation of being the sole represen-tative of Southwestern Deutschtum. The desire among most Südwester, in particular the older generation, to avoid conflicts and present a unified front assisted the delegation in its efforts. However, a number of old-timers saw the election of Dr. Schwietering, a Swakopmund doctor, to the chair-manship of the German League as a "clear 'rape' of the will of the Germans in the mandate region." They believed Voigts better represented them.[11]

The local NSDAP was not completely satisfied with the outcome of the

Bauszus-Wiehl mission. It was especially displeased over the preference given the DB as the designated representative of the Southwestern Germans. Bauszus did not intend to relegate the Nazis to a secondary position, but he was motivated by tactical reasons. The Legislative Assembly had passed a new law, the Criminal Law—commonly known as the Anti-Nazi Law—in August 1933. This law empowered the administrator to ban political organizations as well as unwanted foreign printed materials that threatened the peace and order of the region. It also made punishable the wearing of uniforms and insignias of political organizations and the generation of hostile feelings between the various nationalities. It was a direct reaction to the "loud and alarming appearance" of the National Socialists in SWA. Bauszus thus thought it more prudent to keep the NSDAP out of the public spotlight for a while, and for it to work behind the scenes in its efforts to win people over for the "new" Germany.[12]

The peace within the German population was short-lived. Neuhaus's efforts to dislodge Brenner from Germania, Ltd. ended up in a South African court, with Brenner receiving support from the local party official, Major Weigel; NSDAP and the DB continued to struggle for control of the leadership of the Southwestern German community. Organizational duplication in Germany further complicated matters. Each organization received its orders from a different place—the DB from the AA and the colonial political office in Munich; the local NSDAP from NSDAP's foreign desk in Hamburg, the *Auslandsorganisation der NSDAP* (AO). Thus, there was no single authority to sort out such matters, despite appeals to Germany for clarification.[13]

This structure created a chaotic and untenable circumstance for the German population, especially the older generation. Schauroth regretted that the "unity in our ranks does not exist to the extent that our endangered situation requires"; he said the organization of the league was "not fortified in a manner . . . up for strong shocks."[14] Writing to Lindequist, the former governor and state secretary, he said that "in our internal political life, the Nazi movement, or even more its applications, in all its forms in the Southwest has also brought a great disorder." He noted that almost all associations had splintered into two groups: "On the one side sit the Nazis and their supporters in a closed group, on the other the older population." Schauroth desired a return of the unity that the community once enjoyed and noted the lack of a suitable personality behind whom they could rally: "It is extraordinarily regrettable that we do not have here an appropriate personality on whom the different elements can agree."[15]

Throughout the struggle for "mastery" of the German population, the conflict often degenerated into assaults on personal integrity. The National Socialists and the Brenner camp challenged their opponents' national integrity and identity, accusing them of being unfaithful to the new cause in Germany and thus not having the best interests of SWA Deutschtum in mind. The other side responded that indeed they were good Germans, Neuhaus pointing out the loyalty of the majority in the school association who rejected Brenner. When one of Brenner's allies, R. Matthiessen, equated the majority's rejection of Brenner as a rejection of the new spirit in Germany,[16] Neuhaus retorted that applause produced at the association's assembly by "Brenner's remarks about the national revolt [*nationale Erhebung*] in Germany . . . proved that they welcomed the new spirit of the old Heimat most heartily." Neuhaus added that this majority even reaffirmed their devotion at the assembly where Brenner was relieved of his office.[17] In a move obviously designed to show he was in tune with events in Germany, Neuhaus declared his willingness "to take into the school committee the local Nazi leader (*Landesgruppenführer des NSDAP*) and a few other members of the party and to lead the school association and the school in the national socialist spirit."[18]

Another Südwester accused was Dr. Edgar Wallberg, director of the Oberrealschule and longtime inhabitant of SWA. At the time, Wallberg and his wife were in Germany on vacation. Allies of Brenner accused him "of neglecting or even fighting the national socialist spirit at the school and of showing the mandate government a sympathy dangerous to the German cause."[19] His detractors, claiming that he was a "reactionary" working against their interests, made reference to his criticism of the Nazi attempt to require young Southwestern Germans to give absolute obedience to Hitler. On such grounds, they demanded his dismissal. They appealed to party officials in Germany to prevent his return to SWA and the party promptly worked to fulfill their request.[20] The request was supported by Major Weigel, the local Nazi Party leader, who claimed that although Wallberg was "an outstanding pedagogue and a good German, he was still indifferent about National Socialism."[21] What was not publicly admitted but was undeniably a motivation for the attack on Wallberg was his leading role in the vote against Brenner.

Wallberg was not without allies in SWA. They attested to his loyalty and to his long years of service to Southwestern Deutschtum. Hans Betzler, the school's deputy director, asserted that "Dr. Wallberg served our fatherland at his post in the most faithful German manner."[22] It was admitted that Wallberg did oppose the Hitler oath, but on the grounds that it undermined parental authority,[23] not because he was opposed to National Socialism. Faculty members who were also party members claimed that Wallberg faithfully carried out his duty and spoke in defense of his character. They regretted "that men [like Wallberg] who gave their energy to the Deutschtum in the noblest manner are attacked shamelessly."[24] Giesecke, the new German consul in SWA, also defended Wallberg, as did a DB representative in Germany.[25]

However, the opposition to Wallberg was so strong that even his wife, Gertrud, was not spared. The territorial youth leader of the Nazi Party in SWA, von Lossnitzer, stated that she was "worse than her husband." He described her as "a terrible schemer, who is up to mischief here." Lossnitzer claimed that Frida Voigts, the wife of Albert Voigts and an active member in the community, said that "Mrs. Wallberg continues to arrange the founding of her reactionary coalitions in the south."[26] As in her husband's case, notable individuals came to Gertrud Wallberg's defense, including Frida Voigts. In a letter to Mrs. Agnes von Boemcken, leader of the Women's League of the German Colonial Society in Berlin, Mrs. Voigts denied that she had ever disparaged Mrs. Wallberg; moreover, she praised the work that Gertrud Wallberg had done for the Windhoek chapter of the Women's League and said such criticisms were "ugly things" that she hoped would not be brought up again.[27] Her defense of Mrs. Wallberg was supported by the local chapter of the Women's League; indeed, the deputy leader of the chapter, Klara Drinkuth, said they would do everything they could to defend Gertrud Wallberg from these "infamous accusations."[28]

These personal attacks as well as the issue of Germania, Ltd., and the school association were drawn into the public spotlight. Meinert condemned Brenner's actions in his newspaper the *Allgemeine Zeitung* and demanded that Grönewald publicly apologize for his slanderous remarks at the school association's second assembly. Neuhaus and his associate, Keller, took Brenner to court over the issue of Germania. Foreign Office officials in Germany and the Southwestern National Socialists regretted such actions: they saw in them a danger to Deutschtum, much as colonists and colonial enthusiasts earlier believed that it was important to present a unified front vis-à-vis the Afrikaners as a demonstration of power. Besides, they considered the present issues an internal matter. Brückner, at the Foreign Office, commented that "it is extremely undesirable when quarrels among the Germans, such as the matters of the Germania, Ltd., come before South Africa courts."[29] Thus government officials in Germany informed the local consul to see to it that such public displays, in particular "the publications about the internal happenings within the Deutschtum, were stopped."[30] Eventually, in 1936, Berlin sent Justice Bach to arbitrate the Germania issue.[31]

While the Germans fought among themselves, tensions between the German community and the administration continued to deteriorate; in fact, the two conflicts undeniably reinforced each other.[32] In July 1934, local authorities made use of the new Criminal Law to ban the party (at the height of its power in SWA)[33] and its youth organization. The initial provocation for this action came from the "Day of German Youth" parade in Windhoek on July 8. More than eight hundred young Germans from South and Southwest Africa attended the event. The parade and participants' national socialist fighting songs and speeches, conducted in apparent homage to the Third Reich, provoked local authorities to act. They viewed the parade, as well as the activities of the Nazis in general, as pernicious and a threat to the peace and security of the region. The administration found it intolerable that naturalized Germans belonged to a party that owed allegiance to a foreign power. This incident further exacerbated relations between the Germans and the South Africans.[34] Despite the banning of the party, the South African government still allowed the Nazis to continue their activities, albeit in a decidedly less public manner.[35]

Prior to this event, the German members of the Legislative Assembly had already taken a step toward undermining relations between the two groups. In spring 1934, they gave up their seats. They did this out of protest over the renewed Afrikaner attempt to incorporate SWA into the Union in May. They also resigned from the Advisory Council and the executive. As a result, the UNSWP's resolution that SWA become an administrative unit of South Africa was able to pass. In the elections that followed, in October 1934, the Germans again fared poorly at the ballot box—undeniably because of the Germans' internal divisions and the Afrikaners' larger population. Of the twelve available seats, the Germans won only one. The United National Southwest Party gained eight seats; independents (one against and one for the UNSWP) won two; and the small Economic League gained one seat. In a move apparently meant to reflect population distribution in SWA, the administrator appointed four South Africans and only two Germans to the assembly. Thus the Afrikaners now enjoyed a two-thirds majority, which they promptly used to their advantage. Again they passed a resolution calling for the annexation of SWA by South Africa and passed it on to officials in the Union.[36]

The South African authorities reacted to the resolution in two ways. First, they responded through the administrator, Dr. Conradie, who maintained that South Africa had no interest in incorporating the mandate into the Union as a fifth province. He argued that the Union would not think of infringing upon its entrusted mandate. He further noted that the South African taxpayers would not want to assume the additional burden that would accompany any annexation, claiming that such a decision would be left to the people of Southwest Africa as soon as they had achieved the necessary degree of self-administration.[37] Premier Hertzog had made similar comments as early as 1932. Citing both legal and financial reasons, Hertzog said that annexation did not come into question as long as his party was in power.[38]

The other South African reaction was that the government set up a commission, the so-called Van Zyl Commission, to investigate the conditions in SWA.[39] The task of the commission was twofold. First, it was charged with ascertaining Southwest Africa's degree of preparedness for more self-determination. Second, it hoped to shed some light on the situation in the mandate that had led to the divisions between the two largest populations, the Afrikaners and the Germans. After forty-eight public meetings and 150 witnesses, including Germans (which the new German consul, Hans Oelhafen, described as "unreliable and not representative of the German population"),[40] on March 2, 1936, the commission announced its results. It concluded that the present form of government was a failure and should be replaced. After reading the report and receiving memoranda from the various communities, the Union government declared that it was not convinced that the current form of government was inappropriate and that it saw no reason to incorporate SWA into the Union in order to provide Union citizens with a greater degree of security. However, it agreed with the commission's assessment that relations between the two communities were "impossible."[41]

Indeed, especially within the German community, the government found the current situation intolerable. The DB currently stood under the leadership of a nonnaturalized German, M. Neuendorf (who swore allegiance to a foreign leader), and the South African authorities viewed the membership of naturalized Germans in the league as unacceptable—a position similar to the one it took toward the banned NSDAP. Once again, Germany, a foreign power, exercised undue influence upon Union citizens. The Union government argued that the influence was occasionally unwanted even by some Southwestern Germans and that coercion was often employed in order to obtain their support. This usually, they said, entailed slander, threats of economic and social reprisals, and action against relatives in Germany.[42] Such behavior was unwelcome in SWA, especially since the South African government demanded "from its citizens complete and undivided loyalty." Moreover, it refused to recognize the dual citizenship of its German citizens in SWA.[43]

The Van Zyl Commission and the banning of the Nazi Party resulted in renewed attempts within the German community to achieve some kind of unity. Prior to Weigel being expelled from SWA, he made the older leaders of the German population an offer: he asked Albert Voigts to resume leadership of the DB, with the guarantee that all NSDAP members would unconditionally follow his orders. Until Voigts accepted Weigel's offer in 1935, continuing personality problems led, earlier in the year, to the founding of the Nazi-oriented German Front *(Deutsche Front)* under Neuendorf's control. Voigts opposed this new organization and refused to accept Neuendorf as his second-in-command in the German League, despite party members' and consul von Oelhafen's trying to convince him otherwise. However, with the appearance of the Van Zyl Commission in SWA, a new impetus emerged with the German community to work toward some kind of unity. Especially after the elections and the banning of the NSDAP, Germans in SWA realized the weakness of their position. Consequently, the various German groups, with the assistance of Berlin, achieved a "palace peace": the German Front had to dissolve itself, and Voigts, for the time being, remained the head of the DB. However, as part of the agreement, in 1936 he had to turn it over to Neuendorf.[44]

Yet the German community's attempt to strengthen its own position merely exacerbated its relationship with the administration. After the Union government declared the unacceptability of a non-Union citizen as the head of an organization to which Union citizens belonged, on April 2, 1937, it passed the Southwest African Affairs Proclamation. The proclamation stipulated that only South African citizens could belong to a political organization—and Union citizens were forbidden to swear allegiance to a foreign power or its representatives. Furthermore, the South African government reserved the right to determine which organizations were political.[45]

The Union government's action resulted in widespread complaints from Germans in both Germany and SWA. The German League and the German members of the Legislative Assembly as well as the German government viewed these measures as a direct "political battle announcement against the Deutschtum" of SWA.[46] They claimed that such actions went against the terms of the London Agreement. The German government officially complained that the Germans never fully received cultural, political, linguistic, or, to a certain extent, economic equality, despite the existence of the London Agreement.[47] The German community saw the South African move as an attempt to divide it into two camps: those with British citizenship and those with German citizenship. To some Southwestern Germans, it was an obvious attempt to prevent them from establishing a unified and stronger German front against the administration.[48] It was even argued by one commentator that if any disagreements between segments of the German community existed, it was purely a German affair and none of the administration's business. This writer contended that such differences of opinion were normal among individuals with strong points of view and were in no way a result of one side trying to coerce the other[49]—an assessment that presumably did not take into consideration actions such as those taken against Wallberg and Neuhaus.

Anticipating that the government might declare the league a political organization, the DB tried to label itself as a cultural association. Meanwhile, naturalized Germans, like Dr. Hirsekorn (MdL), desired to establish the DB as an organization independent of Nazi influence and control. However, when the South African government categorized the German League as a political organization, it dissolved itself, against the will of Hirsekorn and other German legislators in the region.[50]

Many oldtimers welcomed this opportunity[51] and took advantage of it to create an organization free from Nazi influence and tied to the mandate. Hence, the naturalized Germans under Hirsekorn's leadership founded a new political organization, the *Deutscher Südwester Bund* (DSWB—German Southwest League) in August 1937. In conscious opposition to the National Socialists, the new association proclaimed "Southwest first," instead of stressing ties with Germany, and set upon a course of close and loyal cooperation with the mandatory government.[52] Nevertheless, like the DB before it, the DSWB aimed "to represent alone the political, cultural, social, and economic interests of the Deutschtum in SWA and to emphasize and strengthen the idea of unity in the Southwest Deutschtum."[53] Hirsekorn claimed that by December 1938 approximately fifteen hundred Germans had joined the organization.[54]

From the DSWB's inception, the German Foreign Office and the AO tried to bring it under the control of Berlin. They ordered Neuendorf and consul Oelhafen to work in that direction, moves that came to Hirsekorn's attention. He complained to the German envoy in Pretoria, Dr. Leitner, about this. Leitner replied merely that Hirsekorn and Oelhafen should try harder to work together. Eventually, Hirsekorn succumbed to the pressure. He agreed to prepare the DSWB ideologically and structurally for a reorientation along National Socialist lines. Beginning in 1939, Berlin ordered Hirsekorn to step down. Dressel, a naturalized member of the NSDAP, became the Southwest League's new leader.[55]

An important step in bringing the DSWB under Nazi control was its eventual close affiliation with the *Verband deutscher Berufsgruppen* (VdB—Union of German Vocational Groups). After the dissolution of the DB, Neuendorf worked to maintain the National Socialist presence in SWA. He did this by establishing several nonpolitical cultural associations and by eventually gaining control of the VdB, schools associations, the Women's League, the so-called Agricultural Chamber, and the German youth organizations. Because the VdB stood under strong Nazi control, it was able to exert a great deal of influence and pressure on Hirsekorn and the DSWB, which eventually helped bring increased Nazi control and influence into the Southwest League.[56]

Not all Southwestern Germans accepted this. They still rejected Nazi influences and saw Southwest Africa, not Germany, as their homeland. Because of their affinity for SWA and their desire to contribute to its future, they continued to demand equal treatment and rights. Consequently, they formed such parties and organizations as the *Deutsch-Afrikanische Partei,* or German-African Party, the SWA League, and the Volksdeutsche Group.[57] The first two included both Germans and Afrikaners as members.[58] Most of these organizations, in particular the German-African Party, openly opposed the Nazis, acknowledged the "just administration" of South-West Africa by the Union Government, and offered naturalized Germans the opportunity for loyal activity "'For our new home—for South West.'"[59]

The German invasion of Poland in September 1939 brought all German political activity in Southwest Africa to an end, however. On September 6, South Africa declared war on Germany. The South African government then banned various German organizations, including the Southwest League and the school associations. Many Germans were interned or placed under house arrest, and the authorities kept files on many Südwester because of their party affiliation or sympathies. The South Africans justified such actions with the claim that most naturalized Germans had played a double game throughout the interwar period, searching for advantages on both sides.[60]

In fact, considering the behavior of the Southwestern Germans during the 1930s, the South African response was not in the least surprising. The South African authorities had acted rather tolerantly and generously, especially over schools; they had met many of the German education demands, providing subsidies for the German private schools beyond their original pledge. Without a doubt, the Southwestern Germans tried to exact the most from their position, playing one side (Germany) against the other (South Africa).

Not all Southwestern Germans betrayed their loyalty to the Union. They saw their future in Southwest Africa. This land had become their new homeland. Nevertheless, the majority desired that the territory either be returned to Germany or be given at least a closer affiliation with the old homeland. Above all, they wanted to resist the annexation of efforts of the Afrikaner element in SWA. Even the older, more established individuals, people such as Voigts and Hirsekorn, pursued this goal.[61] They were not as radical or militant as the younger, newly arrived generation, but they shared a common aim with them. They disagreed over the means to achieve their goals[62] and over what it ultimately meant to be a German, but the nationalistic component of Nazism and Hitler's gains in revising the hated Treaty of Versailles proved appealing to those desiring a return to the "glory" days of the German Empire. It was no wonder that the relatively small group of core National Socialists in the region were able to exercise considerable influence on the local German population and its organizations.

There were, however, limitations on the influence exercised by the Nazis in Southwest Africa. As Hagemann has noted, these included the lack of a coherent policy in the mandate because of the multiplicity of offices in Germany, generational differences within the Southwestern German community, a continuous loyalty conflict resulting from the legal construction of the mandate system, and poor decision making by individuals.[63] One must add to the list the dubious tactics—including coercion—employed by the Nazis to enforce compliance with their views. More importantly, there were the virulent attempts to discredit respected, long-standing members of the German community. While argued in terms of National Socialist ideology, these assaults were often motivated by personal ambition. How, some Südwester asked themselves, could people like the Wallbergs and other members of the school board not be good Germans? They had devoted years of their lives in service to the German community. The attacks undeniably turned some Südwester away from the Nazis and, ultimately, from Germany. They, more than ever, came to realize that their future lay in Southwest Africa, not in Germany.

Long-term inhabitants concluded that their definition of Deutschtum differed from that of the Nazis. However, it was difficult to resist the Nazis, as the example of Hirsekorn and the German Southwest League illustrated. Even though Hirsekorn tried to develop an organization tied to the mandate and representing the naturalized Germans, he was ultimately unable to resist the pressures coming from Germany. Nonetheless, some did resist, and even established new, independent parties such as the German-African Party and the Volksdeutsche Group. Some even volunteered for Union military service after the South African declaration of war. They fully expressed their affinity for Southwest Africa, even if it was under South African control. Nonetheless, this affinity remained problematic for many Southwestern Germans, including those who had lived there for decades and had strong ties to the region.

Conclusion

From Southwestern Germans to
German Südwester

The position of SWA Germans during the war was precarious at best. Many were interned in South Africa or placed under house arrest. In 1942 the Union government took away the British citizenship of automatically naturalized Germans. The new law extended even to their children (even if they had obtained British citizenship *jus soli* in other countries), to their wives (even if they were divorced), and to their widows, regardless of whether they were British citizens before the marriage (the law did, however, exclude those who willingly volunteered for military duty). Although the Southwestern Afrikaners desired even harsher measures, not all South Africans welcomed the denaturalization laws. In the realm of education, however, the situation remained the same as antebellum: both German medium classes and German private schools continued to exist.[1]

At the end of hostilities in Europe, the situation for Germans in SWA remained tenuous. For example, in 1945 Smuts abolished all German private schools and medium classes as well as German as a language of instruction in the Southwestern educational system; and the South African authorities established a commission in 1946 to determine which citizens of German descent they should expel from the Union and the mandate; they feared a possible revival of National Socialist agitation. The commission investigated individuals who had been active National Socialists or sympathizers or who threatened the security of South Africa in the interests of another state. Altogether, the commission reviewed 5,283 cases, the majority of which were Southwestern German foreigners. It recommended the deportation of 254 of them, including 197 Südwester. However, legislative and jurisprudential action delayed the expulsions, and, although the government overcame these obstacles, the general elections in May 1948 changed the political land-scape in South Africa to the benefit of the Germans. The new government, headed by Dr. Malan and his National Party (NP), revoked the expulsion de-crees. In 1949, Malan even made it easier for those Germans who had lost their citizenship in 1942 to regain it.[2]

These were merely the first steps in the reconciliation between the South Africans and Southwestern Deutschtum. In fact, the NP's election vic-tory marked a decisive moment in the history of South and Southwest Africa: Malan made the Südwester "a pillar in the new social order to be established"—the "new social order" being apartheid. Thus, "banned and lawless individuals [the German Südwester] turned into privileged mem-bers of the apartheid society."[3]

In the years following World War II, both Germans and Afrikaans achieved more of their goals than they had through years of opposition. In 1948, when Malan was visiting Windhoek, the Germans declared their loy-alty to the Union and their commitment to working toward a closer union between SWA and South Africa. They also declared their desire not to be treated as foreigners and enemies. Malan's warm reception of their declara-tion signaled a further step toward cooperation between South Africans and Germans and the development of SWA as a "white man's country." Even the opposition leader, Smuts, agreed that the Germans should be treated gener-ously. Until about the mid-1970s, the German community supported Ma-lan's National Party in SWA. With the assistance of the German votes, the NP replaced the United National Southwest Party as the dominant political force in the mandate. However, except in the realm of education and lan-guage and their electoral loyalty to the NP, most remained politically inac-tive. An attempt by the NP to engage the Southwestern Germans in political campaigns failed. Most were satisfied by the guarantee of linguistic and cul-ture autonomy that a parliamentary resolution granted them.[4]

The Southwest African administration made several concessions in the realm of language and culture. It reintroduced German medium classes and financial support for the German private schools in Windhoek, Lüderitz Bay, and Karibib and also agreed to improve German language instruction in the German medium classes (the high school in Windhoek was permitted to offer both the matriculation exam and the Abitur, Lüderitz Bay provided the matriculation exam, and the school in Karibib resembled an elementary and middle school), and in 1958 the SWA Legislative Assembly passed a resolu-tion that raised German to being the third administrative language.[5]

Many of these changes, of course, came at the insistence of Southwestern Germans, a number of whom became active in political life. In 1958, Frey, the former school inspector, was appointed second Southwest African representative in the South African senate, and in the territory's second postwar election, Sartorius von Bach became the first German elected, postwar, to the Legislative Assembly. Several other Germans were active on commissions and in local government.[6]

In essence, the South African government under Malan bought the Southwestern German community's loyalty by guaranteeing them a special position in the new apartheid system. The Germans gained their linguistic and cultural independence in exchange for supporting Malan's program and securing his party as the party of SWA. The Germans were moved in this direction by their failures in the years before the war and by their war experiences. Although the Germans had been interned during the war, the South Africans subsequently treated them with respect and generosity. Out of gratitude for these concessions and this treatment, the Germans agreed to support the National Party.

But the Germans continued to distance themselves from the Afrikaners, believing themselves to be culturally and linguistically superior to their partners in apartheid. They even pointed out their long cultural tradition and its ties to Germany. At the same time, the Southwestern Germans viewed the Germans in Europe—the Germans of the Federal Republic—as outsiders. They saw them as people living in a decadent society and driven by material concerns. To the Southwest Deutschtum, the Federal Republic was a continuation of the industrial society of the nineteenth century from which their forefathers had escaped to create an idyllic image of Germany.[7]

Beginning in the 1960s, there was a further change in the Southwestern Germans' position toward the NP, and politics in general, as the pressure for Namibian independence and the abolition of the apartheid system grew. Around 1960–61 the National Party lost some votes to the newly founded Southwest Party, which campaigned for the full independence of Namibia from South Africa. However, it never enjoyed much electoral success. Most Germans never took the party seriously, and those who had left the NP returned after events in the Belgian Congo convinced them that their future was more secure with a party that guaranteed them a privileged position in society based upon their skin color.[8]

However, international pressure for Namibian independence and an end to apartheid increased in the 1970s. In the face of this pressure and the collapse of the Portuguese colonial empire in 1974–75, many Southwestern Germans realized that the end of white rule in SWA was nearing. The Southwestern Deutschtum reacted to this situation with "a careful politicalization"—essentially moved by selfish and material interests. According to Rüdiger, their "apolitical fatalistic attitude yielded to a real political position with the goal of preserving their material existence and cultural autonomy . . . in an independent Namibia."[9] However, when such behavior took the Southwestern German sensibility across apparently unacceptable lines, such as talks with the black national independence group, SWAPO (the South West African People's Organization of Namibia), most Germans reacted negatively. In fact, the German community was divided on this issue, even though they had a strong group consciousness.[10]

As in the interwar years (and even in the colonial period), it took an apparent threat to the Südwester position and status in society to force them into action. However, like the 1920s and 1930s, they could reach no political consensus. Most were uncertain what role they would play in the future independent Namibia. Some felt they would not have any significant role to play; nor were they sure what role they wanted to play. The majority, despite political abstinence, expressed opposition to "a perpetuation of the apartheid" as well as a rejection of "a seizure of power by SWAPO."[11]

Political abstinence and indecisiveness are distinctive features of German Southwesterndom. They are among the several characteristics that distinguish them from their kin in Germany and what makes them German Südwester and not just Southwestern Germans. These characteristics are the result of formative experiences while living for decades in the region—a process that began during the colonial period and was continued through the interwar and post-WWII years. In the years of German rule, cultural elites attempted to create an unrealistic image of Deutschtum that was supposed to act as a model for the old homeland. They had an intense desire to construct a preindustrial, agrarian vision of Germany bereft of the divisions Germany was suffering as a result of industrialization and nineteenth-century unification. In order to achieve their goal, they pursued directed policies of colonization, inclusion and exclusion, and education. Hence, they advocated the settlement of the educated and propertied classes, and they especially sought women, who as immigrant carriers of culture were supposed to act as guarantors of Deutschtum. They also built schools and replicated German social life in the colony.

To a degree, they were successful. The colonial authorities and supporters of the colonial movement worked to settle segments of the middle Stand, especially educated and well-situated individuals. They could not prevent other segments of the middle and lower Stand (shopkeepers, craftsmen, small-scale farmers) from settling in the colony; nor could they deny former servicemen the right to settle in the protectorate; nevertheless, they created a situation where farmers' interests were paramount even though farmers did not constitute a majority of the population. The colony thus exhibited a decidedly agrarian, nonindustrial character, and the cultural elites believed that the presence of educated and propertied individuals would provide an example to the "other" settlers; they assumed that those below would follow. They held that the middle Stand and those raised to that status—regardless of whether at the upper-middle or lower-middle level—had mutual interests and mutual goals; unfortunately, as their line of reasoning went, not all elements of this group *knew* what they wanted or knew how to comport themselves. "It was the upper-class landowner and not the 'man in the street' . . . who seemed the safest guarantee of this status."[12] It therefore required a transplanted cultural elite to provide a correct model and remind the men and women "of the street" of their responsibilities.

Similarly, as the cultural elite was to be a model for the rest of the SWA German population, Southwest Africa was to be a model for the old homeland. The Südwester claimed that their hospitality, nationalism, nonpartisanship, and loyalty far exceeded the level of those qualities in the Heimat: the homeland, they believed, could learn from them. This applied even in the realm of religion and confessional difference. "There is no room in the local public life for religious particularism. Shouldn't that also be the case in Germany!"[13] The Südwester also made great strides in overcoming the social and regional cleavages that existed in Germany. Though primarily from the middle class, the settlers came from many different regional, professional, and social backgrounds, yet due to the presence of Africans, and even Afrikaners, they were able to achieve a degree of unity.

Such claims and boasts ignored certain realities, however. Appeals to racial unity could, to a degree, enforce conformity within the European community. But this did not hide the fact that divisions existed. So, although the German press appealed to Südwester to consider the common good,[14] SWA, like other settler colonies and the old homeland,[15] suffered from professional and social divisions. Indeed, the various groups that constituted Southwestern society had different interests and wants. Each tried to influence colonial policy for its own benefit. Farmers wanted the colonial government to support agriculture and give them complete power over the African population; businessmen, traders, and craftsmen desired policies that would not restrict them in their endeavors. In order to better represent their various positions, the different groups formed professional associations and had the regional newspapers represent their particular interests. Even among farmers differences existed: large landowners and small homesteaders competed with each other for government assistance. And government officials and missionaries also had their own agendas regarding the African population.[16]

A further factor that affected relationships was length of stay in the colony. Those who lived there for a longer time were called "Old Africans" (*alte Afrikaner*). Dr. Ludwig Külz, a visiting physician, noted that these individuals had an inclination to present themselves as "all-knowing":

> About every theme . . . he knows completely everything and is filled with extreme indignation to hear a deviating opinion. . . . Disagreement is the only means with which he can be most appallingly irritated, especially when the opposition comes from someone who perhaps first came a few months after him into the colony. That is a capital offense.[17]

Külz described such old-timers' feelings toward the colony as unconditional "patriotism."[18] In contrast to the "old Africans" there were "salon Africans" (*Salonafrikaner*), a type that was said to have a "parasitical nature" that could only do the colony harm. Such people, it was said, hoped to obtain after a short stay in the colony advantages that they could utilize in Germany. The "salon Africans" were given the status of guests and were obviously looked down on by the "old Africans."[19]

Thus, in fact, even among the colony's cultural elites—government and military officials and the educated and propertied individual—tensions and divisions ruled as they did in Germany. Indeed, the German Mittelstand— "actually a congeries of social groups with different, sometimes conflicting, interests"[20]—was certainly to be found in SWA. Moreover, as in Germany, confessionalism played a role in Southwestern society, too, although tensions were not as pronounced as in Germany. To a large degree this was due to the colony's strong Protestant character. For example, in 1911, 80 percent of the population was Protestant, while only 17.2 percent was Roman Catholic (the remaining 2.8 percent belonged to other confessions).[21] Nevertheless, confessionalism existed, as evidenced by the colonial administration's stringent supervision of the Catholic schools in Windhoek.

Even though Southwestern Germans claimed to be "true" representatives of German culture, they in fact embodied a hybrid of it conditioned by years of living in the colony. The premise of their right to rule over the indigenous populations and expropriate their land was based on skin color. In many respects, it allowed individuals to attain a status that they would not have otherwise experienced in Germany. Thus the situation and conditions in Southwest Africa differed substantially from those in Germany and made it practically impossible for the homeland to emulate them.

Equally important to the inadequacy of SWA as a model was the fixed and narrow nature of the Deutschtum promoted and maintained there. It ostensibly embodied only a specific, middle-class ideal responding to local conditions. The rules for inclusion assumed a cultural rigidity, and members of the white community could constantly refer to it, especially when an individual transgressed or new settlers arrived. Noncompliance with the norms meant expulsion, while new arrivals had a set of guidelines to follow for acceptance into the community. More important, Südwester used these sociocultural standards to distinguish themselves from the African population, as did white settlers elsewhere (e.g., in Kenya and Southern Rhodesia). Dane Kennedy wrote that

> settler culture . . . was preeminently the expression of the white community's tenuously held position of a predominance in the colonial order. The power to shape and control social identity, to determine the distinctions between themselves and others, was crucial to that predominance. The consequences were profoundly conservative. Although circumstances altered the cultural context of white immigrant's lives, the change followed no linear course of accommodation. No harmonious adjustment of traditional values to new conditions, no integration with Africa, of white with black, took place. On the contrary, the central feature of the settler culture was its renunciation and repression of any substantive adaption to the host environment, its avoidance of contact and interchange with the indigenous population. It was characterized above all by the effort to isolate and institutionalize white settlement within a rigid set of physical, linguistic, social, economic and political boundaries.[22]

However, in SWA, unlike the conditions Kennedy described in Kenya and

Southern Rhodesia, the presence of Afrikaners added a nationalistic content. Southwestern culture was thus not just an expression of *white* identity, but of *white German* identity, vis-à-vis black Africans, the Afrikaners (a mixed race), and white, non-German nationalities. The German community did adapt to the local conditions in some respects, developing a Southwestern identity as unique as a Bavarian or Saxon one,[23] even though SWA did not enjoy as high a degree of independence or autonomy as Bavaria and Saxony.

It was a specific notion of German culture that the Southwest Germans attempted to preserve. The Deutschtum established and maintained in SWA generally corresponded to a middle-class, agrarian ideal of Germany, one ostensibly bereft of the social, regional, and confessional cleavages caused by industrialization and the unfulfilled "national" unification. Urban and discordant images were conspicuously absent from the Southwestern landscape. The elites in both SWA and Germany ostensibly resisted all attempts to change their cultural definition of Deutschtum. This apparent inflexibility and petrification of "German" ideals in the protectorate caused the Südwester to experience "cultural involution."[24] They believed that they were preserving an ideal version of Deutschtum, while the old homeland underwent unwanted and disruptive change. "This was the distinguishing feature of settler culture; not in the cherished values of the settlers' European heritage, but in the centripetal forces that distorted that heritage by securing it against all change."[25]

Yet they themselves and their notion of German culture did evolve. Even as they fixated upon a preindustrial, organic image of Germany, an idyllic, imagined time in Germany's past bereft of the problems besetting Wilhelmine Germany, the local conditions influenced and affected their identity. They were indeed Germans, but with a decidedly Southwest African twist. They exhibited vulgar racism, an almost frenetic nationalism and fanatical devotion to the emperor, parsimony, diligence, an unfettered individualism (however fictitious this actually was), and an adherence to an idealized notion of Germany's past that rejected the "discord" caused by modernization.

This Southwestern reification of Deutschtum continued through the interwar period after Germany lost possession of the territory. However, one aspect of Southwestern identity did not remain static—namely, their affinity for the land, Southwest Africa. Thus, on the one hand, the Germans of SWA desired to return, to reestablish a connection with the old Heimat after the region had come under the control of South Africa, either as German colony again or as an autonomous state with strong ties to the Reich. In fact, the presence of a foreign "master" and the increasing number of Afrikaner and colonial British immigrants actually thrust them into a situation where they felt compelled to express and preserve their Deutschtum. The fact that the Southwestern Germans had, from their own perspective (and leaving out of account that they enjoyed more rights and privileges than the African population), become second-class citizens differentiated their experience from that of other European settlers. So, while the British were consolidating their position in Rhodesia and Kenya, for example, the Germans were fighting to regain their former position of dominance.

Interestingly, they employed many of the same tactics that they had used during the German colonial period. They founded organizations to represent their interests, such as the German League and the Territorial School Union. They were also assisted in their efforts by organizations in Germany, such as the Women's League and the German Colonial Society, as well as government ministries and agencies. Yet the Südwester realized that their activities in the realm of culture had no value if they did not also venture into the political arena. Unlike the colonial period, when Germany utilized military force to subjugate the indigenous population, the country's defeat in the World Wars made such an avenue to reconquering the region impossible. Consequently, they fought through petitions and local elections for the position they felt they deserved and the recognition of German as the third administrative language.

On the other hand, the Southwestern German community slowly realized that its future lay nowhere but in Southwest Africa. The activities of the older generation were indicative of this. They realized they needed to secure their future and that of their children. Some parents allowed their children to take the South African matriculation exam. They were willing to work with South African officials to ameliorate their position. In addition, not all German clubs were exclusively for Germans. There was a growing number of nationally mixed associations. In the years before World War II, some Germans even founded organizations that declared their attachment to SWA, such as Hirsekorn's Southwest League (at least, initially), the Volksdeutsche Group, and the German-African Party.

Another outward expression of affinity for the country was the "Southwestern Song" ("Das Südwesterlied").[26] Composed in 1937 by Heinz Klein-Werner, until 1989 (the year before Namibian independence) the song essentially achieved the status of a national anthem among Germans and Afrikaner in Namibia. Originally, Klein-Werner wanted to provide the Pathfinders with a song that related directly to Southwest Africa instead of one that was tailored for Germany.[27] He was concerned that members of the local Pathfinder chapter in Tsumeb could not identify with the old German songs: "Our old German Pathfinder and country songs *[Landsknechtslieder]* essentially did not say much to a young Südwester." He believed that if the joy in singing was to survive for young people, it had to be with songs "with whose words they [young people] could imagine something." One Saturday afternoon, he wrote the three verses of "The Southwestern Song":[28]

> Hard like camel-thorn wood is our country
> and dry are its river beds.
> The crags, they are burned by the sun
> and shy are the animals in the thicket.
> And should someone ask us:
> What holds you then here fast?
> We could only say:
> We love Southwest!

> But our love is paid dearly
> despite everything, we won't leave you,
> because our worries are eclipsed
> by the bright shining light of the sun.
> And should someone ask us:
> What holds you then here fast?
> We could only say:
> We love Southwest!

> And come you yourself into our land
> and have seen its ranges,
> and have our sun burn you in the heart,
> then can you no longer go.
> And should someone ask you:
> What holds you then here fast?
> You could only say:
> I love Southwest![29]

The song "transmitted a concrete picture of Namibia and the affective relationship of German Namibians to 'their' country." Focused on the region's vegetation, climate, and animals, not people and political events, it transmitted "a subjective feeling of belonging to the land and a special understanding of it."[30]

On a subconscious level, the Southwestern Germans distanced themselves from Germany. They expressed pride in their Deutschtum, yet that Deutschtum was strongly connected to the region—Southwest Africa, which after 1990 came to be known as Namibia. They were wary of conditions in the old homeland. They abhorred the Weimar political system with its multitude of special interest political parties and went to great pains to prevent a similar occurrence in SWA and thus preserve at least a façade of harmony within the German population. Some parents were especially concerned that their children might be exposed to undesirable modes of thinking in Germany, such as socialism and Marxism. They therefore established a continuing education school for women in the mandate in order to "spare" young Southwestern German women from elements foreign to their notion of Deutschtum.

However, the situation was exacerbated by the entry of younger Germans and later by the appearance in the mandate of National Socialism. Although the community was united linguistically and culturally, it could not agree politically. Essentially divided into two camps, it split along generational lines. In general, both sides agreed that they wanted a return to Germany, someday, yet they disagreed over the best means and the time frame. The older generation, more pragmatic, attempted to achieve its aims (e.g., introducing German as an administrative language) by working with South African officials; the newcomers, more aggressive and antagonistic, advocated open agitation and an immediate return to the Reich. The founding of the NSDAP chapter in SWA, and Hitler's seizure of power in Germany, exacerbated the tensions, not only among the Southwestern Germans but also between them and the South Africans. In the ensuing struggle over which organization should represent the German population, the German League or the NSDAP chapter, attempts were made to achieve some semblance of unity, but complications such as communication difficulties, caused by the multiplicity of offices in Germany, further exacerbated the situation. The organizational and generational conflicts often degenerated into expressions of pettiness and hubris; for example, the younger, more nationalist group often called into question the older generation's ability to represent the German community.

Ultimately, the internal conflicts and the open agitation by the Nazis weakened the German position in SWA. A steady increase in the Afrikaner population further threatened the German situation, but the Germans contributed significantly to their own political demise. Prior to 1939, the South

Africans began banning various German organizations, including the DB and the NSDAP. With the outbreak of World War II, the South Africans banned the remaining ones, such as the Women's League, the various youth organizations, and the school associations. In a sense, this was repayment for the German community's apparent lack of loyalty and gratitude to the concessions and leniency shown to it by the South Africans. When, after the war, Malan came to power, the German population's lot improved. Realizing that their destiny was intimately tied to Southwest Africa's, the Germans, in return for cultural autonomy, agreed to support the National Party's program of apartheid. Smuts finally achieved his dream of a "white" colony, albeit under the auspices of his political opponents.

The German/South African cooperation was limited to the Germans' tacit political support of the NP in elections; at other times, the Germans, relishing their autonomy, kept to themselves, venturing only seldom into the realm of politics, and when they did, very often insecurely. In fact, they used their cultural independence to distance themselves from the region's two other main groups of inhabitants: the Afrikaners and, especially, the Africans. Equally important, they distinguished themselves from the Federal Republic's Germans as well, seeing in them everything their ancestors abhorred about Weimar and Wilhelmine Germany. The Germanies of both past and present no longer corresponded to their idea of Deutschtum. Throughout their decades in SWA, they had made great efforts to create and maintain a particular vision of what it meant to be German, and although this vision did not accurately reflect the Germany they had left, the Southwestern environment enabled them to realize much of it. Thus, while Germany moved along a particular path, the Germans in Southwest Africa moved along another.

The Germans in SWA believed that their image of Deutschtum was the correct one. It was, anyway, one that became intimately associated with the region. Through their actions and behavior, they became German Südwester. They still maintained a sense of Deutschtum, but a Germanness grounded in Southwest Africa. Originally part of a sociocultural experiment, these German settlers adapted to and were influenced by the colonial environment. Thus, policies originally intended to create a particular vision of Deutschtum failed in one important aspect: because of the local conditions, as well as time itself, the Southwestern Germans transferred their affinity from the old homeland to the new one.

This has become especially significant since Namibia gained its independence in 1990. The years of apartheid and their cooperation with the

South African regime have placed a black cloud over the German community. Taking into consideration their behavior over the years since 1884, their attitudes toward the black African population have not been not surprising. They came to question the system, but they could not agree on the best means to effect change. They were hindered by an anachronistic value and norm system, political inflexibility, and a strong, self-conscious demarcation vis-à-vis people of other skin colors. Today, as Namibia moves forward, facing many of the same problems that confront South Africa in the postapartheid era, so, as part of Namibia, do the Germans. They see themselves as "part and parcel" of Namibia; Namibia is their Heimat.[31] So far, the German Namibians have benefitted from the national policy of reconciliation and the absence of any fundamental economic and social changes.[32] However, they are still faced with significant questions: Will they maintain their political reticence? Will they still cling to their idyllic, historicized past? The questions are interrelated. Will German history in its current manifestation prove to be a stumbling block to the productive and healthy development of the country?

For the Heimat, Germany, too, these questions remain relevant. Indeed, in the twenty-first century, as Germany still wrestles with national unification, which vision of Germanness will prevail? As the demographics of Europe change, with increasing numbers of people from non-Western states arriving in the European Union, how will Germans respond? As is evidenced by the new dual-citizenship law and growing discussions about multiculturalism, this is an evolving situation.

Epilogue

This study has examined the German experience and German settler colonialism in Southwest Africa, but several relevant issues require further investigation. For instance, *Creating Germans Abroad* makes only limited use of materials detailing the experiences in other European settler colonials. Most comparisons in this book are made with Southern Rhodesia and Kenya, with occasional references to Indochina; in only a few instances are comparisons made to the situations in the other German colonies, which for the most part were colonies of a different type or types, the one exception being German East Africa (present-day Tanzania), and even there the colonial experience differed from that of Southwest Africa. Moreover, while this study refers to the colonial movement in Germany, it does not fully address the scope of the endeavor. The linkage between the domestic rhetoric of imperialism and its application, as in the case of Southwest Africa, remains tenuous at best.

I am addressing these issues in a new project that broadens the scope of study to include not only the situation in Germany's other colonies (e.g., Togo, East Africa, Samoa) but also settler experiences in South America, North America, South Africa, and the Middle East. My current work bridges the gap between the extant research on the connections between imperialism and nationalism that dominated German political culture and the experience of German settler communities that attempted to realize those nationalistic aspirations: it situates German settler colonialism in a larger context—not only that of German imperialism and nationalism but settler colonialism more generally.

Notes

INTRODUCTION

1. For competing explanations of Bismarck's decision to embark upon colonial expansion, see Hartmut Pogge von Strandmann, "Domestic Origins of Germany's Colonial Expansion under Bismarck," *Past and Present* 42 (Feb. 1969): 140–59; and Hans-Ulrich Wehler, "Bismarck's Imperialism, 1862–1890," *Past and Present* 48 (Aug. 1970): 119–55.

2. For instance, see Daniel Bivona, *Desire and Contradiction: Imperial Visions and Domestic Debates in Victorian Literature* (Manchester, U.K.: Manchester University Press, 1990); John MacKenzie, *Propaganda and Empire: The Manipulation of British Public Opinion, 1880–1960* (Manchester, U.K.: Manchester University Press, 1984); MacKenzie, ed., *Imperialism and Popular Culture* (Manchester, U.K.: Manchester University Press, 1986); David Spurr, *The Rhetoric of Empire: Colonial Discourse in Journalism, Travel Writing, and Imperial Administration* (Durham, N.C.: Duke University Press, 1994); and Robert H. MacDonald, *The Language of Empire: Myths and Metaphors of Popular Imperialism, 1880–1918* (Manchester, U.K.: Manchester University Press, 1994). With regard to Germany, see, for example, Woodruff Smith, *The Ideological Origins of Nazi Imperialism* (New York: Oxford University Press, 1986); Susanne Zantop, *Colonial Fantasies: Conquest, Family, and Nation in Precolonial Germany, 1770–1870* (Durham, N.C.: Duke University Press, 1997); Sara Friedrichsmeyer, Sara Lennox, and Susanne Zantop, eds., *The Imperialist Imagination: German Colonialism and Its Legacy* (Ann Arbor: University of Michigan Press, 1998).

3. Works that had a strong influence on my conceptualization of the creation of an identity include Benedict Anderson, *Imagined Communities: Reflections on the Origins and Spread of Nationalism*, rev. ed. (London: Verso, 1991); Leroy Vail, ed., *The Creation of Tribalism in Southern Africa* (Berkeley: University of California Press, 1991); and Eugeen Roosens, *Creating Ethnicity: The Process of Ethnogenesis*, Frontiers of Anthropology, 5 (Newbury Park: Sage, 1989).

4. Most works, however, explore the larger, longer-established settler colonies (e.g., South Africa, Australia) or focus on anthropological phenomena or environmental issues; e.g., see Donald Denoon, *Settler Capitalism: The Dynamics of Dependent Development in the Southern Hemisphere* (Oxford: Clarendon Press, 1983); Tom Griffiths and Libby Robin, eds., *Ecology and Empire: Environmental History of Settler Societies* (Seattle: University of Washington Press, 1997); and Patrick Wolfe, *Settler Colonialism and the Transformation of Anthropology: The Politics and Poetics of an Ethnographic Event* (London: Cassel, 1999).

5. For a discussion of this notion of "incompleteness," see Theodor Schieder, "Grundfragen der neueren Geschichte," *Historische Zeitschrift* 192 (1961): 1–16; see also James Sheehan, "What Is German History? Reflections on the Role of the *Nation* in German History and Historiography," *Journal of Modern History* 53, no. 1 (1981): 16, 22; Roger Chickering, "Language and the Social Foundations of Radical Nationalism in the Wilhelmine Era," in *1870/71–1989/90 German Unifications and the Change of Literary Discourse*, ed. Walter Pape (Berlin; New York: Walter de Gruyter, 1993), 76–77; and Geoff Eley, "State Formation, Nationalism, and Political Culture: Some Thoughts on the Unification of Germany," in *From Unification to Nazism: Reinterpreting the German Past* (Boston: Allen & Unwin, 1986), 61–84. For an explanation and examination of these cleavages, see Stanley Suval, *Electoral Politics in Wilhelmine Germany* (Chapel Hill: University of North Carolina Press, 1985), 4–6, 8; and Thomas Childers, *The Nazi Voter: The Social Foundations of Fascism in Germany, 1919–1933* (Chapel Hill: University of North Carolina Press, 1983), 15–26.

6. A discussion of the various uses of colonialism in Germany can be found in Kenneth Holston's "A Measure of the Nation: Colonial Enthusiasm, Education, and Politics in Germany, 1890–1936," Ph.D. diss., University of Pennsylvania, 1996.

7. Several noteworthy studies examine German colonialism in Namibia, but none of them take a sociocultural approach or consider the period covered by this book. Helmut Bley's work comes closest: Helmut Bley, *South-West Africa under German Rule, 1894–1914*, trans. Hugh Ridley (Evanston, Ill.: Northwestern University Press, 1971); Horst Drechsler, *"Let Us Die Fighting": The Struggle of the Nama and Herero against German Imperialism*, trans. Bernd Zollner (London: Zed Press, 1980). For more recent contributions, see Lora Wildenthal, "Colonizers and Citizens: Bourgeois Women and the Woman Question in the German Colonial Movement, 1886–1914," Ph.D. diss., University of Michigan, 1994; and Krista O'Donnell, "The Colonial Woman Question: Gender, National Identity, and Empire in the German Colonial Society Female Emigration Program, 1896–1914," Ph.D. diss., State University of New York, Binghamton, 1996.

8. The term *Deutschtum* eludes translation. Roughly, it means Germandom or Germanness; it not only connotes German culture, customs, and traditions but can also refer to a German population, usually in a place outside of Germany. Loose translations of the word are wholly inadequate, and in this study, *Deutschtum* itself will primarily be used. *Heimat* translates best as home or homeland, possessing connotations of both. It can refer to a local or regional home or even to one's nation.

9. Dane Kennedy, *Islands of White: Settler Society and Culture in Kenya and Southern Rhodesia* (Durham, N.C.: Duke University Press, 1987).

10. For an examination of the ideological underpinnings of German colonialism, see Woodruff D. Smith, "The Ideology of German Colonialism, 1840–1906," *Journal of Modern History* 46, no. 4 (1974): 641–62; however, Smith's article does not explore the notion of "experimentation" being argued here; in other words, Smith does not fully explore how these ideologies were realized, especially aspects of the "emigrationist" theory.

11. The German word *Stand* translates best into the preindustrial term *estate,* or *rank,* not *class.* The word is based on professional status, not economics, and was used frequently by contemporaries. In historical works it is often used interchangeably with the word *class,* but this study will limit itself to its contemporary usage.

12. Richard V. Pierard, in his "The German Colonial Society, 1882–1914" (Ph.D. diss., State University of Iowa, 1964) provides a standard, though not too insightful, account into the structure and social composition of the organization. For an outstanding analysis of middle Stand character of patriotic organizations, in particular the Pan-German League, see Roger Chickering's *We Men Who Feel Most German: A Cultural Study of the Pan-German League, 1886–1914* (London: Allen & Unwin, 1984) as well as his "Language and the Social Foundations of Radical Nationalism," 76–77. Regarding the supposed nonpartisan nature of the colonial movement, see Holston, "Measure of the Nation."

13. In Namibia, the term *Southwesterners* is a neologism; the more appropriate *Südwester* will be used when referring to German Namibians before Namibian independence.

14. Others view this transformation as taking place later in the mandate years or after World War II, taking only a cursory look at what I believe to be the formative years of the colonial period. For these alternative interpretations, see Klaus H. Rüdiger, *Die Namibia-Deutschen: Geschichte einer Nationalität im Werden* (Stuttgart: Franz Steiner, 1993); Brigitta Schmidt-Lauber, *Die abhängigen Herren: Deutsche Identität in Namibia* (Hamburg: Lit, 1993).

15. Like Southwest Africa, Kenya and Southern Rhodesia, which contained small, rather homogeneous white enclaves within a significantly larger black population, were the primary settler colonies of the metropolitan power (with the exception of South Africa, but it had a "much longer colonial history and a more factionalized white population") and were acquired at the end of the nineteenth century; Kennedy, *Islands of White,* 1–2, 11.

16. Although contemporary Germans used the term *Boer* to refer to the seventeenth-century Dutch descendants living in South Africa, I use the currently more viable term, which today refers to white South Africans who speak Afrikaans; I do, however retain the contemporary *Boer* in quotations to help maintain the integrity of the cited individual's *Weltanschauung* and, hence, a better sense of the times under consideration.

17. Several studies exist that explore political and legal developments during this period; see Werner Bertelsmann, *Die deutsche Sprachgruppe Südwestafrikas*

in Politik und Recht seit 1915 (Windhoek: SWA Wissenschaftliche Gesellschaft, 1979), and Adolf Hagemann, *Südafrika und das "Dritte Reich": Rassenpolitische Affinität und machtpolitische Rivalität* (Frankfurt: Campus, 1989). Two other German historians have written articles about National Socialism in SWA: Heinrich Stuebel, "Die Entwicklung des Nationalsozialismus in Südwestafrika," *Vierteljahrsheft für Zeitgeschichte* 1, no. 2 (1953): 170–76, and Horst Kühne, "Die Fünfte Kolonne des faschistischen deutschen Imperialismus in Südwestafrika (1933–1939)," *Zeitschrift für Geschichtswissenschaft* 8, no. 4 (1960): 765–80. Stuebel's article suffers from a lack of thorough investigation; Kühne's allows a strong adherence to Marxist theories of interpretation to convolute his study.

18. Several studies investigate minorities, including German ones. Although they are studies of other regions and time periods, they nevertheless provide useful insights into the dynamics involved in the formation of minority-group identities; e.g., see Gary B. Cohen, *The Politics of Ethnic Survival: Germans in Prague, 1861–1914* (Princeton: Princeton University Press, 1981); Anders H. Hendriksson, "The Riga German Community: Social Change and the Nationality Question, 1860–1905," Ph.D. diss., University of Toronto, 1978; John A. Armstrong, "Mobilized Diaspora in Tsarist Russia: The Case of the Baltic Germans," in *Soviet Nationality Policies and Practices,* ed. Jeremy R. Azrael (New York: Praeger, 1978), 63–104; Gert Kroeger, "Zur Situation der baltischen Deutschen," *Zeitschrift für Ostforschung* 17 (1968): 601–32.

CHAPTER 1

1. For an account of these early years, see Woodruff D. Smith, *The German Colonial Empire* (Chapel Hill: University of North Carolina Press, 1978), 33–34, 54–56.

2. Bley, *SWA under German Rule,* xxvi, 3–4.

3. See, e.g., see Richard Voeltz, *German Colonialism and the South West Africa Company, 1894–1914* (Athens: Ohio University, Center for International Studies, 1988).

4. Bismarck to Goering, 19 Feb. 1890, BAP Reichskolonialamt, file 6 (hereafter, R1001/file). Dane Kennedy makes a similar argument when he states that in order for whites to maintain their position in the colony vis-à-vis the Africans, more Europeans had to settle in Kenya and Southern Rhodesia; Kennedy, *Islands of White,* 4.

5. Smith, *German Colonial Empire,* 9–12; idem, *Ideological Origins of Nazi Imperialism,* 21–29, esp. 25; idem, "Contexts of German Colonialism in Africa: British Imperialism, German Politics, and the German Administrative Tradition," in *European Impact and Pacific Influence: British and German Colonial Policy in the Pacific Islands and the Indigenous Response,* ed., Hermann J. Hiery and John M. Mackenzie, International Library of Historical Studies (London: Tauris Academic Studies, 1997), 16.

6. Chickering, *We Men,* 111.

7. Ibid.

8. Ibid., 108–11, 185, 187–88, 314–16, 320; see also Pierard, "German Colonial Society," 1–2, 108–12, 370.

9. Richard Hindorf, *Bericht über den landwirtschaftlichen Werth Deutsch-Südwestafrikas, Anlage II zur Denkschrift btr: Das südwestafrikanische Schutzgebiet,* Reichstag, 9. Legislatur-Periode 3, session 1894/95, BAP Deutscher Reichstag, file 1093 (hereafter, R101/file); Karl Dove, *Bericht btr. die Besiedelung Deutsch-Südwestafrikas,* BAP R1001/6492; see also Bley, *SWA under German Rule,* 105.

10. Karl Daeubler, "Die Möglichkeit der Kolonisation und Anpassung der Europäer an die Tropen," *DKZ,* 26 May 1894. Even after a European presence had been established in SWA, debates surfaced periodically on the subject of climate in the colonies, even as late as 1913. For example, see "Die Akklimatisationsfrage in Den Kolonien," *DKZ,* 29 Apr. 1911, 283–85; *Bericht über die 3: Sitzung des Ausschusses btr. Diskussion über den Vortrag des Herrn Oberstabarztes Dr. Kuhn vom 7. Apr. 1911 über den Stand der Akklimatisationsfrage in den Kolonien,* 30 Jan. 1912, BAP German Colonial Society, file 188 (hereafter, 61K01/file); Lohmann, "Zur Akklimatisationsfrage" *DKZ,* 11 Jan. 1913, 20–21; C. von Perbandt, "Sind unsere afrikanischen Kolonien für europäische bezw. speziell deutsche Besiedlung geeignet?" *Jahrbuch über die deutschen Kolonien* 6 (1913): 76–77.

11. Bley, *SWA under German Rule,* 105; DKG, "Notiz für die Presse" [press release], 1892, BAP 61K01/601; Johann Albrecht Herzog zu Mecklenburg, DKG president, *Ausführungen der Deutsche Kolonialgesellschaft btr. Kolonialpolitik,* 1896, BAP 61K01/109; Pierard, "German Colonial Society," 212–93, 370; Geoff Eley, *Reshaping the German Right: Radical Nationalism and Political Change after Bismarck* (Ann Arbor: University of Michigan Press, 1994), 121, 169, 171.

12. See Kennedy, *Islands of White,* 92–93.

13. Or 317,827 square miles (82,347,841 hectares); 1 hectare equals 2.471 acres; 640 acres equals 1 square mile.

14. André du Pisani, *SWA/Namibia: The Politics of Continuity and Change* (Johannesburg: Jonathan Bell, 1986), 25–26; Helga and Ludwig Helbig, *Mythos Deutsch-Südwest: Namibia und die Deutschen* (Weinheim: Beltz, 1983), 125–26.

15. Based on 1903 figures: Crown land (19.3 million ha), concession land (29.2 million ha), white settlers (3.7 million ha), and Africans (31.4 million ha). Leonard Lazar, *Namibia* (London: Africa Bureau, 1972), 95; cited in Pisani, *Politics,* 26.

16. Samassa, "Die Nicht-Lösung der Siedelungsgesellschaft," *Deutsche Zeitung,* 17 Mar. 1907, BAP Pressearchiv des Reichslandbundes, file 6366 (hereafter, R8034II/file).

17. Bley, *SWA under German Rule,* 6–7.

18. Ibid., 7. For a detailed account of Leutwein's pacification program, see ibid., 8–15. For an insightful account of the economic and sociocultural impact of this program, see Walter Nuhn, *Sturm über Südwest: Der Hereroaufstand von 1904 — Ein düsteres Kapital der deutschen kolonialen Vergangenheit Namibias* (Koblenz: Bernard & Graefe, 1989), esp. 324–26.

19. Bley, *SWA under German Rule,* 106–7.

20. Theodor Leutwein, *Elf Jahre Gouverneur in Deutsch-Südwestafrika* (Berlin: Mittler & Sohn, 1906), 410.

21. Ibid.

22. Ibid., 408.

23. Hans Oelhafen, *Die Besiedelung Deutsch-Südwestafrikas bis zum Welt-kriege* (Berlin: Dietrich Reimer [Ernst Vohsen], 1926), 18; Bley, *SWA under German Rule*, 108.

24. For a succinct but detailed description of Leutwein's land policies, see Pisani, *Politics*, 27–29.

25. H. E. Lenssen, ed., *Chronik von Deutsch-Südwestafrika: Eine kurzgefaßte Aufzählung geschichtlicher Ereignisse aus der Deutschen Kolonialzeit von 1883–1915*, 3rd ed. (Windhoek: SWA Wissenschaftliche Gesellschaft, 1988), 67, 74, 84.

26. Leutwein, *Elf Jahre Gouverneur*, 406; idem, *Bedingungen für den öffent-lichen Verkauf von Regierungsfarmen*, 1 Aug. 1899, BAP R1001/1136; idem, *Vorzugs-bedingungen für den Verkauf von Regierungsfarmen für wehrpflichtige Reichsangehörige*, 1 Aug. 1899, BAP R1001/1136.

27. Leutwein, *Elf Jahre Gouverneur*, 408.

28. Ibid., 407.

29. Ibid., 408–10.

30. Lindequist, *Denkschrift über die Besiedelung Deutsch-Südwestafrikas*, 19 Sept. 1906, BAP Kaiserliches Gouvernement in Deutsch-Südwest-Afrika, reel FC14842 (hereafter, R151F/reel).

31. Leutwein to AA, 26 Aug. 1903, BAP R1001/1138; Landrentmeister Junker, *Bericht des Ansiedelungskommission*, 1903, BAP R1001/1138.

32. Leutwein to AA, 26 Aug. 1903, BAP R1001/1138.

33. Leutwein, *Elf Jahre Gouverneur*, 407.

34. Bley, *SWA under German Rule*, 143. Horst Drechsler, citing the official census from 1911, states that only 15,130 Herero out of 80,000 were left, while 9,781 Nama survived out of an original 20,000. Drechsler points out that, because the Germans could not tell them apart from the Herero, the Germans killed one-third of the Berg Damara even though they did not participate in the uprising. Drechsler, *"Let Us Die Fighting,"* 214. These figures came under sharp but dubious criticism by Brigitte Lau. For an examination of her assertions and their implications as well as a strong and thorough refutation of them, see Tilman Dedering, "The German-Herero War of 1904: Revisionism of Genocide or Imaginary Historiography," *Journal of Southern African Studies* 19, no. 1 (1993): 80–88.

35. Paul Rohrbach, settlement commissioner, to imp. govt. [imperial government], Windhoek, 6 Apr. 1906, BAP R151F/FC14851; see also Stuebel, AA, to Mecklenburg, 25 July 1904, BAP R151F/FC14843; Oelhafen, *Die Besiedelung Deutsch-Südwestafrikas*, 38; Bley, *SWA under German Rule*, 170–73; Drechsler, *"Let Us Die Fighting,"* 231.

36. Dernburg, *Erlaß an den Kaiserlichen Gouverneur, Windhoek*, 17 Nov. 1906, BAP R151F/FC14839.

37. Lindequist, *Denkschrift über die Besiedelung Deutsch-Südwestafrikas*, 1906.

38. Rohrbach to imp. govt., Windhoek, 25 July 1906, BAP R151F/FC14842; Lindequist to AA, 19 Sept. 1906, BAP R1001/1142.

39. Lindequist, *Denkschrift über die Besiedelung Deutsch-Südwestafrikas,* 1906.

40. Lindequist, *Organisationsplan für die Wassererschließung in Deutsch-Südwestafrika,* 19 Sept. 1906, BAP R1001/1142; Oskar Hintrager, *Südwestafrika in der deutschen Zeit* (Munich: Oldenbourg, 1955), 85, 88; Oelhafen, *Die Besiedelung Deutsch-Südwestafrikas,* 43–48, 57; Lindequist, *Denkschrift über die Besiedelung Deutsch-Südwestafrikas.* After these monies had been exhausted, the Reichstag allocated no additional funds to aid settlement directly.

41. Lindequist, *Bestimmungen für die Gewährung staatlicher Ansiedlungsbeihilfen,* 12 Sept. 1906, BAP R151F/FC14842.

42. For such an incident, see Schenke, provincial officer, Swakopmund, to imp. govt., Windhoek, 1908, BAP R151F/FC14849.

43. Tecklenburg, imp. govt., Windhoek, to AA, 27 Mar. 1905, BAP R1001/1140; Nuhn, 316, 317.

44. Lindequist, *Denkschrift btr. Viehbeschaffung,* 19 Sept. 1906, BAP R1001/1142.

45. Lindequist, *Denkschrift über die Besiedelung Deutsch-Südwestafrikas,* 1906.

46. The Syndicate for Southwest African Settlement was established in 1892 by the German Colonial Society to promote German colonization in the region. It was succeeded in 1895/96 by the Settlement Company for German Southwest Africa.

47. Rohrbach to imp. govt., Windhoek, 6 Apr. 1906, BAP R151F/FC14851; idem, to govt., Windhoek, 25 July 1906, BAP R151F/FC14842.

48. Lindequist to AA, 28 Apr. 1906, BAP R1001/1141; Hintrager, *Südwestafrika,* 1st ed., 85–86.

49. Lindequist to AA, 28 Apr. 1906.

50. "Zur Frage der Kleinsiedlung," *DSWAZ,* 7 Sept. 1907; "Ein ernstes Wort über Kleinsiedelung," *WN,* 9 May 1908; Hans Berthold, "Kleinsiedlungen und Kleinsiedler in Südwestafrika," *DKZ,* 24 Oct. 1908, 757–58; "Erfolge der Kleinsiedlung in Südwestafrika," *Deutsche Tageszeitung,* 4 Feb. 1911, R8034II/6370; "Die Kleinsiedlung Osona nach 3 Jahren ihres Bestehens," *WN,* 11 Aug. 1909; "Das Siedlungsproblem I," *SWB,* 21 Sept. 1913; "Das Siedlungsproblem II," *SWB,* 24 Sept. 1913; "Das Siedlungsproblem III," *SWB,* 26 Sept. 1913.

51. For a more detailed discussion of the peasant farmer and Lindequist's activities in this direction when he was colonial secretary, see Smith, *Ideological Origins of Nazi Imperialism,* 85–87, 137.

52. Lindequist to AA, 28 Apr. 1906, BAP R1001/1141; Seitz to RKA, 19 Feb. 1914, BAP R1001/6238.

53. SfDSWA, *Geschäftsbericht 1900,* June 1901, BAP R1001/1695; "Aus dem Schutzgebiet," *DSWAZ,* 12 Jan. 1907; "Farm-Volontäre," *DSWAZ,* 14 Aug. 1907; "Jugendliche Hilfskräfte Für Südwest," *WN,* 2 Sept. 1908; "Jugendliche Hilfkräfte für Südwest," *WN,* 30 Sept. 1908; provincial officer, Karibib to imp. govt., Windhoek, 13 Jan. 1907, BAP R151F/FC14845; Sander, DKG secretary, to Zafa, 15 Oct. 1907, BAP 61Ko1/110.

54. Fabarius to governor, Windhoek, 27 Oct. 1908, BAP R151F/FC14845; provincial officer, Omaruru to imp. govt., Windhoek, 13 Nov. 1909, BAP R151F/FC14845; provincial officer, Omaruru, to imp. govt., Windhoek, 25 Nov. 1909, BAP R151F/FC14845; Lindequist, *Denkschrift über die Besiedelung Deutsch-Südwestafrikas*, 1906.

55. Fabarius, *Denkschrift über einige kolonialpolitische und Siedelungsaufgaben, vetreten durch die Deutsche Kolonialschule*, 1906, BAP R151F/FC14844.

56. Schuckmann, *Runderlaß an Imperial Bezirks- (Distrikts-) Ämter*, 29 Oct. 1907, BAP R151F/FC14842.

57. Lenssen, *Chronik von Deutsch-Südwestafrika*, 203–4.

58. Schuckmann, *Runderlaß an Imperial Bezirks- (Distrikts-) Ämter*, 29 Oct. 1907.

59. Schuckmann, *Erlaß an die Kaiserlichen Bezirks- and Distriktämter*, 24 Apr. 1908, BAP R1001/2044.

60. Theodor Seitz, *Vom Aufstieg und Niederbruch Deutscher Kolonialmacht: Erinnerungen*, vol. 3, *Die Gouverneursjahre in Südwestafrika* (Karlsruhe i.B.: E. F. Müller, 1929), 28, 32, 34; idem, *Erlaß an Inspektion der Landespolizei*, 23 June 1913, BAP Schutzbegiet Deutsch-Südwestafrika, file 2579 (hereafter, R1002/file); Seitz to RKA, 19 Feb. 1914, BAP R1001/6238.

61. Bley, *SWA under German Rule*, 111.

62. Von Perbandt, "Sind unsere afrikanischen Kolonien für europäische bezw. speziell deutsche Besiedlung geeignet?" 81.

63. Hans Berthold, "Die Besiedlung Deutsch-Südwestafrika," *Jahrbuch über die deutschen Kolonien* 4 (1911): 202.

CHAPTER 2

1. Fromm, provincial officer, Windhoek, to imp. govt., Windhoek, 22 May 1911, BAP R151F/FC14854; *Deutsch-Südwestafrika: Amtlicher Ratgeber für Auswanderer* (Berlin: Dietrich Reimer [Ernst Vohsen], 1912), 39; Paul Rohrbach, *Deutsch Südwest-Afrika ein Ansiedlungs-Gebiet?* (Berlin-Schöneberg: Hilfe, 1906), 9.

2. SfsS, *Notizen für Ansielder in Deutsch-Südwestafrika*, Apr. 1893, BAP 61K01/600a.

3. *Bericht über die Sitzung des Vorstandes der DKG btr. Auskunftsstelle für Auswanderer*, 1 Dec. 1900, BAP 61K01/108; "Politischer Tagesbericht betreffend Zafa," *Norddeutsche Allgemeine Zeitung*, 29 Aug. 1902, BAP R1001/6275; Zafa, *Deutsch-Südwestafrika*, BAP R1001/6275; Zafa, *Belehrung bei Ausreise in eine deutsche Kolonie*, BAP 61K01/109; *Bericht über die 2. Sitzung des Auskunftsbeirats*, 20 May 1903, BAP 61K01/108; *Bericht über 3. Sitzung des Auskunftsbeirats*, 9 May 1904, BAP 61K01/109; Graf Pfeil, Zafa Director, *Denkschrift über Auskunftserteilung und Besiedlung*, 31 Jan. 1907, BAP R151F/FC14853; Lindequist to AA, 24 July 1906, BAP R1001/1141; *Bericht über die 8. Sitzung des Auskunftsbeirats*, 26 May 1909, BAP 61K01/110.

4. *Deutsch-Südwestafrika: Amtlicher Ratgeber für Auswanderer.*

5. For example, Walter Mittelstaedt, "Südwestafrika als Ansiedelungsgebiet für deutsche Auswanderer," *Koloniale Zeitschrift,* 11 July 1913, 433–37; Georg Haverland, "Zur Besiedlung von Deutsch-Südwestafrika," *DKZ,* 2 May 1891, 57–58; "Winke für die Auswanderung nach Südwestafrika," *KuH* 2, no. 3 (1908/09): N1; "Zur Auswanderung nach Deutsch-Süd-West-Afrika," *Berliner Neueste Nachrichten,* 19 Aug. 1899, BAP R8034II/6326; "Planmäßige Besiedelung Deutsch-Südwestafrikas," *Deutsche Tageszeitung,* 13 Jan. 1903, BAP R8034II/6333; "Zur Frage der Besiedlung Deutsch-Südwestafrikas," *Vossische Zeitung,* 19 Sept. 1902, BAP R1001/1136; "Koloniales. Auskunfterteilung über Auswanderung nach D-SWA," *Norddeutsche Allgemeine Zeitung,* 1 Oct. 1908, BAP R1001/224.

6. Hubert Janson, "Aus dem Farmerleben in Südwest," *KuH* 1, no. 23 (1907/08): 3.

7. *Jahresbericht über die Entwicklung von Deutsch-Südwestafrika im Jahre 1898/99 an den Deutschen Reichstag,* 10. Legislatur-Periode 1, session 1898/99, BAP R101/1094; *Bevölkerungsstatistik D-SWA, Anlage D.1. zur Denkschrift über die Entwicklung der deutschen Schutzgebiete . . . an den Reichstag,* 11. Legislatur-Periode 1, session 1903/05, BAP R101/1096; *Bevölkerungsstatistik, Anlage zur Denkschrift über die Entwicklung der Schutzgebiete . . . an den Deutschen Reichstag,* 12. Legislatur-Periode 2, session 1909/10, BAP R101/1101; Karl Dove, *Die Deutschen Kolonien IV: Südwestafrika* (Berlin; Leipzig: Göschen'sche Verlagshandlung GmbH, 1913), 65–67.

8. U. U. Jäschke, "Der Siedlungsraum SWA/Namibia mit drei Fallbeispielen zur Farmentwicklung," in *Namibia—Ausgewählte Themen der Exkursionen 1988,* ed. Heinrich Lamping, Frankfurter Wirtschafts- und Sozialgeographische Schriften, 53 (Frankfurt am Main: Institut für Wirtschafts- und Sozialgeographie der Universität Frankfurt, 1989), 201–5.

9. Bley, *SWA under German Rule,* 108.

10. ADV, *Die Bureneinwanderung nach Deutsch-Südwestafrika, Vertraulich!* Apr. 1900, BAP R1001/1149; ADV to AA, 8 Nov. 1902, BAP R1001/1137.

11. Caprivi, *Denkschrift btr das südwestafrikanische Schutzgebiet . . . an den Deutschen Reichstag,* 9. Legislatur-Periode 2, session 1893/94, BAP R101/1093.

12. Leutwein, *Elf Jahre Gouverneur,* 414–16; Johannes Nickol, "Gefährdetes Deutschtum in Südwestafrika," *Die Deutschen Kolonien* 10:4 (1911), BAP R151F/FC14842.

13. "Südwestafrika. Buren Planen Einen Putsch," *DKZ,* 7 Oct. 1905, 431; "Südwestafrika. Das Burenkomplott," *DKZ,* 14 Oct. 1905, 438; "Südwestafrika. Das Burenkomplott," *DKZ,* 21 Oct. 1905, 450; Nickol, "Gefährdetes Deutschtum in Südwestafrika"; Konrad Fischer, "Habt Acht auf das Deutschtum Im Südbezirk von Südwest!," *KuH* 1, no. 19 (1907-8): 9; Erich Mayer, "Burenfragen," *WN,* 1. Beilage, 17 Jan. 1907; Samassa, "Die Burenfrage in Südwest," *WN,* 3 June 1908.

14. Estorff, imp. govt., Windhoek, to AA, 14 Nov. 1902, BAP R1001/1152; idem, *Bedingungen für die Ansiedlung holländischer Afrikaner in Deutsch-Südwestafrika,* 13 Nov. 1902, BAP R1001/1152; "Die Bureneinwanderung in Deutsch-Südwestafrika," *Deutsche Tageszeitung,* 20 Jan. 1902, BAP R8034II/6331; Ministerial

Councillor Gerstenhauer, "Das Deutsche Schulwesen in Südwestafrika," *DKZ*, 22 Jan. 1903, 33–35; Leutwein to AA, 24 Nov. 1903, BAP R1001/1153; *Liste der auf Grund der Berliner Verhandlungen in Deutsch-Südwestafrika eingewanderten noch dort befindlichen Buren*, 1903, BAP R1001/1153; Tecklenburg to AA, 18 May 1905, BAP R1001/1153; Tecklenburg to German consulate-general, Cape Town, 7 Nov. 1904, BAP R1001/1153.

15. "Das Rassenproblem in Südwestafrika (Schluß)," *SWB*, 4 Apr. 1913.

16. Christopher Fyfe, "Race, Empire, and the Historians," *Race & Class* 33, no. 4 (1992): 18–19.

17. Bley, *SWA under German Rule*, 170–73; Drechsler, *"Let Us Die Fighting,"* 231.

18. John Comaroff, "Images of Empire, Contests of Conscience: Models of Colonial Domination in South Africa," *American Ethnologist* 16 (Nov. 1989): 672–73.

19. Clara Brockmann, *Briefe eines deutschen Mädchens aus Südwest* (Berlin: Mittler & Sohn, 1912), 50; Külz, "Arbeiternot und Eingeborenenpflege in Südwestafrika," *DKZ*, 29 Apr. 1911, 281–82; Hans Wulff, "Vorschläge Zur Abhilfe der Arbeiternot," *SWB*, 10 May 1911; "Vorschläge Zur Abhilfe der Arbeiternot. Eine Entgegnung," *SWB*, 24 May 1911; Bley, *SWA under German Rule*, 149–69; Gottlieb Haussleiter, *Zur Eingeborenen-Frage in Deutsch-Südwest-Afrika: Erwägungen und Vorschläge* (Berlin, 1906), 8–9, 33–34.

20. See, e.g., Dane Kennedy's brief treatment of this issue in Kenya and Southern Rhodesia and how it was combated; Kennedy, *Islands of White*, 174–79.

21. See Stoler, "Making Empire Respectable: The Politics of Race and Sexual Morality in Twentieth-century Colonial Cultures," *American Ethnologist* 16 (Nov. 1989): 638; and idem, "Sexual Affronts and Racial Frontiers: European Identities and the Cultural Politics of Exclusion in Colonial Southeast Asia," *Comparative Studies in Society and History* 34 (July 1992): 550.

22. Kennedy, *Islands of White*, 4; "Die deutsche Frau in den Kolonien," *WN*, 2. Blatt, 6 Mar. 1909.

23. Kolonialrat, *Bericht des Ausschusses über die ihm zur Vorberatung überwiesene Frage: Beschränkung der Einwanderung mittelloser Personen in die deutschen Kolonien*, V. Sitzungsperiode 1898/1901, no. 20, Nov. 9–10, 1899, BAP R1001/6294; Lindequist to AA, 14 Dec. 1905, BAP R1001/1141.

24. Lindequist to AA, 14 Dec. 1905, BAP R1001/1141.

25. Quoted in Leutwein, *Elf Jahre Gouverneur*, 232–33.

26. Hintrager to AA, 5 Oct. 1905, BAK, Nachlass Hintrager, file 8 (hereafter, N1037/file); Tecklenburg to AA, 23 Oct. 1905, BAP R1001/5417.

27. Hintrager to AA, 5 Oct. 1905, BAK N1037/file; Tecklenburg to AA, 23 Oct. 1905, BAP R1001/5417.

28. See, e.g., Rudolf Hermann, "Mischehen und Grundeigentum in Deutsch-Südwestafrika," *ZfKKK* 8 (1906): 134–41; Fleischmann, "Die Mischehenfrage," *ZfKKK* 12 (1910): 83–87.

29. Pierard, "The Transportation of White Women to German Southwest Africa, 1898–1914," *Race* (1970–71): 317.

30. Lindequist, *Vertrauliche Rundverfügung an die Bezirksämter,* 20 Dec. 1905, BAP 61K01/175; see also Pierard, "Transportation," 317. The term *Bastard* refers to the Basters—descendants of Dutch settlers at the Cape of Good Hope and Khoisan. A group of Basters moved to SWA in 1868.

31. George Mosse, *Nationalism and Sexuality: Respectability and Abnormal Sexuality in Modern Europe* (New York: H. Fertig, 1985), 16–18; idem, *Toward the Final Solution: A History of European Racism* (New York: H. Fertig, 1978), 82; Chickering, *We Men,* 108–18, 197, 304; Stoler, "Making Empire Respectable," 643–45; Kennedy, *Islands of White,* 4, 188.

32. Schreiber, "Zur Frage der Mischehen zwischen Weißen und Eingeborenen im deutschen Schutzgebiete Südwestafrika," *ZfKKK* 11 (1909): 88.

33. Ibid.

34. For a detailed account of the debates in Germany surrounding these issues, see Franz-Josef Schulte-Althoff, "Rassenmischung im kolonialem System. Zur deutschen Kolonialpolitik im letzten Jahrzehnt vor dem Ersten Weltkrieg," *Historisches Jahrbuch* 105 (1985): 52–94.

35. "Ein Einwanderungsverbot für Südwestafrika," *Deutsche Tageszeitung,* 24 Feb. 1906, BAP R8034II/6364; "Warnung vor der Entsendung Mittelloser Ansiedler," *DKZ,* 22 Jan. 1903, 38–39; "Unerwünschte Einwanderer," *DKZ,* 15 Sept. 1904, 370.

36. Lindequist, *Verordnung btr. Einwanderung in das Deutsch-Südwestafri-kanisches Schutzgebiet,* Jan. 1906, BAP R1001/2042; see also idem, *Rundverfügung an die Bezirksämter btr. Verordnung über Einwanderung in das Schutzgebiet,* 15 Dec. 1905, BAP R1001/2042.

37. Böhmer, provincial officer, Lüderitz Bay, to governor, 26 Aug. 1909, BAP R1001/1144. Anti-Semitism was not limited to the ranks of lower officials. Governor Schuckmann demonstrated his blatant anti-Semitism by extending the requirements for immigration to include the ability to write one's name in a European language, not Hebrew. He justified his decision by claiming it was necessary to stop the tide of undesirables from entering the colony since the discovery of diamonds. He wrote that "alone in Lüderitz Bay more than 55 foreign Jews have immigrated since Jan. 1, 1909, and the signatures in Hebrew are multiplying alarmingly." See Schuckmann, *Verordnung btr. Ergänzung der Einwanderungsverordnung vom 15. Dezember 1905,* 12 June 1909, BAP R1001/1144; Schuckmann to RKA, 12 June 1909, BAP R1001/1144.

38. For British, Dutch, Belgian, and French concerns over the "presence of non-productive men" in their colonies, see Stoler, "Making Empire Respectable," 645.

39. Expelled Germans occasionally contested this power, as in the case of *Victor von Alten vs. German Empire,* but without success. The courts ruled that not all German laws applied to the protectorates, even though they were German possessions, and that authority over them derived solely from the chancellor and his representatives, including the Colonial Office but not the Reichstag; see Barlach, attorney, to AA, n.d., BAP R1001/7547; 11th Civil Senate of the Royal Chamber Court, Berlin, *Victor von Alten vs. the German Reich,* 3 Dec. 1909, BAP R1001/7547; "Das Ausweisungsrecht

der Gouverneure," *WN*, 30 Oct. 1909; Kurt von Stengel, "Die Zulässigkeit der Ausweisung von Reichsangehörigen und von Ausländern aus den Schutzgebieten," *WN*, 2. Blatt, 19 Jan. 1910; Stengel, "Die Zulässigkeit der Ausweisung von Reichsangehörigen und von Ausländern aus den Schutzgebieten (Fortsetzung)," *WN*, 2. Blatt, 22 Jan. 1910; Stengel, "Die Zulässigkeit der Ausweisung von Reichsangehörigen und von Ausländern aus den Schutzgebieten (Schluß)," *WN*, 2. Blatt, 26 Jan. 1910.

40. State Secretary Lindequist, RKA, *Runderlaß an die kaiserlichen Gouverneure der deutschen Schutzgebiete*, 25 Jan. 1911, BAP R1001/7547; RKA, *Aufzeicnungen über die Ausweisungen aus den Schutzgebieten*, BAP R1001/7547.

41. Imp. govt., Windhoek, *Ausweisungsgefehl für Techniker Karl Ernst Bartenwerfer*, 13 Feb. 1913, BAP R151F/FC5233.

42. Mayor Houtermans, Windhoek, to imp. district office, Windhoek, 15 May 1912, BAP R151F/FC5233; provincial officer, Windhoek, to imp. govt., Windhoek, 21 June 1912, BAP R151F/FC5233; imp. govt., Windhoek, *Verfügung btr. Ausweisung Rosinger*, 11 July 1912, BAP R151F/FC5233.

43. Fock to imp. govt., Windhoek, 26 Mar. 1910, BAP R1001/1918.

44. Schneidenberger, provincial officer, Okahandja, to imp. govt., Windhoek, 20 Aug. 1910, BAP R1001/1918.

45. Brill, provincial officer, Windhoek, to imp. govt., Windhoek, 1 Sept. 1910, BAP R1001/1918.

46. Fyfe, 20; Kennedy, *Islands of White*, 188.

47. *Testimony of Aug. Martin given to Schneidenberger, Imperial District Officer, Okahandja*, 30 Aug. 1910, BAP R1001/1918; provincial court, Windhoek, *Strafsache gegen Aug. Martin zu Windhuk*, 21 Oct. 1910, BAP R1001/1918.

48. Brückner, imp. govt., Windhoek, *Ausweisungsbefehl für Aug. Martin*, 7 Oct. 1910, BAP R1001/1918; Brückner to RKA, 7 Nov. 1910, BAP R1001/1918; president, Authority for Public Juvenile Care, to Senate Commission for Imperial and Foreign Affairs, Hamburg, 6 Jan. 1911, BAP R1001/1918; Brückner to RKA, 18 Feb. 1911, BAP R1001/1918; Martin Hennig, director, Rauhe House, Hamburg, to RKA, 3 Dec. 1913, BAP R1001/1918; Hennig to RKA, 4 Oct. 1916, BAP R1001/1918; Hennig to RKA, 3 Mar. 1917, BAP R1001/1918.

49. Mosse, *Nationalism and Sexuality*, 19, 90, 98; idem, "Nationalism and Respectability: Normal and Abnormal Sexuality in the Nineteenth Century," *Journal of Contemporary History* 17, no. 2 (1982): 224, 229.

50. Mosse, *Nationalism and Sexuality*, 20; idem, "Nationalism and Respectability," 232.

51. Edward Ross Dickinson, *The Politics of German Child Welfare from the Empire to the Federal Republic* (Cambridge: Harvard University Press, 1996), 43–44.

52. Tecklenburg, *Rundverfügung an die Kaiserliche Standesämter*, 23 Sept. 1905, BAP R151F/FC14857; Bley, *SWA under German Rule*, 212; Martha Mamozai, *Schwarze Frau, weiße Herrin: Frauenleben in den deutschen Kolonien* (Reinbek bei Hamburg: Rowohlt, 1989), 126.

53. Bley, *SWA under German Rule*, 212; Mamozai, *Schwarze Frau*, 126; district chief, Bethanien, to provincial office, Keetmanshoop, 14 Apr. 1908, BAP

R151F/FC5180; Hintrager, *Erlaß an das Kaiserliche Bezirksamt in Keetmanshoop*, 6 June 1908, BAP R151F/FC5180; imp. govt., Windhoek, to Schiefer, 23 Dec. 1910, BAP R151F/FC5181; provincial court, Windhoek, *Ada Maria (Hererofrau) vs. Kaspar Friedrich Leinhos (Deutscher)*, 1908, BAP R151F/FC5180; imp. high court, Windhoek, *Ada Maria vs. Leinhos*, 10 Nov. 1909, BAP R1001/5423.

54. State Secretary Solf, RKA, *Erlaß an den Gouverneur in Windhuk*, 17 May 1913, BAP R1001/5424; Brill, provincial officer, Windhoek, to imp. govt., Windhoek, 29 Apr. 1911, BAP R151F/FC5181; imp. high court, Windhoek, *Entscheidung über Frau Denk gegen Herrn Denk wegen Nichtbestehens der Ehe*, 26 July 1911, BAP R151F/FC5181.

55. Dernburg, *Verordnung des Reichskanzlers btr. die Selbstverwaltung in Deutsch-Südwestafrika*, 29 Jan. 1909, BAP R1001/2058; Lindequist, *Bestimmungen für die Gewährung staatlicher Ansiedlungsbeihilfen*, 12 Sept. 1906, BAP R151F/FC14842.

56. Schuckmann to Carl Becker, Vaalgras, 11 Oct. 1909, BAP R1001/2058; Dernburg, *Erlaß an den Gouverneur in Windhuk*, 11 Dec. 1909, BAP R1001/2058.

57. Becker to Schuckmann, 1 Sept. 1909, BAP R1001/2058.

58. Lora Wildenthal, "Race, Gender, and Citizenship in the German Colonial Empire," in *Tensions of Empire: Colonial Cultures in a Bourgeois World*, ed. Frederick Cooper and Ann Stoler (Berkeley: University of California Press, 1997), 269-72.

59. Kennedy, *Islands of White*, 4, 188-89.

60. For a discussion of the importance of associations in Germany, see Thomas Nipperdey, "Verein als soziale Struktur im späten und frühen 19. Jahrhundert," in *Geschichtswissenschaft und Vereinswesen im 19. Jahrhundert*, ed. Hartmut Boockmann, et al. (Göttingen: Vandenhoeck & Ruprecht, 1972), 1-44.

61. For example, *Satzungen des Turnverein Windhuk in Deutsch-Südwestafrika*, 14 Apr. 1904, BAP R1001/1736; *Satzungen des Männer-Turnvereins Swakopmund*, 10 Sept. 1910, BAP R1001/1737; *Satzungen des Männerturnvereins Lüderitzbucht*, 1 Mar. 1912, BAP R1001/1738; *Satzungen des Schützen-Vereins zu Karibib*, 26 Apr. 1913, BAP R1001/1739.

62. C. Wandres, president of the Protestant Mission in Nama country, *Bemerkungen über Mischehen und Mischlinge aus der Praxis für die Praxis*, n.d., BAP R1001/5423; Pastor Hasenkamp, "Unsere Stellung zum Verbot der Rassenmischehe," *Evangelisches Gemeindeblatt für Deutsch-Südwestafrika*, July 1913, BAP R1001/5424.

63. Haussleiter, 36-37; Missionary Director T. Öhler, chairman, Committee of German Protestant Missions, to Solf, RKA, 3 Sept. 1912, BAP R1001/5417; Lothar Engel, *Kolonialismus und Nationalismus im Deutschen Protestantismus in Namibia 1907 bis 1945: Beiträge zur Geschichte der deutschen Evangelischen Mission und Kirche im ehemaliggen Kolonial- und Mandatsgebiet Südwestafrika* (Frankfurt am Main: Peter Lang, 1976), 36-37; Bley, *SWA under German Rule*, 213.

64. Accordingly, the courts refused to hear any cases involving individuals of mixed parentage since they dispensed justice only for Europeans. In one instance, the imperial high court in Windhoek threw out the decision of a lower court because

the accused was a "native" and as such had to be tried before the "native" courts"; see high court, Windhoek, *Urteil in der Strafsache gegen Diplom-Ingenieur Baumann*, 12 Mar. 1913, BAP R1001/5424; "Ein Beitrag Zur Frage der Reinlichen Rassenscheidung," *KuH* 6, no. 32 (1912/13): N1–2.

65. Gesine Krüger, *Kriegsbewältigung und Geschichtsbewußtsein: Realität, Deutung, und Verarbeitung des deutschen Kolonialkriegs in Namibia, 1904 bis 1907* (Göttingen: Vandenhoeck & Ruprecht, 1999), 62–68.

66. Imp. govt., Windhoek, to Schiefer, 23 Dec. 1910, BAP R151F/FC5181; Dernburg, *Erlaß an den Gouverneur in Windhuk*, 19 Nov. 1908, BAP R1002/2728; Kunze, deputy provincial officer, Karibib, to imp. govt., Windhoek, 1 Sept. 1908, BAP R1002/2728.

67. Bley, *SWA under German Rule*, 170–73, 213–14, 260–79.

68. Holleben to Imperial Chancellor Bethmann Hollweg, 28 June 1912, BAP R1001/5417; Seitz to RKA, 24 Feb. 1911, BAP R1001/5423; Seitz to RKA, 26 Oct. 1911, BAP R1001/5423; "Verordnung des Gouverneurs von Deutsch-Südwestafrika über die Mischlingbevölkerung vom 23. Mai 1912," *Amtsblatt für das Schutzgebiet Deutsch-Südwestafrika*, 3/12 (June 1912), BAP R1001/1951.

69. Hintrager, *Verordnung an die Kaiserliche Bezirks- Distriktsämter btr. Handhabung der Verordnung über die Mischlingsbevölkerung*, 31 July 1912, BAP R1001/5424.

70. Seitz, *Erlaß an das Kaiserliche Distriktsamt in Bethanien*, 28 Feb. 1914, BAP R151F/FC5181.

71. "Weiss oder farbig?" *WN*, 8 Aug. 1907; and "Weiss oder farbig?" *WN*, 2. Blatt, 8 Aug. 1907; Wildenthal, "Race, Gender, and Citizenship," 273–77.

72. Bley, *SWA under German Rule*, 214.

CHAPTER 3

1. Mosse, *Nationalism and Sexuality*, 16–18.

2. Clara Brockmann, *Die Deutsche Frau in Südwestafrika: Ein Beitrag zu Frauenfrage in unseren Kolonien* (Berlin: Mittler & Sohn, 1910), 5.

3. Ibid., 6.

4. Franz Richter, "Die Frau und die Kolonien," *ZfKKK* 7 (1905): 712.

5. H. Ladeburg, "Die koloniale Frauengrage," *WN*, 2. Blatt, 3 Nov. 1909.

6. Seitz, *Die Gouverneursjahre in Südwestafrika*, 110.

7. "Der Kolonialverein," *Hallesche Zeitung*, 1. Beilage, 24 Apr. 1910, BAK Nachlass Külz, file 33 (hereafter, N1042/file).

8. Chickering, "'Casting Their Gaze More Broadly': Women's Patriotic Activism in Imperial Germany," *Past and Present* 118 (Feb. 1988): 179.

9. Lecture held before the Women's League on Dec. 3, 1909. "Dr. Külz-Bückeburg über Südwestafrika," *Tägliche Rundschau*, Morgen Ausgabe, 4 Dec. 1909, BAK N1042/33.

10. Hintrager, "Deutsch-Südwestafrika wirtschaftliche Entwicklung, 1906–10"; lecture before the DKG in Stuttgart and Reutlingen, Feb. 1911, BAK N1037/2.

11. They did this even though they knew that the actual reason for sending them there was a result of German men's sexual behavior. Thus, women were required to correct the deficiencies of their male counterparts; see Wildenthal, "'She Is Victor': Bourgeois Women, Nationalist Identities, and the Ideal of the Independent Woman Farmer in German Southwest Africa," *Social Analysis* 33 (Sept. 1993): 76.

12. Pierard, "Transportation," 317; Mertens, DKG treasurer, to Kuhn, Cassel, 23 Aug. 1899, BAP 61Ko1/174; *Bericht über die Sitzung des Ausschusses über Schreiben des AA, btr. die Übersiedlung von deutschen Frauen und Mädchen nach SWA*, 5 Jan. 1897, BAP 61Ko1/170; *Bericht über die Sitzung des Vorstandes, btr. Bewilligung eine Zuschuß zu Bestreitung der Kosten der Überfahrt der Frau von H. und ihrer vier Kinder und der Frau C.*, 11–12 June 1897, BAP 61Ko1/170; *Bericht über die 1. Sitzung des Verwaltungsrats, Antrag auf Bewilligung von Mitteln in Höhe von 20,000 Mark zur Entsendung von Frauen und Mädchen nach D-SWA*, 31 Oct. 1898, BAP R1001/7071.

13. Adolf Sachse, DKG executive vice-president, Kretzschmar, DKG Dresden, 28 Dec. 1898, BAP 61Ko1/172; Sachse to Leutwein, 9 July 1898, BAP 61Ko1/171; A. Seidel, DKG secretary, to Aline Krieß, 31 Aug. 1898, BAP 61Ko1/171; DKG to Woermann-Linie, 15 May 1907, BAP 61Ko1/176; Ahlhorn, provincial officer, Okahandja, *Bescheinigung über Farmer Andreas Sell*, 2 June 1914, BAP 61Ko1/185.

14. Leutwein to Richthofen, 30 Mar. 1897, BAP 61Ko1/170.

15. Richthofen, state secretary, to Mecklenburg, 17 May 1897, BAP 61Ko1/170; *Bericht über die Sitzung des Ausschusses des DKG*, 17th session, 22 July 1897, BAP 61Ko1/170.

16. DKG to imp. govt., DSWA, 10 Dec. 1907, BAP 61Ko1/176.

17. Mertens to Kuhn, Cassel, 23 Aug. 1899, BAP 61Ko1/174.

18. Mertens to Kuhn, 23 Aug. 1899, BAP 61Ko1/174; Mertens to Lina Wagner, 5 Sept. 1898, BAP 61Ko1/172; DKG, *Auskunft über Übersiedelung deutscher Frauen und Mädchen nach D-SWA*, Jan. 1898, BAP 61Ko1/171; Seidel to Therese Schöndach, 3 July 1899, BAP 61Ko1/174.

19. Seidel to Margarethe Stumpe, Liegnitz, 1 Nov. 1898, BAP 61Ko1/172; DKG, letter to imp. govt., DSWA, 19 Sept. 1907, BAP 61Ko1/176; Seidel to Minna Einsenkel, 25 Jan. 1899, BAP 61Ko1/173.

20. Pastor Regeler, *Wie deutsche 'gute Hausfrauen' für Südwestafrika gemietet werden*, 1898, BAP 61Ko1/172; DKG, *Erwiderung auf die Hauptangriffspunkte des Herrn Pastors Regeler*, 1898, BAP 61Ko1/172; Minna Cauer, "Die Übersiedelung deutscher Frauen nach den Kolonien," *Die Frauenbewegung: Revue für die Interessen der Frauen*, 1 Aug. 1899, BAP 61Ko1/174.

21. Sachse to Kretzschmar, 22 Nov. 1898, BAP 61Ko1/172.

22. Pierard, "Transportation," 318.

23. FB, *Aufruf! Frauen Deutschlands, helft, daß unsere Kolonien innerlich deutsche Länder werden*, 1912, BAP R1001/7430.

24. DKG Berlin, *Antrag auf engere Gemeinschaft mit dem Deutschkolonialen Frauenbund*, 1908, BAP 61Ko1/153; *Abmachungen zwischen dem Präsidenten der DKG und der Vorsitzenden des Deutschkolonialen Frauenbundes btr. die Hinaus-*

sendung von deutschen Frauen und Mädchen, 1908, BAP R1001/6693; Holleben to Volkmann, Charlottenburg, 1908, BAP 61K01/176; *Frauenbund der Deutschen Kolonialgesellschaft,* 1907, BAP 61K01/153; "Aufforderung zum Eintritt in den Deutschen Kolonialen Frauenbund,'" *WN,* 6 June 1907; "Frauenbund der Deutschen Kolonialgesellschaft," *DKZ,* 26 Sept. 1908, 683; FB, *Aufruf! Frauen Deutschlands, helft unsere Kolonien arbeiten!* 1914, BAP 61K01/157.

25. Winkler, "Aussendung von Frauen und Mädchen nach Deutsch-Südwestafrika," *DKZ,* 30 Sept. 1911, 653; see also, "Aussendung von Frauen und Mädchen nach Südwest," *DKZ,* 13 Aug. 1910, 551–52, and Winkler, "Zur Frauenauswanderung in Deutsch-Südwestafrika," *DKZ,* 29 Mar. 1913, 209–10.

26. Hatten, "Die Frauenfrage in den deutschen Kolonien," *KuH* 6, no. 16 (1912–13): 8; Buchmann to imp. govt., DSWA, 14 Sept. 1908, BAP R1002/2579.

27. Hatten, "Die Frauenfrage"; Buchmann to imp. govt., DSWA, 14 Sept. 1908; Hedwig Heyl, FB chair, to Mecklenburg, 7 Aug. 1913, BAP 61K01/156; Mecklenburg to Heyl, 16 Aug. 1913, BAP 61K01/156; Heyl to Mecklenburg, 22 Aug. 1913, BAP 61K01/156; Winkler to Zafa, 29 Oct. 1913, BAP 61K01/111.

28. Hatten, "Zur Fraueneinwanderung in die Deutschen Kolonien," *FBuE,* 1 Nov. 1912, 1, HLA, 56–253(3).

29. Franz Strauch, DKG deputy president, to Dernburg, 9 Dec. 1909, BAP R1001/1951.

30. "Gebildete Mädchen für Deutsch-Südwest," *Deutsche Tageszeitung,* 19 Mar. 1909, BAP R8034II/6368.

31. Brill, provincial officer, Windhoek, to imp. govt., Windhoek, 22 Apr. 1911, BAP R151F/FC14855.

32. Hatten, "Zur Fraueneinwanderung"; idem, "Die Frauenfrage," 9.

33. "Das Ende der Kolonial-Frauenschule," *WN,* 2. Blatt, 30 Nov. 1910; "Weibliche Hilfskräfte," *SWB,* 29 Aug. 1913; Kolonial-Frauenschule in Bad Weilbach, *Jahresbericht 1912/13,* BAP R151F/FC14855; Mamozai, *Schwarze Frau,* 144; quoted material in *Deutsche Kolonial-Frauenschule zu Witzenhausen,* 1908, BAP R151F/FC14845.

34. Countess Zech, "Die Kolonialfrauenschule in Witzenhausen," *KuH* 3, no. 25 (1909–10): 6–7; Mamozai, *Schwarze Frau,* 144.

35. Wolff to Winkler, 6 July 1912, BAP 61K01/607; Hoffmann, chair, supervisory board of Colonial Women's School, to imp. govt., DSWA, 9 Apr. 1912, BAP R151F/FC14855.

36. "Die Lehrfarm für Mädchen und Frauen in Brakwater bei Windhuk, DSWA" [press release], 1912, BAP 61K01/606; "Die Lehrfarm in Südwest-Afrika für junge Mädchen" [press release], 1909, BAP R1001/1951; "Deutsch-Südwest-Afrika. Lehrfarm Brakwater bei Windhuk (advertisement)," *FBuE,* 1 June 1911, 2, HLA, file 56–253(3).

37. Die Lehrfarm in Südwest-Afrika für junge Mädchen [press release], 1909, BAP R1001/1951.

38. "Wie kleiden wir uns in Südwest," *KuH* 3, no. 10 (1909–10): 9; V., "Die Ausrüstung für Südwestafrika," *KuH* 2, no. 15 (1908–9): 8; M.H., "Vorkehrungen für die

Reise nach Südwest," *KuH* 6, no. 44 (1912–13): 8; M.H., "Haus- und Kücheninventar in Südwest," *KuH* 6, no. 4 (1912–13): 8; "Die Bedeutung hygienischer Fragen für Frauen, die nach den Kolonien gehen," *KuH* 6, no. 1 (1912–13): 8; "Gesundheitsverhältnisse und Körperpflege in Südwest," *KuH* 3, no. 11 (1909–10): 9–10.

39. M. Lorenz, "Der Garten der südwestafrikanischen Farmersfrau," *KuH* 1, no. 4 (1907–8): 13; "Geflügelzucht auf einer Südwestafrikanischen Farm," *KuH* 3, no. 24 (1909–10): 8–9; Maria Karow, "Die Bächerei auf einer Farm in Südwest: 1. Brot und Semmeln," *KuH* 3, no. 19 (1909–10): 8–9; idem, "Die Bäckerei auf einer Farm in Südwest: 2. Kuchen und Allerei Kleinbackwerk," *KuH* 3, no. 20 (1909–10): 8–9; Brandeis, "Die deutsche Hausfrau in den Kolonien: Wie soll man in den Tropen kochen, um gesund zu bleiben?" *KuH* 1, no. 12 (1907–8): 12.

40. I borrow this expression from MacMillan in her analysis of British women in India; Margaret MacMillan, *Women of the Raj* (New York: Thames & Hudson, 1988), 11.

41. See, e.g., George Orwell, "Shooting an Elephant," in *Shooting an Elephant and Other Essays* (London: Secker & Warburg, 1950), 1–10.

42. Brockmann, *Briefe eines deutschen Mädchens,* 102, 112.

43. Brockmann, "Deutsches Frauenleben in Südwest: 2. Unsere Eingeborenen Hilfskräfte," *KuH* 2, no. 15 (1908–9): 3.

44. Ibid.

45. Brandeis, "Die deutsche Hausfrau in den Kolonien."

46. Brockmann, *Briefe eines deutschen Mädchens,* 110.

47. Mamozai, *Schwarze Frau,* 154–55. I was unable to find any examples of such incidents.

48. While no recorded examples exist for SWA, there were certainly examples of this in Germany's Pacific colonies; see Hermann J. Hiery, *Das Deutsche Reich in der Südsee, 1900–1921* (Göttingen: Vandenhoeck & Ruprecht, 1995), 40–58, esp. 41.

49. Leutwein, "Zur Frauenfrage in unseren Kolonien," clipping, newspaper unknown, 1898, BAK Nachlass Leutwein, file 2 (hereafter, N1145/file).

50. "Das Elisabeth-Haus (Wöchnerinnenheim) in Windhuk," *WN,* 16 May 1908; *Bericht über die Sitzung des Kuratoriums des Elisabethhauses,* 30 Sept. 1913, BAP 61K01/188; *Bericht über die Elisabethhäuser in Deutsch-Südwestafrika auf der Hauptversammlung der DKG in Danzig,* 5–6 June 1914, BAP 61K01/188; Rhode, DKG, *Vorlage für die Ausschußsitzung am 30. März 1906,* 16 Mar. 1906, BAP 61K01/190; "Das Frauen-Heim in Deutsch-Südwestafrika," *SWB,* 19 Feb. 1913; *Bericht über die Sitzung des Kuratoriums der Elisabethhäuser,* 26 Mar. 1914, BAP 61K01/209.

51. Karow, "Die Erziehung der deutschen Jugend in Südwest," *KuH* 5, no. 18 (1911–12): 6.

52. Ibid., 7; Brockmann, *Die Deutsche Frau in Südwestafrika,* 8.

53. Michael Townson, *Mother-tongue and Fatherland: Language and Politics in Germany* (Manchester, U.K.: Manchester University Press, 1992), 93; Chickering, "Language and the Social Foundations of Radical Nationalism," 70, 73, 75.

54. "Der Kampf um die Deutsche Sprache und das Deutschtum in den deutschen Kolonien," *DKZ,* 5 Nov. 1903, 455–56; "Für die Reinheit der Sprache,"

DSWAZ, 24 July 1902; Seitz, *Rundverfügung an alle Regierungsschulen . . . btr. Verkehr von Kindern mit Eingeborenen*, 5 June 1918, BAP R1002/2125.

55. Karow, "Die Erziehung der deutschen Jugend in Südwest," 6.

56. Frobenius, "Die Arbeiten des Frauenbundes der Deutschen Kolonialgesellschaft: Das Jugendheim in Lüderitzbucht," in *10 Jahre Frauenbund*, 18–20.

57. The home in Lüderitz Bay served a dual function: not only was it a *Jugendheim*, it was also a home for young, unmarried women, or *Mädchenheim*. The FB set up the Mädchenheim as a refuge for women who were either employed or living alone in the area—a place where they could find contact with colleagues and get some social stimulation. The FB intended it also to provide accommodations for those who had just arrived from Germany; ibid., 18–20; and "Die Eröffnung des Lüderitzbuchter Jugendheims," *KuH* 5, no. 31 (1911–12): 8.

58. "Die Eröffnung des Lüderitzbuchter Jugendheims," 8. Regarding the kindergarden in Windhoek, see Leutwein, *Elf Jahre Gouverneur*, 235.

59. Antonie Brandeis, "Die deutsche Hausfrau in den Kolonien," *KuH* 1, no. 4 (1907–8): 13.

60. H.I., "Wenn Gäste überraschend kommen," *KuH* 6, no. 46 (1912–13): 8; H.I., "Wenn Gäste überraschend kommen," *KuH* 6, no. 47 (1912–13): 9.

61. O'Donnell describes several additional examples; see, "Colonial Woman Question," 271–76.

62. Schmidt, provincial officer, Keetmanshoop, to imp. govt., Windhoek, 1908, BAP R151F/FC14854.

63. Narciß, provincial officer, Windhoek, to imp. govt., Windhoek, 1 June 1907, BAP R151F/FC14859.

64. Beyer, provincial officer, Warmbad, to imp. govt., Windhoek, 1 May 1914, BAP R151F/FC14858; Heilingbrunner, provincial officer, Keetmanshoop, to imp. govt., Windhoek, 15 May 1914, BAP R151F/FC14858; Seitz to Solf, RKA, 2 June 1914, BAP R1001/1144; Solf to Mecklenburg, 23 July 1914, BAP 61K01/178.

65. Kauffmann, provincial officer, Lüderitz Bay, to imp. govt., Windhoek, 2 May 1914, BAP R151F/FC14858.

66. Wildenthal, "'She Is Victor'": 81–85, esp. 82; Mamozai, *Schwarze Frau*, 143, 146–47; Kerstin Engelhardt, "Missionarinnen und Siedlerinnen: Deutsche Kolonialistinnen," in *Namibia; Frauen mischen sich ein*, ed. Florence Hervé (Berlin: Orlanda Frauenverlag, 1993), 31.

67. Brockmann, "Deutsches Frauenleben in Südwest: 1. Frauentypen," *KuH* 2, no. 11 (1908–9): 3.

68. Engelhardt, "Missionarinnen und Siedlerinnen," 32.

69. *Sitzung des Bezirksbeirats Keetmanshoop*, 21 Nov. 1908, BAP R151F/FC5244.

70. Fuchs, provincial officer, Swakopmund, *Polizeiverfügung btr. das Verhalten der Prostituierten in Swakopmund*, 7 Sept. 1904, BAP R151F/FC5243.

71. Provincial officer, Swakopmund, to imp. govt., Windhoek, 7 Apr. 1909, BAP R151F/FC5243.

72. Fuchs, *Polizeiverfügung*, 1904; provincial court, Swakopmund, *Strafsache gegen E. Schmidt, S. Leda und A. Lebrun*, 9 June 1905, BAP R151F/FC5243.

73. For Germany, see Ute Frevert, *Women in German History: From Bourgeois Emancipation to Sexual Liberation,* trans. Stuart McKinnon-Evans (New York: Berg, 1990), 87. For the Transvaal, see Charles van Onselen, "Prostitutes and Proletarians, 1886–1914," in *Studies in the Social and Economic History of the Witwatersrand, 1886–1914,* vol. 1: *New Babylon* (New York: Longman, 1982), 103–62, esp. 105.

74. Police Sergeant Weber, Swakopmund, to provincial office, Swakopmund, 15 Oct. 1904, BAP R151F/FC5243; provincial officer, Swakopmund, to Lindequist, 22 Jan. 1906, BAP R151F/FC5243.

75. Weber to provincial office, Swakopmund, 15 Oct. 1904; provincial officer, Swakopmund, to imp. govt., Windhoek, 17 Oct. 1904, BAP R151F/FC5243.

76. Winkler, "Zur Fraueneinwanderung in Deutsch-Südwestafrika," *DKZ,* 29 Mar. 1913, 210.

77. Kuhn and Lieut. W. Harbers, "Die Auswanderung von Frauen und Kindern in die britischen Kolonien," *ZfKKK* 12 (1910): 833–58.

78. O'Donnell attributes the low percentages after 1910 to sparse and biased data collection and late emigration; O'Donnell, "Colonial Woman Question," 244.

79. See table 3.2; *Liste der mit Unterstützung der DKG nach D-SWA ausgereisten Personen für 1909,* 1910, BAP 61K01/177; imp. govt., Windhoek, *Liste der im Jahre mit Unterstützung der DKG nach Deutsch-Südwestafrika übergesiedelten Personen,* 1914, BAP 61K01/182; O'Donnell, "Colonial Woman Question," 7.

80. *Bevölkerungsstatistik D-SWA, Anlage D.1 zur Denkschrift . . . an den Reichstag,* 11. Legislatur-Periode 1, session 1903/05; *Bevölkerungsstatistik, Anlage zur Denkschrift . . . an den Deutschen Reichstag,* 12. Legislatur-Periode 2, session, 1909/10.

81. *Die deutschen Schutzgebiete in Afrika und der Südsee, 1912/13: Amtliche Jahresberichte,* 22.

82. Eric Hobsbawm, *Nations and Nationalism since 1780: Programme, Myth, Reality* (Cambridge: Cambridge University Press, 1991): 169.

83. For an examination of those opposed to German colonialism, see Helmut Stoecker and Peter Sebald, "Enemies of the Colonial Idea," in *Germans in the Tropics: Essays in German Colonial History,* ed. Arthur Knoll and Lewis Gann (New York: Greenwood Press, 1987): 59–72.

84. Mamozai, *Schwarze Frau,* 190; Engelhardt, "Missionarinnen und Siedlerinnen," 31.

85. O'Donnell, "Colonial Woman Question," 261–64.

86. Mamozai, *Schwarze Frau,* 190.

87. Chickering, "'Casting Their Gaze,'" 160; see also Mosse, *Nationalism and Sexuality,* 17.

88. Engelhardt, "Missionarinnen und Siedlerinnen," 31.

89. "Die deutsche Frau und die Kolonien," *SWB,* 15 Oct. 1913; "Frauenstimmrecht in den Kolonien?" *DKZ,* 23 Oct. 1909, 707; Mamozai, *Schwarze Frau,* 189–90.

90. Chickering, "'Casting Their Gaze,'" 178.

91. Hans Jenny, *Südwestafrika: Land zwischen den Extremen* (Stuttgart: W. Kohlhammer, 1966), 66.

92. Chickering, "'Casting Their Gaze,'"160.

93. For example, see Donal Lowry, "'White Woman's Country': Ethel Tawse Jollie and the Making of White Rhodesia," *Journal of Southern African Studies* 23, no. 2 (1937): 259–81.

94. See Chila Bulbeck, "New Histories of the Memshahib and Missus: The Case of Papua New Guinea," *Journal of Women's History* 3, no. 2 (1991): 98; Margaret Strobel, *European Women and the Second British Empire* (Bloomington: Indiana University Press, 1991); and Pat Barr, *The Dust in the Balance: British Women in India, 1905–1945* (London: Hamish Hamilton, 1989); MacMillan, *Women of the Raj,* 125.

95. Mamozai, *Schwarze Frau,* 152, 154.

96. Ibid., 155–56; Ann Stoler, "Rethinking Colonial Categories: European Communities and the Boundaries of Rule," *Comparative Studies in Society and History* 31 (Jan. 1989): 147–48.

97. Chickering, "'Casting Their Gaze,'" 179–80.

98. Wildenthal, "'She Is Victor'": 83.

CHAPTER 4

1. Franz Wenzel, "Sicherung von Massenloyalität und Qualifikation der Arbeitskraft als Aufgabe der Volksschule," in Schule und Staat im 18. und 19. Jahrhundert: Zur Sozialgeschichte der Schule in Deutschland (Frankfurt am Main: Suhrkamp, 1974), 337–39; Katharine D. Kennedy, "Regionalism and Nationalism in South German History Lessons, 1871-1914," *German Studies Review* 12 (Feb. 1989): 19–26; idem, "A Nation's Readers: Cultural Integration and Schoolbook Canon in Wilhelmine Germany," *Paedagogica Historica* 33 (1997): 461–62, 463, 476.

2. Kennedy, *Islands of White,* 169–70. In Kenya, public education for Europeans started in 1909, though not on a major scale. It was not until the late 1920s that any major improvements took place, and the first secondary school did not open until 1931. Meanwhile, in Southern Rhodesia state education began in 1899 and first underwent a major expansion in 1923. Compulsory education for whites was not introduced there until 1930.

3. Hans Amrhein, *Die deutsche Schule im Auslande* (Leipzig, 1905): 29–30.

4. "Der Bur und das Deutschtum in Deutsch-Südwestafrika," Deutsche Tageszeitung, 4 June 1903, BAP R1001/1950.

5. Kennedy, *Islands of White,* 172–74.

6. Gerstenhauer, "Das deutsche Schulwesen in Südwestafrika," DKZ, 22 Jan. 1903, 34.

7. Thus, even though East Africa was Germany's largest African colony, white settlement there remained small compared with SWA. For example, in 1912 SWA had 14,816 whites, while East Africa had only 4,866: Cynthia Cohen, "'The Natives Must First Become Good Workmen': Formal Educational Provision in German Southwest Africa and East Africa Compared," *Journal of Southern African Studies* 19 (Mar. 1993): 128–29.

8. Cited in Helene v. Falkenhausen, *Ansiedlerschicksale: Elf Jahre in Deutsch-Südwestafrika, 1893–1904,* 2nd ed. (Berlin: Dietrich Reimer [Ernst Vohsen], 1905), 36; see also Eduard Moritz, *Das Schulwesen in Deutsch-Südwestafrika* (Berlin: Dietrich Reimer [Ernst Vohsen], 1914), 3, 149–54; Hohenlohe, imp. chancellor, "Denkschrift btr. das sudwestafrikanische Schutzgebiet," to the Reichstag, 9. Legislatur-Periode 3, session 1894/95, 1894, BAP, German Reichstag, file 1093 (hereafter, R101/file), BAP; Hohenlohe, Jahresbericht über die Entwicklung von Deutsch-Südwestafrika im Jahre 1896/97, to the Reichstag, 9. Legislatur-Periode 5, session 1897/98, 1898, BAP R101/1094; C. P. Heese, "Das Erziehungswesen in Südwestafrika unter der deutschen Regierung bis 1915," in *SWA Journal,* ed. J. Fischer and P. Meinert (Windhoek: John Meinert, 1986), 135; Cohen, "'Natives,'"125.

9. Moritz, *Das Schulwesen,* 3, 155–56.

10. Denkschrift über die Entwicklung Deutsch-Südwestafrika an den Deutschen Reichstag, 10. Legislatur-Periode 2, session 1900/1903, 1903, BAP, R101/1095; Moritz, *Das Schulwesen,* 3–4, 103–4.

11. Moritz, *Das Schulwesen,* 4–5, 104–6; Bericht über die Sitzung des Ausschusses der DKG, 13 Nov. 1900, BAP, R1001/1949; Valois, DKG executive vice-president, to Bülow, imp. chancellor, 7 Feb. 1901, BAP, R1001/1949; Steubel, Colonial Department director, to Valois, 21 May 1901, BAP, R1001/1949.

12. Moritz, *Das Schulwesen,* 4.

13. Kennedy, *Islands of White,* 169–70.

14. Lindequist, Begründung der Verordnung des Gouverneurs von D-SWA btr. die Einführung der Schulpflicht, 1906, BAP R1001/1950; Moritz, *Das Schulwesen,* 4. Regarding support for the measure, see, e.g., Fuchs, provincial officer, Swakopmund, to imp. govt., Windhoek, 18 May 1905, BAP R1001/6489; "Das Schulwesen in Deutsch-Südwestafrika," *WN,* 2. Blatt, 5 Sept. 1907.

15. Lindequist, Verordnung . . . btr. die Einführung der Schulpflicht, 20 Oct. 1906, BAP R1002/2125; idem, Ausführungsbestimmungen zur Schulpflicht, 1906, BAP R1002/2125; idem, Begründung . . . die Einführung der Schulpflicht, 1906.

16. Alfred Zedlitz, Vorschläge zu einem Gesetzentwurf, btr. weitere räumliche Ausdehnung der Schulpflicht, 1 May 1909, BAP R1002/2729; see also Brill, provincial officer, Windhoek, to imp. govt., Windhoek, 5 Oct. 1909, BAP R151F/FC4737; Schenke, provincial officer, Swakopmund, to imp. govt., Windhoek, 9 Sept. 1909, BAP R151F/FC4737; imp. govt., Windhoek, to RKA, 30 June 1910, BAP R1001/1951.

17. Seitz, Verordnung . . . zur Ergänzung der Verordnung vom 20. Oktober 1906 btr. die Einführung der Schulpflicht, 28 Oct. 1911, BAP R1002/2125; Seitz to RKA, 28 Oct. 1911, BAP R1001/1951; Moritz, *Das Schulwesen,* 9.

18. Lindequist to AA, 26 Mar. 1906, BAP R1001/1950; *Satzungen des Schulgemeinde, bzw. des Schulvorstandes zu Windhoek,* 1906, BAP R1001/1950; Moritz, *Das Schulwesen,* 6–7; Heese, "Das Erziehungswesen," 128.

19. Schuckmann to RKA, 8 Sept. 1908, BAP R1001/1951; Conze, RKA, to imp. treasury, 7 Oct. 1908, BAP R1001/1951; *Denkschrift über die Errichtung von Schulverbände in D-SWA,* 1908, BAP R1001/1951; Schuckmann, *Erlass des Staatssekretärs des Reichskolonialamts,* 15 June 1909, BAP R1002/2729; *Bezirksgesetz für den*

Bezirksverband Warmbad btr. die Erhebung einer Schulsteuer, 30 Aug. 1910, BAP R1001/1951; "Selbsverwaltung. 1. Die Schulfrage," WN, 12 Sept. 1908; Heese, "Das Erziehungswesen," 128.

20. Schuckmann to RKA, 8 Sept. 1908.

21. Brückner, Windhoek, *Rundverfügung an Lehrer und Lehrerinnen,* 1910, BAP R1002/2125.

22. Lindequist, RKA, *Bericht über die Dientsreise nach DSWA vom 19. Juni bis 2. Nov. 1907,* 25 Oct. 1907, BAP Alte Reichskanzlei, file 927 (hereafter, 07.01/file).

23. See, e.g., Moritz, *Das Schulwesen,* 3, 155–56.

24. Ibid., 3, 156–58.

25. Seitz to RKA state secretary, 1913, BAP R1001/1952.

26. Hintrager to RKA, 30 Dec. 1911, BAP R1001/1951; idem, *Rundverfügung btr. Überweisung von Pensionaten an Bezirksverbände* (Gemeinde), 15 June 1912, BAP R1001/2125; Hintrager to RKA, 3 Jan. 1912, BAP R1001/1951; Heinrich Schnee, RKA state secretary, to imp. treasury, 23 Feb. 1912, BAP R1001/1951; Seitz, *Rundverfügung btr. Pensionsbeihilfe,* 30 May 1912, BAP R1001/2125; Hintrager, *Rundverfügung btr. Pensionsbeihilfe,* 13 Jan. 1913, BAP R1001/2125; idem, *Rundverfügung btr. Pensionsbeihilfe,* 12 Mar. 1913, BAP R1001/2125; Moritz, *Das Schulwesen,* 12.

27. Golinelli, RKA, to DKG, 3 Oct. 1907, BAP 61Ko1/948; Theodor von Holleben, DKG executive vice-president, to provincial officer, Windhoek, 18 June 1907, BAP 61Ko1/948; Holleben to Schuckmann, Windhoek, 25 Oct. 1907, BAP 61Ko1/948; ADV Committee for the Boer School Fund to imp. govt., Windhoek, 15 June 1910, BAP R1002/2729.

28. *Jahresbericht über die Entwicklng der Schutzgebiete . . . 1907/08, Teil E: DSWA,* 1909; *Denkschrift über die Entwicklung der Schutzgebiete . . . 1908/09, Teil: DSWA* an den Reichstag, 12. Legislatur-Periode 2, session 1909/10, BAP R1001/6541; Moritz, *Das Schulwesen,* 6, 8–9, 43–46, 28–29.

29. "Jahresbericht über die Entwicklung von Deutsch-Südwestafrika im Jahre 1906/07, 4. Schule und Mission," WN, 4 Apr. 1908, 2. Blatt; Moritz, *Das Schulwesen,* 8, 111–12.

30. Blumhagen, DSWA, to RKA, 12 Nov. 1913, BAP R1001/1952; Hejdebrand, govt. assessor, *Vermerk zu Blumhagens Bericht btr. Prüfungs-Kommission,* 18 Dec. 1913, BAP R1001/1952; Conze, RKA, to Seitz, 19 Mar. 1914, BAP R1001/1952; Seitz to RKA, 7 May 1914, BAP R1001/1952; Gerstmeyer, RKA, to Interior Ministry, 25 June 1914, BAP R1001/1952; Kelch, Reich School Commission chair, Interior Ministry, 8 Aug. 1914, BAP R1001/1952; state secretary, Interior Ministry, to RKA, 19 Aug. 1914, BAP R1001/1952.

31. Heinz Stübig, *Bildung, Militär, und Gesellschaft in Deutschland: Studien zur Entwicklung im 19. Jahrhundert, Studien und Dokumentationen zur deutschen Bildungsgeschichte,* ed. Christoph Führ and Wolfgang Mitter, vol. 54 (Cologne: Böhlau, 1994), 139.

32. Realschule—a form of secondary high school that, compared with one based on a more classical education, emphasized modern instruction.

33. "Das Schulwesen in Deutsch-Südwestafrika," WN, 2. Blatt, 5 Sept. 1907;

Denkschrift über die Entwicklung des höheren Schulwesens im südwestafrikanischen Schutzgebiet, Beilage 2 zum Etat für das südwestafrikanische Schutzgebiet auf das Rechnungsjahr 1912, 1911, BAP R1001/1951; "Realschule Windhoek," *WN,* 21 Mar. 1908; Hinträger to RKA, 19 Nov. 1912, BAP R1001/1951; Moritz, *Das Schulwesen,* 168-69.

34. The Lüderitz Bay school closed after operating for only approximately six months due to a lack of financial support. Moritz, *Das Schulwesen,* 120-21, 139-40.

35. Heese, "Das Erziehungswesen," 134.

36. Schuckmann to RKA, 6 Oct. 1908, BAP R1001/1951.

37. Ibid.

38. Even city officials in Swakopmund preferred to hire Protestants; see Swakopmund city administration to imp. govt., Windhoek, 27 Feb. 1914, BAP R1001/1952.

39. Heese, "Das Erziehungswesen," 135.

40. *Allgemeine Bestimmungen über das Volksschulwesen in Deutsch-Südwestafrika (zum Zwecke der Ausarbeitung von Lehrplänen),* 1911, BAP R1001/2125; K. F. Hoeflich, "Das Deutsche Sprach- und Schulproblem in S.W.A.," in *Ein Leben für Südwestafrika: Festschrift für Dr.h.c. Heinrich Vedder,* ed. W. Drascher and H. J. Rust (Windhoek, 1961), 115; Cohen, "'Natives,'" 127.

41. Wenzel, "Sicherung von Massenloyalität," 342-43, 364-65, 377-78; Bernd Schönemann, "Nationale Identität als Aufgabe des Geschichtsunterrichts nach der Reichsgründung," *Internationale Schulbuchforschung* 11:2 (1989): 107-27. According to Wenzel, the Prussian schools also emphasized religious instruction, but in the colonial setting it did not appear to receive any greater attention: however the colony possessed strong church communities; see chapter 5.

42. Moritz, *Das Schulwesen,* 107, 157; *Allgemeine Bestimmungen über das Volksschulwesen,* 1911, BAP R1001/2125.

43. Kennedy, "Regionalism," 25.

44. Ibid., 26.

45. Celia Applegate, *A Nation of Provincials: The German Idea of Heimat* (Berkeley: University of California Press, 1990), 11.

46. Hinträger, *Rundverfügung an alle Bezirks- (Distrikt-) Ämter,* 5 Sept. 1913, BAP R10012/2125.

47. Foreword and table of contents, *Land und Leute: Eine Heimatkunde für Deutschlands Jugend und Volk,* ed. Bernhard Voigt (Stuttgart, 1913); Hinträger to RKA, 23 Jan. 1913, BAP R1001/1952; Heese, "Das Erziehungswesen," 130.

48. Oskar Wallberg to imp. govt., Windhoek, 4 Sept. 1912, BAP R1001/1951; Hinträger to RKA, 21 Sept. 1912, BAP R1001/1951; e.g., see Royal Bavarian State Ministry of the Royal Household and of Foreign Affairs to RKA, 7 Dec. 1912, BAP R1001/1951; Seitz to RKA, 4 Nov. 1913, BAP R1001/1952.

49. George Mosse, *The Nationalization of the Masses: Political Symbolism and Mass Movements in Germany from the Napoleonic Wars through the Third Reich* (Ithaca, N.Y.: Cornell University Press, 1991), 65.

50. Moritz, *Das Schulwesen,* 32.

51. Seitz, *Rundverfügung,* 12 July 1913, BAP R1002/2125.

52. Kennedy, "A Nation's Reader," 461.

53. "Die Regierungsschule in Windhoek," *WN*, 13 June 1907.

54. Moritz, *Das Schulwesen*, 33; Hintrager, *Rundverfügung an die Regierungs-schulen*, 7 Sept. 1912, BAP R1002/2125; Hintrager, *Rundverfügung an die Kaiserliche Bezirks- (Distrikts-) Ämter*, 7 Sept. 1912, BAP R1002/2125.

55. Cohen, "'Natives,'" 126; Hintrager to RKA, 19 Nov. BAP R1001/1951; Seitz to RKA, 28 July 1913, BAP R1001/1952.

56. Seitz, *Rundverfügung an die Regierungsschule btr. die Austellung von Lehr-plänen*, 1 Nov. 1911, BAP R1002/2125; Rosenberg, Windhoek, *Rundverfügung btr. das Einreichen eines Lehrplanes*, 27 July 1911, BAP R1002/2125; Hintrager, *Rund-verfügung btr. Abänderung der Rundverfügung vom 27. Apr. 1911*, 23 Jan. 1914, BAP R1002/2125.

57. *Dienstvorschrift für den Schulinspektor*, 31 July 1913, BAP R1002/2125; Cohen, "'Natives,'" 128; Heese, "Das Erziehungswesen," 129.

58. Lindequist, RKA, Bericht über die Dienstreise nach DSWA vom 19. Juni bis 2. Nov. 1907, 25 Oct. 1907, BAP 07.01/927; von Blaul, Royal Govt., from Mittelfran-ken, Chamber of the Interior, to Royal School Commission in Nuremberg, 19 July 1913, BAP R1002/1785.

59. Taken from Zedlitz's Diensteid, 17 Feb. 1908, Windhoek, BAP R1002/2004.

60. See, e.g., Vertrag zwischen Margerethe v. Eckenbrecher und Windhuker Schule, 29 Aug. BAP R1002/387; Chamber of Commerce for Duchy of Braunschweig, Department for Commercial Education, Zeugnis über Eckenbrecher, 25 Mar. 1914, BAP R1002/387; Höhere Privatmädchenschule und Lehrerinnenbildungsanstalt zu Stift Keppel, Prüfungszeugnis für die Schulamts-Kandidantin, Eckenbrecher, 1914, BAP R1002/387.

61. Zastrow, provincial officer, Grootfontein, to Seitz, 19 Dec. 1911, BAP R151F/FC4750.

62. Entwurf einer Hausordnung für Pensionate, n.d., BAP R1002/2125.

63. Blumhagen, Windhoek, Erlaß an die Kaiserliche Bezirks- (Distrikts-) Ämter, 15 June 1913, BAP R151F/FC4737.

64. See "Das Jugendheim in Lüderitzbucht," 18–20.

65. Cohen, "'Natives,'" 118.

66. Bericht über die Sitzung des Vorstandes der DKG, 5 Dec. 1896, Berlin, BAP R1001/7306.

67. Moritz, *Das Schulwesen*, 87–88.

68. Bernhard Voigt, *Grundlagen und Weiterentwicklung des Volksschulwesens im Schutzgebiet Deutsch-Südwestafrika*, 1 Sept. 1917, BAP R1002/2125.

69. Calculations based upon Table 4.1.

70. Moritz, *Das Schulwesen*, 47.

71. See, e.g., Bernhard Voigt, *Besichtigung der Regierungsschule zu Swakop-mund*, 22 Mar. 1917, BAP R1002/2127; idem, *Revision der Regierungsschule zu Grootfontein*, 7 June 1917, BAP R1002/2127; idem, *Revision der Regierungsschule zu Karibib*, 2 July 1917, BAP R1002/2127.

72. Voigt, *Grundlagen und Weiterentwicklung*, 1917.

73. "Wie die Sehnsucht ergreifet mein Herze sehr/Nach dem Lande, das gar so weit über'm Meer!/Wie mein Herze stets klopfet voll Jubel empor,/Wenn heimatlich' Klänge berühren mein Ohr,/Wo an die Scholle mich knüpfet manch liebendes Band,/ Da ist meine Heimat, das Hereroland!" "Mein Heimatland," *WN*, 27 June 1908.

74. Voigt, Grundlagen und Weiterentwicklung, 1917.

75. Ibid.

76. Ibid.

CHAPTER 5

1. Lucie Möller, "Deutsche Ortsnamen Südwestafrikas im Rahmen einer historisch-onomastischen Darstellung," *Afrikanischer Heimatkalender* (1984): 47, 52–53; idem, "Deutsche Ortsnamen Südwestafrikas im Rahmen einer historisch-onomastischen Darstellung," *Afrikanischer Heimatkalender* (1986): 42; idem, "Deutsche Ortsnamen Südwestafrikas im Rahmen einer historisch-onomastischen Darstellung," *Afrikanischer Heimatkalender* (1987): 90–95.

2. Heinrich Lamping, "Namibia—Entwicklungen und Perspektiven," in *Namibia: Ausgewählte Themen der Exkursionen 1988*, ed. H. Lamping, Frankfurter Wirtschafts- und Sozialgeographische Schriften 53 (Frankfurt am Main: Institut für Wirtschafts- und Sozialgeographie der Universität Frankfurt, 1989), 12.

3. Hintrager, *Südwestafrika*, 1st ed., 179.

4. N. Mossolow, *Windhoek damals/Die Windhoek van weleer/This Was Old Windhoek*, 2nd ed. (Windhoek: N. Mossolow, 1965), 33, 38.

5. Guido G. Weigend, "German Settlement Patterns in Namibia," *Geographic Review* 75 (Apr. 1985): 163.

6. Bley, *SWA under German Rule*, 125–26, 130–31; Walter Peters, *Baukunst in Südwestafrika 1884–1914: Die Rezeption Deutscher Architektur in der Zeit von 1884 bis 1914 im ehemaligen Deutsch-Südwestafrika (Namibia)* (Windhoek: SWA Wissenschaftliche Gesellschaft, 1981), 80, 122, 142, 188, 249, 253.

7. Hintrager, *Südwestafrika*, 1st ed., 175; Weigend, 163.

8. M. J. Bonn, *Wandering Scholar* (New York: John Day, 1948), 135. Bonn was critical of the entire colonial endeavor and described himself as less conservative and more "liberal."

9. "Deutsches Leben in Südwest," *KuH* 5, no. 15 (1911–12), 4.

10. Peters, *Baukunst*, 168.

11. Lamping, "Namibia—Entwicklungen und Perspektiven," 12–13.

12. R. von Schumann, "Hauptorte in Südwestafrika in ihrer historisch-geographischen Entwicklung—Otjimbingwe, Omaruru, Windhoek," in *Namibia: Ausgewählte Themen der Exkursionen, 1988*, ed. H. Lamping, Frankfurter Wirtschafts- und Sozialgeographische Schriften 53 (Franfurt am Main: Institut für Wirtschafts- und Sozialgeographie der Universität Frankfurt, 1989), 172.

13. Ibid., 160–73; Lamping, "Namibia—Entwicklungen und Perspektiven," 12–21.

14. Mossolow, *Windhoek damals*, 32, 34, 46.

15. *Kolonial-Handels-Adreßbuch*, 7 (1903): 21–27; 12 (1909): 167–78; 17 (1913): 123–45.

16. Hulda Rautenberg, *Das alte Swakopmund, 1892–1919. Swakopmund zum 75. Geburtstag* (Neumünster: Karl Wachholtz, 1867), 119–20, 217–18.

17. *Kolonial-Handels-Adreßbuch*, 4 (1900): 19–23; 7 (1903): 21–27; 12 (1909): 167–78; 17 (1913): 123–45.

18. "Die Entwicklung deutschen Lebens in der Kolonie," *KuH* 2, no. 22 (1908–9): N2.

19. *Kolonial-Handels-Adreßbuch*, 4 (1900): 19–23; 9 (1905): 25–31; 11 (1907): 36–42; 15 (1911): 224–48; 18 (1914): 112–43.

20. *Kolonial-Handels-Adreßbuch*, 7 (1903): 21–27; 12 (1909): 167–78; 18 (1914): 112–43.

21. *Kolonial-Handels-Adreßbuch*, 7 (1903): 21–27; 11 (1907): 36–42; 18 (1914): 112–43.

22. Hintrager, *Südwestafrika*, 1st ed., 179.

23. Rautenberg, *Das alte Swakopmund*, 251.

24. "Deutsches Leben in Südwest," *KuH* 5, no. 15 (1911–12): 4–5, provides a short but insightful account of life in Windhoek in the early 1900s.

25. "Die Turnvereine im deutschen Volksleben," *SWB;* see also Mosse, *Nationalization of the Masses,* 125.

26. Brockmann, *Briefe eines deutschen Mädchens,* 9.

27. Bley, *SWA under German Rule,* 77.

28. Ibid., 75, 77; Mamozai, *Schwarze Frau,* 145–47.

29. Bley, *SWA under German Rule,* 87–88.

30. Ibid., 75, 86–88; Mamozai, *Schwarze Frau,* 148.

31. Schmidt-Lauber, *Die abhängigen Herren,* 66.

32. Ibid., 62.

33. Bley, *SWA under German Rule,* 203.

34. Margarethe v. Eckenbrecher, *Was Afrika mir gab und nahm: 1. Erlebnisse einer deutschen Frau in Südwestafrika, 1902–1936,* 8th ed. (Berlin: Mittler & Sohn, 1940), 154–57.

35. For example, Falkenhausen, *Ansiedlerschicksale;* Eckenbrecher, *Was Afrika mir gab und nahm* and *Deutsch-Südwestafrika: Kriegs- und Friedensbilder* (Berlin-Leipzig: Mittler und Sohn, 1907); Brockmann, *Die deutsche Frau in Südwestafrika* and *Briefe eines deutschen Mädchens;* Lydia Höpker, *Um Scholle und Leben. Schicksale einer deutschen Farmerin in Südwest-Afrika* (Minden in Westfalen: Wilhelm Köhler, 1927); Bernhard Voigt, *Südwestafrika, einst und jetzt* (Bochum: F. Kamp, 1939); idem, *Du meine Heimat Deutschsüdwest: Ein afrikanisches Farmleben* (Berlin: Safari, 1925); and idem, *Auf dorniger Pad: Aus Deutsch-Südwestafrikas alten Tagen* (Berlin: Safari, 1926); and Paul Leutwein, *"Du weitest Deine Brust, der Blick wird freier," Kriegs- und Wanderfahrten in Südwest* (Berlin: Deutscher Kolonial-Verlag, 1909).

36. Höpker, *Um Scholle und Leben,* 21; quoted in Amadou Booker Sadji, "African Nature and German Culture: Colonial Women Writers on Africa," in *Blacks*

and German Culture, ed. Reinhold Grimm and Jost Hermand (Madison: University of Wisconsin Press, 1986), 27.

37. Eckenbrecher, *Was Afrika mir gab und nahm* (1904), 146; quoted in Sadji, "African Nature and German Culture," 26.

38. Sadji, "African Nature and German Culture," 23-24, 27; see also Sibylle Benninghoff-Lühl, *Deutsche Kolonialromane 1884-1914 in ihrem Entstehungs- und Wirkungszusammenhang* (Bremen Übersee-Museum Bremen, 1983), 167-69.

39. Brockmann, "Deutsche Frauen in Südwestafrika," *KuH* 2, no. 22 (1908-9): 2; see also John Noyes, *Colonial Space: Spatiality in the Discourse of German South West Africa, 1884-1915* (Chur, Switzerland: Harwood Academic, 1992), 252-63; Benninghoff-Lühl, *Deutsche Kolonialromane*, 163, 180.

40. See Amadou Booker Sadji, *Das Bild des Negro-Afrikaners in der deutschen Kolonialliteratur, 1884-1945: Ein Beitrag zur literarischen Imagologie Schwarzafrikas* (Berlin: Dietrich Reimer, 1985), esp. chapter "Hausfrauen- und Ansiedlerliteratur"; idem, "African Nature and German Culture," 29-31; and Benninghoff-Lühl, *Deutsche Kolonialromane*, 169-70.

41. Helbig and Helbig, *Mythos Deutsch-Südwest*, 134.

42. Ibid.

43. Bley, *SWA under German Rule*, 174-201; see also Schmidt-Lauber, *Die abhängigen Herren*, 60-61, 66.

44. Bley, *SWA under German Rule*, 189-90; Dernburg, *Verordnung des Reichskanzlers btr. die Selbstverwaltung in Deutsch-Südwestafrika*, 29 Jan. 1909, BAP R1001/2058; Schuckmann, *Verordnung btr. Ausführung der Verordnung über die Selbstverwaltung*, 15 May 1909, BAP R1001/2058; idem, *Verordnung btr. Ausführung der Verordnung über Selbstverwaltung*, 16 Aug. 1909, BAP R1001/2058; Hintrager, *Erlaß an die Kaiserliche Bezirks- Distrikts- Ämter*, 15 July 1910, BAP R1002/2726.

45. Die Wahlrechtsfrage," *WN*, 24 Oct. 1908; "Die Verstimmung über die Selbstverwaltung," *DKZ*, 22 May 1909, 355; "Die Verstimmung über die Selbstverwaltung," *DKZ*, 29 May 1909, 363-64; "Was uns not tut, I." *WN*, 2 Mar. 1910; "Was uns not tut, II." *WN*, 5 Mar. 1910; and "Was uns not tut, III." *WN*, 9 Mar. 1910.

46. Wilhelm Föllmer, "Das Wahlrecht in unseren Kolonien," *WN*, 2. Blatt, 15 Aug. 1908.

47. Wilhelm Külz, *Die Selbstverwaltung für Deutsch-Südwestafrika* (Berlin: Wilhelm Süsseroff, 1909), 52.

48. "Dr. Külz-Bückeburg über Südwestafrika," *Tätgliche Rundschau*, Morgen Ausgabe, 4 Dec. 1909, BAK N1042/33; Seitz, *Die Gouverneursjahre in Südwestafrika*, 9-10; Bley, *SWA under German Rule*, 195.

49. Bley, *SWA under German Rule*, 196; Seitz, *Die Gouverneursjahre in Südwestafrika*, 17.

50. Schmidt-Lauber, *Die abhängigen Herren*, 66-67; Bley, *SWA under German Rule*, 213-14, 217, 240.

51. Antonie Brandeis, "Menus aus Landesprodukten der Tropen," *KuH* 1, no. 19 (1907-8): R3.

52. Mamozai, *Schwarze Frau*, 148.

53. For the role of print media in the "creation" of a larger community or nation, see Anderson, *Imagined Communities*, chapter 5, "Old Languages, New Models."

54. "Südwestafrikanische Landeshymne," *Fest-Kommers anläßlich der Fahnenweihe des Kriegervereins Karibib-Lieder-Texte*, 11 Apr. 1914, BAP R151F/FC5241.

55. Celia Applegate, "What Is German Music? Reflections on the Role of Art in the Creation of the German Nation," *German Studies Review*, special issue: *German Identity* (winter 1992): 30, 22.

56. "Heimat," *SWB*, 25 Jan. 1914.

57. "Mein Heimatland," *WN*, 27 June 1908.

58. A. Hermkes, "Der deutsche Farmer in Südwest!" *SWB*, 2. Blatt, 7 Sept. 1913.

59. Wolfgang Hardtwig, "Nationsbildung und politische Mentalität: Denkmal und Fest im Kaiserreich," chapter in *Geschichtskultur und Wissenschaft* (Munich: Deutscher Taschenbuch, 1990), 266, 265.

60. See, e.g., Mossolow, *Windhoek damals*, 37; "Das Landesfest am Kaisertage," *SWB*, 31 Jan. 1912. For the significance of these holidays in Germany, see Fritz Schellack, "Sedan- und Kaisergeburtstagsfeste," in *Öffentliche Festkultur: Politische Feste in Deutschland von der Aufklärung bis zum Ersten Weltkrieg*, ed. Dieter Düring, Peter Friedemann, and Paul Münch (Reinbek bei Hamburg: Rowohlt, 1988), 278–97; and Monika Weinfurt, "Kaisergeburtstagsfeiern am 27. Jan. 1907: Bürgerliche Feste in den Städte des Deutschen Kaiserreichs," in *Bürgerliche Feste: Symbolische Formen politischen Handelns im 19. Jahrhundert*, ed. Manfred Hettling and Paul Nolte (Göttingen: Vandenhoeck & Ruprecht, 1993), 157–91.

61. Joseph Perry, "Frontweihnachten, 1914–1917: A Community of Longing," paper given at Second Annual Transatlantic Seminar in German History, Bochum, Germany, Apr. 17–20, 1996, photocopy, 6.

62. "Deutsche Weihnacht!" *SWB*, 24 Dec. 1913; see also "Ostern," *SWB*, 15 Apr. 1911; "Südwestafrikanische Ostergedanken," *SWB*, 12 Apr. 1914.

63. "Die Südwester bei der Völkerschlachtfeier in Leipzig," *SWB*, 26 Nov. 1913. There is a growing historiography surrounding this event, especially in terms of using the jubilation accompanying the celebration as a means to explain the enthusiasm expressed at the outbreak of World War I; see, e.g., Wolfram Siemann, "Krieg und Frieden in historischen Gedenkfeiern des Jahres 1913," in *Öffentliche Festkultur*, 298–20, and Ute Schneider, "War in Mind: Celebrations and War Enthusiasm in the Rhineland, 1913," in *Festive Culture in Germany and Europe from the Sixteenth to the Twentieth Century*, ed. Karin Friedrich (Lewiston: Edwin Mellon, 2000), 265–80. However, a recent essay by Smith rejects this idea; see Jeffrey Smith, "The Monarchy versus the Nation: The 'Festive Year' 1913 in Wilhelmine Germany," *German Studies Review* 23, no. 2 (2000): 270–72.

64. Hintrager, *Südwestafrika*, 1st ed., 179; Lenssen, *Chronik von Deutsch-Südwestafrika*, 80; Mossolow, *Windhoek Damals*, 39; idem, *Windhoek: Drei historische Wahrzeichen/Drie geskiedkundige Kentekens/Three Historical Landmarks* (Windhoek: John Meinert, 1972), 65; Hans Hartmut Diehl, "Brief History of the Evangelical Lutheran Church in Namibia (GELC)," in *Lutheran Churches in*

Namibia: A Brief Historical Survey of the Three Lutheran Churches in Namibia, trans. E. Hoffmann (Windhoek: ELOC, 1995), 17; Carl J. Hellberg, *Mission, Colonialism, and Liberation: The Lutheran Church in Namibia, 1840–1966* (Windhoek: New Namibia, 1997), 129.

65. Hellberg, *Mission, Colonialism, and Liberation*, 129.

66. N. Mossolow, *Windhoek*, 66–67; Hintrager, *Südwestafrika*, 1st ed., 131.

67. Mossolow, *Windhoek*, 67.

68. Hintrager, *Südwestafrika*, 131.

69. Mossolow, *Windhoek damals*, 47.

70. Ibid.; idem, *Windhoek*, 67; Hintrager, *Südwestafrika*, 131; Schumann, "Hauptorte in Südwestafrika," 166.

71. Bley, *SWA under German Rule*, 131.

72. Quoted in Hintrager, *Südwestafrika*, 1st ed., 169.

73. Hans Grimm, "Aus Gustav Voigts' Leben," chapter in *Das Deutsche Südwester Buch* (Munich: Albert Langen, 1929), 120.

74. "Südwestafrikanische Landesausstellung 1914" [press release], 1914, BAP 61Ko1/37.

75. "Die erste südwestafrikanische Landesausstellung zu Windhuk vom 29. bis 31. Mai 1909," *DKZ*, 24 July 1909, 497–99.

76. R. Matthiessen, Territorial Fair Propaganda Committee, to DKG, 19 June 1914, BAP 61Ko1/37.

77. "Heimat," *SWB*, 25 Jan. 1914.

78. "Das Nationalbewußtsein unserer Kolonisten," *SWB*, 29 Aug. 1913.

79. Joachim Warmbold, *Germania in Africa: Germany's Colonial Literature*, Studies in Modern German Literature, ed. D. G. Brown, vol. 22 (New York: Peter Lang, 1989), 163.

80. Reinhart Koselleck, "Kriegerdenkmale als Identitätsstiftungen der Überlebenden," in *Identität*, 2nd ed., ed. Oda Marquard and Karlheinz Stierle (Munich: Wilhelm Fink, 1996), 256, 259.

81. Thomas Nipperdey, "Nationalidee und Nationaldenkmal in Deutschland im 19. Jahrhundert," *Historische Zeitschrift* 206, no. 3 (1968): 529–85; Hardtwig, "Nationsbildung und politische Mentalität," 265–66.

82. For example, the Windhoek Troop Garden commemorating those who fell in the Witboo War in April 1897 or the Marine Memorial in Swakopmund honoring those marines who lost their lives in the 1904–7 uprisings; Lenssen, *Chronik von Deutsch-Südwestafrika*, 89; Mossolow, *Windhoek damals*, 36; Peters, *Baukunst*, 203.

83. Gustav Zelle, "Rund um den Reiter von Südwest in Windoek . . . und ein kleiner Mosaik—Beitrag zu aktuellen Thema südliches Afrika," in *Symbol für Südwestafrika, der Reiter von Südwest: die ehemalige deutsche Schutztruppe und ihr Beitrag zur Erforschung und Entwicklung des Landes und seiner Menschen*, ed. Hans Schmiedel, Shriftenreihe zur Familien- und Sippenkunde für Heimat und Geschichte, 25 (Düsseldorf: G. Zelle, 1979), 54–58; Mossolow, *Windhoek damals*, 47; Noyes, *Colonial Space*, 257.

84. Alon Confino, "The Nation as Local Metaphor: Heimat, National Memory,

and the German Empire, 1871–1918," *History and Memory* 5, no. 1 (1993): 59–60; see also Martin Roth, *Heimatmuseum: Zur Geschichte einer deutschen Institution,* Berliner Schriften zur Museumkunde, vol. 7 (Berlin: Gebrüder Mann, 1990); Heinz Reif, Sigrid Heinze und Andreas Ludwig, "Schwierigkeiten mit Tradition: Zur kulturellen Praxis städtischer Heimatmuseen," in *Das historische Musem: Labor, Schaubühne, Identitätsfabrik,* ed. Gottfried Korff and Martin Roth (Frankfurt: Campus, 1990), 231–47.

85. W. Külz, *Die Selbstverwaltung,* 5.

86. General Louis Botha, "Bekanntmachung," 9 July 1915, BAK N1037/17; Stoecker, "Der erste Weltkrieg," in *Drang nach Afrika: Die deutsche koloniale Expansionspolitik und Herrschaft in Afrika von den Anfängen bis zum Verlust der Kolonien,* ed. Stoecker (Berlin: Akademie, 1991), 240–41; William Roger Louis, *Great Britain and Germany's Lost Colonies, 1914–1919* (Oxford: Clarendon Press, 1967), 51–54; Pisani, *Politics,* 47; Byron Farwell, *The Great War in Africa, 1914–1918* (New York: Norton, 1986), 86–104.

87. Pisani, *Politics,* 47; Stoecker, "Der erste Weltkrieg," 241; Adolf Rüger, "Das Streben nach kolonialer Restitution in den ersten Nachkriegsjahren," in *Drang nach Afrika,* 280.

88. Stoecker, "Der erste Weltkrieg," 241; Rüger, "Das Streben nach kolonialer Restitution," 280.

89. For a more detailed discussion, see Maynard W. Swanson, "South West Africa in Trust, 1915–1939," in *Britain and Germany in Africa,* ed. Prosser Gifford and Wm. Roger Louis (New Haven: Yale University Press, 1967), 631–46; Pisani, *Politics,* 46.

90. DKG to Frau Geh.Reg.Rat Hanna Methner (z.Zt. Berlin-Schöneberg), 22 Dec. 1914, BAP 61Ko1/179.

91. RKA to Finanzrat O. Loy, 17 Aug. 1918, BAP R1001/1145.

92. Swanson, "SWA in Trust," 648–49.

93. Höpker, *Um Scholle und Leben,* 120.

94. Schmidt-Lauber, *Die abhängigen Herren,* 69; Swanson, "SWA in Trust," 648–49.

95. Regarding the Ovambo, see Patricia Hayes, "'Cocky' Hahn and the 'Black Venus': The Making of a Native Commissioner in South West Africa, 1915–46," *Gender and History* 8, no. 3 (1996): 364–92; re. the Ovambo and Bondelwarts, see Helbig and Helbig, *Mythos Deutsch-Südwest,* 185–87.

96. Bernhard Voigt, *Wiedereröffnung der Schulen nach der feindlichen Besetzung und das Verhalten einiger Lehrkräfte mit Anlagen,* 10 June 1917, BAP R1002/2133; Ullmann, *Kommentar zum Bericht über die Revision der Regierungsschule am 17.-19. Juli 1917 mit Abschrift der Revision,* 28 July 1917, BAP R1002/2127; Voigt to Karlowa, 6 Aug. 1917, BAP R1002/2127; Karlowa to Ullmann, 6 Aug. 1917, BAP R1002/2127; Voigt to Karlowa, 18 Jan. 1918, BAP R1002/2127; Kastl, *Rundverfügung,* 6 Mar. 1916, BAP R1002/2125; *Schulbericht aus Pomona,* 20 June 1917, BAP R1002/2125; Voigt, *Lehrplan der südwestafrikanishen Schulen,* 1918, BAP R1002/2125.

97. Voigt, Grundlagen und Weiterentwicklung.

98. "Ansiedlung südafrikanischer Bürger in Deutsch-Südwest," *Deutsche Tageszeitung*, 30 July 1915, BAP R8034II/6372.

99. Eckenbrecher, *Was Afrika Mir Gab und Nahm*, 214.

100. Lindequist, "Was wird aus Südwestafrika?" *Tägliche Rundschau*, 11 July 1918, BAP R8034II/6372.

101. George F. Kohn, "The Organization and Work of the League of Nations," supplement to *The Annals of the American Academy of Political and Social Sciences* 114 (July 1924): 71.

102. Byron Dextor, *The Years of Opportunity: The League of Nations, 1920–1926* (New York: Viking, 1967), 49. The A mandates were the "former Turkish territories which have reached a stage of development which permits them to be independent nations, but which need certain administrative supervision until they are able to 'stand alone.'" Britain and France became mandatories for these territories. The B mandates were the Central African colonies (Togo, Cameroon, and Tanganyika) "whose development is at a stage 'that the mandatory must be responsible for the administration of the territory under conditions that will guarantee the freedom of conscience or religion'" for the indigenous population with certain limitations in the interest of security and peace. France, Britain, and Belgium received territory under this category. The C mandates were Southwest Africa and the Pacific Islands, "'which, owing to the sparseness of their population or their small size, or their remoteness from the centres of civilization, or their geographical contiguity to the territory of the mandatory, and other circumstances, can best be administered under the laws of the mandatory as integral portions of its territory, subject to the safeguards . . . mentioned in the interests of the indigenous population.'" These territories went to the non-European powers. Kohn, "League of Nations," 71.

103. Helbig and Helbig, *Mythos Deutsch-Südwest*, 191.

104. The most notable were Hans Grimm, *Volk ohne Raum* (München: Lippoldsberg, 1926), idem, *Dreizehn Briefe aus Deutsch-Südwest-Afrika* (Munich: Albert Langen, 1928), and *Das Deutsche Südwester Buch;* and Heinrich Schnee, *German Colonization, Past and Future: The Truth about the German Colonies* (New York: Knopf, 1926).

105. Hans Ernst Blumhagen, *Die Doppelstatigkeit der Deutschen im Mandatsgebiet Südwestafrika und ihre völkerrechtlichen Auswirkungen* (Berlin: D. Reimer, 1938); Kurt Wiedern, *Deutsche Staatsangehörigkeit im C-Mandat Südwestafrika* (Greifswald, 1934); Hugo Blumhagen, *Entscheidungsjahre in Deutsch-Südwestafrika* (Berlin: Dieter Reimer/Ernst Vohsen, 1939).

106. Rüger, "Das Streben nach kolonialer Restitution," 262–77; Hartmut Pogge von Strandmann, "Imperialism and Revisionism in Interwar Germany," *Imperialism and After: Continuities and Discontinuities*, ed. Wolfgang Mommsen and Jürgen Osterhammel (London: Allen & Unwin, 1986), 92–97; Wolfe W. Schmokel, *Dream of Empire: German Colonialism, 1919–1945* (New Haven: Yale University Press, 1964), 58–72; Adolf Rüger, "Imperialismus, Sozialreformismus und antikoloniale demokratische Alternative," *Zeitschrift für Geschichtswissenschaft* 23, no. 11

(1975): 1293–308; Andrew J. Crozier, *Appeasement and Germany's Last Bid for Colonies* (New York: St. Martin's, 1988).

107. Swanson, "SWA in Trust," 645–46.

108. Helbig and Helbig, *Mythos Deutsch-Südwest*, 190; Pisani, *Politics*, 52.

109. Schmidt-Lauber, *Die abhängigen Herren*, 70, 72–73. Schmidt-Lauber argues that they idealized the German period, which they undeniably did. I would nonetheless argue that their heightened sense of identity in the interwar years undoubtedly built upon the foundations established during the time of German control.

110. *Korag Richtlinien*, 8 June 1925, BAP 61 Ko1/561.

111. Schmidt-Lauber, *Die abhängigen Herren*, 72.

CHAPTER 6

1. Gerstmeyer to DKG, 4 Nov. 1919, BAP 61 Ko1/178.

2. A. Stauch, Lecture about Southwest Africa at VfDSW's membership assembly, 15 Dec. 1926, 61 Ko1/533. The VfDSW was founded in 1916 with the goal of promoting settlement in Germany itself and of strengthening Deutschtum abroad. Various associations belonged to it, including the DKG, VDA, and the Pan-German League, as well as other patriotic organizations pursuing similar goals; see also Jung, RWA, *Vereinigung für Deutsche Siedlung und Wanderung*, no. 183, 27 Feb. 1920, BAP 61 Ko1/126.

3. Seitz to Woermann-Linie, Hamburg, 5 Jan. 1927, BAP 61 Ko1/533.

4. Hinträger, "Unsere Frauenauswanderung," *Koloniale Frauenarbeit* (1930): 23, BAK N1037/4.

5. A. G. Sappeur-Flury to Korag, 1927, BAP 61 Ko1/578.

6. *Südwester* to RKA, 29 May 1918, BAP R1001/1145; Südwester, *Erläuterungen zu der Hingabe der Südwest-Afrikaner an das RKA! Warum Südwest deutsch bleiben muß!* 1918, BAP R1001/1145; *Südwester* to the German Armistice Commission, 7 Jan. 1919, BAP R1001/1145; Bertelsmann, *Die deutsche Sprachgruppe Südwestafrikas*, 15.

7. Pisani, *Politics*, 52.

8. Winkler, DKG, to Miss Paul, Berlin-Wilmersdorf, 5 June 1919, BAP 61 Ko1/180; DKG to Max Göbel, Riesenthal, 10 June 1919, BAP 61 Ko1/180; Blumhagen, Reich migration office, to German consulate, Rotterdam, 14 Jan. 1920, BAP R1001/1226; German consulate, Rotterdam, to Reich migration office, 26 Jan. 1920, BAP R1001/1226; Winkler to Ernst Wache, 5 Jan. 1921, BAP 61 Ko1/181; Winkler to Günther Hertwig, Meiningen, 6 Jan. 1921, BAP 61 Ko1/181; Bertelsmann, *Die deutsche Sprachgruppe Südwestafrikas*, 16–17.

9. Vice-consul Bräuer, Pretoria, to AA, 11 Aug. 1924, BAP 61 Ko1/531; Bertelsmann, *Die deutsche Sprachgruppe Südwestafrikas*, 83.

10. Bräuer to AA; Hinträger to AA, 21 July 1924, BAP 61 Ko1/146; Stark, *Ansiedlungsbedingungen für Südwestafrika* (Windhoek, 1925), BAP R1001/1145; Bertelsmann, *Die deutsche Sprachgruppe Südwestafrikas*, 16, 23–24, 83–84.

11. Statistics from Grimm, *Die Dreizehn Briefe*, 91, and M. Neuendorf, "Geschlossenes Volkstum in weiter Steppe," *Wir Deutsche in der Welt*, ed. Verband Deutscher Vereine im Ausland e.V. (Berlin, 1937), 129; cited in Bertelsmann, *Die deutsche Sprachgruppe Südwestafrikas*, 85.

12. Hintrager, "Ein Wiedersehen mit Südwestafrika"; lecture held before the full assembly of the Syndicate for German Migration, 10 Dec. 1930, BAP 61Ko1/125.

13. Bertelsmann, *Die deutsche Sprachgruppe Südwestafrikas*, 85–86.

14. Blank to Hintrager, 30 Sept. 1926, BAP 61Ko1/125.

15. Eltester, AA, to Hartmann, Rothstock/Oderbruch, 19 Nov. 1931, BAP R1001/7427; Oelhafen to AA, 4 Mar. 1938; see also table 6.1.

16. Bertelsmann, *Die deutsche Sprachgruppe Südwestafrikas*, 84.

17. Seitz to H. Roeckl, Munich, 2 Nov. 1927, BAP 61Ko1/534.

18. S.S., SWA, "Südwestafrika als Ziel deutscher Auswanderer," *DA* 9, no. 22 (1926): 715–16; Aenne Klatt-Müller, "Die Berufsstätigkeit unserer Kolonialdeutschen in Südwest," *DKZ* 50 (1938): 233–34.

19. Hans Denk, lecture about Southwest Africa, 26 Oct. 1928, BAP 61Ko1/125.

20. H. Mehnert, *Koloniesationsmöglichkeiten in Deutsch-Süd-West-Afrika-Mandat*, 1927, BAP 61Ko1/533.

21. *Besprechung über die Unterbringung von Neueinwanderern*, Windhoek, 1 June 1926, BAP R1001/1771.

22. Franz, German consul, SWA, to AA, 28 Nov. 1927, BAP R1001/1146.

23. Sofie von Uhde, *Deutsche unterm Kreuz des Südens: Bei den Kolonialsiedlern in Südwest und Ostafrika* (Berlin: Dietrich Reimer/Ernst Vohsen, 1934), 74.

24. Franz, German consul, SWA, to AA, 28 Nov. 1927, BAP R1001/1146.

25. *Besprechung über die Einwanderung nach Südwest*, Windhoek, 27 May 1926, BAP R1001/1771; *Besprechung über die Unterbringung von Neueinwandern*; Franz to AA, 10 June 1926, BAP R1001/1771.

26. RfA, *Südwestafrika*, leaflet no. 5, 1926, BAP R1001/1146.

27. RWA, *Die Pflichten des deutschen Auswanderers im Auslande*, leaflet no. 38, 1921, BAP 61Ko1/126.

28. *Protocol of the Founding Meeting of the Colonial Reich Syndicate*, Halle, 1922, BAP 61Ko1/559; *Politische Ziele der Koloniale Reichsarbeitsgemeinschaft*, 1925/6, BAP 61Ko1/559.

29. RfA, *Farmangebote in Südwestafrika*, leaflet no. 666, 15 Jan. 1925, BAP 61Ko1/124; RfA, *Farmangebote in Südwestafrika*, leaflet no. 670, 22 Jan. 1925, BAP 61Ko1/125; Rische, Duisburg-Meiderich, to DKG, 31 Aug. 1930, BAP 61Ko1/118.

30. Bielfeld, AA, to Foreign Currency Exchange, Berlin, 30 May 1939, BAP R1001/1168.

31. RfA, *South West Land and Settlement Company, Ltd.*, leaflet no. 833, 22 Feb. 1927, BAP 61Ko1/125.

32. Regarding the craftsmen, see Seitz to AA, 20 Apr. 1926, BAP R1001/1165; Hintrager, RfA, to AA, 15 May 1926, BAP R1001/1165; F. W. Kegel, Tsumeb, to Franz, 23 Aug. 1926, BAP R1001/1165; Franz to German consulate-general, Pretoria, 14 Sept. 1926, BAP R1001/1165; AA to Seitz, 27 Oct. 1926, BAP R1001/1165. With regard

to the Volga Germans, see Seitz to AA, 20 Jan. 1927, BAP 61Ko1/125; Reich Interior Ministry to RfA, 19 Jan. 1927, BAP R1001/1166; RfA to AA, 28 Jan. 1927, BAP R1001/1166; RfA to AA, 18 Mar. 1927, BAP R1001/1166.

33. Denk, lecture about Southwest Africa, 26 Oct. 1928.

34. Franz to AA, 10 June 1926, BAP R1001/1771; Franz to RfA, 9 Apr. 1926, BAP R1001/1146; Franz to AA, 28 Nov. 1927, BAP R1001/1146.

35. Franz to RfA, 8 Feb. 1926, BAP 61Ko1/349; Paul Barth, FWG secretary, to RfA, 3 May 1927, BAP 61Ko1/125; Barth to Seitz, 19 Nov. 1928, BAP 61Ko1/351; Barth to Seitz, 6 July 1927, BAP 61Ko1/351; Barth to DKG, 31 Jan. 1929, BAP 61Ko1/351.

36. Barth to RfA, 3 May 1927, BAP 61Ko1/125.

37. Hinträger to AA, 21 July 1924, BAP 61Ko1/146.

38. S.S., "Südwestafrika als Ziel deutscher Auswanderer," 716; Barth to RfA, 3 May 1927; Barth to AA, 15 Dec. 1927, BAP 61Ko1/351; RfA, *Farmvolontäre in Südwestafrika,* leaflet no. 740, 3 Sept. 1925, BAP 61Ko1/124; RfA, *Verzeichnis der Farmer in Südwestafrika, die Volontäre aufnehmen,* 1925, BAP 61Ko1/124; Franz to RfA, 13 July 1926, BAP R1001/1146.

39. Hinträger, RfA, *Erlaß btr. Farmvolontäre in Südwestafrika,* 28 Mar. 1927, BAP 61Ko1/125.

40. Excerpt from a letter by Gustav Frenzel, Otjivero, SWA, 20 Mar. 1927, BAP 61Ko1/125.

41. Franz to AA, 5 Nov. 1928, BAP R1001/1146; see also Hinträger to AA, 28 Oct. 1926, BAP R1001/1772.

42. Hinträger to AA, 28 Oct. 1926.

43. Franz to RfA, 17 May 1925, BAP R1001/1145.

44. Ibid.; RfA, *Verzeichnis der Vertrauensleute,* 1925, BAP 61Ko1/124; Franz to AA, 20 June 1925, BAP R1001/1145.

45. Paul Barth, VdR secretary, *Geschäftsbericht 1925,* 20 July 1925, BAP 61Ko1/346; VdR, "Landsleute! Reichsdeutsche!," leaflet, July 1925, BAP 61Ko1/346.

46. Franz to AA, 28 Nov. 1927; Barth, *Geschäftsbericht 1925;* Barth to Seitz, 15 Apr. 1929, BAP 61Ko1/346a.

47. Seitz to Brenner, DB chair, 28 Aug. 1925, BAP 61Ko1/346; VdR to DB, 14 Sept. 1925, BAP 61Ko1/346a; de Haas, AA, to German consulate-general, Pretoria, 31 Aug. 1926, BAP R1001/1773; VdR to Seitz, 27 Dec. 1925, BAP 61Ko1/346a; Barth to Seitz, 7 Aug. 1926, BAP 61Ko1/533.

48. Franz to AA, 4 Oct. 1928, BAP R1001/1773; Pastor Winfried Ebers, Windhoek, to Herzog zu Mecklenburg, 14 July 1925, BAP 61Ko1/346a; *Verzeichnis der Optanten in SWA,* 1925, BAP 61Ko1/346; DKG to German Municipal Congress *(Städetag),* Berlin, 16 Aug. 1928, BAP 61Ko1/346a; Hinträger, RfA, to Reich Interior Ministry, 14 Aug. 1928, BAP R1001/1773.

49. Agnes von Boemcken, FB deputy chair, to AA, 6 July 1926, BAP R1001/1197.

50. Hinträger, RfA, to Reich Minister of the Interior and to AA, 2 Mar. 1928, BAP R1001/1146.

51. Hinträger to AA, 23 May 1928, BAP R1001/1197.

52. Idem, 12 Dec. 1927, BAP R1001/1197.

53. Idem, 4 Apr. 1928, BAP R1001/1197.

54. Idem, 10 July 1926, BAP R1001/1197; Brückner, AA, to FB, 29 Sept. 1926, BAP R1001/1197; idem, 23 May 1928; Brückner to RfA, 13 Nov. 1928, BAP R1001/1197; Hintrager to Reich Interior Ministry and AA, 2 Mar. 1928.

55. *Satzungen des FB der DKG*, 1927, BAP R1001/6693; Boemcken to AA, 15 Mar. 1925, BAP R1001/6693; Mamozoi, *Schwarze Frau*, 204.

56. FB, *Richtlinien für Reisebeihilfen*, 1928, BAP R1001/1197; Margarete Schnitzket, "Bericht über die Stellenvermittlung nach Südwestafrika," *Koloniale Frauenarbeit* (1927): 24–27, BAP R1001/6693; Hintrager, "Die deutsche Frauenauswanderung nach Afrika," *Mitteilungen des Frauenbundes der Deutschen Kolonialgesellschaft*, no. 6 (Sonderdruck, 1931), BAP R1001/6694; Frida Voigts, speech at the FB Conference, Windhoek, 17–18 Oct. 1929, BAP R1001/1197.

57. FB to Reich Institute for Employment and Unemployment Insurance, 22 Feb. 1936, BAP R1001/6695.

58. FB, *Richtlinien für Reisebeihilfen*, 1928.

59. Schnitzket, "Bericht über die Stellen-Vermittlung nach Südwestafrika."

60. Hintrager, "Die deutsche Frauenauswanderung nach Afrika."

61. Sofie von Uhde, "Farmersfrau in Südwest," *Das Illustrierte Blatt der Frau: Fürs Haus*, 29 June 1933, BAP R1001/1941.

62. These numbers refer to the total number of whites immigrating to SWA from overseas. South African officials made no national distinctions in their data collection. For the actual number of Germans, only figures for 1928 exist: according to Hintrager, in that year 325 German men and 281 German women went to the mandate from Germany; for 1926–28, Hintrager to AA, 8 Jan. 1930, BAP R1001/1197; for 1924 and 1925, see Hintrager to AA, 2 Mar. 1928.

63. Frida Voigts, speech at the Women's League Conference, 17 or 18 Oct. 1929.

64. Hintrager to AA, 8 Nov. 1929, BAP R1001/1197.

65. FB, *Übersicht über das Ergehen der nach Südwest- und Ostafrika gesandten Mädchen 1929*, 1930, BAP R1001/1198.

66. Hintrager, "Die deutsche Frauenauswanderung nach Afrika."

67. FB, *Übersicht über das Ergehen der nach Südwest- und Ostafrika gesandten Mädchen 1929*, 1930.

68. FB, *1930 Jahresbericht über die Auswandererhilfe und Stellenvermittlung*, 15 Jan. 1931, BAP R1001/1198.

69. Schmidt, RfA, to AA, 2 June 1930, BAP R1001/1198.

70. F. Voigts, speech to Women's League conference, 17 or 18 Oct. 1929.

71. Franz to AA, 8 Jan. 1930, BAP R1001/1197.

72. Hintrager to AA, 8 Jan. 1930.

73. Ibid.

74. Franz to AA, 8 Jan. 1930.

75. Hintrager to AA, 8 Jan. 1930.

76. Eltester, AA, to RfA, 14 Apr. 1931, BAP R1001/1198; Eltester to Reich Interior Ministry, 21 Apr. 1931, BAP R1001/1198.

77. Bertelsmann, *Die deutsche Sprachgruppe Südwestafrikas*, 88–89.

Chapter 7

1. Fock, LdDS, to VDA, 19 Feb. 1920, BAP 61Ko1/957.

2. Uhde, *Deutsche Unterm Kreuz des Südens*, 44.

3. Bernhard Voigt, *Bericht btr. die Übernahme der Deutschen Schulen als Regierungsschulen durch die Regierung*, 14 Apr. 1921, BAP 61Ko1/958; Eckenbrecher, *Was Afrika Mir Gab und Nahm*, 267; H.-V. Gretschel, "The Lost 'Umlaut': The German Language in Namibia, 1915-1939—a Suppressed Language?" *Logos* 13 (1993): 51; Bertelsmann, *Die deutsche Sprachgruppe Südwestafrikas*, 17-18.

4. Fritzsche, Windhoek, to Seitz, DKG president, 28 Sept. 1920, BAP 61Ko1/957.

5. Bertelsmann, *Die deutsche Sprachgruppe Südwestafrikas*, 18.

6. Voigt, *Bericht btr. die Übernahme der Deutschen Schule*, 1921.

7. Walter Ahlhorn to DKG directorate, 4 Mar. 1920, BAP 61Ko1/957; "Der Kampf um die deutschen Schulen in Südwestafrika," Magdeburgische Zeitung, 30 May 1920, BAP R1001/1953; Bertelsmann, *Die deutsche Sprachgruppe Südwestafrikas*, 18.

8. "Ein Erfolg des Deutschtums in Südwestafrika," Deutsche Zeitung, 1 Dec. 1921, BAP R1001/1953; "Deutschtum im Ausland, ein Burenblatt über das deutsche Schulwesen in Südwest," Weser-Zeitung, 6 Aug. 1921, BAP 61Ko1/147; Seitz to Lotz, LdDS chair, 1 Sept. 1921, BAP 61Ko1/958; Bertelsmann, *Die deutsche Sprachgruppe Südwestafrikas*, 18-19.

9. Eckenbrecher, *Was Afrika mir gab und nahm*, 267; "Der Kampf um die deutschen Schulen in Südwestafrika"; Bertelsmann, *Die deutsche Sprachgruppe Südwestafrikas*, 19.

10. Voigt, *Bericht btr. die Übernahme der Deutschen Schulen*, 1921.

11. Ibid.; Bertelsmann, *Die deutsche Sprachgruppe Südwestafrikas*, 19.

12. Voigt, *Bericht btr. die Übernahme der Deutschen Schulen*, 1921.

13. Ibid.; Bertelsmann, *Die deutsche Sprachgruppe Südwestafrikas*, 19-20.

14. Voigt, *Bericht btr. die Übernahme der Deutschen Schulen*, 1921; Lotz to Overseas Industry and Commerce Corp. (OICC), Berlin, 22 July 1921, BAP 61Ko1/958; LdDS, Beschluß des Gesamtvorstands-Sitzung, 16-17 July, BAP 61Ko1/958.

15. Lotz to OICC, 1921.

16. Bertelsmann, *Die deutsche Sprachgruppe Südwestafrikas*, 20.

17. LdDS to Hofmeyr, Windhoek, 20 Oct. 1921, BAP 61Ko1/959; LdDS, *Bericht über den derzeitigen Stand der deutschen Schulfragen in Südwest-Afrika*, 20 May 1922, BAP 61Ko1/960; Bertelsmann, *Die deutsche Sprachgruppe Südwestafrikas*, 20-21; Hoeflich, 124-25; Gretschel, "The Lost 'Umlaut,'" 51-52.

18. Gretschel, "The Lost 'Umlaut,'" 52.

19. H. Richter, LdDS secretary, *Kurze Aufzeichnungen zur Frage der deutschen Schulsache in Südwest-Afrika*, 1 Feb. 1922, BAP 61Ko1/959; LdDS to Hofmeyr, 23 May 1922, BAP 61Ko1/960.

20. Frey, "Die Deutschen Regierungsschulen in Südwestafrika," *DtSchA* 16, no. 11 (1924): 292-96; see also Renner, German consul-general, Pretoria, to AA, 8 Oct. 1924, BAP R1001/1953/1.

21. Frey, "Die Deutschen Regierungsschulen in Südwestafrika," 296-97.

22. Ibid., 292, 297.

23. Eckenbrecher, *Was Afrika mir gab und nahm,* 270, 278.

24. Brückner to Fricke, German consul, Windhoek, 25 Nov. 1931, BAP R1001/1954.

25. Seitz to AA, 1926, BAP R1001/1953/1.

26. Freytag, AA, to Seitz, 27 Nov. 1926, BAP R1001/1953/1.

27. Quote from *Beschluß der 1. Konferenz der Schulvorstände und Schulleiter der deutschen Privatschulen Südwestafrikas,* 5–6 Dec. 1925, BAP R1001/1953/1; see also Körner, "Vom deutschen Schulwesen in Südwestafrika," *DtSchA* 18, nos. 9/10 (1926): 238; Wallberg, *Die deutschen Schüler des Mandatslandes Südwestafrika,* 1933, BAP R1001/1954.

28. "Dienstanweisung für die Direktoren, Schulleiter und Lehrer an den deutschen Privatschulen Südwestafrikas," *DtSchA* 19, nos. 1–3 (1927): 17–22, 47–52, 78–83.

29. *Beschluß der 1. Konferenz der Schulvorstände und Schulleiter,* 5–6 Dec. 1925; Bertelsmann, *Die deutsche Sprachgruppe Südwestafrikas,* 73.

30. Entwicklung des Schulwesens, 1929.

31. Haug, Pretoria, to AA, 3 Feb. 1925, BAP R1001/1953/1; see also Haug to AA, 23 Dec. 1926, BAP R1001/1953/1.

32. Körner, "Vom deutschen Schulwesen in Südwestafrika," 239; Professor Gries, "Die deutsche Realschule in Windhoek, 1919-1924," *DtSchA* 16, nos. 8, 9, 10 (1924): 217-31, 259-65; idem, Dritter Bericht der Deutschen Realschule zu Windhoek, 1919-24, BAP R1001/1953; Wallberg, *Fünfter Bericht der Deutschen Oberrealschule Windhoek nebst Reformrealgymnasium,* 1928-29, BAP 61K01/964; "Zu welchen Berechtigunen in Deutschland eröffnen die deutschen Privatschulen Südwests den Weg?" (newspaper clipping), BAP 61K01/960/2.

33. Giesecke, German consulate for SWA, to AA, 26 Sept. 1934, BAP R1001/1955.

34. Bertelsmann, *Die deutsche Sprachgruppe Südwestafrikas,* 74; Engel, *Kolonialismus und Nationalismus,* 349.

35. LdDS to AA and to VDA, Berlin, 13 Apr. 1920, BAP 61K01/957. For a description of the economic hardships confronting the Südwester, see Lotz to Ministry for Reconstruction, KZV, 20 June 1921, BAP 61K01/958.

36. Bertelsmann, *Die deutsche Sprachgruppe Südwestafrikas,* 73; Hoeflich, 125-26; state subsidy to German Schools, 1925, BAP R1001/1953/1; Franz to German consulate-general, Pretoria, 9 July 1925, BAP R1001/1953/1.

37. Wiehl, German Embassy, Cape Town, to AA, 13 Feb. 1936, BAP R1001/1956.

38. Lotz to C. Kettler, Bremen, 10 Mar. 1922, BAP 61K01/959; Meyer-Gerhard, Reich Ministry for Reconstruction, KZV, to Reich Finance Ministry, 23 Nov. 1921, BAP 61K01/959; Lindequist, Aufzeichnung der Besprechung über südwestafrikanische Schulangelegenheiten, 11 Jan. 1930, BAP 61K01/960/4; Siller, Reich Finance Ministry to Reich Ministry for Reconstruction, KZV, 2 Dec. 1921, BAP 61K01/959; Aufstellung über die den deutschen Schulen in den ehemaligen deutschen Kolonien im Etatsjahr 1930 gewährten Reichszuschüsse, 3 Sept. 1931, BAP R1001/1954; Bielfeld, AA, *Aufzeichnung einer Besprechung btr. deutsche Privatschulen in SWA,* 29 Dec. 1939, BAP R1001/1958.

39. Seitz to LdDS, 1 Sept. 1921, BAP 61Ko1/958.

40. Winkler to LdDS, 22 Apr. 1921, BAP 61Ko1/957; DKG to Paul Müller, Saalfeld, 23 May 1921, BAP 61Ko1/957; LdDS to DKG, 19 Aug. 1921, BAP 61Ko1/958; Seitz, *Antrag auf Bewilligung von 500.000M zur Unterstützung der deutschen Schulen in SWA*, 5 Nov. 1920, BAP 61Ko1/957; Seitz to Verwaltungsrat der Wohlfahrtslotterie, 12 Mar. 1921, BAP 61Ko1/957; Verwaltungsrat der Wohlfahrtslotterie, *Bericht über die Sitzung der Kommission für die Lehrerausreisen nach SWA*, 4 Feb. 1921, BAP 61Ko1/957.

41. Bredow to DKG directorate, 6 Jan. 1920, BAP 61Ko1/1031; see also Bredow to DKG, 15 Apr. 1921, BAP 61Ko1/1031; Winkler, DKG, to FB, 10 Oct. 1921, BAP 61Ko1/1031; Zastrow, DKG Berlin chapter, to DKG, 2 May 1929, BAP 61Ko1/1031; DKG to FB, 14 May 1929, BAP 61Ko1/1031; *Vereinbarung btr. Bücherversorgung der deutschen Kolonien zwischen VDA, DKG und FB*, 12 June 1929, BAP·61Ko1/1031.

42. LdDS to Seitz, 18 Dec. 1920, BAP 61Ko1/957; Winkler to FB, 16 Apr. 1921, BAP 61Ko1/957; LdDS to DKG, 1921, BAP 61Ko1/957; Frieda Lotz, "Schülerheim in Südwestafrika," *Koloniale Frauenarbeit* (1927): 12–17, BAP R1001/6693; Beschlüsse btr. Deutschtumspflege in der Besprechung beim FB der DKG, 29 Oct. 1930, BAP 61Ko1/960/4; Körner, "Vom deutschen Schulwesen in Südwest," *Koloniale Frauenarbeit* (1930): 13–16, BAK N1037/4.

43. *Entwicklung des Schulwesens*, 1929.

44. Margarethe von Zastrow, "Fortbildung afrikanischer Jugend in Deutschland," Koloniale Frauenarbeit (1930): 31, BAK N1037/4. 32; Boemcken, FB chair, *Referat über Spipendienfürsorge, aus dem Protokoll der Vorstands-Sitzung des FB*, Aachen, 13 June 1930, LAB rep.42, acc.2147, no.26164.

45. *Entwicklung des Schulwesens*, 1929.

46. Boemcken, *Referat über Stipenienfürsorge;* Gunzert, AA to Embassy Treasurer, 18 May 1936, BAP R1001/6695.

47. Mrs. Prof. Werner, FB, "Über die Erziehung afrikanischer Kinder in Deutschland," lecture held in the FB's board meeting, 31 May 1928, LAB rep.42, acc.2147, no.26164.

48. Ibid.; M. von Zastrow, "Südafrikanische Erziehungsfragen," *Koloniale Frauen-Arbeit* (1926): 9–13, HLA A/a/3/bb no. 28; M. von Zastrow, "Fortbildung afrikanischer Jugend in Deutschland," 32–34.

49. Haug, Pretoria, to AA, 21 Oct. 1927, BAP R1001/1953/1.

50. Werner, "Über die Erziehung afrikanischer Kinder in Deutschland."

51. Seitz, Aufzeichnung btr. weitere Ausbildung für Mädchen, 12 July 1929, BAP 61Ko1/960/3.

52. M. von Zastrow, "Südwestafrikanische Erziehungsfragen," 9.

53. Seitz, *Aufzeichnung btr. weitere Ausbidlung für Mädchen*, 1929.

54. Ibid.; Lotte Sanita Ebers, Warum brauchen wir eine Fortbildungsschule für deutsche Mädchen in Südwestafrika?, 1929, BAP 61Ko1/960/3.

55. Ebers to Seitz, 6 Aug. 1929, BAP 61Ko1/960/3; Wallberg, "Die Hedwig Heyl-Haushaltungsschule in Windhuk," *DtSchA* 26, no. 5 (1934): 157.

56. Hermann Leusner, *Die Entwicklung des Schulwesens in den deutschen afrikanischeen Kolonien, jetzigen Mandatsgebieten, vom Ende des Weltkrieges bis*

zur Gegenwart (Köln: Buchdruckerei Orthen, 1938), 58–59; see also Else Frobenius, *30 Jahre Koloniale Frauenarbeit* (1936), 29.

57. Rautenberg, "Die Hedwig Heyl-Haushaltungsschule," *Afrikanischer Heimatkalender* (1986): 97–100; Wallberg, "Die Hedwig Heyl-Haushaltungsschule in Windhuk," 157; "Deutsch-Südwestafrika. Hedwig-Heyl-Haushaltungsschule in Windhuk," *DtSchA* 28, no. 3 (1936): 92; "Arbeitsplan der Hedwig-Heyl-Haushaltungsschule," *DtSchA* 28, no. 9 (1936): 294.

58. "Deutsch-Südwestafrika. Hedwig-Heyl-Haushaltungsschule in Windhuk," 92.

59. Wallberg, "Die Hedwig Heyl-Haushaltungsschule in Windhuk," 157.

60. See Rautenberg, "Die Hedwig Heyl-Haushaltungsschule," 100.

61. *Tätigkeitsbericht des Ausschusses für Auslandsdeutschtum des HKSCV*, 1931, BAP R1001/1954; Herbert Ludwig, HKSCV, to Hintrager, 20 Feb. 1931, BAP R1001/1954; "Die Werkschule der Deutschen Oberrealschule in Windhuk (Südwestafrika)," *DtSchA* 23, no. 7 (1931): 231–32; "Die deutsche Werkschule in Windhuk, eine Stiftung der deutschen Corpsstudenten im Kösener S.C. Verband," *DtSchA* 23, no. 7 (1931): 232–33; quote from Ramsay, HKSCV, to Emil Althaus, 27 Feb. 1930, BAP 61Ko1/964.

62. Ramsay to Brückner, 5 June 1931, BAP 61Ko1/964; Brückner, AA, to Ramsay, 6 June 1931, BAP 61Ko1/964; Ludwig to Hinstrager, 20 Feb. 1931; Ramsay to Althaus, 27 Feb. 1930; *Tätigkeitsbericht des Ausschusses für Auslandsdeutschtum;* "Grundsteinlegung zum Werkunterrichtshaus der Deutschen Oberrealschule in Winhuk," *Allgemeine Zeitung* (Windhoek), 22 Feb. 1930, BAP 61Ko1/964.

63. Hans Wunderlich to Reich Minister Külz, 23 Mar. 1927, BAP 61Ko1/960/2.

64. Haug to AA, 26 Aug. 1927, BAP R1001/1953/1.

65. H. H. G. Kreft, education director, to German School Association, Swakopmund, 24 Feb. 1928, BAP 61Ko1/960/2; German School Association, Swakopmund, to Education Department, Windhoek, 28 Aug. 1928, BAP 61Ko1/960/2; German School Association, Swakopmund, to DB, 23 Jan. 1928, BAP 61Ko1/960/2; DB, Abänderungsvorschläge des DB zum Angebot des Administrators vom 24. Februar 1928, 16 Mar. 1928, BAP 61Ko1/960/2.

66. Seitz to A. Voigts, 19 Apr. 1928, BAP 61Ko1/960/2; Karl Hess, DKG Greiz chapter, to DKG, Berlin, 1 Aug. 1928, BAP 61Ko1/960/2; German School Association, Swakopmund, Rundschreiben, 15 Aug. 1928, BAP 61Ko1/960/2; Bertelsmann, *Die deutsche Sprachgruppe Südwestafrikas*, 76; Voigts to Seitz, 9 Mar. 1928, BAP 61Ko1/960/2.

67. Voigts to Seitz, 9 Aug. 1928, BAP 61Ko1/960/2; German Realschule, Swakopmund, *Aufruf zur Erhaltung der Schule in Swakopmund,* 1928, BAP 61Ko1/960/2; German School Association, Swakopmund, *Rundschreiben,* 15 Aug. 1928; Schulze, Berlin, to AA, Education Department, 12 Sept. 1928, BAP 61Ko1/960/2; Blank to AA, Education Department, 24 Sept. 1928, BAP 61Ko1/960/2; Körner, Berlin, to Seitz, 4 Oct. 1928, BAP 61Ko1/960/3; Körner, *Einige Bemerkungen zu der Denkschrift der deuschen Schule Swakopmund . . . über die Erhaltung und den Ausbau der deutschen Schule Swakopmund,* 1928, BAP 61Ko1/960/2; quote from R. Blank, DB, Zusammenfassung der Verhandlungen wegen der Swakopmunder Privatschule, 1928, BAP R1001/1954.

68. Hintrager to AA, 18 Apr. 1929, BAP R1001/1954.

69. Abkommen zwischen dem Administrator für Südwestafrika . . . und dem Deutschen Schulverein von Swakopmund, 13–14 Apr. 1929, BAP R1001/1954; Gretschel, "The Lost 'Umlaut,'" 53.

70. Bertelsmann, *Die deutsche Sprachgruppe Südwestafrikas*, 77–79; *Die Entwicklung der Deutschen Höheren Schule in Swakopmund*, 1931, BAP 61Ko1/960/4; Parents' Council, Swakopmund, to Kreft, 7 Jan. 1932, BAP R1001/1954; Fricke, German consulate, Windhoek, to AA, 21 Jan. 1932, BAP R1001/1954; Hoeflich, 127.

71. Fricke to AA, 11 July 1931, BAP R1001/1954; Fricke to L. Roeder, Tsumeb School Association, 17 Sept. 1931, BAP R1001/1954; Fricke to AA, 8 Dec. 1931, BAP R1001/1954; H. H. G. Kreft, education director, to Roeder, 28 Aug. 1931, BAP R1001/1954; Fricke, *Bemerkungen btr. den Lehrplan für die Einrichtung der Regierunsschule in Tsumeb*, 1931, BAP R1001/1954; Fricke to AA, 29 Dec. 1931, BAP R1001/1954; *Ergebnisse der Verhandlungen zwecks Übergabe der Deutschen Privatschule Tsumeb*, 5 Aug. 1931, BAP R1001/1954.

72. Lindequist to Tsumeb School Association, 24 Sept. 1931, BAP R1001/1954.

73. Lindequist to DB for SWA, 24 Sept. 1931, BAP 61Ko1/350/1.

74. Lindequist to Tsumeb School Association, 5 Mar. 1932, BAP R1001/1954.

75. Hugo Blumhagen, *Südwestafrika, einst und jetzt* (Berlin: Dietrich Reimer/ Ernst Vohsen, 1934), 65–66; Victor Dick, Lüderitz Bay School Association, to AA, 20 Mar. 1931, BAP R1001/1954; Bredow, FB chair, to Dick, 11 May 1931, BAP R1001/1954; Dick to Bredow, 20 May 1931, BAP R1001/1954; Bredow to Detzner, AA, 30 May 1931, BAP R1001/1954; Detzner to Bredow, 11 June 1931, BAP R1001/1954; Bertelsmann, *Die deutsche Sprachgruppe Südwestafrikas*, 75.

76. *Notizen über Südwestafrika*, c.1930, BAP R1001/1954.

77. Franz, *Verzeichnis über das Südwester Vereinswesen*, Sept. 1926, BAP R1001/1740; Franz, *Ergänzendes Verzeichnis über das Südwester Vereinswesen*, Oct. 1926, BAP R1001/1740.

78. Engel, *Kolonialismus und Nationalismus*, 293; *Notizen über Südwestafrika*, c.1930.

79. *Notizen über Südwestafrika*, c.1930.

80. Engel, *Kolonialismus und Nationalismus*, 293, 296–97, 303–5.

81. Diehl, "Brief History," 18.

82. Karl Seidelmann, *Die Pfadfinder in der deutschen Jugendgeschichte: Teil 1—Darstellung* (Hannover: Hermann Schroedel, 1977), 25, 27ff, 197.

83. *Entwicklung des Schulwesens*, 1929.

84. See Seidelmann, *Die Pfadfinder*, 91.

85. R. Strunck, league leader of the German Pathfinder League for SWA, *Allgemeine Richtlinien für einen Jugendpfleger in Südwestafrika*, 1933, BAP R1001/1955.

86. Ibid.; Gries, *Deutsches Schulwesen im Mandatsgebiet Südwestafrika*, 1938, BAP R1001/1956; Hildegard Rutkowski, "Deutsches Schul- und Erziehungswesen in unseren Kolonien seit dem Weltkrieg," *DKZ* 53 (1941): 63.

87. Gretschel, "The Lost 'Umlaut,'" 53.

88. Wallberg, *Gründe für die Erhaltung der deutschen Privatschulen in Südwest*, 14 Apr. 1932, BAP 61Ko1/350/1.

CHAPTER 8

1. Swanson, "SWA in Trust," 645–46.

2. *Windhuk Advertiser,* 22 Sept. 1920; quoted in Gretschel, "The Lost 'Umlaut,'" 47.

3. Gretschel, "The Lost 'Umlaut,'" 46–47.

4. Ibid., 4.

5. Cohen, *Politics,* 14.

6. "Das frühere Deutsch-Südwestafrika heute noch deutsch," *Deutsches Volksblatt,* 27 Nov. 1931, BAK N1037/3.

7. Bertelsmann, *Die deutsche Sprachgruppe Südwestafrikas,* 22–23.

8. *Die London Verständigung von 23. Oktober 1923 über die Deutschen in Südwestafrika,* 1923, BAP 61K01/531; de Haas to Smuts, 23 Oct. 1923, BAP 61K01/531.

9. Swanson, "SWA in Trust," 644; Franz to AA, 15 Nov. 1924, BAP 61K01/532.

10. Carl Cranz, "Ein Schicksalstag für Deutsch-Südwestafrika. Auf letztem Kolonialposten," *Deutsche Zeitung,* 14 Mar. 1925, BAP R8034II/6353; see also Gretschel, "The Lost 'Umlaut,'" 47.

11. Franz to German consulate-general, Pretoria, 29 Feb. 1924, BAP 61K01/531.

12. Günzert, AA, to Winkler, DKG, 10 June 1924, BAP 61K01/147; Gretschel, "The Lost 'Umlaut,'" 47; Schmidt-Lauber, *Die abhängigen Herren,* 70–71.

13. Haug to Hans Müller, Windhoek, 19 Feb. 1923, BAP 61K01/531.

14. Bertelsmann, *Die deutsche Sprachgruppe Südwestafrikas,* 38–39; Gretschel, "The Lost 'Umlaut,'" 47.

15. Bertelsmann, *Die deutsche Sprachgruppe Südwestafrikas,* 39.

16. Blumhagen, *Südwestafrika, einst und jetzt,* 47; see also Hans Hirsekorn, "Naturalisation und ihre Durchführung," Dec. 1929 (clipping; newspaper unknown), BAP 61K01/350/1.

17. Swanson, "SWA in Trust," 662–63; Bertelsmann, *Die deutsche Sprachgruppe Südwestafrikas,* 40–41; quoted material from Swanson, "SWA in Trust," 662.

18. Franz to German consulate-general, Pretoria, 28 Jan. 1926, BAP 61K01/532; Bertelsmann, *Die deutsche Sprachgruppe Südwestafrikas,* 42.

19. *Satzungen der Deutschen Bundes für Südwestafrika,* 15 Apr. 1928, BAP 61K01/960/3; see also "Deutsche Vereine im Ausland: Windhuk," *DA* 8, no. 10 (1925): 288.

20. *Tagung des Deutschen Bundes,* 11 Apr. 1925, BAP R1001/1771.

21. Franz to AA, 15 May 1925, BAP R1001/1771.

22. "Deutsche Vereine im Ausland: Windhuk," 288

23. Seitz to Albert Voigts, 13 July 1925, BAP 61K01/532.

24. *Jahresbericht des Deutschen Bundes für Südwestafrika,* BAP R1001/1771.

25. VdR, "Landsleute! Reichsdeutsche!"; Seitz to Brenner, 28 Aug. 1925, BAP 61K01/346; de Haas, AA, to Haug, 31 Aug. 1926, BAP R1001/1773; Haug, German consul-general, Pretoria, to AA, 6 Nov. 1926, BAP R1001/1772; Hintrager to Reich Interior Ministry, 14 Aug. 1928, BAP R1001/1773.

26. Seitz to Hintrager, 7 Sept. 1925, BAP 61K01/532; Seitz to Voigts, 13 July 1925; Seitz to Matthiessen, SWA, 13 Feb. 1926, BAP 61K01/532.

27. For example, see Larry Eugene Jones, *German Liberalism and the Dissolution of the Weimar Party System, 1918–1933* (Chapel Hill: University of North Carolina Press, 1988); idem, "'The Dying Middle': Weimar Germany and the Fragmentation of Bourgeois Politics," *Central European History* 5, no. 1 (1972): 23–54; idem, "Inflation, Revaluation, and the Crisis of Middle-class Politics: A Study in the Dissolution of the German Party System, 1923–28," *Central European History* 12, no. 2 (1979): 143–68; idem, "Crisis and Realignment: Agrarian Splinter Parties in the Late Weimar Republic, 1928–33," in *Peasants and Lords in Modern Germany: Recent Studies in Agricultural History,* ed. Robert G. Moeller (Boston: Allen & Unwin, 1986), 198–232; and Childers, "Interest and Ideology: Anti-System Politics in the Era of Stabilization, 1924–1928," in *Die Nachwirkungen der Inflation auf die deutsche Geschichte, 1924–1933,* ed. Gerald D. Feldman (Munich: Oldenbourg, 1985), 1–20.

28. Pisani, *Politics,* 73–74; Eletester, AA, to Korag, 31 May 1926, BAP 61Ko1/562; Engel, *Kolonialismus und Nationalismus,* 333; Blumhagen, *Entscheidungsjahre,* 4.

29. Bielfeld, German consulate-general, Windhoek, to AA, 1 July 1927, BAP 61Ko1/534. UNSWP's reference to "the Southwest's African population" (meaning the whites and denying population status to blacks) is typical of the time.

30. Ibid.

31. Voigts to Hintrager, 24 Sept. 1926, BAP R1001/1772; Franz to AA, 19 Dec. 1927, BAP R1001/1772; Franz to German consulate-general, Pretoria, 20 Apr. 1928, BAP R1001/1772.

32. Schauroth, DB secretary, *Vorschläge zur Vorbereitung für die nächsten Wahlen,* 9 Feb. 1928, BAP 61Ko1/350; *Protocol of the Meeting of the Central Election Committee,* 6 Feb. 1929, BAP 61Ko1/534; Franz to AA, 15 Apr. 1929, BAP 61Ko1/1772; DB, *Unsere politische Lage vor den Wahlen am 3. Juli 1929,* 22 May 1929, BAP 61Ko1/350.

33. *Protocol of the Meeting of the Central Election Committee,* 7 Feb. 1929, BAP 61Ko1/534.

34. Engel, *Kolonialismus und Nationalismus,* 335; Blumhagen, *Entscheidungsjahre,* 4. It is uncertain whether the administrator's decision reflected the growing numerical superiority of Afrikaners in the mandate, which meant that they should have the majority of seats. If one takes this perspective, then the administrator was actually rather generous in 1926 since even then the Afrikaner community was larger than the German; see table 6.1.

35. Engel, *Kolonialismus und Nationalismus,* 335.

36. Hirsekorn, "Naturalisation und ihre Durchführung"; Engel, *Kolonialismus und Nationalismus,* 335.

37. *Protocol of the Extraordinary Assembly of the German League,* 6–7 Oct. 1929, BAP 61Ko1/960/3; *Joint Meeting between the DB and the UNSWP,* 19–20 Mar. 1932, BAP 61Ko1/350/1; Engel, *Kolonialismus und Nationalismus,* 337–38; Bertelsmann, *Die deutsche Sprachgruppe Südwestafrikas,* 51–52.

38. Bertelsmann, *Die deutsche Sprachgruppe Südwestafrikas,* 52–55; Engel, *Kolonialismus und Nationalismus,* 338; Voigts to Schnee, DKG president, 1932, BAP 61Ko1/350/1; Reichstag Foreign Affairs Committee, 12 May 1932, BAP R1001/7255;

"Memorandum der Besprechungen," *Allgemeine Zeitung für die Interessen aller Berufsständen in Südwest Afrika,* 13 Apr. 1932, BAP 61Ko1/350/1.

39. Bertelsmann, *Die deutsche Sprachgruppe Südwestafrikas,* 55-56; Engel, *Kolonialismus und Nationalismus,* 338.

CHAPTER 9

1. Hagemann, *Südafrika,* 49.

2. Ibid., 49-50; Bertelsmann, *Die deutsche Sprachgruppe Südwestafrikas,* 57; Engel, *Kolonialismus und Nationalismus,* 338; James Denby, U.S. consul, Cape Town, to secretary of state, Washington, D.C., 11 Apr. 1939, in *The Nazis in Africa,* ed. L. Smythe Barron, *Lost Documents on the Third Reich,* vol. 111 (Salisbury, N.C.: Documentary Publications, 1978), 149-82, specifically 151; Keena, U.S. legation, Cape Town, to secretary of state, Washington, D.C., 9 July 1938, in Barron, *Lost Documents,* 72-89, specifically 72. Hagemann's study provides the best and most comprehensive examination of the effects of National Socialism on the Southwestern German community.

3. Hagemann, *Südafrika,* 54; Bertelsmann, *Die deutsche Sprachgruppe Südwestafrikas,* 57.

4. Fricke, consulate-general, SWA, to AA, 21 Aug. 1933, BAP R1001/1955; see also Hagemann, *Südafrika,* 54; Engel, *Kolonialismus und Nationalismus,* 346.

5. Fricke to AA, 21 Aug. 1933; Hagemann, *Südafrika,* 54.

6. H. Grönewald, speech before the assembly of the German School Association, Windhoek, 9 Aug. 1933, BAP R1001/1955.

7. Fricke to AA, 21 Aug. 1933.

8. Hagemann, *Südafrika,* 54-55; Bach, ombudsman of the Court of Arbitration, Stellungnahme zu den Streitfragen Germania Ltd./Deutscher Schulverein Windhuk, Anlage 21, 26 Feb. 1936, BAP R1001/1957.

9. Hagemann, *Südafrika,* 56-57.

10. Ibid., 59; Brückner, Vermerk btr. Brenner, 16 Aug. 1933, BAP R1001/1955.

11. Hagemann, *Südafrika,* 56-58; Engel, *Kolonialismus und Nationalismus,* 347-48; quoted material in Hagemann, *Südafrika,* 56.

12. Hagemann, *Südafrika,* 57-59; Bertelsmann, *Die deutsche Sprachgruppe Südwestafrikas,* 60; Ralph J. Totten, U.S. legation, Pretoria, to secretary of state, Washington, D.C., 1 Aug. 1933, in Barron, *Lost Documents,* 3-6; Totten to secretary of state, Washington, D.C., 10 Aug. 1933, in Barron, *Lost Documents,* 7-8.

13. Hagemann, *Südafrika,* 60; Engel, *Kolonialismus und Nationalismus,* 349; Schauroth to Ritter von Epp, KPA, Munich, 1 June 1934, BAP R1001/1955.

14. Schauroth to Epp, 1 June 1934.

15. Schauroth to Lindequist, 1933, BAP R1001/1955.

16. Matthiessen to AA, 1 Oct. 1933, BAP 61Ko1/535; Matthiessen to Schnee, German Colonial Society president, BAP 61Ko1/535.

17. Neuhaus, Eklärung über Brenner, 1933, BAP R1001/1955.

18. Neuhaus to German consulate, SWA, 6 Feb. 1934, BAP R1001/1955.

19. Faculty and NSDAP members, Oberrealschule, Windhoek, to AA, 9 Aug. 1934, BAP R1001/1955.

20. Territorial Youth leader, SWA, to Reich Youth leadership, Berlin, 25 June 1934, BAP R1001/1955; Engel, *Kolonialismus und Nationalismus,* 349; Matthiessen to AA, 1 Oct. 1933; Nazi activities in South West Africa, 9.

21. Giesecke, German consulate in SWA, to AA, 13 Aug. 1934, BAP R1001/1955.

22. Hans Betzler to German consulate, SWA, 13 Aug. 1934, BAP R1001/1955.

23. Matthiessen to AA, 1 Oct. 1933.

24. Faculty and NSDAP members, Oberrealschule, Windhoek, to AA, 9 Aug. 1934, BAP R1001/1955.

25. Giesecke, German consulate, SWA, to AA, 13 Aug. 1934, BAP R1001/1955; Hunold, DB deputy leader, Berlin, to AA, 22 Aug. 1934, BAP R1001/1955.

26. Territorial Youth leader to Reich Youth leadership, 25 June 1934.

27. Frida Voigts to Agnes Boemcken, FB leader, 10 Sept. 1934, BAP R1001/1955.

28. Klara Dinkuth, FB deputy leader, Windhoek chapter, to A. Boemcken, 9 Sept. 1934, BAP R1001/1955.

29. Brückner, AA, to Jung, Reichsleitung der NSDAP, Kolonialreferat, Munich, 28 Feb. 1934, BAP R1001/1955.

30. Brückner, *Vermerk btr. Brenner,* 16 Aug. 1933; see also Matthiessen to Schnee, 7 Oct. 1933.

31. The documentation for this process is extensive; the main points of contention and their resolution are contained in Wiehl to AA, 22 Apr. 1936, BAP R1001/1957.

32. Pisani, *Politics,* 82.

33. Heinrich Stuebel places party membership at 80 to 95 percent of the German population, but provides no supporting evidence. Stuebel, "Die Entwicklung des Nationalsozialismus," 176. Hagemann argues more convincingly that by the end of 1933 and the beginning of 1934, approximately only 10 percent of the Southwestern Germans belonged to the party, and that this was the highest rate of membership the party had ever attained in the region. Hagemann does, however, contend that the party had achieved a relatively high degree of organization; Hagemann, *Südafrika,* 60. U.S. diplomats in 1939 placed Nazi membership at circa one-sixth of the white population, or one-half of the German population: Denby to secretary of state, 11 Apr. 1939.

34. Totten to secretary of state, Washington, D.C., 17 July 1934, in Barron, *Lost Documents,* 20–21; Pisani, *Politics,* 79; Bertelsmann, *Die deutsche Sprachgruppe Südwestafrikas,* 61; Hagemann, *Südafrika,* 61; Engel, *Kolonialismus und Nationalismus,* 449–50; Blumhagen, *Entscheidungsjahre,* 1–2; Hintrager, "Der Bericht der Südwestafrika-Kommission vom 2. März 1936," Koloniale Rundschau 28 (1937): 281–82.

35. Within the small historiography about the national socialist influence in SWA, a difference of opinion exists about the South Africans' ability to control the party's spread and influence. On the one hand, historians such as Maynard Swanson and Heinrich Stuebel have argued that the NSDAP pursued a very rational course of action and that the South African government was unable to contain the Nazi threat without offering much evidence in support. On the other hand, Albrecht Hagemann

contends most convincingly that Nazi activities were actually chaotic and that the South Africans had things under control the whole time. Similarly, Bertelsmann believes that the South Africans consciously permitted NSDAP to continue to work in order to feed the tensions and discord already present within the German population and thus had matters under control; see Swanson, "SWA in Trust," 664–65; Stuebel, "Die Entwicklung des Nationalsozialismus," 170–76; Hagemann, *Südafrika*, 49–64, esp. 49; Bertelsmann, *Die deutsche Sprachgruppe Südwestafrikas*, 61.

36. Bertelsmann, *Die deutsche Sprachgruppe Südwestafrikas*, 44; Engel, *Kolonialismus und Nationalismus*, 339–40; Pisani, *Politics*, 79; Blumhagen, *Entscheidungsjahre*, iii, 4–5; Totten to secretary of state, 17 July 1935; U.S. legation, Pretoria, to secretary of state, Washington, D.C., 22 May 1934, in Barron, *Lost Documents*, 15–17; Irving N. Linnell, U.S. legation, Pretoria, to secretary of state, Washington D.C., 5 Nov. 1934, in Barron, *Lost Documents*, 22–23; "Südwestafrika soll der Union eingegliedert werden. Entschließung der gesetzgebenden Versammlung," *Deutsche Allgemeine Zeitung*, 24 May 1934, BAP R8034II/6354/i.

37. "Keine Eingliederung Deutsch-Südwestafrika in die Südafrikanishce Union," *Völkischer Beobachter*, 15 Dec. 1934, BAP R8034II/6354/i; "Südwest-Mandat bleibt gewährt," *Der Tag*, 7 June 1934, BAP R8034II/6354/i; see also Engel, *Kolonialismus und Nationalismus*, 341.

38. Bielfeld, German consulate-general, Pretoria, to AA, 6 Dec. 1932, BAP 61K01/535.

39. Blumhagen, *Entscheidungsjahre*, 5.

40. Oelhafen, German consul, SWA, to AA, 9 Oct. 1939, BAP R1001/1956.

41. Hintrager, "Der Bericht der Südwestafrika-Kommission vom 2. März 1936," 279, 289; Blumhagen, *Entscheidungsjahre*, 6; Bertelsmann, *Die deutsche Sprachgruppe Südwestafrikas*, 62; Hagemann, *Südafrika*, 63.

42. Engel, *Kolonialismus und Nationalismus*, 350; Keena to secretary of state, 9 July 1938; Keena to secretary of state, 3 Sept. 1938, in Barron, *Lost Documents*, 94–95; see also Stuebel, "Die Entwicklung des Nationalsozialismus," 173, Schmidt-Lauber, *Die abhängigen Herren*, 76.

43. Blumhagen, *Entscheidungsjahre*, 15–18, 38–39; see also Bertelsmann, *Die deutsche Sprachgruppe Südwestafrikas*, 62; Keena to secretary of state, 9 July 1938.

44. Pisani, *Politics*, 81; Hagemann, *Südafrika*, 62–63; Bertelsmann, *Die deutsche Sprachgruppe Südwestafrikas*, 61–62; Engel, *Kolonialismus und Nationalismus*, 351–53. Totten, Pretoria, to secretary of state, Washington, D.C., 21 May 1935, in Barron, *Lost Documents*, 35–36.

45. Engel, *Kolonialismus und Nationalismus*, 353–54; Hagemann, *Südafrika*, 63; Bertelsmann, *Die deutsche Sprachgruppe Südwestafrikas*, 62–63; "Proklamation des Generalgouverneurs der Südafrikanischen Union vom 2. Apr. 1937," in Blumhagen, *Entscheidungsjahre*, 105–6.

46. "Ausnahmegesetz in Südwest-Afrika: Ein Schlag gegen das Deutschtum," *Deutsche Allgemeine Zeitung*, 3 Apr. 1937, BAP R8034II/6373; "Kampferlaß gegen das Deutschtum," *Völkischer Beobachter*, 4 Apr. 1937, BAP R8034II/6356; see also Blumhagen, *Entscheidungsjahre*, 30–35; Hagemann, *Südafrika*, 63.

47. Bertelsmann, *Die deutsche Sprachgruppe Südwestafrikas,* 63.

48. "Südwest-Administrator versucht Spaltung der Deutschen," *Berliner Tageblatt,* 27 Apr. 1937, BAP R8034II/6373.

49. Blumhagen, *Entscheidungsjahre,* 38–39. As Engel and Stuebel have demonstrated, this was certainly not the case.

50. Hagemann, *Südafrika,* 63; Bertelsmann, *Die deutsche Sprachgruppe Südwestafrikas,* 63; "Neue deutsche Partei in Deutsch-Südwest," *Völkischer Beobachter,* 3 July 1937, BAP R8034II/6373.

51. Engel, *Kolonialismus und Nationalismus,* 354.

52. Ibid., 354; Hagemann, *Südafrika,* 63–64; Bertelsmann, *Die deutsche Sprachgruppe Südwestafrikas,* 64; Pisani, *Politics,* 82.

53. Blumhagen, *Entscheidungsjahre,* 41.

54. Hirsekorn to Leitner, German envoy, Pretoria, 12 Dec. 1938, BAP R1001/1740.

55. Bertelsmann, *Die deutsche Sprachgruppe Südwestafrikas,* 64; Engel, *Kolonialismus und Nationalismus,* 356–57; Hagemann, *Südafrika,* 64; Pisani, *Politics,* 83; Hirsekorn to Leitner, 12 Dec. 1938; Hirsekorn to Leitner, 18 Dec. 1938, BAP R1001/1740; Leitner, to AA, 23 Dec. 1938, BAP R1001/1740.

56. Lembcke, directorate of the AO, NSDAP, to AA, 21 Jan. 1939, BAP R1001/1236; Bismarck, AA, to directorate of the AO, NSDAP, 26 Apr. 1938, BAP R1001/1236; Engel, *Kolonialismus und Nationalismus,* 355; Bertelsmann, *Die deutsche Sprachgruppe Südwestafrikas,* 64.

57. A Volksdeutsche is someone not born in Germany, the Reich; a Volksdeutsche does not possess German citizenship (cf. *Reichsdeutsche*).

58. Engel, *Kolonialismus und Nationalismus,* 359; Pisani, *Politics,* 82, 87. Heinrich Stuebel estimated that the Volksdeutsche Group had approximately four hundred members. Unfortunately, he provides no evidence for this figure and his gross exaggeration of Nazi party membership during this period casts further doubts on the validity of this number. Nonetheless, it is the only figure available for this organization. Stuebel, "Die Entwicklung des Nationalsozialismus," 176.

59. Denby, Cape Town, to secretary of state, Washington, D.C., 18 Mar. 1939, in Barron, *Lost Documents,* 144–45; Keena, Cape Town, to secretary of state, Washington, D.C., 29 Mar. 1939, ibid., 148.

60. Bertelsmann, *Die deutsche Sprachgruppe Südwestafrikas,* 66–68; see also Engel, *Kolonialismus und Nationalismus,* 359.

61. Schmidt-Lauber, *Die abhängigen Herren,* 78.

62. Hagemann, *Südafrika,* 64.

63. Ibid.

CONCLUSION

1. Bertelsmann, *Die deutsche Sprachgruppe Südwestafrikas,* 67–68, 79.

2. Bertelsmann, *Die deutsche Sprachgruppe Südwestafrikas,* 69, 79–80, 96–97; Rüdiger, *Die Namibia-Deutschen,* 15.

3. Rüdiger, *Die Namibia-Deutschen*, 15.

4. Ibid., 15–17; Bertelsmann, *Die deutsche Sprachgruppe Südwestafrikas*, 94–95.

5. Rüdiger, *Die Namibia-Deutschen*, 17; Bertelsmann, *Die deutsche Sprachgruppe Südwestafrikas*, 117–18, 103–6.

6. Rüdiger, *Die Namibia-Deutschen*, 17; Bertelsmann, *Die deutsche Sprachgruppe Südwestafrikas*, 98–103.

7. Rüdiger, *Die Namibia-Deutschen*, 151.

8. Ibid., 17.

9. Ibid., 18.

10. Ibid., 19.

11. Ibid.

12. Bley, *SWA under German Rule*, 111.

13. "Der Streit der Konfession in Deutschland," *SWB*, 15 Jan. 1913.

14. Bley, *SWA under German Rule*, 188, 192–93.

15. For the situation in Germany, see, e.g., Suval, *Electoral Politics*, 120–60; Chickering, *We Men;* Geoff Eley, *Reshaping the German Right*, 41–98; Robert Gellately, *The Politics of Economic Despair: Shopkeepers and German Politics, 1890–1914* (London: Sage, 1974); Shulamit Volkov, *The Rise of Popular Antimodernism in Germany: The Urban Master Artisans, 1873–1896* (Princeton: Princeton University Press, 1978). For the situation in other settler colonies, see Frederick Cooper and Ann Stoler, "Tensions of Empire: Colonial Control and Visions of Rule," *American Ethnologist* 16 (Nov. 1989): 609–21; and Comaroff, "Images of Empire," 661–85.

16. Bley, *SWA under German Rule*, 186–87; Mamozai, *Schwarze Frau*, 188; Schmidt-Lauber, *Die abhängigen Herren*, 61; Engelhardt, "Missionarinnen und Siedlerinnen," 31; O'Donnell, "Colonial Woman Question," 261.

17. Ludwig Külz, *Tropenarzt im afrikanischen Busch*, 3rd ed. (Berlin: Süsserott, 1943), 142.

18. Ibid., 144.

19. Ibid., 144; Schmidt-Lauber, *Die abhängigen Herren*, 62.

20. David Blackbourn, "The *Mittelstand* in German Society and Politics, 1871–1914," *Social History* 2, no. 4 (1977): 409–33, quote from p. 410; see also Chickering, *We Men*, 113–14.

21. Dove, *Die Deutschen Kolonien*, 67.

22. Kennedy, *Islands of White*, 189.

23. James Retallack, "'Why Can't a Saxon Be More Like a Prussian?' Regional Identities and the Birth of Modern Political Culture in Germany, 1866–67," *Canadian Journal of History* 32, no. 1 (1997): 26–55.

24. Kennedy, *Islands of White*, 191.

25. Ibid., 192.

26. Although composed in Southwest Africa, the song is known in Germany and counted among German folk songs; in fact, it is still used as a means to identify the German Südwester. A quick search on the internet revealed three sites that refer to the song. Two are specifically about German folk songs ("Welcome to the Leader in Lieder mit Midi Melodies" <http://ingeb.org/Lieder/hartwiek.html>; and Robert Kopp, "Deut-

sche Volkslieder/German Folksongs" <http://www.acronet.net?~robokopp/Lieder/sudwest.html>. The other is an on-line travel journal operated by the *Süddeutsche Zeitung,* one of Germany's largest daily newspapers, which uses the opening line from the melody to talk about travel in Namibia. Sabine and Theo Allofs, "Hart wie Kameldornholz," *SzonNet: Reisejournal, Fernweh-Extra* (Munich: Süddeutsche Zeitung, 1998) <http://www.sueddeutsche.de/reise/fernweh/namibia/service/buchttip_1.html>.

27. Schmidt-Lauber, *Die abhängigen Herren,* 109.

28. Gerhard Gellrich, "Das Südwesterlied 'Hart wie Kameldornholz'—Ursprung und Varianten," *Afrikanischer Heimatkalender* (1986): 106.

29. Reprinted in Erwin Sandelowsky, *Anekdoten, Lieder mit Noten, und die alten Geschichten von Deutsch-Südwestafrika* (Windhoek: John Meinert, 1973), 83.

30. Schmidt-Lauber, *Die abhängigen Herren,* 108–9.

31. Ibid., 100–7.

32. Rüdiger, *Die Namibia-Deutschen,* 152.

Bibliography

ARCHIVAL MATERIALS

Federal Archive, Potsdam

Alte Reichskanzlai 07.01
    Deutsch-Südwestafrika
        927 Bd. 2 (May 1907–March 1910)

Deutsche Kolonialgesellschaft 61 Ko1
    SWA Landesausstellung 1914
        37 August 1913–May 1921
    Zentralauskunftsstelle für Auswanderer
        108 Bd. 1 (May 1900–May 1907)
        109 Bd. 2 (June 1901–October 1905)
        110 Bd. 3 (January 1906–December 1910)
        111 Bd. 4 (April 1911–December 1920)
    Auswanderungsfrage
        118 Bd. 2 (July 1926–September 1930)
    Reichswanderungsamt
        124 Bd. 1 (June 1918–November 1925)
        125 Bd. 2 (March 1919–September 1931)
        126 Bd. 3 (June 1919–November 1924)
    Reichskolonialministerium
        146 Bd. 1 (January 1911–October 1924)
        147 Bd. 2 (January 1911–September 1925)
    Deutsch Kolonialer Frauenbund (Frauenbund der DKG)
        153 Bd. 1 (March 1907–July 1909)
        156 Bd. 4 (January 1912–December 1913)
        157 Bd. 5 (January 1914–September 1927)

Hinaussendung deutscher Frauen nach DSWA
    170 Bd. 1 (July 1896–January 1898)
    171 Bd. 2 (January 1898–August 1898)
    172 Bd. 3 (August 1898–August 1899)
    173 Bd. 4 (January 1899–April 1899)
    174 Bd. 5 (May 1899–October 1900)
    175 Bd. 6 (November 1900–March 1907)
    176 Bd. 7 (March 1907–June 1909)
    177 Bd. 8 (July 1909–December 1910)
    178 Bd. 9 (January 1911–January 1923)
Hinaussendung
    179 Bd. 1 (January 1911–January 1915)
    180 Bd. 2 (May 1919–February 1920)
    181 Bd. 3 (May 1920–December 1926)
Frauenfrage: Listen übergesiedelter Personen
    182 Bd. 1 (April 1903–May 1914)
Übersiedlung von Frauen und Mädchen
    185 (February 1912–January 1919)
Elisabethhäuser in DSWA
    188 Bd. 1 (December 1913–January 1924)
Wöchnerinnenheim in Windhuk
    190 Bd. 1 (December 1905–October 1906)
Wöchnerinnenheim in Grootfontein
    209 (July 1913–July 1914)
Verband der Reichsdeutschen in SWA
    346 Bd. 1 (July 1925–February 1926)
    346a Bd. 2 (August 1925–May 1929)
Verband südwestafrikanischer Farmer
    349 (February 1926–March 1926)
Deutscher Bund in Windhuk
    350 Bd. 1 (April 1926–November 1929)
    350/1 Bd. 2 (December 1929–October 1932)
Farmwirtschaftsgesellschaft für SWA
    351 (January 1928–December 1929)
Politische Verhältnisse in SWA
    531 Bd. 1 (August 1920–October 1924)
    532 Bd. 2 (December 1924–August 1926)
    533 Bd. 1—SWA (June 1926–September 1927)
    534 Bd. 2—SWA & SA (June 1927–August 1935)
Südwestafrika
    535 (February 1930–January 1934)
Koloniale Reichsgemeinschaft, Gründungsvorbereitungen
    559 (June 1922–May 1926)

Korag
    561 Bd. 1 (December 1922–December 1925)
    562 Bd. 2 (December 1925–January 1927)
Drucksachen der Korag, Rundschreiben
    578 (January 1926–May 1936)
Syndikat
    600a (1892–95)
Siedlung SWA
    601 Bd. 1 (1892)
    602 Bd. 2 (April 1892–November 1895)
Lehrfarm in DSWA für Mädchen
    606 Bd. 1 (March 1909–December 1910)
    607 Bd. 2 (August 1911–December 1913)
Schulwesen in Kolonien
    948 (May 1904–May 1910)
Schulwesen in SWA
    957 Bd. 1 (March 1920–May 1921)
    958 Bd. 2 (June 1921–October 1921)
    959 Bd. 3 (September 1921–March 1922)
    960 Bd. 4 (April 1922–December 1924)
Schulvereine in SWA
    960/2 (October 1928–December 1929)
    960/3 (August 1929–October 1932)
    960/4 (January 1930–November 1932)
Schulverein Windhuk
    964 Bd. 1 (June 1927–June 1931)
Bücherdienst für Ost- und Südwestafrika—Sendungen
    1031 Bd. 1 (January 1920–1929)

Deutscher Reichstag R101
    SWA Schutzgebiet
        1093 Bd. 2 (December 1892–October 1896)
        1094 Bd. 3 (November 1896–October 1902)
        1095 Bd. 4 (January 1903–November 1904)
        1096 Bd. 5 (January 1904–February 1905)
        1101 Bd. 10 (May 1909–March 1910)

Filme der Akten des Kaiserlichen Gouvernements in Deutsch-Südwest-Afrika
R151F
    Unterrichtswesen
        FC4737, FC4749, FC4750
    Rechtspflege gegen Nichteingeborene
        FC5180, FC5181
    Strafpolizei (Ausweisungen)
        FC5233

Sicherheitspolizei: Vereine: Turnvereine, Bürgervereine, DKG, 1902–1914
  FC5241
Maßregeln gegen geschlechtliche Ausschweifung: Generalia, Specialia, 1899–1914
  FC5243, FC5244
Besiedlungssachen, Farm- und Landwirtschaft (Allgemeines)
  FC14839, FC14842-5, FC14849, FC14851, FC14853-9

Pressearchiv des Reichslandbundes R8034II
Kolonialpolitik, Allgemeines
  6326 Bd. 3 (April 1899–August 1899)
  6331 Bd. 8 (November 1901–June 1902)
  6333 Bd. 10 (October 1902–March 1903)
  6353 Bd. 31 (January 1925–November 1927)
  6354/i Bd. 33 (January 1933–May 1935)
  6356 Bd. 35 (March 1937–April 1938)
SWA, Allgemeines
  6364 Bd. 1 (1905-6)
  6366 Bd. 3 (1907-8)
  6368 Bd. 5 (1909)
  6370 Bd. 7 (1910-11)
  6372 Bd. 9 (1912-19)
  6373 Bd. 10 (1919-40)

Reichskolonialamt R1001
Fotokopien u. Abschriften von Akten des ehemaligen RKA aus dem Besitz von
Georg Thiemann
  6
Auskunftserteilung über Auswanderung in die deutschen Kolonien
  224 Bd. 1 (November 1895–October 1911)
Ansiedlungen in DSWA, Allgemeines
  1136 Bd. 3 (December 1899–September 1902)
  1137 Bd. 4 (September 1902–May 1903)
  1138 Bd. 5 (May 1903–February 1904)
  1140 Bd. 7 (January 1905–November 1905)
  1141 Bd. 8 (October 1905–October 1906)
  1142 Bd. 9 (September 1906–February 1907)
  1144 Bd. 11 (July 1908–July 1914)
  1145 Bd. 12 (October 1914–August 1925)
  1146 Bd. 13 (August 1925–September 1937)
Beförderung der Einwanderung von Buren in DSWA
  1149 Bd. 3 (August 1894–October 1900)
  1152 Bd. 6 (July 1902–June 1903)
  1153 Bd. 7 (July 1903–August 1908)
Auswanderung deutscher Handwerker nach SWA
  1165 (April 1926–October 1926)

Ansiedlung von Wolga–Deutschen in SWA
    1166 (January 1927–January 1930)
Juden und Halbjuden in SWA
    1168 (December 1935–May 1939)
Auswanderung von Frauen nach DSWA
    1197 Bd. 1 (March 1925–February 1930)
    1198 Bd. 2 (March 1930–October 1931)
Rückwanderung von Ansiedlern in das ehemalige DSWA
    1226 (July 1919–August 1939)
Deutsche Arbeitsfront in SWA
    1236 (June 1935–April 1940)
Besiedlung von Klein-Windhuk
    1695 Bd. 11 (April 1900–December 1901)
Vereine in D-SWA
    1736 Bd. 1 (March 1903–March 1910)
    1737 Bd. 2 (April 1910–March 1912)
    1738 Bd. 3 (April 1912–November 1912)
    1739 Bd. 4 (December 1912–July 1914)
    1740 Bd. 5 (April 1914–January 1939)
Deutscher Bund für SWA
    1771 Bd. 1 (November 1924–October 1926)
    1772 Bd. 2 (October 1926–December 1929)
Verband der Reichsdeutschen in SWA
    1773 (June 1925–November 1928)
Ausweisungen aus SWA
    1918 Bd. 1 ([1891] September 1906–October 1920, 1938)
Veröffentlichungen
    1941 (January 1912–March 1939)
Schulen in DSWA
    1949 Bd. 1 (July 1890–May 1901)
    1950 Bd. 2 (March 1901–February 1907)
    1951 Bd. 3 (May 1907–June 1913)
    1952 Bd. 4 (February 1913–December 1914)
    1953 Bd. 5 (September 1914–September 1924)
    1953/51 Bd. 6 (August 1924–December 1927)
    1954 Bd. 8 (November 1928–April 1933)
    1955 Bd. 9 (May 1933–January 1935)
    1956 Bd. 10 (February 1935–December 1939)
    1957 Bd. 10 (Abschriften)
    1958 Bd. 11 (December 1939–February 1940)
Rundverfügungen des Kaiserlichen Gouvernements von D-SWA
    2042 Bd. 1 (May 1905–December 1906)
    2044 Bd. 3 (January 1908–December 1908)

Einricthung einer Kommunal- und Selbstverwaltung
    2058 Bd. 2 (December 1908–December 1909)
Mischehe und Mischlinge
    5417 (January 1906–12)
Mischehen und Mischlinge in rechtlicher Beziehung
    5423 Bd. 1 (June 1889–January 1913)
    5424 Bd. 2 (January 1913–April 1919)
Auskunftserteilung über Auswanderung in die deutschen Kolonien
    6238 Bd. 2 (November 1911–July 1918, 1940)
Zentralauskunftsstelle für Auswanderer
    6275 Bd. 1 (July 1902–October 1906)
Unterstützung, Verpflegung und Heimschaffung mittelloser Personen aus den
Kolonien
    6294 Bd. 1 (March 1894–February 1902)
Jahresberichte aus DSWA
    6489 Bd. 5 (May 1904–December 1905)
Besiedlungsmöglichkeiten DSWA
    6492 (December 1894–February 1895)
Denkschriften über die Entwicklung in DSWA
    6541 (1907–9)
Frauenbund des DKG
    6693 Bd. 1 (1907–17, March 1926–August 1930)
    6694 Bd. 2 (September 1930–December 1932)
    6695 Bd. 3 (January 1933–August 1936)
Sitzung des Verwaltungsrats
    7071 Bd. 1 (October 1898–June 1905)
Verhandlungen des Reichstages und Bundesrats, bzw. Reichsrats über die Lage
und Verwaltung in den Kolonien
    7255 Bd. 3 (May 1924–May 1932)
Schulwesen in Kolonien und Deutschland-Allgemeines
    7306 Bd. 1 (April 1895–97)
Bevölkerungsstatistik der deutschen Kolonien
    7427 (April 1890–August 1916, November 1931–January 1939)
Bevölkerungsstatistik über DSWA
    7430 Bd. 1 (February 1891–April 1913)
    7431 Bd. 2 (January 1913–May 1939)
Ausweisungen aus den Kolonien
    7547 (May 1887–February 1914)

Schutzgebiet Deutsch-Südwest Afrika R1002
    Personalakten
        387 Eckenbrecher, Margarethe v. (Lehrerin), Bd. 1
        1785 Tworeck, Eugen (Lehrer), Bd. 1
        2004 Zedlitz, Alfred (Oberlehrer), Bd. 1

Unterrichtswesen—Generalia
  2125 Bd. 1 (July 1910, April 1915–October 1919)
Unterrichtswesen—Revisionen
  2127 Bd. 1 (June 1916–July 1919)
Regierungsschulen außer Maltahöhe
  2133 Bd. 1 (November 1915–August 1919)
Besiedlung, Heraussendung von Frauen usw. durch DKG
  2579 Bd. 1 (May 1908–June 1913)
Selbstverwaltung
  2726 Bd. 1 April 1908–February 1913
Standesamtssachen
  2728 Bd. 1 (March 1908–October 1914)
Schulangelegenheiten
  2729 Bd. 1 (April 1908–December 1914)

Federal Archive, Koblenz

Nachlass Dr. Oskar Hintrager N1037
Nachlass Dr. Wilhelm Külz N1042
Nachlass Dr. Paul Leutwein N1145

State Archive, Berlin/Helene-Lange-Archiv

Amtsgericht Charlottenburg: Frauenbund der Deutschen Kolonialgesellschaft
  (Rep.42, Acc.2147, Nr.26164)
Helene-Lange-Archiv Brochure Collection

PERIODICALS/GOVERNMENT PUBLICATIONS

Afrikanischer Heimatkalender (Windhoek)
Der Auslandsdeutsche (Germany)
Deutsche Kolonialzeitung (Berlin)
Die Deutsche Schule im Auslande (Germany)
Die deutschen Schutzgebiete in Afrika und der Südsee: Amtliche Jahresberichte
  (Berlin)
Deutsch-Südwestafrikanische Zeitung (Swakopmund)
*Frauenberuf und -Erwerb: Beilage zum Centralblatt des Bundes Deutscher
  Frauenvereine* (Germany)
Koloniale Rundschau (Germany)
Kolonial-Handels-Abreßbuch (Germany)
Koloniale Zeitschrift (Germany)
Kolonie und Heimat (Berlin)
Der Südwestbote (Windhoek)
Windhuker Nachrichten (Windhoek)
Zeitschrift für Kolonialpolitik, Kolonialrecht und Kolonialwirtschaft (Berlin)

BIBLIOGRAPHY

GOVERNMENT DOCUMENTS

Barron, L. Smythe, *The Nazis in Africa: Lost Documents on the Third Reich*, vol. 111 (Salisbury, N.C.: Documentary Publications, 1978).

CONTEMPORARY WORKS

Amrhein, Hans. *Die deutsche Schule im Auslande.* Leipzig: G. J. Göschen, 1905.

Berthold, Hans. "Die Besiedlung Deutsch-Südwestafrika." *Jahrbuch über die deutschen Kolonien* 4 (1911): 200–206.

Blumhagen, Hans Ernst. *Die Doppelstatigkeit der Deutschen im Mandatsgebiet Südwestafrika und ihre völkerrechtlichen Auswirkungen.* Berlin: D. Reimer, 1938.

Blumhagen, Hugo. *Entscheidungsjahre in Deutsch-Südwestafrika.* Berlin: Dieter Reimer/Ernst Vohsen, 1939.

———. *Südwestafrika einst und jetzt.* Berlin: Dieter Reimer/Ernst Vohsen, 1934.

Bonn, M. J. *Wandering Scholar.* New York: John Day, 1948.

Brockmann, Clara. *Die deutsche Frau in Südwestafrika: Ein Beitrag zur Frauenfrage in unseren Kolonien.* Berlin: Mittler & Sohn, 1910.

———. *Briefe eines deutschen Mädchens aus Südwest.* Berlin: Mittler & Sohn, 1912.

Deutsch-Südwestafrika: Amtlicher Ratgeber für Auswanderer. Berlin: Dietrich Reimer/Ernst Vohsen, 1912.

Dove, Karl. *Die Deutschen Kolonien IV: Südwestafrika.* Berlin; Leipzig: Göschen'sche Verlagshandlung GmbH, 1913.

Eckenbrecher, Margarethe v. *Was Afrika mir gab und nahm: 1. Erlebnisse einer deutschen Frau in Südwestafrika, 1902–1936.* 8th ed. Berlin: Mittler & Sohn, 1940.

———. *Deutsch-Südwestafrika: Kriegs- und Friedensbilder.* Berlin: W. Weicher, 1907.

Falkenhausen, Helene v. *Ansiedlerschicksale: Elf Jahre in Deutsch-Südwestafrika, 1893–1904.* 2nd ed. Berlin: Dietrich Reimer/Ernst Vohsen, 1905.

Frobenius, Else. *10 Jahre Frauenbund der Kolonialgesellschaft.* Berlin: Kolonie und Heimat Verlagsgesellschaft, 1918.

———. *30 Jahre Koloniale Frauenarbeit.* Aachen: Reichskolonialbund, 1936.

Grimm, Hans. *Das deutsche Südwester-Buch.* Munich: Albert Langen, 1929.

———. *Dreizehn Briefe aus Deutsch-Südwest-Afrika.* Munich: Albert Langen, 1928.

———. *Volk ohne Raum.* München: Lippoldsberg, 1926.

Haussleiter, Gottlieb. *Zur Eingeborenen-Frage in Deutsch-Südwest-Afrika: Erwägungen und Vorschläge.* Berlin: M. Warneck, 1906.

Hintrager, Oskar. *Südwestafrika in der deutschen Zeit.* 1st and 2nd ed. München: R. Oldenbourg, 1955, 1956.

Höpker, Lydia. *Um Scholle und Leben: Schicksale einer deutschen Farmerin in Südwest-Afrika.* Minden in Westfalen: Wilhelm Köhler, 1927.

Kohn, George F. "The Organization and Work of the League of Nations." Supplement to *Annals of the American Academy of Political and Social Sciences* 114 (July 1924): 1–79.

Külz, Ludwig. *Tropenarzt im afrikanischen Busch.* 3rd ed. Berlin: Süsserott, 1943.

Külz, Wilhelm. *Die Selbstverwaltung für Deutsch-Südwestafrika.* Berlin: Wilhelm Süsseroff, 1909.

Lenssen, H. E. *Chronik von Deutsch-Südwestafrika: Eine kurzgefaßte Aufzählung geschichtlicher Ereignisse aus der Deutschen Kolonialzeit von 1883–1915.* 3rd ed. Windhoek: SWA Wissenschaftliche Gesellschaft, 1988.

Leusner, Hermann. *Die Entwicklung des Schulwesens in den deutschen afrikanischen Kolonien, jetzigen Mandatsgebieten, vom Ende des Weltkrieges bis zur Gegenwart.* Cologne: Buchdruckerei Orthen, 1938.

Leutwein, Paul. *"Du weitest Deine Brust, der Blick wird freier." Kriegs- und Wanderfahrten.* Berlin: Deutscher Kolonial-Verlag, 1909.

Leutwein, Theodor. *Elf Jahre Gouveneur in Deutsch-Südwestafrika.* Berlin: Mittler & Sohn, 1906.

Moritz, Eduard. *Das Schulwesen in Deutsch Südwestafrika.* Berlin: Dietrich Reimer/Ernst Vohsen, 1914.

Nazi Activities in South West Africa (as stated in the Report of Southwest Africa Commission, March, 1936). Friends of Europe Publication, no. 43. London: Friends of Europe, 1936.

Oelhafen, Hans. *Die Besiedelung Deutsch-West-Afrika bis zum Weltkriege.* Berlin: Dietrich Reimer/Ernst Vohsen, 1926.

von Perbandt, C. "Sind unsere afrikanischen Kolonien für europäische bezw. speziell deutsche Besiedlung geeignet?" *Jahrbuch über die deutschen Kolonien* 6 (1913): 76–94.

Rohrbach, Paul. *Deutsch-Südwest-Afrika ein Ansiedlungsgebiet?* Berlin-Schöneberg: Hilfe, 1906.

Schnee, Heinrich. *German Colonization, Past and Future: The Truth about the German Colonies.* New York: Knopf, 1926.

Seitz, Theodor. *Vom Aufstieg und Niederbruch deutscher Kolonialmacht: Erinnerungen.* Bd. 3, *Gouverneursjahre in Südwestafrika.* Karlsruhe i.B.: E. F. Müller, 1929.

Uhde, Sofie von. *Deutsche Unterm Kreuz des Südens: Bei den Kolonialsiedlern in Südwest- und Ostafrika.* Berlin: Dietrich Reimer/Ernst Vohsen, 1934.

Voigt, Bernhard. *Auf dorniger Pad. Aus Deutsch-Südafrikas alten Tagen.* Berlin: Safari, 1926.

———. *Deutsch-Südwestafrika, Land und Leute: Eine Heimatkunde für Deutschlandsjugend und Volk.* Stuttgart: Strecker & Schröder, 1913.

———. *Du meine Heimat Südwest: Ein afrikanisches Farmleben.* Berlin: Safari, 1925.

———. *Südwestafrika, einst und jetzt.* Bochum: F. Kamp, 1939.

10 Jahre Frauenbund der Deutschen Kolonialgesellschaft. Berlin: 'Kolonie und Heimat,' 1918.

Wiedern, Kurt. *Deutsche Staatsangehörigkeit im C-Mandat Südwestafrika.* Greifswald: [n.p.?], 1934.

SECONDARY LITERATURE

Anderson, Benedict. *Imagined Communities: Reflections on the Origin and Spread of Nationalism.* London: Verso, 1992.

Applegate, Celia. *A Nation of Provincials: The German Idea of Heimat.* Berkeley: University of California Press, 1990.

———. "What Is German Music? Reflections on the Role of Art in the Creation of the German Nation." *German Studies Review,* special issue, *German Identity* (winter 1992): 21–32.

Armstrong, John A. "Mobilized Diaspora in Tsarist Russia: The Case of the Baltic Germans." In *Soviet Nationality Policies and Practices,* ed. Jeremy R. Azrael, 63–104. New York: Praeger, 1978.

Barr, Pat. *The Dust in the Balance: British Women in India, 1905–1945.* London: Hamish Hamilton, 1989.

Benninghoff-Lühl, Sibylle. *Deutsche Kolonialromane, 1884–1914, in ihrem Entstehungs- und Wirkungszusammenhang.* Bremen: Übersee-Museum Bremen, 1983.

Bertelsmann, Werner. *Die deutsche Sprachgruppe Südwestafrikas in Politik und Recht seit 1915.* Windhoek: SWA Wissenschaftliche Gesellschaft, 1979.

Bivona, Daniel. *Desire and Contradiction: Imperial Visions and Domestic Debates in Victorian Literature.* Manchester, U.K.: University of Manchester, 1990.

Blackbourn, David. "The *Mittelstand* in German Society and Politics, 1871–1914." *Social History* 2, no. 4 (1977): 409–33.

Bley, Helmut. *South-West Africa under German Rule, 1894–1914.* Trans. Hugh Ridley. Evanston, Ill.: Northwestern University Press, 1971.

Bulbeck, Chila. "New Histories of the Memshahib and Missus: The Case of Papua New Guinea." *Journal of Women's History* 3, no. 2 (1991): 82–105.

Chickering, Roger. "'Casting Their Gaze More Broadly': Women's Patriotic Activism in Imperial Germany." *Past and Present* 118 (February 1988): 156–85.

———. "Language and the Social Foundations of Radical Nationalism in the Wilhelmine Era." In *1870/71–1989/90: German Unifications and the Change of Literary Discourse,* ed. Walter Pape, 61–78. New York: de Gruyter, 1993.

———. *We Men Who Feel Most German: A Cultural Study of the Pan-German League, 1886–1914.* London: Allen & Unwin, 1984.

Childers, Thomas. "Interest and Ideology: Anti-System Politics in the Era of Stabilization, 1924–1928." In *Die Nachwirkungen der Inflation auf die deutsche Geschichte, 1924–1933,* ed. Gerald D. Feldman, 1–20. Munich: R. Oldenbourg, 1985.

———. *The Nazi Voter: The Social Foundations of Fascism in Germany, 1919–1933.* Chapel Hill: University of North Carolina Press, 1983.

Cohen, Cynthia. "'The Natives Must First Become Good Workmen': Formal Educational Provision in German Southwest Africa and East Africa Compared." *Journal of Southern African Studies* 19 (March 1993): 115–34.

Cohen, Gary B. *The Politics of Ethnic Survival: Germans in Prague, 1861–1914.* Princeton, N.J.: Princeton University Press, 1981.

Comaroff, John L. "Images of Empire, Contests of Conscience: Models of Colonial Domination in South Africa." *American Ethnologist* 16 (November 1989): 661–85.

Confino, Alon. "The Nation as Local Metaphor: Heimat, National Memory and the German Empire, 1871–1918." *History and Memory* 5, no. 1 (1993): 42–86.

Cooper, Frederick, and Ann L. Stoler. "Tensions of Empire: Colonial Control and Visions of Rule." *American Ethnologist* 16 (November 1989): 609–21.

Crozier, Andrew J. *Appeasement and Germany's Last Bid for Colonies.* New York: St. Martin's Press, 1988.

Dedering, Tilman. "The German-Herero War of 1904: Revisionism of Genocide or Imaginary Historiography." *Journal of Southern African Studies* 19, no. 1 (1993): 80–88.

Denoon, Donald. *Settler Capitalism: The Dynamics of Dependent Development in the Southern Hemisphere.* Oxford: Clarendon Press, 1983.

Dextor, Bryon. *The Years of Opportunity: The League of Nations, 1920–1926.* New York: Viking, 1967.

Dickinson, Edward Ross. *The Politics of German Child Welfare from the Empire to the Federal Republic.* Cambridge: Harvard University Press, 1996.

Diehl, Hans Hartmut, "Brief History of the Evangelical Lutheran Church in Namibia (GELC)." In *Lutheran Churches in Namibia: A Brief Historical Survey of the Three Lutheran Churches in Namibia,* 17–20, trans. E. Hoffmann. Windhoek: ELOC Printing, 1995.

Drechsler, Horst. *"Let Us Die Fighting": The Struggle of the Nama and Herero against German Imperialism.* Trans. Bernd Zollner. London: Zed Press, 1980.

Eley, Geoff. *Reshaping the German Right: Radical Nationalism and Political Change after Bismarck.* Ann Arbor: University of Michigan Press, 1991.

———. "State Formation, Nationalism, and Political Culture: Some Thoughts on the Unification of Germany." In *From Unification to Nazism: Reinterpreting the German Past.* Boston: Allen & Unwin, 1986.

Engel, Lothar. *Kolonialismus und Nationalismus im Deutschen Protestantismus in Namibia 1907 bis 1945: Beiträge zur Geschichte der deutschen Evangelishen Mission und Kirche im ehemaligen Kolonial- und Mandatsgebiet Südwestafrika.* Frankfurt am Main: Peter Lang, 1976.

Engelhardt, Kerstin. "Missionarinnen und Siedlerinnen: Deutsche Kolonialistinnen." In *Namibia: Frauen mischen sich ein,* ed. Florence Hervé, 21–37. Berlin: Orlanda Frauenverlag, 1993.

Farwell, Byron. *The Great War in Africa, 1914–1918.* New York: Norton, 1986.

Frevert, Ute. *Women in German History: From Bourgeois Emancipation to Sexual Liberation.* Trans. Stuart McKinnon-Evans. New York: Berg, 1990.

Friedrichsmeyer, Sara, Sara Lennox, and Susanne Zantop, eds. *The Imperialist Imagination: German Colonialism and Its Legacy.* Ann Arbor: University of Michigan Press, 1998.

Fyfe, Christopher. "Race, Empire, and the Historians." *Race and Class* 33 (April–June 1992): 15–30.

Gellately, Robert. *The Politics of Economic Despair: Shopkeepers and German Politics, 1890–1914.* London: Sage, 1974.

Gellrich, Gerhard. "Das Südwesterlied 'Hart wie Kameldornholz'—Ursprung und Varianten." *Afrikanischer Heimatkalender* (1986): 105–14.

Gretschel, H.-V. "The Lost 'Umlaut': The German Language in Namibia, 1915–1939: A Suppressed Language?" *Logos* 13 (1993): 44–60.

Griffiths, Tom, and Libby Robin, eds. *Ecology and Empire: Environmental History of Settler Societies.* Seattle: University of Washington Press, 1997.

Hagemann, Adolf. *Südafrika und das "Dritte Reich": Rassenpolitische Affinität und machtpolitische Rivalität.* Frankfurt: Campus, 1989.

Hardtwig, Wolfgang. "Nationsbildung und politische Mentalität: Denkmal und Fest im Kaiserreich." In *Geschichtskultur und Wissenschaft.* Munich: Deutscher Taschenbuch, 1990.

Hayes, Patricia. "'Cocky' Hahn and the 'Black Venus': The Making of a Native Commissioner in South West Africa, 1915–46." *Gender and History* 8, no. 3 (1996): 364–92.

Heese, C. P. "Das Erziehungswesen in Südwestafrika unter der deutschen Regierung bis 1915." In *SWA Journal,* ed. J. Fischer and P. Meinert, 127–35. Windhoek: John Meinert, 1986.

Helbig, Helga, and Ludwig Helbig. *Mythos Deutsch-Südwest: Namibia und die Deutschen.* Weinheim: Beltz, 1983.

Hellberg, Carl J. *Mission, Colonialism, and Liberation: The Lutheran Church in Namibia, 1840–1966.* Windhoek: New Namibia Books, 1997.

Hendriksson, Anders H. "The Riga German Community: Social Change and the Nationality Question, 1860–1905." Ph.D. diss., University of Toronto, 1978.

Hiery, Hermann J. *Das Deutsche Reich in der Südsee, 1900–1921.* Göttingen: Vandenhoeck & Ruprecht, 1995.

Hobsbawm, Eric. *Nations and Nationalism since 1780: Programme, Myth, Reality.* Cambridge: Cambridge University Press, 1991.

Hoeflich, K. F. "Das Deutsche Sprach- und Schulproblem in S.W.A." In *Ein Leben für Südwestafrika: Festschrift für Dr.h.c. Heinrich Vedder,* ed. W. Drascher and H. J. Rust, 111–36. Windhoek: SWA Wissenschaftliche Gesellschaft, 1961.

Holston, Kenneth. "A Measure of the Nation: Colonial Enthusiasm, Education and Politics in Germany, 1890–1936." Ph.D. diss., University of Pennsylvania, 1996.

Jäschke, U. U. "Der Siedlungsraum SWA/Namibia mit drei Fallbeispielen zur Farmentwicklung." In *Namibia—Ausgewählte Themen der Exkursionen 1988,* ed. Heinrich Lamping, 181–212. Frankfurter Wirtschafts- und Sozialgeographische Schriften, 53. Frankfurt am Main: Institut für Wirtschafts- und Sozialgeographie der Universität Frankfurt, 1989.

Jenny, Hans. *Südwestafrika: Land zwischen den Extremen.* Stuttgart: W. Kohlhammer, 1966.

Jones, Larry Eugene. "Crisis and Realignment: Agrarian Splinter Parties in the Late Weimar Republic." In *Peasants and Lords in Modern Germany: Recent Studies in Agricultural History,* ed. Robert G. Moeller, 198–232. Boston: Allen & Unwin, 1986.

———. "'The Dying Middle': Weimar Germany and the Fragmentation of Bourgeois Politics." *Central European History* 5, no. 1 (1972): 23–54.

———. *German Liberalism and the Dissolution of the Weimar Party System, 1918–1933.* Chapel Hill: University of North Carolina Press, 1988.

———. "Inflation, Revaluation, and the Crisis of Middle-Class Politics: A Study in the Dissolution of the German Party System, 1923–28." *Central European History* 12, no. 2 (1979): 143–68.

Kennedy, Dane. *Islands of White: Settler Society and Culture in Kenya and Southern Rhodesia.* Durham, N.C.: Duke University Press, 1987.

Kennedy, Katharine D. "A Nation's Readers: Cultural Integration and Schoolbook Canon in Wilhelmine Germany." *Paedagogica Historica* 33 (1997): 459–80.

———. "Regionalism and Nationalism in South German History Lessons, 1871–1914." *German Studies Review* 12, no. 1 (1989): 11–33.

Koselleck, Reinhart. "Kriegerdenkmale als Identitätsstiftungen der Überlebenden." In *Identität,* 2nd ed., ed. Oda Marquard and Karlheinz Stierle, 255–76. Munich: Wilhelm Fink, 1996.

Kroeger, Gert. "Zur Situation der baltischen Deutschen." *Zeitschrift für Ostforschung* 17 (1968): 601–32.

Krüger, Gesine. *Kriegsbewältigung und Geschichtsbewußtsein: Realität, Deutung, und Verarbeitung des deutschen Kolonialkriegs in Namibia 1904 bis 1907.* Göttingen: Vandenhoeck & Ruprecht, 1999.

Kühne, Horst. "Die Fünfte Kolonne des faschistischen deutschen Imperialismus in Südwestafrika, 1933–1939." *Zeitschrift für Geschichtswissenschaft* 8, no. 4 (1960): 765–80.

Lamping, Heinrich, ed. *Namibia—Ausgewählte Themen der Exkursionen 1988.* Frankfurter Wirtschafts- und Sozialgeographische Schriften, 53. Frankfurt am Main: Institut für Wirtschafts- und Sozialgeographie der Universität Frankfurt, 1989.

———. "Namibia—Entwicklungen und Perspektiven." In *Namibia: Ausgewählte Themen der Exkursionen 1988,* ed. H. Lamping, 5–36. Frankfurter Wirtschafts- und Sozialgeographische Schriften 53. Frankfurt am Main: Institut für Wirtschafts- und Sozialgeographie der Universtität Frankfurt, 1989.

Louis, William Roger. *Great Britain and Germany's Lost Colonies, 1914–1919.* Oxford: Clarendon Press, 1967.

Lowry, Donal. "'White Woman's Country': Ethel Tawse Jollie and the Making of White Rhodesia." *Journal of Southern African Studies* 23, no. 2 (1937): 259–81.

MacDonald, Robert H. *The Language of Empire: Myths and Metaphors of Popular Imperialism, 1880–1918.* Manchester, U.K.: Manchester University Press, 1994.

MacKenzie, John, ed. *Imperialism and Popular Culture*. Manchester, U.K.: Manchester University Press, 1986.

———. *Propaganda and Empire: The Manipulation of British Public Opinion, 1880–1960*. Manchester, U.K.: Manchester University Press, 1984.

MacMillan, Margaret. *Women of the Raj*. New York: Thames & Hudson, 1988.

Mamozai, Martha. *Schwarze Frau, weiße Herrin: Frauenleben in den deutschen Kolonien*. Reinbek bei Hamburg: Rowohlt, 1989.

Möller, Lucie. "Deutsche Ortsnamen Südwestafrikas im Rahmen einer historisch-onomastischen Darstellung." *Afrikanischer Heimatkalender* (1984): 45–54.

———. "Deutsche Ortsnamen Südwestafrikas im Rahmen einer historisch-onomastischen Darstellung." *Afrikanischer Heimatkalender* (1986): 41–49.

———. "Deutsche Ortsnamen Südwestafrikas im Rahmen einer historisch-onomastischen Darstellung." *Afrikanischer Heimatkalender* (1987): 89–102.

Mosse, George L. *Toward the Final Solution: A History of European Racism*. New York: H. Fertig, 1978.

———. "Nationalism and Respectability: Normal and Abnormal Sexuality in the Nineteenth Century." *Journal of Contemporary History* 17, no. 2 (1982): 221–46.

———. *Nationalism and Sexuality: Respectability and Abnormal Sexuality in Modern Europe*. New York: H. Fertig, 1985.

———. *Nationalization of the Masses: Political Symbolism and Mass Movements in Germany from the Napoleonic Wars through the Third Reich*. Ithaca, N.Y.: Cornell University Press, 1991.

Mossolow, N. *Windhoek damals/Die Windhoek van weleer/This Was Old Windhoek*. 2nd ed. Windhoek: N. Mossolow, 1965.

———. *Windhoek: Drei historische Wahrzeichen/Drie geskiedkundige Kentekens/Three historical landmarks*. Windhoek: John Meinert, 1972.

Nipperdey, Thomas. "Nationalidee und Nationaldenkmal in Deutschland im 19. Jahrhundert." *Historische Zeitschrift* 206:3 (June 1968): 529–85.

———. "Verein als soziale Struktur im späten und frühen 19. Jahrhundert." In *Geschichtswissenschaft und Vereinswesen im 19. Jahrhundert*, ed. Hartmut Boockmann et al., 1–44. Göttingen: Vandenhoeck & Ruprecht, 1972.

Nöckler, Herbert C. *Sprachmischung in Südwestafrika*. Munich: Max Hueber, 1963.

Noyes, John. *Colonial Space: Spatiality in the Discourse of German South West Africa, 1884–1915*. Chur, Switzerland: Harwood Academic, 1992.

Nuhn, Walter. *Sturm über Südwest: Der Hereroaufstand von 1904—Ein düsteres Kapital der deutschen kolonialen Vergangenheit Namibias*. Koblenz: Bernard & Graefe, 1989.

O'Donnell, Krista. "The Colonial Woman Question: Gender, National Identity, and Empire in the German Colonial Society Female Emigration Program, 1896–1914." Ph.D. diss., SUNY, Binghamton, 1996.

Onsalen, Charles van. "Prostitutes and Proletarians, 1886–1914." In *Social and Eco-*

nomic History of Witwatersrand: Vol. 1, *New Babylon.* New York: Longman, 1982.

Orwell, George. "Shooting an Elephant." In *Shooting an Elephant and Other Essays.* London: Secker & Warburg, 1950.

Perry, Joseph. "Frontweihnachten, 1914–17: A Community of Longing." Paper presented at the Second Annual Transatlantic Seminar in German History, Bochum, Germany, 19 April 1996. Photocopy.

Peters, Walter. *Baukunst in Südwestafrika, 1884–1914: Die Rezeption Deutscher Architektur in der Zeit von 1884 bis 1914 im ehemaligen Deutsch-Südwestafrika (Namibia).* Windhoek: SWA Wissenschaftliche Gesellschaft, 1981.

Pierard, Richard V. "The German Colonial Society, 1882–1914." Ph.D. diss., State University of Iowa, 1964.

———. "The Transportation of White Women to German Southwest Africa, 1898–1914." *Race* (1970–71): 317–22.

Pogge von Strandmann, Hartmut. "Domestic Origins of Germany's Colonial Expansion under Bismarck." *Past and Present* 42 (February 1969): 140–59.

———. "Imperialism and Revisionism in Interwar Germany." In *Imperialism and After: Continuities and Discontinuities,* ed. Wolfgang Mommsen and Jürgen Osterhammel, 90–119. London: Allen & Unwin, 1986.

du Pisani, André. *SWA/Namibia: The Politics of Continuity and Change.* Johannesburg: Jonathan Bell, 1986.

Rautenberg, Hulda. "Die Hedwig-Heyl-Haushaltungsschule in Windhuk." *Afrikanischer Heimatkalender* (1986): 93–104.

———. *Das alte Swakopmund, 1892–1919: Swakopmund zum 75. Geburtstag.* Neumünster: Karl Wachholtz, 1967.

Reif, Heinz, Sigrid Heinze, and Andreas Ludwig. "Schwierigkeiten mit Tradition: Zur kulturellen Praxis städtischer Heimatmuseen." In *Das historische Museum: Labor, Schaubühne, Identitätsfabrik,* ed. Gottfried Korff and Martin Roth, 231–47. Frankfurt: Campus, 1990.

Retallack, James. "'Why Can't a Saxon Be More Like a Prussian?' Regional Identities and the Birth of Modern Political Culture in Germany, 1866–67." *Canadian Journal of History* 32, no. 1 (1997): 26–55.

Roosens, Eugeen. *Creating Ethnicity: The Process of Ethnogenesis.* Frontiers of Anthropology, 5. Newbury Park, Calif.: Sage, 1989.

Roth, Martin. *Heimatmuseum: Zur Geschichte einer deutschen Institution.* Berliner Schriften zur Museumkunde, vol. 7. Berlin: Gebrüder Mann, 1990.

Rüdiger, Klaus H. *Die Namibia-Deutschen: Geschichte einer Nationalität im Werden.* Stuttgart: Franz Steiner, 1993.

Rüger, Adolf. "Imperialismus, Sozialreformismus, und antikoloniale demokratische Alternative." *Zeitschrift für Geschichtswissenschaft* 23, no. 11 (1975): 1293–308.

———. "Das Streben nach kolonialer Restitution in den ersten Nachkriegsjahren." In *Drang nach Afrika: Die deutsche koloniale Expansionspolitik und Herr-*

schaft in Afrika von den Anfängen bis zum Verlust der Kolonien, ed. Helmuth Stoecker, 202–83. Berlin: Akademie, 1991.

Sadji, Amadou Booker. "African Nature and German Culture: Colonial Women Writers on Africa." In *Blacks and German Culture*, ed. Reinhold Grimm and Jost Hermand, 22–34. Madison: University of Wisconsin Press, 1986.

———. *Das Bild des Negro-Afrikaners in der Deutschen Kolonialliteratur, 1884–1945: Ein Beitrag zur literarischen Imagologie Schwarzafrikas*. Berlin: Dietrich Reimer, 1985.

Sandelowsky, Erwin. *Anekdoten, Lieder mit Noten, und die alten Geschichten von Deutsch-Südwestafrika*. Windhoek: John Meinert, 1973.

Schellack, Fritz. "Sedan- und Kaisergeburtstagsfest." In *Öffentliche Festkultur: Politische Fest in Deutschland von der Aufklärung bis zum Ersten Weltkrieg*, ed. Dieter Düring, Peter Friedemann, and Paul Münch, 278–97. Reinbek bei Hamburg: Rowohlt, 1988.

Schieder, Theodor. "Grundfragen der neueren deutschen Geschichte." *Historische Zeitschrift* 192, no. 1 (1961): 1–16.

Schmidt-Lauber, Brigitte. *Die abhängigen Herren: Deutsche Identität in Namibia*. Hamburg: Lit, 1993.

Schmokel, Wolfe W. *Dream of Empire: German Colonialism, 1919–1945*. New Haven: Yale University Press, 1964.

Schneider, Ute. "War in Mind: Celebrations and War Enthusiasm in the Rhineland, 1913." In *Festive Culture in Germany and Europe from the Sixteenth to the Twentieth Century*, ed. Karin Friedrich, 265–80. Lewiston: Edwin Mellon Press, 2000.

Schönemann, Bernd. "Nationale Identität als Aufgabe des Geschichtsunterrichts nach der Reichsgründung." *Internationale Schulbuchforschung* 11 (1989): 107–28.

Schulte-Althoff, Franz-Josef. "Rassenmischung im kolonialen System: Zur deutschen Kolonialpolitik im letzten Jahrzeht vor dem ersten Weltkrieg." *Historisches Jahrbuch* 105 (1985): 52–94.

von Schumann, R. "Hauptorte in Südwestafrika in ihrer historisch-geographischen Entwicklung—Otjimbingwe, Omaruru, Windhoek." In *Namibia: Ausgewählte Themen der Exkursionen 1988*, ed. H. Lamping, 141–80. Frankfurter Wirtschafts- und Sozialgeographische Schriften 53. Franfurt am Main: Institut für Wirtschafts- und Sozialgeographie der Universität Frankfurt, 1989.

Seidelmann, Karl. *Die Pfadfinder in der deutschen Jugendgeschichte: Teil 1—Darstellung*. Hanover: Hermann Schroedel, 1977.

Sheehan, James. "What Is German History? Reflections on the Role of the *Nation* in German History and Historiography." *Journal of Modern History* 53, no. 1 (1981): 1–23.

Siemann, Wolfram. "Krieg und Frieden in historischen Gedenkfeiern des Jahres 1913." In *Öffentliche Festkultur: Politische Feste in Deutschland von der Aufklärung bis zum Ersten Weltkrieg*, ed. Dieter Düring, Peter Friedemann and Paul Münch, 298–320. Reinbek bei Hamburg: Rowohlt, 1988.

Smidt, Karen. *"Germania führt die deutsche Frau nach Südwest": Auswanderung, Leben und soziale Konflikte deutscher Frauen in der ehemalige Kolonie Deutsch-Südwestafrika, 1884–1920. Eine sozial- und frauengeschichtliche Studie.* Ph.D. diss., Otto-von- Euericke-Universität Magdeburg, 1995.

Smith, Jeffrey. "The Monarchy versus the Nation: The 'Festive Year' 1913 in Wilhelmine Germany." *German Studies Review* 23, no. 2 (2000): 257–74.

Smith, Woodruff D., *The German Colonial Empire.* Chapel Hill: University of North Carolina Press, 1978.

———. *The Ideological Origins of Nazi Imperialism.* New York: Oxford University Press, 1989.

———. "The Ideology of German Colonialism, 1840–1906." *Journal of Modern History* 46, no. 4 (1974): 641–62.

———. "Contexts of German Colonialism in Africa: British Imperialism, German Politics, and the German Administrative Tradition." In *European Impact and Pacific Influence: British and German Colonial Policy in the Pacific Islands and the Indigenous Response,* ed. Hermann J. Hiery and John M. Mackenzie, 9–21. International Library of Historical Studies. London: Tauris Academic Studies, 1997.

Spurr, David. *The Rhetoric of Empire: Colonial Discourse in Journalism, Travel Writing, and Imperial Administration.* Durham, N.C.: Duke University Press, 1994.

Stoecker, Helmut, ed. *Drang nach Afrika: Die deutsche koloniale Expansionspolitik und Herrschaft in Afrika von den Anfängen bis zum Verlust der Kolonien.* Berlin: Akademie, 1991.

Stoecker, Helmut, and Peter Sebald. "Enemies of the Colonial Idea." In *Germans in the Tropics: Essays in German Colonial History,* ed. Arthur Knoll and Lewis Gann, 59–72. New York: Greenwood Press, 1987.

Stoler, Ann. "Making Empire Respectable: The Politics of Race and Sexual Morality in Twentieth-century Colonial Cultures." *American Ethnologist* 16 (November 1989): 634–60.

———. "Rethinking Colonial Categories: European Communities and the Boundaries of Rule." *Comparative Studies in Society and History* 31 (January 1989): 134–61.

———. "Sexual Affronts and Racial Frontiers: European Identities and the Cultural Politics of Exclusion in Colonial Southeast Asia." *Comparative Studies in Society and History* 34 (July 1992): 514–51.

Strobel, Margaret. *European Women and the Second British Empire.* Bloomington: Indiana University Press, 1991.

Stuebel, Heinrich. "Die Entwicklung des Nationalsozialismus in Südwestafrika." *Vierteljarhsheft für Zeitgeschichte* 1, no. 2 (1953): 170–76.

Stübig, Heinz. *Bildung, Militär, und Gesellschaft in Deutschland: Studien zur Entwicklung im 19. Jahrhundert.* Studien und Dokumentationen zur deutschen Bildungsgeschichte, ed. Christoph Führ and Wolfgang Mitter, vol. 54. Cologne: Böhlau, 1994.

Sudholt, Gerd. *Die deutschen Eingeborenenpolitik in Südwestafrika: Von den Anfängen bis 1904.* Hildesheim: Georg Olms, 1975.

Suval, Stanley. *Electoral Politics in Wilhelmine Germany.* Chapel Hill: University of North Carolina Press, 1985.

Swanson, M. H. "South West Africa in Trust, 1915–1939." In *Britain and Germany in Africa,* ed. Prosser Gifford and William Roger Louis, 631–65. New Haven: Yale University Press, 1967.

Townson, Michael. *Mother-tongue and Fatherland: Language and Politics in Germany.* Manchester, U.K.: University of Manchester Press, 1992.

Vail, Leroy, ed. *The Creation of Tribalism in Southern Africa.* Berkeley: University of California Press, 1991.

Voeltz, Richard. *German Colonialism and the South West Africa Company, 1894–1914.* Athens: Ohio University, Center for International Studies, 1988.

Volkov, Shulamit. *The Rise of Popular Antimodernism in Germany: The Urban Master Artisans, 1873–1896.* Princeton, N.J.: Princeton University Press, 1978.

Walters, F. P. *A History of the League of Nations.* London: Oxford University Press, 1967.

Warmbold, Joachim. *Germania in Africa: Germany's Colonial Literature.* Studies in Modern German Literature, vol. 22, ed. D. G. Brown. New York: Peter Lang, 1989.

Wehler, Hans-Ulrich. "Bismarck's Imperialism, 1862–1890." *Past and Present* 48 (August 1970): 119–55.

Weigend, Guido G. "German Settlement Patterns in Namibia." *Geographic Review* 75 (April 1985), 156–69.

Weinfurt, Monika. "Kaisergeburtstagsfeiern am 27. Januar 1907: Bürgerliche Feste in den Städte des Deutschen Kaiserreichs." In *Bürgerliche Feste: Symbolische Formen politischen Handelns im 19. Jahrhundert,* ed. Manfred Hettling and Paul Nolte, 157–91. Göttingen: Vandenhoeck & Ruprecht, 1993.

Wenzel, Frank. "Sicherung von Massenloyalität und Qualifikation der Arbeitskraft als Aufgabe der Volksschule." In *Schule und Staat im 18.und 19. Jahrhundert: Zur Sozialgeschichte der Schule in Deutschland,* ed. Ursual Aumüller et al., 323–86. 2nd ed. Frankfurt am Main: Suhrkamp, 1979.

Wildenthal, Lora. "Colonizers and Citizens: Bourgeois Women and the Woman Question in the German Colonial Movement, 1886–1914." Ph.D. diss., University of Michigan, 1994.

———. "Race, Gender, and Citizenship in the German Colonial Empire," in *Tensions of Empire: Colonial Cultures in a Bourgeois World,* ed. Frederick Cooper and Ann Stoler, 263–83. Berkeley: University of California Press, 1997.

———. "'She Is Victor': Bourgeois Women, Nationalist Identity, and the Ideal of the Independent Woman Farmer in German Southwest Africa." *Social Analysis* 33 (September 1993): 68–88.

Wolfe, Patrick. *Settler Colonialism and the Transformation of Anthropology: The Politics and Poetics of an Ethnographic Event.* London: Cassel, 1999.

Zantop, Susanne. *Colonial Fantasies: Conquest, Family, and Nation in Precolonial Germany, 1770–1870.* Durham, N.C.: Duke University Press, 1997.

Zelle, Gustav. "Rund um den Reiter von Südwest in Windoek . . . und ein kleiner Mosaik—Beitrag zu aktuellen Thema südliches Afrika." In *Symbol für Südwestafrika, der Reiter von Südwest: Die ehemalige deutsche Schutztruppe und ihr Beitrag zur Erforschung und Entwicklung des Landes und seiner Menschen,* ed. Hans Schmiedel, 41–86. Shriftenreihe zur Familien- und Sippenkunde für Heimat und Geschichte, 25. Düsseldorf: G. Zelle, 1979.

Index

www.ingramcontent.com/pod-product-compliance
Lightning Source LLC
Chambersburg PA
CBHW032121020426
42334CB00016B/1025